Elvis
up close

Elvis up close

in the words of those who knew him best

edited by
ROSE CLAYTON AND DICK HEARD

Turner Publishing, Inc.
ATLANTA

Copyright © 1994 by Rose M. Clayton and Richard M. Heard
Illustrations copyright © 1994 by Jerry Tiritilli

All rights reserved under international copyright conventions. No part of the contents of this book may be reproduced or utilized in any form or by any means, electronic or mechanical, including photocopying, recording, or by any information storage and retrieval system, without the written consent of the publisher.

Published by Turner Publishing, Inc.
A Subsidiary of Turner Broadcasting System, Inc.
1050 Techwood Drive, N.W.
Atlanta, Georgia 30318

Library of Congress Cataloging-in-Publication Data
Heard, Dick, 1936–
    Elvis up close: in the words of those who knew him best/by Dick Heard and Rose Clayton.—1st ed.
      p. cm.
    ISBN 1-57036-058-8: $22.95
    1. Presley, Elvis, 1935–1977. 2. Rock musicians—United States—Biography.
I. Clayton, Rose, 1939–. I. Title.
    ML420.P96H53 1994
    782.42166'092—dc20
    [B]   94-12812
                                                                                                           CIP
                                                                                                           MN

Distributed by Andrews and McMeel
A Universal Press Syndicate Company
4900 Main Street
Kansas City, Missouri 64112

Walton Rawls-Vice President, Editorial
Katherine Buttler-Editorial
Lauren Emerson-Copy Chief
Michael Walsh-Vice President, Design
Karen Smith-Book Design
Marty Moore-Picture Editor
Anne Murdoch-Production Manager

First Edition 10 9 8 7 6 5 4 3 2 1

Printed in the U.S.A.

*To Jackie Heard Streett
for all the good times.
D. H.*

*To Elvis
and all of our mutual friends
who made this story possible.
R. C.*

Contents

CHAPTER ONE
"Poor as Job's Turkey"
1935-1948 7

CHAPTER TWO
"They'll Run Us
Out of Town!"
1949-1954 31

CHAPTER THREE
"Beautiful Hunk of
Forbidden Fruit"
1954-1955 55

CHAPTER FOUR
"Crazy Mad for Me"
1955-1956 81

CHAPTER FIVE
"On a Rocket Ride"
1957 109

CHAPTER SIX
"Everything I Have
Is Gone"
1958-1959 135

CHAPTER SEVEN
"Where He Left Off"
1960 165

CHAPTER EIGHT
"Just Having a Ball"
1961-1963 181

CHAPTER NINE
"While the Iron Is Hot"
1963-1967 205

CHAPTER TEN
"Eye of the Tiger"
1967-1971 227

CHAPTER ELEVEN
"He Tried to Behave
Himself."
1972-1974 259

CHAPTER TWELVE
"Down a Blind Alley"
1975-1976 287

CHAPTER THIRTEEN
"Treadmill to Oblivion"
1976-1977 317

CHAPTER FOURTEEN
"When the Light Is Gone"
1977 335

CHAPTER FIFTEEN
"Something That Was
Lasting"
1977-1994 361

THOSE WHO KNEW HIM BEST 379
Index 399
Acknowledgments 405

Elvis
up close

"Poor as Job's Turkey"
1935-1948

s the Great Depression draws to a close, little do the people of East Tupelo, Mississippi, suspect the impact the events of January 8, 1935, will eventually have on their rural community and, indeed, on the whole world. This is the birthdate of Elvis Aaron Presley.

Amid the daily challenge for survival, Elvis's relatives, Harold Loyd and Annie, Christine, and Wayne Presley, do not note the specific details of his birth, an event filled not only with joy but with tragedy. They do, however, remember how the little family is affected. In those early years of struggle and bad luck, the Presleys move around so much that it is difficult even for relatives to detail exactly where they live when. What they do recall is the love that binds them all together. Through such childhood playmates as Guy Harris and Odell Clark, Elvis is seen as a busy little kid playing hard and getting into trouble. Classmates like Becky Martin and Joe Savery reveal some of Elvis's schoolday antics and his early interest in music.

It is from the precious memories of those in Tupelo that we learn the advantage of growing up in hard times when the quality of life is affected less by one's ability to acquire than by one's capacity to share.

> "Everybody has their own version of their relationship with and to Elvis. That's natural. That's folklore. That's where folklore springs from. It's wonderful."
>
> MARY REEVES DAVIS (friend)

HAROLD LOYD *(cousin and playmate)*: East Tupelo, Mississippi, was just nothin', a wide spot in the road.... It was very small, and a few people owned the better part of it. It was hard to get work unless you wanted to work in the fields.

JANELLE MCCOMB *(family friend)*: Like the rest of the country, East Tupelo had just come through the Depression. Times were really tough, and farming was one of the largest industries. We had a cotton mill where a few people worked, but other than that, if you didn't own your own business or hadn't inherited your granddaddy's farm or something like that, it was rough.

HAROLD LOYD: Gladys [Smith] was twenty-one and Vernon [Presley] only seventeen when they run off to Pontotoc [Mississippi] to get married [June 17, 1933]. Most all the family on Gladys's side, the Smith side, and Vernon and his family, we all lived within throwin' distance—meanin' you could almost throw a rock from one of their houses to the other. Gladys was younger than my mother, Rheta. They was sisters. Vernon and his relations and all the Smiths, we were all close and visited quite a bit and always helped each other whenever we could.

    Vernon and his brother Vester, they always worked at somethin'. Sometimes they would have a little truck patch, you know, a little garden, and they did public work. The times was much harder on Vernon and Gladys than it was on my mama and father and us, because we lived on a farm. At least we had plenty to eat.

CHRISTINE ROBERTS PRESLEY *(great aunt)*: Vernon and Gladys were like us, poor as Job's turkey.

HAROLD LOYD: That little house Vernon built [on Old Saltillo Road, Elvis's birthplace] wasn't much of a house. It didn't have no ceilin', just the roof. It was real small, but they were real proud of it. I understand the land belonged to Orville Bean. He loaned Vernon the hundred and eighty dollars to buy the lumber to build the house. Vernon was supposed to pay it back with interest—like rent payments.

VESTER PRESLEY (*uncle*): Elvis was born sometime between four and five o'clock in the morning [January 8, 1935]. I don't know the exact time. Vernon had to be at work at five o'clock in the morning, and he got up at four. So, he said it was just like clockwork. Vernon got up at four and Gladys was having some trouble, so he got the doctor.

JIMMY VELVET (*friend and memorabilia collector*): My wife and I bought the instruments from Dr. [William Robert] Hunt's daughter that her father used to deliver Elvis. She told us she wasn't certain that the time of birth—4:35 A.M. on Elvis's birth certificate—was correct. She said her father told her that he waited several days to write it down.

ELOIS BEDFORD (*first girlfriend*): My grandmother had this thing she did: she went from house to house tending to sick people. Back then they didn't go to the hospital for everything. They had people who helped each other, waited on people who were sick, and such as that. My family tells me that my grandmother, who was a midwife, was up there the night Elvis was born.
 Gladys had complications with the twins. They were born at the house, and then they had to carry her to the hospital.

JANELLE MCCOMB: The doctor who delivered Elvis was my granddaddy's best friend, Dr. Will Hunt. Dr. Will was a Sunday school teacher when I was a little girl. There wasn't but about five thousand people in Tupelo, and everybody knew, or knew of, just about everybody else. When Elvis was born, Dr. Hunt announced in church that the Presleys had given birth to twins, and one of the twins had died. Some of the congregation went to visit and took things.

JOE SAVERY (*classmate*): You hear a lot about Elvis's twin brother Jesse Garon. I have the death certificate on him here in the office, but there's no name. It was called "stillborn, child of Vernon Presley." Gladys's name is not even on it. Another thing about this death certificate is that they had the date wrong on it. [It is dated January 9, rather than January 8.] It was just a mistake. But, it was the original certificate, and Dr. Hunt was the doctor that attended and declared the other twin dead at the house.

One of the strangest things, that I don't understand, is nobody really knows where that child was buried. Now I do know that Mrs. Presley was not in any condition to go to a funeral; however, I know that somebody in the family had bound to made arrangements or something. They said they buried the child at Priceville [cemetery]. Later on, Elvis tried to find out, but nobody knew where the child was buried. You would think somebody in the family would have known where they buried that child, but I have never known anybody that does.

HAROLD LOYD: It was rough back in the mid-thirties right after Elvis was born. We didn't have much of nothing. 'Course, being kids, you don't worry about where the next meal is comin' from, but I'm sure it was hard on all the parents.

Early on, my family lived on a farm, and we raised just about every darn thing we ate. We had plenty to can. My mother always canned vegetables, and she would get out and roam the hills and pick berries. She would put 'em up in glass jars. We called it "cannin'." We always had a hog to kill in the wintertime—plenty of chickens, thousands of eggs. Vernon and Gladys and little Elvis would come to visit. I remember a while before they'd get ready to go, my mother would go out to the smokehouse where we had our sausage hangin', cut off a big piece of ham, get 'em some sausage, jars of beans and things. She'd package it all up and give it to them. Be enough to last 'em maybe a week. We shared.

JANELLE MCCOMB: The Presleys were just people. I've got to tell it like it is, there was no blue halo or no lightning flash back then; Elvis was just another kid on the block. Nobody, and I don't care who you ask, is gonna tell you any earth-shattering thing that they remember about Elvis in East Tupelo, because not even Elvis would realize how earth-shattering he would become!

HAROLD LOYD: My mom and I went to Vernon's little house just right after Elvis was born. We went lots of times visitin'. But, of course, all us kids big enough to play, we'd stay out in the yard playin'. I can't tell you anymore what that kid looked like when he was a baby than the man in the moon. I'm sure I went in there and looked at him, but I can't remember.

When Elvis was about two or three years old, old enough to get around and play with me and the other kids, I guess that's when I really got to know him, got closer to him.

ANNIE CLOYD PRESLEY *(cousin-in-law)*: Vernon just was not the type, and neither was my husband, to really show their affection. They showed it in action but not in words and outside deeds. They did it more privately, if you understand what I'm saying. I don't know whether that was a Presley trait, but all of 'em was like that. They did not show affection in public, yet there was not a one of them that didn't help around the house or tend to the kids occasionally.

CHRISTINE ROBERTS PRESLEY: Vernon was full of life. He'd holler and speak to everybody and was friendly. Around the house, he'd pick at Gladys. I'd hear 'em pick at one another on the porch and I'd hear him and her laughing in the house. I'd just imagine Vernon had pulled a joke on her. He was a mess. They was a happy family. Foot, yeah!

HAROLD LOYD: Gladys was a good mother and a good wife. She was like a second mother to me, but, of course, there was a very strong bond between her and Elvis after his twin was born dead. As I understood it, Gladys couldn't have any more kids. Somethin' happened to her during the childbirth, so that drew her closer to Elvis. She was so protective of him. If Elvis just whimpered, she would run to him. I always played with Elvis real gentle when he was a kid, 'cause I knew how Gladys was.

CHRISTINE ROBERTS PRESLEY: She'd sing to that boy and seen that the family got what they needed if she could afford it. Vernon would work day labor with Mr. Bean whenever he could use him, putting up pasture fence and wire, posts, and everything like that.

Elvis was sweet. I don't know what it was about that boy, but you could just love him to death. One day I said, "Come here, Elvis, and hug my neck." He sort of smiled and come over and put his arm around my neck. I said, "You're the sweetest little ol' young'un that I ever seen." And he said, "Thank you." Just as smart.

HAROLD LOYD: Elvis was always real hyper. He would run and play so hard he'd just wear himself out, then he'd go over to the couch and lay down and be asleep the second he put his head down. Just wore himself out playin'.

CHRISTINE ROBERTS PRESLEY: Elvis had a little ol' coal bucket. Gladys would tell him to bring in some coal, and he would put a few pieces in and bring it to the house. He liked to clean up the yard. I've seen him pick up sticks that were scattered around out there that Gladys might have told him to get. He was a smart little ol' boy.

HAROLD LOYD: Vernon sold Mr. Bean a hog and felt like, I guess, he didn't get paid enough for the hog, so he changed the amount on the check. Well, Mr. Bean prosecuted him, and Vernon was sent to Parchman [Penitentiary], a state institution prison. Him and Uncle Travis Smith, which was Gladys's oldest brother, and one other guy, they got convicted of alterin' that check. Wasn't for very much money. The check was made out for four dollars, and they changed it to fourteen dollars or somethin'. Anyhow, they went off to prison for that. Got three years, I think.

ANNIE CLOYD PRESLEY: We all felt sorry for Gladys and Elvis when Vernon went to prison. My father-in-law [Noah Presley, Elvis's great uncle] tried to help 'em all he could.

CHRISTINE ROBERTS PRESLEY: Noah said that he just cried. He begged Mr. Bean. See, Mr. Bean was a good friend of Noah's, so he begged him not to prosecute Vernon. Noah said, "I'll double that money for you if you will just not send Vernon to prison. He didn't mean to beat you. He told me he didn't." Mr. Bean said, "No, Vernon needs to be taught a lesson."

ANNIE CLOYD PRESLEY: Gladys would get somebody to take her to Parchman just about every weekend. Mr. Noah would take a load down there sometimes. He drove us in a school bus.

HAROLD LOYD: While Vernon was in prison, they got behind on their rent or house payments and lost that little house. Gladys wasn't workin', and there was no money comin' in. The landlord kicked 'em out.

WAYNE E. PRESLEY (cousin): When Elvis and them moved into Tupelo, we lived in the other side of the [duplex] house. I seen Gladys every day there. Vernon wasn't around. They said he was in prison.
    Rent back then wasn't much—ten or twelve dollars a month, or something like that; but they didn't have but two rooms.
    Of course, they were poor people just like everybody was—on commodities. You know what you call commodities? Well, that's where the government gives you cheese, sugar, beans, and stuff. They brought 'em in old boxcars down to the fairground, and you'd go there and pick 'em up. It helped you survive.

HAROLD LOYD: But Vernon wasn't down in prison very long. He just barely got in, and somehow Gladys got him out. He served about six to nine months. [Some sources report Vernon was released five months short of serving a three-year sentence.] I was just a kid myself, so I don't remember all the details. She got him out, on I think they called it a "hardship case," so he could help provide for her and Elvis.

ANNIE CLOYD PRESLEY: Elvis being an only child, he didn't have to have that much discipline really. If Gladys ever whipped him, I never did know about it. When she said, "No!" he knew she meant it. She had at a young age learned him that she meant what she said. So she didn't have to do that much discipline.

I'd tell Elvis, "Don't do that or you have to go home." That's the way we did. If kids were at my house and wouldn't behave, they went home. Well, Elvis never had to go home because he'd quit whatever bad he was doing.

CHRISTINE ROBERTS PRESLEY: Elvis was the best little ol' thing. He was so polite. I'd fix him a sandwich of some kind; sometimes I had bologna. He ate bologna and just cereal. He wasn't big as a split minnow.

HAROLD LOYD: I went to the same church that Gladys and Vernon went to in East Tupelo and I noticed real early on when the choir group would be singin' some hymn, Elvis—when he was just a little fellow—would be singin' right along with 'em in that little squeaky voice. He always wanted to go right up there to the front and sing with them, but Gladys and Vernon would hold him back. One time he pulled loose and got away from them. I wasn't there when it happened, but Gladys used to laugh about it. He got loose and ran up front and started singin'. The preacher and all of 'em thought it was cute, so they got to where they would let him stand up there and sing with 'em. Yeah, I noticed when he was very young, five or six years old, he was already singin' lots.

WAYNE E. PRESLEY: Elvis had a little old pasteboard guitar. It didn't really play. It was just a toy. I'd say, "Rap on that guitar and try to sing," and he would.

CHRISTINE ROBERTS PRESLEY: Elvis always wanted to get out and play around in the yard and throw rocks. All my boys did that. They didn't throw at nobody's house. They just had a good time. They would play pitch in the yard and sometimes they'd have a bat out there. I didn't have to watch Elvis, and I didn't ever have to get after him. Elvis was a good boy. He could get along with anybody.

WAYNE E. PRESLEY: We used to play together out in the yard. I pulled Elvis around in that little ol' red wagon. Elvis wasn't contrary or nothing. If you said, "Well, I ain't gonna pull you in that wagon." He'd say, "Okay."

HAROLD LOYD: One time I had Elvis ridin' in a little red wagon out in the backyard, and I was pullin' him around. I turned the wagon a little too sharp too fast. It flipped over and Elvis fell out. Well, it didn't hurt him none, but it scared him and he started cryin'. I thought, "Oh, god! Gladys is going to come out here and kill me!"

I couldn't say, "Elvis" 'til I was almost grown. I called him "Hiss." So I grabbed him up and said, "Hiss! Hiss!" I was scared to death. I could just see Gladys coming out the back door with a darn broom. You know how a hen will protect her baby chicks? That's the way Gladys was. And she wasn't scared to take a broom to you, neither.

CHRISTINE ROBERTS PRESLEY: It didn't seem like Gladys was well after the twins were born. Her nerves were just really bad. Somehow Gladys was able to keep her house going. Now she might have felt bad—that I didn't know nothing about—but I know she was awfully nervous. She would tell me she had the worst nerves and she'd had 'em since them babies was born.

My son Bobby threw a rock against the old storm cellar door one time, and it popped so loud we thought it was a gun. We thought Bobby and Elvis had slipped the gun out of the house. The muscles in the back of Gladys's legs were just a-twitchin'. All that high temper Gladys had, honey, it was just weakness from her nerves.

Sometimes Gladys had to take medicine. She'd say, "Sometimes I just can't sleep—just can't settle down." I said, "Yeah, I know a whole lot about that. I've seen the time I didn't sleep but fifteen minutes before I seen daylight. I lost a baby, too, and you know what? That will kill you quicker than anything."

ANNIE CLOYD PRESLEY: It's a wonder Elvis hadn't grown up being as nervous and scary as Gladys was. It's a wonder he hadn't been real scary, but he wasn't.

CHRISTINE ROBERTS PRESLEY: Gladys read Bible stories to Elvis. She taught Elvis how to live and what to do, and that's the reason he didn't bother nobody.

She always took him to church, too. It was a Holy Roller church. That's what people used to call them back then, "Holy Rollers." Nobody had no use for them. They would "shout"—scared me to death. I didn't know what they were shouting about—me, just a kid.

CORENE RANDLE SMITH *(pastor's wife)*: There was a few people that got so happy [in church] they called it "shouting," but about all they did was stand there and move their feet up and down real fast. It wasn't really a dance of any kind. They'd just get excited and full of joy.

ANNIE CLOYD PRESLEY: Gladys was very devout in her religion. We talked religion a good bit. That's about all we talked about really. The [Assembly of God] church thought it was a sin to go to movie shows. They thought it was a sin to do this, do that. Fact, you couldn't hardly do nothing.

CORENE RANDLE SMITH: The church was strict. We couldn't wear much makeup and not much jewelry. We were taught to be moderate. Dancing was taught against. In those days women didn't ever wear shorts and whatever. They hardly ever had swimsuits. Back then, I guess, people thought if a woman had on shorts or a swimsuit she was just terrible.

ANNIE CLOYD PRESLEY: There was singings always somewhere. Sunday morning was always church, Sunday school and preaching. If they was having a revival, we went every night if at all possible. Mr. Brown had an old flatbed truck, and we'd load that truck down on Sunday evenings—even before I had any kids. We'd load that truck down and go around to these little churches, whenever they were having all-day service. My husband and Vernon and Gladys all sang, and occasionally I'd try to sing alto. We sang in church together, and we'd gather up at each other's house. That was our entertainment—gathering at each other's house and singing and having a good time.

I remember one night we went up to Gladys and Vernon's and—this is funny (a little dirty, too)—Vernon always said what he thought. We were all sitting around singing, and Elvis was singing with us. Elvis had his little hand in his pocket dangling his ding-a-ling. Vernon all at once just stopped singing. Vernon could say anything and never crack a grin. So Vernon said, "Son, if you'd just quit playing with that thing a little bit, you might could sing." Embarrassed that kid to death! We all just hollered.

CHRISTINE ROBERTS PRESLEY: I know one thing: they was as close of a family as anybody could be.

CORENE RANDLE SMITH: Gladys was just the typical mother, and Vernon, I would say, was just like everybody else around. Everybody was friends. We all knew where everybody lived. We went to see about them if they needed help. Just being a good neighbor and a good Christian was the normal thing to do back then.

CHRISTINE ROBERTS PRESLEY: Elvis would love on his mother. He'd tell her he loved her and that he was going to do this and going to do that when he got big. Gladys told me that he would tell her that she wouldn't have to worry about something to eat when he got big. Just like my Bobby did me.

I'd have a chill and I'd be out pickin' cotton until I'd 'bout faint. My son would pat me on the hand and say, "Mama, when I get big, you won't never have to work. I'm gonna buy you a big house, and I'm gonna buy you a lot of food and a lot of pretty things to go in it." Kids are just like that, you know; they build air castles.

:◉:◉:◉:

GUY HARRIS *(neighborhood friend)*: People ask me, "What did you and Elvis do when you were little?" Well, hell, nothing. We didn't have much of nothing to do anything with.

ODELL CLARK *(neighborhood friend)*: We lived at 906 Kelly Street out here in East Tupelo. Elvis lived next door to us at 904 for a long time. The old house that they lived in was just like ours; it had pillows [columns] on the front. Elvis would hang on those pillows and just sing. I said, "My god! There must be something wrong with that boy!" Elvis would sing all the time as loud as he could.

LAVERNE FARRAR *(neighborhood friend)*: I lived next door to Elvis, and we grew up together. Elvis was an only child, but there were five of us. He always wanted to play. He'd come up to the house and stay with us awhile and eat. The main thing is that Elvis was a good boy—wasn't no smart- or ugly-talker or nothing.

ODELL CLARK: The Presleys had some old silverleaf poplar trees—I never will forget them—in the yard up there. We played under them a lot.

We had some homemade coaster wagons, and we would coast down that hill up there, see who could coast the farthest, and we would brag about this, that, and the other.

LAVERNE FARRAR: We had a swing made out of a tire in our front yard on the tree. We'd swing on that. Boy, that was the best swing you ever saw.

ODELL CLARK: One time this Morgan boy who lived down here got some old fifty-pound lard cans, and he cut the bottom out of them 'til they was about six-inches high. He put one on a two-by-four and put strings on it and made a guitar out of it. He traded that to Elvis for something, and Elvis banged on that thing. He would rattle your ears with it—just that boom, boom, boom, same old thing with no tune or anything to it.

ANNIE CLOYD PRESLEY: Elvis was just an average little boy. He'd get out there and play and wrestle and what have you. I remember one day him and one of the neighbor boys was wrestlin' between the two houses on a vacant lot out there, and Elvis broke the little boy's hip. I mean, they were really wrestling! Elvis broke his hip, but neither parent got mad. It was just an accident, you know.

LAVERNE FARRAR: I remember that red wagon. My mama took a picture. Elvis was standin' up in it, had on blue-striped pants and a kinda white shirt. Me and my brother and Guy Harris and Junior Harris [Guy Harris's brother] and all of us was sittin' in the wagon. Mama liked to take pictures, and that's how come us with all those pictures of Elvis. Nearly all of them was made at my house.

Elvis liked to stay up at my house. We'd always ask the blessing 'fore we ate. He knew that. Elvis bowed his head just like we did.

CHRISTINE ROBERTS PRESLEY: I'll tell you one thing, nobody run over Elvis down there. One night I seen Gladys get a stick after this boy that lived out there, and that tickled me slap to death. That boy thought he was so smart. He said something about Elvis, and, boy, Gladys picked up a broomstick. That boy ran and hid. She said, "Boy, you come out of there, or I'll whip you 'til you can't even walk. Come on out and say that to my face." He didn't do it. When he got out, he got gone in a hurry, 'cause he was real scared.

ODELL CLARK: I remember Gladys one time wearing some people out with her brush broom. Have you ever seen a brush broom? People back then used to get a bunch of branches and bind them up pretty tight and use them to sweep their yards with. I remember some folks next door jumped on Elvis one day, and Gladys wore two or three of them out with her brush broom—parents and all.

GUY HARRIS: Gladys got a hold of us pretty strong one day 'cause we got out and got sun-blistered pretty bad. I can't remember what we were doing. She fixed our lunch, and Elvis claimed he was too blistered to eat. He was trying to stay outside and away from her as much as he could, 'cause he didn't want the old switch.

ODELL CLARK: Elvis had two small dogs. One of them was white with brown specks on it, and the other was a little brownish-red-looking dog. He gave them strange names. One he called "Woodlawn," and the other he called "Muffy Dee." I never will forget the names of those dogs. Elvis really loved his pets.

If you had a dog or a cat or anything back then, you took care of it. That was your main job, but I know Elvis still had to carry water just like we did, and he had to run up to the store for his mother for groceries.

:◎:◎:◎:

HAROLD LOYD: Elvis always loved music, but he didn't always shake and carry on like he did in the later years, after he got into the business. He loved music, country and western, and, of course, gospel. Might have been he got it from Vernon.

Vernon, he would be doing somethin' around the house, and he would be just a-hummin'. Vernon had a darn good voice. I believe that if he'd ever really tried, he could have made somethin' out of himself. Gladys and Vernon and Elvis, all three of them, loved to sing, and they had a lot of rhythm. They bought Elvis a guitar. Gave it to him for his birthday.

Sometimes when I'd be visitin' or stayin' with 'em, Gladys would tell Elvis, "Son, run get your guitar." He'd pretend he didn't hear. Gladys would say, "Elvis! Go in there and get your guitar, and let's sing some good gospel songs—the three of us. He'd say, "Oh, Mama, I can't pick that guitar and I can't sing." But she'd say, "Oh, yes you can. I've heard you. Now go and get it." He wouldn't do it—too shy to pick in front of me, I guess. But in a little while he'd take that guitar and go off in another room and shut the door, and we'd hear him in there just a-beatin' on that guitar and singin' like crazy. Now if you opened the door just a little bit—let him catch you watchin'—he'd throw the guitar down on the bed and take off out the door. He was very shy. I never did understand how he got out of all that shyness. Back then he didn't want nobody watchin' him. But just leave him alone, he would do great.

ODELL CLARK: He was shy, but Elvis never was what you call a "sissy." It was just the way of life out here. You had to fight; if you didn't, all the kids would run over you all the time—jump on you. I don't remember Elvis ever being bruised up or anything too much. But sometimes he would get a black eye or a bloody nose.

:◎:◎:◎:

ANNIE CLOYD PRESLEY: Gladys and Vernon and me and Sales were just always together. We went down to Pascagoula during the war, World War II. My husband, Sales, he could always get a job. I mean, no matter what. He could quit this morning and go to work somewhere else before dinner. Well, Sales was working down there at the ammunition factory 'til he decided he wanted to go work in the shipyard in Pascagoula. So he went, got a job, and then came back and got me and the kids. We hadn't been down there long 'til Vernon and Gladys and Elvis came and stayed down there. We rented cabins, just little one-room cabins was what they had built there close to the shipyard. You slept, ate, and everything in that one little ol' room. We'd get together every morning.

Elvis watched after my kids. He was a good baby-sitter, I guess you'd call it. He was real good with children. He would watch after 'em and play with 'em just to have somebody to play with, 'cause Gladys was particular who Elvis played with, where he went, and all this.

They usually played out there in the road—played house, hide-and-seek, you know, just regular games. They didn't have many toys.

Sales didn't want me living down there [in Pascagoula] away from my family when I had my next baby, so he brought me home. We caught the bus to Mobile, and we had to change in Mobile before we caught the bus to Tupelo. We got out in Mobile and went into a little restaurant beside the bus station. We was eating and looked up and Gladys and Vernon and Elvis was coming in the door.

I said, "What are y'all doing here?" Gladys said, "You think I'm staying down here and you not here? You're crazy. I'm going home, too." So we came home, and Sales and Vernon went back to Pascagoula and worked 'til they worked their notice out. When they came home, they went to driving a truck for L. P. McCarty. Sales drove the truck for L. P. in the daytime and washed the streets at night for the city.

BECKY MARTIN *(friend)*: My daddy owned a store out on the highway. I remember there was sugar and different staples like that that were rationed because it was during the war. You had to have stamps to buy sugar back then, and a family was only allowed so many stamps. If you ran out of sugar or stamps, you couldn't buy anymore. You had to borrow from someone.

My daddy sold driver's licenses at the store. You could get your driver's license for about a quarter in those days. Gasoline and tires were rationed 'cause of the war, but there weren't many cars back then, anyway.

ODELL CLARK: We had about two or three water wells out here in East Tupelo. The whole community used them. We would all go to the well and pump our water.

The women had these old pots that they boiled clothes in, usually, and they would make lye soap. They would put their clothes in this big wash pot and put the soap and water in there. Then they built a fire around the outside of those old galvanized tubs. Usually after they boiled those clothes for awhile, they would take them out and wash them on an ol' rub board, as they called it. They would rub the clothes awhile and then hang them out on the fence to dry.

For drinking water we had two-gallon water buckets. Everybody used the same bucket, and everybody drank out of the same dipper in each family. We had to go to that well pretty regular, you know. We had to go get drinking water and water we used to take a bath in and everything else. The kids toted. Everybody did. Elvis did. Sure did.

LAVERNE FARRAR: We didn't have no air conditioners or fans. Now, ain't that a sight? We didn't have no bath in the house or no electricity to fix a stove or nothing like that. We just had lights, and that's all. But we didn't think nothing about it. We had an outdoor toilet, and we bathed in tin tubs. Ain't that hard?

GUY HARRIS: Everybody had an old icebox, they called it. They'd put some ice up in the top, and then the cold air would filter down through. The Clarks ran an ice route—in other words, Mr. Clark would go to the ice plant and buy ice. We'd get ice in hundred-pound, fifty-pound, and twenty-five-pound blocks. The ice would last probably two or three days.

LAVERNE FARRAR: Gladys went barefooted all the time. She wore these little housedresses—just slip 'em on, you know, no sleeves, and cut out at the neck. I can just see her in that today, getting a Toni permanent. She'd get Toni home permanents back then.

HAROLD LOYD: After my mother died in '41, my stepdad remarried, and I left home and lived with Elvis and his folks for a while. Then I stayed with Vester [Elvis's uncle] and different ones of my family folks until I got old enough to take care of myself.

I was almost six years older than Elvis. He was a typical kid, but his mother was very strict. When he was real young, she wouldn't let him out of her sight. Many times I heard him say, "Mama, can I go out and play?" And she would say, "Yeah, you can go out and play in the yard, but don't you get too far away that you can't hear me if I call you. You better be able to hear me." So he had to stay right around the house.

The rest of us would wander off, go down in the bottom, and go swimming in the channel, all except Elvis. He couldn't do that. He had to stay right there close to the house.

LAVERNE FARRAR: In Tupelo we didn't have but one swimming pool, and it cost to go in. It was about a mile-and-a-half from our house to that swimming pool, so we never did get to go.

BECKY MARTIN: The boys would go swimming in the creek [or channel] in their birthday suits; they didn't have swimmin' suits. The girls couldn't go swimmin' with them in the creek, anyway.

HAROLD LOYD: It was dangerous just going down to the channel—falling in or something. I almost drowned once. I heard that Elvis did slip off one time with some kids and went down there to the channel, and Gladys went out looking for him. When she finally did find him, she tore his rear end up. So he never done that anymore.

ANNIE CLOYD PRESLEY: At one time we all lived there on Berry Street. One day a friend of ours [Ruby Brown] who lived right direct across the street from me was painting her house. Me and Gladys and her and a couple more women went out there about ten or ten-thirty that morning. We took a coffee break—we'd call it that, or a rest period—and we'd gang up and get the news of a morning before we started our dinner [lunch]. Ruby took us all in the house and fixed us coffee and cake.

All at once we started hearing something going *glub, glub, glub*, like water or something pouring out. So we jumped up and run to the door. My Sybil, my third daughter (she was, what, fourteen months old?) she had took that gallon of paint (Ruby had failed to get the lid on it good) and somehow or another she had got that bucket turned bottom-side upwards on top of her head, and paint was—I mean, she was white as a sheet. I mean, just paint!

Well, before I could get to her, Gladys got to her. She picks her up under her arms and runs out in the middle of the road. Vernon's on top of their house there putting a roof on it, and Elvis is out in the yard playing. Gladys is a-holdin' that child out like this [out in front of her, at arm's length] saying, "Oh, look-a-here. Look-a-here, Vernon!" Elvis got so tickled, he got down on the ground and rolled and rolled. He was laughing so! They all thought it was just so funny. It was funny, later. Right then it wasn't funny to me. I liked to never got that paint off her.

:◉:◉:◉:

BECKY MARTIN: Between East Tupelo and downtown, what is now called East Main, was a dirt, one-lane road we called "the levee." Then it became a two-lane highway. Elvis and them had to cross that to get to school. Lawhon [East Consolidated School on Lake Street, which Elvis attended, 1941–1946] was a big, wood-frame building back in the '40s. It was just fields and levee between East Tupelo and Tupelo then, and it took about twenty-five to thirty minutes to walk it. East Tupelo was still a city of its own at that time.

ODELL CLARK: Before we started to school every year, we went over to Lee County Health Department or the nurses came out to a little store up here on East Main. They would have certain days we would go and take all our shots.

I don't remember Elvis being sick any. He never looked sick to me, but he was skinny. Elvis sure was skinny!

GUY HARRIS: Gladys was real strict on Elvis, but everybody's parents was. My parents was on me. We didn't cross the highway unless we were going to school or down to the schoolhouse for some kind of function. Usually our parents went with us because everybody was real protective of their kids back in those days. Gladys might take us somewhere, or maybe my mother, or maybe some of the other Presleys. There was a lot of Presleys lived out there in East Tupelo.

LAVERNE FARRAR: We had a path we made between two houses. We'd go through that path to the highway, then we'd all go across the highway together. Lots of times Elvis walked to school with me and my sister and brothers and Odell Clark and Junior Harris and all of 'em; then we'd walk home to eat dinner [lunch] and walk back to school. After school we all walked home together.

BECKY MARTIN: Seems like I remember we had to take our lunch in the first few years of going to school. If we didn't go home for lunch, we'd eat at our desk in the classroom. We'd take peanut butter and jelly sandwiches and drink milk we'd get out of the school cafeteria. Everybody around here liked peanut butter and jelly sandwiches. That was one of Elvis's favorites.

SHIRLEY JANE JONES *(classmate)*: I remember one thing sticks in my mind about how Elvis looked. His hair was always really neat. A lot of boys didn't comb their hair that well at that age, but Elvis's hair was always neatly combed.

When you went to school everyday, your mother seen to it that you was clean. She would wash you with a bath rag and soap.

ELOIS BEDFORD: We'd catch rainwater and let the sun heat it. We'd take baths two or three times a week, or sometimes, if it rained, we'd stand out in the rain.

ODELL CLARK: Didn't have any running water at all. You got you a small pan, put some water in it, and just took a bath anywhere you could find the privacy. We had outhouses.

LAVERNE FARRAR: Elvis was good. That's all I can ever say about him. He wore little checkered pants sometimes and a little white shirt. And he wore overalls a lot, you know, like my brothers.

ELOIS BEDFORD: Sometimes they might make a smirky remark about something Elvis wore—different colors of clothes that other kids didn't wear. But I didn't see anything wrong with what he wore.

ODELL CLARK: We went barefoot in the summertime. In the fall our parents would go buy us a pair of shoes: clodhoppers, just ol' lace-up shoes. That's what farmers used, you know. Elvis just had hand-me-downs. You could tell they were way too big for him, but he stayed clean in them. He wasn't raggedy.

LAVERNE FARRAR: When we'd come home from school, we'd pull our school clothes off and hang 'em up and wear 'em again next day. We was proud of what we had. We didn't know no difference.

BECKY MARTIN: I got more acquainted with Elvis when he got in our fifth grade class. Mrs. [Oleta] Grimes was our teacher, and she was a good, firm teacher. Everybody in that class learned everything that we were told to learn. We had to learn the poem "Crossing the Bar," and I bet everybody in that fifth grade still remembers it. Sometimes we had to go to the front of the room and recite. I don't remember Elvis being nervous about it. The hardest thing we all had to learn was the Gettysburg Address. We had to memorize the states, and capitals, and presidents. They were real easy for us to learn because they were in alphabetical order. I can still say them all. My grandfather thought that was the greatest thing in the world. He wanted us to get on the radio and say the states and capitals, and the presidents.

SHIRLEY JANE JONES: The school was really small [there were two grades in one room], but the fifth grade had its own separate room. I don't know why I remember fifth grade so well, but I do. We'd meet for about thirty minutes or an hour each morning in a small auditorium, kind of in the middle of the school. It was a larger room, and we gathered there for what we called "chapel" back then. We had prayer and we sang. It was wartime in those days, so we'd sing a lot of songs like "God Bless America." Elvis was the only one that I knew of that had a guitar or any kind of instrument, so we kind of relied on him to do the playing for us. I remember singing "You Are My Sunshine" with Elvis; he and I singing and him playing the guitar.

BECKY MARTIN: My brothers and sisters, we were all taught to say, "Yes, ma'am" and "No, ma'am" to everybody. I still do it. They say Elvis still did that 'til the day he died.

ODELL CLARK: I don't remember Elvis ever getting in trouble in school. He was just about average, you know. The only thing was he just liked to sing. If he could get one person to listen to him, he would sing their ear off.

BECKY MARTIN: The boys would play together, and the girls would play together; not too many mixed girls and boys. My best friend, Elois Bedford, was Elvis's first girlfriend.

ELOIS BEDFORD: We were childhood sweethearts from probably second or third grade. We just did the things that childhood sweethearts do: write notes, walk along together, talk, see each other on the school ground. I think we went a couple of times to the Halloween carnival—they had cakewalks and things like that, you know. But I don't remember a whole lot about that.

What I do remember was that little smile Elvis had. I can close my eyes now and still see him walking toward me. I remember the day he told me he liked someone else. We must have been in about fifth grade. I was just about to get on the school bus to go home that afternoon, and Elvis handed me a note and told me that he liked another girl. Her name was Magdalene Morgan. I lost him that day.

:◎:◎:◎:

SHIRLEY JANE JONES: Mrs. Grimes gave her students encouragement. She made you feel like you could do something. I guess that helped Elvis to get his start. She'd give you confidence.

I think Elvis had drive. I really do. Elvis was really devoted to his music even back then. You could tell.

BECKY MARTIN: Elvis always went to church. Even if his parents didn't go, he did. I'm sure his mother instilled that in him.

HAROLD LOYD: I remember Gladys saying to Elvis, "Son, I'm proud of you, but always remember . . . no matter what happens when you grow up, never look down on others or think you are better than they are because in the eyes of God we are all equal. We are all God's children."

ODELL CLARK: Elvis and I both lived about a half block from the Assembly of God Church. They had a public address system at the church, and you could hear the preaching without going inside, but if you did go in, everybody was real quiet. We listened to the preacher.

BROTHER FRANK W. SMITH (pastor): Elvis's parents were members of the church where I was pastor. They bought Elvis a book that showed how to make chords, and I had gone to his house a time or two to show Elvis how to make chords or some runs [on his guitar].

SHIRLEY JANE JONES: I remember my part of the talent contest that Elvis was in at the fair because I won first place. Mr. Franks—Tracy Franks—he announced at school they were going to have a talent show for anyone that wanted to enter, and the first prize would be twenty-five dollars and a trophy. There were three trophies. One was bigger, and then smaller, and smaller. First prize, second prize, and third prize.

I remember Elvis sang "Old Shep." Elvis didn't win anything as far as money. Fourth place is what I always remember Elvis winning.... He was really disappointed that he didn't win. I could tell it by the look on his face.

LAVERNE FARRAR: When Elvis sang "Old Shep," well, all of us kids thought that was so silly. You know how silly kids are. But now Elvis didn't smile or nothing. He sang it right out from his heart.

ANNIE CLOYD PRESLEY: Gladys would walk by my house with Elvis with his guitar. They would walk to Tupelo, and Elvis would sing on them amateur hours on the radio on WELO on Saturday evening.

SHIRLEY JANE JONES: We didn't have television in those days. Radio was our main entertainment. They just had little different-type local radio shows. The show that I sang on was a little variety show. I don't remember Elvis singing on that particular show that I was on, but I think that he played with Mississippi Slim on his radio show. Mississippi Slim played guitar, and I think he wrote some. He had gone to Nashville, I think, and made some recordings.

ANNIE CLOYD PRESLEY: Gladys did push Elvis into music more than Vernon did. That I'll say. But Vernon was in there, too. I mean Vernon loved Elvis's singing. He was proud of him.

:◎:◎:◎:

ODELL CLARK: All people in East Tupelo were poor, just about. I remember when me and Elvis was nine or ten years old, his father would be worn out when he would get home every evening. He had to walk about two miles over and back from L. P. McCarty's. It was a wholesale company where Vernon worked that delivered flour, meal, and stuff. Vernon would have dust all on him; I guess it was flour or something.

Guy Harris: Our parents started letting us walk to the movies probably when I was seven, and Elvis was about ten. They'd trust us to do that. From where we lived in East Tupelo, it was probably a little over a mile to the Strand, which was right there on Main Street. The Lyric was over on Broadway, which was two or three blocks further away.

Odell Clark: We saw Gene Autry and Roy Rogers and Tex Ritter. That's mostly all they had at that theater. We would have enough money to go to the movie, but we didn't have any money to buy anything like popcorn, Cokes, and stuff like that.

Laverne Farrar: The continued serial would be "Flash Gordon." We never would miss that. Then my oldest brother started showing movies at the theater, and he'd bring 'em home and show 'em at the house on Friday nights. My brother would put the loud speakers on the front porch and have Ernest Tubb singing "Walking the Floor Over You." Well, the kids knowed it was time for the show. So, they started gangin' in. All of us would go and get in that one room. We'd hang a big ol' sheet up on the wall, and I'm telling you that was fun. My brother'd charge some of us a dime, and some of us he didn't charge nothin' much. Elvis would come every time.

Odell Clark: We played cowboys and Indians and stuff like that. Elvis wanted to sing all the time. I don't remember him ever trying to sing like Gene Autry or Roy Rogers or anybody, but it seems like he liked to hear Eddy Arnold after we were about grown.

Guy Harris: We weren't allowed to be out after dark. You had to be home. If you went anywhere, you'd go with your parents over to, maybe, the Presleys' house and play. Sometimes we'd have a little ol' neighborhood party and invite all the kids around, spend-the-night parties and stuff like that. We'd play games like spin the bottle, but nothing real strong.
    There wasn't any street lights. That's one reason that everybody was real protective of their kids back then. I guess really they just didn't want their kids to get out and get in trouble. The only trouble you could get into was maybe throwing rocks at somebody's house. That would

probably be it; but when you got your butt torn up, you wished you hadn't even seen that rock.

ODELL CLARK: We had air raids [drills] every once in awhile. Everybody had to turn their lights out, or they had to buy these black shades to put over their windows. We were scared to death. I never will forget when they said something about dropping the atomic bomb. People around here especially, we didn't know what they were talking about. They said it might set off a chain reaction to destroy the whole world. Now that scared us kids worse than anything else. We were probably about ten or eleven years old. I remember Elvis and all us kids were talking about it. We listened to President [Franklin D.] Roosevelt on the radio. We really liked his speeches.

Seems like that war went on forever. I know it was over in five years at the most, but it seemed like to me, when I was a kid, it went on forever and ever.

:◎:◎:◎:

JOE SAVERY: When Elvis came [to Milam Junior High] from Lawhon school, East Tupelo was like a county. It was a municipality taken over by the City of Tupelo. They had their own little government there. Of course, it was segregated schools back then. Elvis was new to the school system—just like moving into town really.

ELOIS BEDFORD: Elvis was a loner. He liked people, but he was quiet.

JOE SAVERY: Elvis lived somewhere over where the jail is now. There was a low-income black section, what they called "Shakerag," across the tracks. I never went with Elvis to Shakerag, and I never heard him talk about going. I heard some people say that he went over there and got some of his musical ideas. He could have. I don't know. I've been over and through there a lot of times, but I don't ever remember anybody playing music or anything.

HAROLD LOYD: One time I was staying with Gladys and Vernon. I was in the Navy—home on boot leave. They had indoor facilities by then. Most places didn't, but they had 'em. They even had a bathtub, so I took me a bath. I had a habit that when I got finished taking a bath, I'd catch some water and rinse the tub down. Gladys liked that. "Elvis," she called, "come here." "What do you want, Mama?" he asked. "Come here!" she hollered back at him. So he came in, and she said, "Look a-here. See how clean that tub is? Harold, when he gets through taking a bath, he cleans it. Now it's ready for the next person. You should do that, you know." And Elvis said, "Oh, Mama, you called me all the way in here for that?"

CHRISTINE ROBERTS PRESLEY: Elvis was always a-helpin' when he came to stay with me. I had this old wringer-type of washing machine. He would put the clothes in for me and wash them when I would be making up beds, but Elvis wouldn't let the clothes wash long enough. I would have to take them all back down off the line and rewash them.

JOE SAVERY: Elvis wasn't a person that was trying to get everybody's attention. He wasn't loud or anything like that. He was well-behaved, very well-behaved, really.

I played with Elvis all the time at Milam Junior High School in sixth grade. All the playground was out in the front. They had a shed where they kept the bicycles, and we used to play around there. Elvis was very quiet to have become the showman that he did. It's a funny thing. I mean, he was just one of the gang. We would go out and play softball and touch football occasionally. By the way, Elvis wasn't a very good athlete.

Elvis wasn't taking a guitar out there in the playground like some people say either. Homerooms would get together back then. We're talking about very small classes, eighteen or nineteen. Maybe not that many. There was a boy named James Gault that carried the accordion, and Elvis had a guitar, and they would play together. I don't remember Elvis singing much, but I remember them playing. It was terrible.

GUY HARRIS: They'd let school out for Children's Day at the fair. It's about the only day we got to go to the fairground. If you marched in the Children's Day parade, then you got in the fair free.

My mom would fix lunch, and we'd take our lunch with us so we wouldn't spend any money for any kind of food. My mom usually fixed us a little-ol' jar of tea and some kind of sandwich, probably bologna, and we'd take it with us.

JOE SAVERY: My dad was president of the fair. I could have gone in anyway, but Elvis and I tried to go under the fence one time. There was an opening there that we were trying to go in and got caught. Later on people said Elvis got arrested trying to slip in. I've heard it said that the guards threw us out, but they didn't.

Mr. Parham, the guard that caught us, had known me for a long time. . . . He told my dad, "I want you to see who I caught trying to slip in the back gate!" They all laughed at us and told us not to try to slip in again. Then my dad let Elvis and me in the pass gate.

:◎:◎:◎:

BECKY MARTIN: One thing that bugs me, seems like it's always been insinuated that Elvis came from trash. That's wrong.

SHIRLEY JANE JONES: He wasn't a hillbilly. This is not hillbilly country.

We got the cream of the crop on this side of the tracks. There's lots of people, not just Elvis Presley, came from this side of town, the east side of the tracks, that has made good professional people that have good professional jobs, high quality and well thought of.

LAVERNE FARRAR: You talking about the "Beverly Hillbillies," that's who we was; but we loved it. We didn't know no difference. Everybody loved one another back then and didn't nobody try to get no better than nobody else.

HAROLD LOYD: You know, somebody started a rumor that Vernon and Gladys and Elvis moved to Memphis 'cause Elvis had got some little girl pregnant, and her parents were fixin' to force marriage on 'em. That's a bunch of crap. Elvis might have had a girlfriend while he was still living in Tupelo, you know how kids are when they're that age. But they were just girl "friends." That's all.

"They'll Run Us Out of Town!"
1949-1954

After arriving in Memphis, the Presleys find that the pattern dictated by hard times in East Tupelo continues: moving, only to move again; finding new jobs, only to lose them.

According to his new neighborhood buddies, Buzzy Forbes, Paul Dougher, and Ronnie Trout, young Elvis is always game for the three "G's" of life: good times, guitars, and girls. Classmate Fred Fredrick and Elvis's trusty confidants, George Klein and Ronnie Smith talk about his not-so-trusty wheels and his zoot-suitin' ways.

Cousin Harold Loyd pops in from Tupelo just in time to accompany Elvis to Memphis Recording Service, where a three dollar investment and some good ol' boy charm make a believer out of a young lady named Marion Keisker. With a simple flip of a switch, Marion sets in motion events that land Elvis an audition with her boss, record producer Sam Phillips. Musicians Scotty Moore, Stan Kesler, and Jack Clement reminisce about the uninhibited, unorthodox climate at Sun Records and the lucky accident that gives birth to rock 'n' roll.

> "He burst on the scene when the world needed a hero, when everybody needed a sunrise. We'd come through a depression. We'd come through a war. Everybody was ready to give vent to their emotions."
>
> Janelle McComb

Harold Loyd: Vernon and Gladys and Elvis moved on up to Memphis, where Vernon finally got him a job at United Paint Company. Got to be a foreman there. He was mixin' paint, but he picked up a five-gallon can of paint, pulled something in his back, and he was out of work quite a bit; so Gladys went to work at one of the hospitals as a helper, cleanin' rooms, emptyin' bedpans, and stuff like that.

Bill Perry *(paperboy)*: Elvis lived in a housing project. Now, the house we lived in wasn't anything to shout about; it wasn't a mansion or anything. But we didn't live in public housing, either.

Buzzy Forbes *(neighborhood friend)*: The first time I met Elvis was right about 1949. We lived in this same building in the Lauderdale Courts. The building was very big; it had multiple units on each end and in the middle. Elvis lived in one section of the same building where I lived. I had already met Paul Dougher, who became one of our mutual friends, and I was going to visit him. As I was going up the steps—well, Elvis was there. That's the first time I ever saw him. He was talking to one of the girls in the apartments there, Billie Wardlow. He said, "Hello." I had some comic books that I was carrying up to my friend, and they were rolled up. I reached over and slapped Elvis on the back of the head with them as I went by, and, pow, he slapped me back, on the back of the head. I turned around with fire in my eyes, and we like to have got into a fight the first time I ever met him. We glared at each other for a second or two, then he grinned, and I did, too, and I shook hands and went on upstairs.

Paul Dougher *(neighborhood friend)*: Billie Wardlow was Elvis's first real girlfriend as far as I knew. She lived on the second floor, and we all saw each other every day. She used to hang out the window and talk to the guys. She said she couldn't come out because she didn't have any clothes to wear. Elvis took her a pair of blue jeans and gave them to her.

BUZZY FORBES: I can't say that Elvis's mother never followed him to school in her lifetime—the first day, or whatever—but I never saw her go to school with him. Hell, Paul and Farley [Guy, another neighborhood friend] and Elvis and I were going to school all the time. Heck, we walked through the Courts together, and walked across the bayou, to and from school.

PAUL DOUGHER: In school Elvis was real quiet. He didn't associate in groups. He wasn't one to just have people around him all the time, and he was different as far as his dress went, so some people just thought he was kinda strange. But he always had two or three close friends.

BUZZY FORBES: The kids in Lauderdale Courts were all day long trying to figure ways to have fun, things to do without much money. Most of the kids didn't have jobs, and, of course, most of them were from one-parent families. So, you had a lot of time on your hands, and kids spent a lot of time playing and doing stuff together.

PAUL DOUGHER: There was a swimming pool down the street several blocks away. It was the old Malone swimming pool. Me and Buzzy, Farley, and Elvis would go. Of course, Elvis had to have permission to go anywhere. His mother was really strict on knowing where he was at and wanting to protect him and things like that. Of course, we would have to beg her to let him go, a lot of times. My mother would have to go, too, in order for Elvis to go. My mother and his mother were good friends. Elvis's mother wouldn't go to the swimming pool, but she knew my mother would go and watch and see that we didn't get into any trouble.

Sometimes we'd just hang out with the other kids in the neighborhood and talk and ride bikes. Sometimes we'd go to the movies. I think it cost a dime. If Elvis didn't have the money, I might have it; or if I didn't have it, maybe Buzzy would have it. Times were simple as far as what we did.

RONNIE TROUT *(classmate and friend)*: We would play kick-the-can in Lauderdale Courts. It was like hide-and-go-seek. My girlfriend liked to go and hide with Elvis to make me jealous. I thought it was kind of silly because I knew what she was doing. At that time I thought I had more going for me than Elvis did.

PAUL DOUGHER: Elvis and Billie [Wardlow] started sitting outside at night together, and that sort of thing.

He'd take her to the local ice cream place. She was a pretty girl, real pretty girl at that age. He really did like her. Had he been older, they would have probably gotten married. I don't doubt it, 'cause he talked about her all the time when we were together—as far as how much he liked her.

There was a lot of good times at the Lauderdale Courts when we were thirteen, fourteen, and fifteen years old. We had good times playing ball and chasing the girls around there.

BUZZY FORBES: Elvis really liked cork ball. In fact, I don't know any kids that grew up at that time that didn't. Cork ball was a little like baseball, only you used a broom handle for a bat and a piece of cork wrapped with tape for a ball.

PAUL DOUGHER: Elvis was a good athlete, very quick, but he didn't really like team athletics. In his younger years he didn't want to be on a team like a baseball team. He played ball in the field, sandlot and football, and he was good at it—a lot better than some of us. He was a lot faster than I was. If he had put his mind to it, he could have been a good football player.

BUZZY FORBES: All the boys used to play football. In fact, on Saturdays sometimes when it wasn't football season, we would go to other people's neighborhoods to have football contests. It wasn't unusual to put up ten or fifteen cents a game.

We was playing football down there one day, and when we got through we come in. I'd done been bounced off the concrete, and my elbows were blue and bloody and messed up. We walked in the living room there, and Mrs. Presley looked at me, and she just burst into tears. She was soft-hearted. She couldn't take a whole lot of that sort of stuff.

BILL PERRY: I delivered papers to the Presleys' apartment. 'Course these people were not my friends, but I knew their son. I didn't like Vernon. He was mean, cranky. I didn't like to talk to him. A lot of people have a tendency to treat children like second-class citizens, and that's the way Vernon treated me. He never had any money; he would never pay me. Elvis's mother always paid me. Whether he had any money I don't know, but I always considered Vernon to be just a bum, just a man that didn't take very good care of his family. I believe that he drank, I really do. If I remember, I think he was intoxicated quite a bit. Or not quite a bit, but, you know, several times that I saw him. Again, I understand where he was raised men did drink like that.

I thought Gladys was a very nice lady. When I think about the days I saw her, it seems like she was rather unhappy. She looked tired all the time. She had these dark spots under her eyes, and she was heavy, too. But I always kind of felt sorry for her. I thought she probably deserved more than she was getting.

BARBARA PITTMAN *(neighborhood friend)*: Elvis's mother and my mother worked together. They were best friends. They used to have Stanley parties in the housing projects to get money together. That's how I knew Gladys. That's how I knew the family. My family did manage to get into a new housing project, Hurt Village. It was beautiful then; it was like townhouses. Elvis was so jealous of that; he used to come over there and say, "How in the world? We never had anything like this in the projects."

PAUL DOUGHER: We knew we didn't have what other kids had. We could see that at school. We could see the way they dressed, but it didn't make any difference back then whether a guy was dressed nicer than me or not if he was a friend.

BUZZY FORBES: We knew we were poor, but it wasn't like it was something wrong with being poor. I don't know of anyone that was hungry, but we didn't have a lot of extra money to throw away.

RONNIE TROUT: Elvis and his mother and his grandmother would go to the Poplar Street Mission together at night for the preaching and the gospel music. Brother Denson was the evangelistic preacher, and his mission on Poplar was down on skid row. They would take down-and-outers and give them a place to sleep and breakfast and so on. They had boxes there of clothes that were donated. These were for the transients that needed clothing of different types. Of course, when people discard their clothes, they discard all manner of clothes. The Denson folks let Elvis look through the box and see if there was anything in there that he could wear. Elvis would dig out some of the clothes that he really liked, and that was, supposedly, where Elvis got a lot of the dress pants, sport coats, and things like that that he would put together as an outfit.

PAUL DOUGHER: I would go into the Presleys' apartment, and Gladys and Vernon and sometimes Elvis would be sitting and talking. Gladys and

Vernon were real nice people. I would go in, and if they were eating she'd say, "Sit down. Have something to eat." We would listen to the radio, 'cause back then none of us had TV.

Elvis always wanted to sing. He sang a lot of gospel around the house. When we would sit in his room, he would sing gospel songs and popular songs, too, but he never expressed the fact to me that, "I'm going to be a singer," or "I'm going to be in the movies." That never came out. He might have thought it in his mind, but he never said it to me.

BUZZY FORBES: We used to have parties in some of our apartments. We would invite kids from the school and what have you. We'd have Cokes, and listen to music, and all of us would be dancing. Well, Elvis didn't dance. All of us would be dancing, and Elvis would be mimicking the guitar to the beat of the record. He was doing his own gyrations even back then—the identical gyrations that you saw when he turned professional. It was just feeling and movement that he had when he played music. It was the feeling you got from listening to the bop beat that was popular back at that time.

PAUL DOUGHER: Elvis was real bashful playing at first; but he'd turn the radio on, hear a new song, and in thirty minutes time he could play it.

Finally, Elvis got to where come night he would sit out on the porch and start playing his guitar—just us, and my mother, and his mother and father, all of us sitting out there. Before long he would have a little crowd out there in the front yard. It kinda got to be a ritual of doing that, you know. Two or three nights a week he would sit out there and sing and give everybody a little concert.

We all liked Elvis's singing. My mother liked it, and all the kids did. If they heard him singing, they would come up and sit down until he decided to quit. He would play for an hour and a half, sometimes. He could sing good then. Of course, he got better the older he got.

FRED FREDRICK *(classmate and friend)*: Our friendship at school was simple; I admired Elvis because he was nice to me. I always remember that I was a younger guy that Elvis spent some time with for no apparent reason other than just either to help me out or whatever, but I liked it.

MACK GURLEY *(friend)*: I met Elvis in about 1950, when we were in high school. I had a car and he didn't then, so I was always giving him a ride.

For a long time he would have me drop him off a couple of blocks from home because he was embarrassed about living in the projects, and he didn't want me to know.

We both loved music, and the subjects any time we had discussions were music, girls, and cars—same as most red-blooded American boys. Elvis was always tapping with the music on the radio, or humming, or he'd burst out with a line, even in those days.

We'd listen to rhythm and blues, either country or rhythm and blues—that's the only stations we'd listen to—and, of course, to gospel music.

JAMES BLACKWOOD *(gospel singer)*: The Blackwood Brothers had a daily radio broadcast at noon on WMPS in Memphis from 1950 until about 1955. People would take noon break and come up and sit in the studio and watch the broadcast.

It was quite a large radio studio, and they had seats in it for people to come and watch. Bob Neal was our radio announcer. We would sing, and Bob Neal would do the commercials. This was in the days before tape. We had to do it live.

J. D. SUMNER *(gospel singer)*: Elvis used to attend our gospel concerts in Memphis every month when I was with the Blackwood Brothers. He would come to the concerts when he was a kid—fourteen years old—and come around backstage. At that time I didn't even know his name. He was just a nice kid, and we were friends from the very beginning. I used to let him in the back door for our shows for nothing; and then the first thing I knew, [after he became famous] he let me in the back door of his concerts for nothing. And when he needed a gospel quartet, well, he'd contact me.

:◉:◉:◉:

RONNIE SMITH *(musician and friend)*: Vernon had an old Lincoln [Zephyr] that Elvis was driving when he went to work at Precision Tools. They made artillery shells for the Army down there.

GEORGE KLEIN *(classmate and friend)*: There was a rumor that Elvis was fired from Precision Tools because his hair was too long, but that's not true. He was let go because he was too young to work there—but he did have slightly long hair.

RONNIE TROUT: A lot of people had long hair, and a lot of people had the ducktails and so forth; but Elvis was one of the first that wore sideburns —long sideburns.

The greasy thing was in. The guys back in the forties used Vitalis or whatever on their hair, but in the fifties you used water. You just wet your hair at the school fountain, or whatever, and combed it, and it stayed that way. During the summer, there wasn't no air conditioning back then, so just the natural oil would make your hair look greasy.

Elvis and I were in the bathroom at wood shop one time. There was this big wash basin where you would wash all the stain and shellac and glue and stuff off your hands; so we were in there cleaning up. Elvis was combing his hair, and I was washing my hands. He says, "Hey, Ronnie, how do you like my hair?" Some guys were teasing him by saying Elvis had a "Toni home permanent." They just referred to any permanent back then as a "Toni," and some boys got them. Elvis had dyed his hair black and had gotten what looked like a permanent wave in the front. I said, "Well, Elvis, it looks really good. I like it like that." I felt sorry for him, because people would mess him around 'cause he looked different and acted different.

BARBARA PITTMAN: I'll never forget the time when Elvis put black shoe polish on his hair to see how he would look black-headed. That was before he dyed it. We were doing a show out on Jackson Avenue at the [Little Flower] Catholic church, and after the show it started pouring down rain. Elvis's daddy's old car wouldn't start. We had to push it down Faxon Avenue, and the black shoe polish was coming out all over Elvis's face. He could almost do an Al Jolson.

Tony Curtis was Elvis's idol. So Elvis said, "To look like Tony Curtis, you have to have black hair." Elvis wanted to be a matinee idol—just had to be. He said, "Look, there is no blonde-headed idol except James Dean." Elvis just worshiped Tony Curtis and Rudolph Valentino.

BILL PERRY: Elvis kind of puffed his hair up in the front. (What do you call it? Pompadour.) And he always wore unusual clothing. He had good taste, but his clothing was unusual. Just like the day he came to school wearing pink trousers. He bought the trousers in a tailor shop on North Main—Ike's or the Tiger Shop—that mostly catered to people of color rather than to white people.

GEORGE KLEIN: While everybody else was wearing T-shirts and Levi's, Elvis was wearing dress pants and maybe a sports shirt or a sport coat with the collar turned up and a stripe down the side of the sleeve; you know, something different. The guys would kid him quite a bit, but he took it good-naturedly.

RONNIE TROUT: I had never seen Elvis in blue jeans, but one day he wore a pair to school. One thing that got my attention was they weren't Levi's like everybody else's. They were the blue-jean blue jeans with baggy legs that you couldn't wear and still be a cool guy back then. They were about the least expensive you could get. The reason I knew a little about it was 'cause I had been working selling jeans at Lansky's. But, anyway, that particular day Elvis told me, almost apologetically, when he sat down, "Hey, Ronnie, I had to wear my blue jeans today." I thought, "Well, what's that?" He said, "All my other pants are in the cleaners." Elvis said it like he was apologizing for having to wear jeans—and that's what everyone else wore. I've thought about it a lot. It might have been that Elvis thought maybe I'd be disappointed because he was only wearing jeans. It's like he had an appearance he had to keep up at all times, and that particular day he couldn't do it. . . .

The first time my [future] wife ever saw Elvis, we were at a football game. At half-time, people would just walk around the track. So Elvis was down walking around the track. He had on his whole get-up. He had his sunglasses on, even though it was at night, and he got my wife's attention. She said, "Who is that guy down there?"

Anytime anybody was different, people would make fun of them. They would do that with Elvis because of the way he dressed. He would wear dress pants or a shirt open at the collar to school. He would take a scarf and kinda fashion it like an ascot, tie it like a movie producer. Then he'd wear a sport coat, like a one-button coat that looked kinda like a zoot suit. All the other guys were wearing denim, T-shirts, loafers, moccasins, things like that. So, Elvis stood out. When you do that, you're asking for it, especially in North Memphis at Humes High School.

MACK GURLEY: I didn't go to the same school, but Elvis was always joking about the fact that he had failed music. My wife looked up his school records one time, and, sure enough, he did fail music. Other than that, he was an average student.

FRED FREDRICK: Elvis and I were in wood shop together. We didn't have any chairs or desks or anything, just five or six massive worktables, and everybody had an area. Just by chance, we were kind of together in one area.

Anyway, we talked a lot. I remember so well Elvis talking about various girlfriends, but especially Dixie [Locke]. You know how guys will talk: "this girl's got nice hips . . . her hair smells good . . . she's well-built," and that type of thing. The talk was always about how Elvis admired women. He was very protective, extremely protective of who the conversation was about. You could hear the respect in everything that Elvis talked about, how he wanted to meet certain ones, how he was gonna go to the dance with this particular one; you know.

RONNIE SMITH: I remember Elvis coming down Mississippi Boulevard; I guess he was going to see Patty Philpot—she lived on Mississippi. Then he'd go down to see Dixie Locke. Neither one of them knew about the other one. Elvis stopped and asked me about Patty. I told him, "I don't know, but she's sure spent a lot of money on lipstick. I'll put it that way." Elvis said, "Oh, me!" He was supposed to see them both that night.

:◎:◎:◎:

FRED FREDRICK: Elvis liked the ladies, and he loved football. He just wasn't very big at the time, but he played. We played a lot of touch football during recess out on the football field, so there was always some activity there. I remember there was always a big day at Humes when you had junior/senior fights—the juniors in a game against the seniors—and Elvis would play. There was no sissy about Elvis at all.

BUZZY FORBES: Elvis, he wasn't overly muscular—on the front end, you wouldn't have been afraid of him—but if it came to a scrap, someone would have had a surprise coming. Elvis had real good, quick reflexes; I've never known him to lose a scrap, and I've seen him in quite a few.
  Contrary to what you may have heard, Elvis was not kicked off the football team at Humes High School. I think he started in the spring practice of the eleventh grade. He was part of the team, and he liked it. His desire was there, but he wasn't big enough and developed enough to be on the first team. He quit because he just didn't have time. Elvis needed to get a job and he did. He went to work at the theater.

PAUL DOUGHER: Elvis liked working at the Loew's State theater 'cause he was making money. He got to see girls down there, and he got to see movies free. He talked me into getting a job with him. He said, "I'll get you a job, and we can work together." So, I went down there with him and he got the guy to hire me. We were ushers. It was fun. There was always something going on. One night it was real slow in the theater, and he said, "I think I'll just run down the stairs and holler 'Fire!'" I said, "You won't do that." He said, "Yeah, I will." And he did it!

Down the stairs he went, "Fire!" All these people jumped up and run out, and here comes the manager, wantin' to know what was going on. Elvis said, "Well, I thought there was a fire upstairs. He went back up there and, of course, there wasn't nothing, and he said, "I must been mistaken." The guy didn't say anything, but all the people were standing outside. Elvis had a strange sense of humor.

BERNARD LANSKY (*Beale Street [Memphis] clothier*): When Elvis started working at the Loew's theater, he used to walk down to the corner on coffee break and look in the window. Beale Street in its heyday was a dynamite street; it was fantastic. We were the first door, right off the corner from Main Street. People would come down and see what was happening. Elvis would stand there looking, and I'd say, "Come in and let me show you around." Elvis laughed and said, "I don't have no money, but when I get rich, I'll buy you out." I said, "No, don't buy me out, just buy it from me."

:◎:◎:◎:

GEORGE KLEIN: The day our senior class show came, the same guys who had been kidding Elvis were standing up and cheering for him. He had that ability of winning you over—that charisma.

RONNIE TROUT: It was not a talent contest. There were no prizes given. All these kids were just on the program because they had some kind of talent.

FRED FREDRICK: There was like fifteen hundred students there. It was the seventh through the senior year, and you had parents; so there was a lot of people there. After the talent show, people were much friendlier to Elvis.

Elvis was very active, but he wasn't active in the drama club or the glee club. He was in R.O.T.C. It was a very military-type, regimented-type thing. He liked the military. He liked the uniform. And he liked wood shop.

Wood shop was the last class of the day; so whenever the bell rang, we all left. If you helped Elvis push his car off—'cause it never would start on its own—he'd give you a ride home.

Paul Dougher: That old twelve-cylinder Lincoln could really drink gas. You'd just go around the block and it seemed like it drank up two or three dollars worth of gas. Elvis would say, "Y'all want to go for a ride?" We'd say, "Yeah." "Well, y'all chip in money for the gas." We would chip in, and around the block we would go; but only two or three times around. Then Elvis would stop and say, "Okay, that's it." And he'd let us out, but he would have enough gas to go wherever he wanted to go. It was funny. We would say, "We didn't get no ride; you just took us around the block." And he'd laugh and go on.

After Elvis moved out of the Courts and down on Alabama [Street], we'd go looking for him, 'cause he had a car and we didn't. Usually he wouldn't be around. He would be gone somewhere. He said he went down to Beale Street and listened to the gospel or the guys sing down there on the street.

Buzzy Forbes: We went to the Suzore [theater], and we'd pass the Green Owl, which was on Market and Main. On Friday and Saturday nights some guys would be outside with a bucket and strings, playing that sorta stuff. They were good, and we liked to watch them. They were good enough to appreciate, but we didn't sit there and spend hours watching them. Beale Street is not where—as much as people try and say it—that's not where Elvis got his feelings about singing.

Jerry Baxter *(friend)*: The whole way that Elvis carried himself and everything, I think that was original. He just had a style of his own. I think he learned most of his moves at the Catholic [CYO, Catholic Youth Organization-sponsored] dances.

Everybody went stag to the dances back then. You would just dance with everybody and have jam sessions and cut in. When you left, everybody would load up [in cars] and go over across the bridge—there wasn't but one bridge then—to West Memphis, Arkansas.

Fred Fredrick: This went on for five years. There was a steady stream right down Jackson [Avenue] to the bridge, right across the bridge to Danny's. In West Memphis there were three night clubs [popular with the teenagers]: The Plantation Inn, The Cotton Club, and Danny's. The Cotton Club you couldn't get in unless you were armed to the teeth. Danny's was a bad-assed place to go, too. That's where the real, *real* dancers went. Later when Willie Mitchell became the house band at Danny's, that kind of took our group away from the Plantation Inn.

Willie played all kinds of his own music. Elvis went to Danny's because of Willie Mitchell—because of the music. It was different; it wasn't white hillbilly and it wasn't the black blues. It was a danceable music deal. It was the only band playing the music we wanted to dance to, and that was the difference. Every Saturday night at Danny's they would have a big revue, and two little guys would get out on the floor and dance—like break dancing.

I never saw Elvis dance other than slow dance with a girl back then, but he would watch. He got into that. I always kidded him about being in time with the music, but he did some really good foot music. Those clubs gave Elvis an awful lot of his music.

BUZZY FORBES: Elvis was a little unique. Certain things were more important to him. The way he dressed was important to him. For people to like him was important to him. To be able to stand on his own two feet and take care of himself was important to him. And he exerted effort to make sure these things happened as best he could.

RONNIE TROUT: Elvis had some black pants that had a loose look, but they were pegged at the bottom, tight around the ankle, and had that zoot-suit look. Elvis's taste was strictly for something far out. He wanted to be seen. He wanted to make a statement: "Hey, look at me." That's a paradox, because Elvis was one of the shiest humans that I knew at Humes High School—just morbidly shy.

BERNARD LANSKY: When Elvis was in high school, I put his junior-senior prom suit coat on him. It was pink and black. Pink and black was hot. I put his first tuxedo on him when he graduated.

BUZZY FORBES: The only high school picture people really ever see of him is that graduation picture. Elvis liked all his friends' curly hair, so he done put a little bit of curl into his hair, too, and it's terrible. It's not Elvis. That's the worst picture I've ever seen of him.

RONNIE TROUT: Elvis was proud of his high school diploma—coming from absolutely zero. Anything that was of any note, such as graduating from high school or even being in a high school program, he was proud of as a personal accomplishment. I think it made him happy, too, because he knew it pleased his family.

LARRY GELLER *(hair stylist)*: Elvis said to me once, "You know, I don't know why they gave me a diploma. I don't know how I got out of high school. I would sit there, and I'd just be looking out the window. I had no idea what the teacher was saying. I'd be thinking about Tony Curtis and Marlon Brando, and being a star, and singing. My whole life is a dream. I was dreaming."

:◎:◎:◎:

HAROLD LOYD: I never did hear Elvis talk about wantin' to get in the music business. But we went down to Sun [Memphis Recording Service] to make a record for Gladys, and that's how he got started—just pure accident.

RONNIE SMITH: I was trying to figure out why Elvis went down to Sun. Everybody says it was to make a birthday present [record] for his mother, but it couldn't have been. It wasn't her birthday.

Besides, back then they had these discs, they were a carryover from the Second World War, 'cause a lot of people, instead of writing letters, would go in and make a little record and send it to their husbands or boyfriends. You could buy blank records at Grants or Sears or anywhere and go make your own little records.

EDDIE BOND *(disc jockey and band leader)*: Everybody knew what everybody else was doing in those days. Everybody was going there, trying to get Sam Phillips [owner of Sun Records] to listen or something. Sam had black music on his mind—totally, one hundred percent. No white person had a chance, not a chance.

HAROLD LOYD: Mrs. [Marion] Keisker was workin' there in the office at Sun and was the one that recorded that first song ["My Happiness," August, 1953] for Elvis. She made herself a copy, too.

JACK CLEMENT *(musician friend)*: The way I understand it, Sam was at a wedding, taping, that Saturday, and Marion was there looking after the office, as well as doing those four-dollar records for people. She knew how to set the mike up and run the lathe to cut the disc. Sam had taught her how to do all that stuff. There wasn't much to it. Anyway, Sam wasn't there the first day Elvis came in, and Marion was.

MARION KEISKER *(Sun Records employee)*: Now for some reason Sam doesn't want to give me credit for being the first one to believe in Elvis, but I was.

Elvis came in to make a record one Saturday. Sam was off somewhere doing something, and I was really busy. Elvis had to wait awhile (there were a lot of people there), but I finally got around to him. He was very polite. While I was getting ready, I asked him what kind of singer he was. He told me he sang all kinds of songs. I asked him, "Well, who do you sound like?" He said, "I don't sound like nobody." We got all set up—he had a guitar with him—and he recorded two songs, "That's When Your Heartaches Begin" and "My Happiness," and something struck me about him. I'm not quite sure what, but about the middle of the first song, I flipped on the tape recorder and made a copy for Sam to hear later and wrote down his name and his neighbor's phone number.

Sam was always telling people he wished he could find a white boy who could sing like a black boy, so I kept trying to get Sam to listen to the tape I had made with this Presley kid, but it took months and months. . . .

:◎:◎:◎:

FRED FREDRICK: Elvis had started working for Crown Electric as an apprentice electrician—making a pretty good living. He was delivering electrical parts from place to place. He was driving a little pickup truck with a Crown Electric logo on the side. Everybody thinks Elvis was a big truck driver. No, no, no!—little bitty truck, little black Chevrolet, like a fifty model.

PAUL BURLISON *(musician friend)*: Elvis swept the floor, put up stock, and unloaded trucks when they came in with materials. Him being an apprentice (you'd get to be an electrician in four years) he had to learn the material, couplings, connectors, et cetera.

One day I happened to go into the shop, and I heard this guitar there in the back playing. So I stuck my head in the door, and Elvis was sitting up on the table playing chords and singing. It was lunch time, so I walked in there and told him it sounded "pretty good." Elvis was doing some country song, and he just said, "Thanks." Elvis was kinda shy back then; he really was.

RONNIE SMITH: The first time Elvis ever played before a live audience was at this Moose Lodge meeting thing at the Columbia Mutual Towers. I put together this band, Elvis and me, but a couple of guys didn't like Elvis and they wouldn't get up there onstage. So we got up and sang every song we knew.

Later on when I was playing guitar with Eddie Bond's band at the Hi-Hat, I told Elvis to come out and let Eddie hear him sing because we needed a singer real bad. Elvis had been sittin' in playin' around town, and he really wanted a gig. But before Eddie could hire him, Elvis got his call from Sun Records.

MARION KEISKER: Almost a year after Elvis recorded "My Happiness," Sam got all excited about a new song he'd found, but couldn't find anyone to sing. I mentioned Elvis to him again. We got Elvis to come in and try, but he couldn't do the song to satisfy Sam. That might have been the end of it, but something stirred Sam's interest, so he got Scotty Moore to work with the kid and see what they could come up with.

SCOTTY MOORE *(musician)*: It was something that I'd always wanted to do. I was always putting one group or another together. I'd had a country group [the Starlite Wranglers] in Memphis, and they'd cut one record with Sam on Sun. I think there was six of us and we sold six copies. Sam and I were talking every day, about, you know, "Well let's try this. What do you think's gonna happen next?" All this evolved into getting Elvis to come in.

JACK CLEMENT: Sun was just a place that was a lot more experimental than most. I think that is the main thing that made it happen. It was just the only place them weirdos could go.

STAN KESLER *(songwriter)*: I remember how much fun it was in the early days, how relaxed it was—the easy feeling, the good feeling. At Sun you always felt at home. Sam had a way of making everybody feel like a king when he walked in the door.

PAUL BURLISON: We [musicians] would just sit in a circle, and everybody would nod at each other. No drum booth. No singer's booth. Nothing. Just put a mike out there on the floor and sing. That's the way we did it.

SCOTTY MOORE: It was just an audition. [The day they accidentally cut Elvis's first hit.] That's the only reason there was just Bill Black and myself in the studio. We just needed enough music to see what Elvis sounded like on tape, 'cause the first recording he did was on acetate. We were just searching around. Sam was just trying to get a line on his voice. Did he sing this kind of song or tempo better?

STAN KESLER: That's when it all happened; it was an accident really. Sam says they were just trying things, and during a break Elvis picked up his guitar and started singing. Then Bill started slapping the bass, just clowning around. Well, Sam heard it, and Sam's very perceptive about things like that—things that are different. That's what he was looking for: something that was different, because Memphis couldn't compete with Nashville on just ordinary country records. When Sam heard the guys cutting up out in the studio, he said, "Wait a minute. Start that over." Scotty got his guitar and joined in.

SCOTTY MOORE: Up until we did "That's All Right (Mama)," all Sam would say was, "That's pretty good. We might come back and try that again later." But when we did "That's All Right (Mama)," Sam said, "What are y'all doing?" We said, "We don't know." No more instruments than we had, I was just trying to make as much noise as we could. That's probably what we thought it was while we were doing it. But when we heard a playback, we knew we had some kind of rhythm, a little different rhythm, but none of us knew what to call it, so we didn't call it anything at that time.

CARL PERKINS *(musician, songwriter, friend)*: The music we did in the early fifties, what they call "rockabilly," was basically country music. I think the very bottom line of rockabilly music was country boys influenced with country music and then Southern black spirituals—maybe not altogether the black spirituals, but that rhythm—that feel—that black music had.

SAM PHILLIPS *(owner of Sun Records and Memphis Recording Service)*: Rock 'n' roll and rhythm and blues tended not to be something you wanted to copy exactly. You wanted to feel it. We tried to get in the general bag of it and hope that it was successful. There were enough copyists. We did not want to copy Nashville and the good singers they had there.

EDDIE BOND: I think the sound was discovered accidentally. Scotty and Bill were playing real country. Scotty was a country guitar picker, but he loved Chet Atkins. I don't know if you have followed Chet Atkins's music, but that's exactly what Scotty done. Scotty took Chet Atkins's guitar [style]. (He couldn't play Chet Atkins very good, but he played what he did know like Chet Atkins would have if Chet Atkins didn't know how to play. I guess you could say it something like that.) It came out like something new. The slapping bass had been around for a long time, but they really made it dominate. It was almost like beating the drum.

SAM PHILLIPS: Without rhythm we would have been dead. [The early Sun sound] was a spontaneous rhythm thing no matter what the tempo of the song. Tempo should not have that much to do with rhythm. If you've got a good rhythm section that is cookin', if there is that movement, it tends to universalize the feel.

JACK CLEMENT: Elvis was the whole rhythm section on a whole bunch of his first records, the first four at least. Wasn't no drums on there, just him and a bass, with Scotty playing lead guitar. Elvis could have been a hell of a musician, I think. But, he just never bothered to learn more chords. He didn't need to, really. He was having a ball—really enjoying it.

SCOTTY MOORE: When we finished doing the songs, Sam played 'em back for us. We got excited, but we just shook our heads. I said, "Good god! They'll run us out of town when they hear this!"

Sam said he'd take it down to Dewey Phillips [a WHBQ disc jockey] and play it for him.

ABE SCHWAB *(proprietor, A. Schwab's Dry Goods on Beale Street)*: Dewey was something! Every day a radio station gets a stack of records this high, and the secretary takes them to the garbage can and throws them in. Nobody wants them. Ain't nobody interested. Un-uh! Dewey Phillips listens to every record. He hears one that's different; he takes and hides it way in the back somewhere for about a week. Everybody else'll get rid of their copy. Then he comes out with his new hit, and he's got the only copy in the city of Memphis. Everyone had to listen to Dewey's show to know what's new!

STAN KESLER: Dewey Phillips was the first one to play an Elvis record. I have to give him credit; he did get Elvis started. He's really the one. It was July 7, 1954.

MARTY LACKER *(schoolmate)*: In July of 1954 there was this buddy of mine from school—Monty Weiner was his name. We were driving down Vollintine Avenue in Memphis in his car at night listening to the Dewey Phillips radio show. Dewey was saying, "We got this boy here from Humes High School, and this is his first record, and the first time we're playing it. I want to see what y'all like about it." Of course, Monty and I looked at each other and said, "Humes High! Who the hell is that?" Dewey played the record and it sounded great to us. It was so different. We were really into what then was called "race music," you know, R&B, black music. Well, the record plays, and we said, "Man, that was a great record!" When the record ended and Dewey said, "That's Elvis Presley," Monty almost ran into a pole! He screeched the car to a stop, and we both looked at each other and we said, "Elvis?"

EDDIE BOND: Dewey didn't call him "Elvis" though; he called him "Elton Preston." He didn't know his name or maybe couldn't pronounce his name: "Elton Preston's got a new record here."

RONNIE SMITH: At first we couldn't believe that they let Elvis sing on the radio. We didn't believe at first that it was a record. We couldn't figure it out.

EDDIE BOND: I remember Dewey Phillips played Elvis's record six times straight. Dewey says, "It's gonna be a hit! It's gonna be a hit! Elvis, if you're out there listening, come on down here. I want to talk to you." Elvis went down and talked to him.

STAN KESLER: When I first heard Elvis's first record on the air, it just flabbergasted me. I said, "Gosh, who is this? What kind of music is this?" I think the disc jockeys were in the same boat: "This don't fit. I'm playing Webb Pierce and Faron Young. He don't sound like them. Is he black?" And of course, the black disc jockeys, they were saying, "Well, this guy's got to be white, but he don't sound it. Where does he fit?"

JACK CLEMENT: One morning in Memphis, I turned on my radio and Sleepy-Eyed John [Lepley] said, "Here's that record everybody's been raving about." And here comes "Blue Moon of Kentucky." That woke me right up! I loved it! It was kind of a revelation. It was like, "Hey, I've been waiting for that." The same reaction was instantaneous around Memphis. The record was just so uninhibited, so fresh, and it just didn't sound like anything else. When I heard it, I said, "Why didn't I think of that?" It was so obvious: somebody just goes into the studio and just does it, not like they're making a record. It was the amateurishness of the whole thing, I think, that made it float. Just the uninhibitedness of it all.

I didn't particularly hear black music in his style. I didn't make that kinda connection. To me he was more like a bluegrasser that was having fun without a banjo.

PAUL DOUGHER: From that time on, the people that really knew Elvis realized he had something special and was going to make it. I always knew he could sing from hearing him every day—but to hear him on the air!

JACK CLEMENT: In Memphis, Elvis was a star overnight.

EDDIE BOND: After the record was first released [July 19, 1954], I heard that [songwriter] Bill Monroe said, "He ruined my damn song." He told a lot of people that. I heard it all over Nashville. "He ruined my damn song!"

BILL MONROE *(star of the Grand Ole Opry, writer of "Blue Moon of Kentucky)*: What kinda bothered me, you know, was changing it from my way of singing, the bluegrass style, to another style. That's the only thing. I didn't know how it was going to work out.

:◎:◎:◎:

SCOTTY MOORE: We started doing a few little shows around Memphis, and then started spreading out.

JACK CLEMENT: Bob Neal had been around Memphis for years. He was always into dramatics, and he used to produce a lot of plays and stuff on radio there in Memphis on WMPS. That was a powerful station. In the beginning Neal would go out on the road to do shows, and sometimes he took Elvis and Bill and Scotty along. He was quite well-known and respected around Memphis before he branched off into management. People would come to see Bob back then, not Elvis.

SONNY NEAL *(friend)*: Dad [Bob Neal] was promoting shows in the Memphis area, and we did all the shows there at Ellis Auditorium. Then he'd take the shows we had at Ellis, and we'd tour out through Arkansas and Mississippi—everywhere within about a two hundred-mile radius.

During the summertime we did shows out at the shell in Overton Park. Dad put Elvis on one of his shows there when "Blue Moon of Kentucky" came out.

SLIM WHITMAN *(recording artist)*: The first time I met Elvis I was headlining at a show in the Overton Park Shell in Memphis. Bob Neal was the one that brought us in. I didn't know Elvis then, but after that show I sure did. He only had out one record, "Blue Moon of Kentucky" backed with "That's All Right (Mama)."

BILLY WALKER *(recording artist)*: Slim Whitman and I were both working the Louisiana Hayride and booking out of Shreveport, Louisiana. I'd had three hits, and Slim was coming off a million seller, "Indian Love Call." So when Bob Neal asked us in Memphis if we would care if this new kid went on and did a couple of numbers, I said, "Man, it don't make any difference to me. Put him on the show." I wasn't worried about a newcomer.

Talk about being unknown, they called him "Elvin" when they introduced him.

PAUL BURLISON: I was just standing around with some friends of mine when they introduced them. I remember them going onstage ... I thought Elvis was shaking because he was nervous, but I think Scotty was more scared than Elvis.

SCOTTY MOORE: The girls went crazy! Elvis didn't know why; none of us knew why. When we came off stage, somebody told Elvis it was because he was shaking his leg. That was a natural thing for him. It wasn't planned. Most guys would stand flat-footed, play guitar, and pat their foot. Well, Elvis would just kinda roll up on the balls of his feet—kinda in a tense way—and with his arm playing rhythm and everything. He was wearing those big, baggy pants back in those days, and his britches' leg would just start going crazy. Naturally, once he found out what was happening, he started embellishing on that real quick. I mean, he was smart.

:◎:◎:◎:

JACK CLEMENT: When I met Elvis, I was playing at a place called the Eagle's Nest. It was promoted by Sleepy-Eyed John, the disc jockey. It was Sleepy-Eyed John's deal. He rented the Eagle's Nest and hired my band and hired Elvis. I was the lead singer and the emcee, and Elvis was the floor show. He was the one that drew the crowd. When Elvis got up there with them three pieces, the crowd went nuts. Everybody was dancing, dancing better than they were to our eight-piece, western swing band.

RONNIE SMITH: John Lepley [Sleepy-Eyed John] was the manager at the Eagle's Nest. Anyway, Elvis was booked out there, playing one night, and John brought him outside. Reg [Reggie Young] and I was sitting out there with our guitars, and John was cussing and talking to Elvis bad. The argument had to do with songs. John said, "I told you before to quit singing that song," blah, blah, blah, and dammit this and dammit that. Elvis just listened.

Later when we got into the car, Elvis was laughing: "I ain't paying no attention to him. I don't have to be out there." It was that kind of an attitude, but he was very polite and taking all that stuff when nobody I knew would have done it. Any other guy would have left John laying there on the floor.

JACK CLEMENT: Elvis was great, a lot of fun, except when he tried to pick up my girlfriend when I would be up onstage singing. (I was going with this very lovely young lady—actually, I later married her.) I had to bring Elvis onstage, then I had to follow him. Anyway, when I would be up onstage, he would be over there at the table with my girlfriend—kind of schmoozing her. But in this movie, I got the girl.

SCOTTY MOORE: In the very early, early days, we were getting twenty-five to fifty bucks a night, maybe. I'm talking about short hops around Memphis. We just kept spreading out, and the further we went, the bigger the price. I mean, fifty or sixty dollars. And we were glad to get it, so we could buy gas to get home.

PAUL BURLISON: They didn't any of them have a car. That was Scotty's girlfriend's car they were using, and they almost burned it up. They were eating bologna sandwiches a lot of times, driving up and down the road together.

Elvis was just playing places here and there. They would run down to Mississippi and play a few little old clubs in Arkansas. Bob Neal was just booking wherever he could.

Elvis, Scotty, and Bill played the auditorium at the wrestling matches. They played inside the ring. I was there. They also played on a flatbed truck at Katz Drug Store when it opened.

MARTY LACKER: Katz Drug Store was opening in a new shopping center on Lamar, and for the grand opening they had entertainment. It was Elvis. So, during one of my breaks from my job, I went to see him. He was performing on a flatbed truck. I hadn't seen him since high school, and I had never seen him perform. He was shaking up a storm on the truck, and I was right down in front of him. He was looking down at me, smiling, and he made a pistol out of his hand, like you know, just saying, "Hi, how you doing?" The crowd was really enjoying him. In 1954 that was something new for Memphis.

"Beautiful Hunk of Forbidden Fruit"
1954-1955

Following the release of his first record, Elvis had become an overnight sensation—at least in Memphis. Country music stars Slim Whitman and Billy Walker spread the news of the astonishing new singer when they return home to Shreveport, Louisiana.

Talent agent Tillman Franks and Horace Logan, director of the Louisiana Hayride radio show, remember making a deal for Elvis that dramatically affects his future; announcer Frank Page recalls Elvis's unimpressive debut—a debut that nonetheless catapults Elvis and his band to stardom throughout the South.

With their characteristic enthusiasm, country superstars Faron Young and Porter Wagoner describe life behind the scenes with "The Hillbilly Cat." It's a whirlwind of one-night stands, as guitarist Scotty Moore and drummer D. J. Fontana relive the excitement of Elvis's early success both onstage and off.

Along the way, girlfriends Wanda Jackson and June Juanico reveal personal memories of private moments they share with the newly proclaimed "King of Western Bop."

Elvis soon outshines his competition. He begins collecting new fans like Jimmy Velvet and new friends like Mae Axton. Both provide eyewitness accounts of the growing hysteria as Elvis's popularity increases.

> "I'll never forget hearing Elvis's first records, 'That's All Right (Mama)' and 'Blue Moon of Kentucky.' I remember thinking, 'What a wild sound! What a great record!' His records just stirred something in me. Then, and for the rest of my life, there was nobody like him."
>
> WAYLON JENNINGS, *(recording artist and friend)*

T. TOMMY CUTRER *(country music disc jockey)*: Dewey Phillips, I guess, was the first guy that played Elvis's record on the air, and then Bob Neal was probably the second guy. I was probably the third guy. I got Elvis hot in Shreveport [Louisiana].

I had a show on KCIJ, Shreveport—a little five-thousand-watt independent daytimer. But my show could be heard all over the Arkansas, Louisiana, and Texas area.

Sam Phillips and I had worked together at WREC [radio] in Memphis back in the forties. Back then Sam was a studio engineer, and I was the announcer at WREC, in the old Peabody Hotel. Then I moved to Louisiana. He called me for one of those old-time friendly favors: "Help me with this boy." He sent me a copy of the first Presley record, and I played it. It got a fantastic reaction immediately. Good god, it was a phenomenon! People were saying, "Play that record again." My god, those telephones lit up! I would have to play the record two or three times an hour. In just a period of a couple of weeks, hell, he was the hottest thing in that part of the country.

TILLMAN FRANKS *(talent manager and show promoter)*: One day I was talkin' to T. Tommy, and I said, "That nigger record you're playing is really wild." He said, "It ain't no nigger. It's a white boy. Sam Phillips has got him." I said, "You've got to be kidding." I put it all in the back of my mind.

HORACE LOGAN *(program director of radio station KWKH, Shreveport, Louisiana)*: I was the talent scout [for the Louisiana Hayride show], cleaned up the stage—and any damn thing that needed to be done I did it. The Hayride was a stepping-stone for about twenty-five artists who came there utterly unknown and left there nationally famous.

Frank Page *(music director, radio station KWKH, and Louisiana Hayride announcer)*: The Hayride was the hottest thing in country music from about '47 to '57. In those ten years we formed more stars and found more talent than probably any other show. At that time the Hayride was more important than even the Grand Ole Opry.

Slim Whitman: The Hayride was broadcast live and had a huge Saturday-night radio audience. It was popular from Louisiana to Texas, Arizona, and even California. You could sell fifty thousand records off the stage of the Louisiana Hayride.

Horace Logan: When Slim Whitman and Billy Walker came back from up there in Memphis, Slim came in my office and sat down. He used to stutter pretty bad, and he said, "We h-had a kinda unusual thing happen up there. I p-put a b-b-boy on the s-show in Memphis, and he s-stole it away from me." I asked what the boy's name was, and he said, "I d-don't know, some f-f-funny name, but I'll think of it."

Billy Walker gave me the same report but remembered the kid's name was Elvis Presley.

Tillman Franks: I was trying to get Horace Logan to let my artists Jimmy and Johnny off for a night 'cause I had an opportunity for a five hundred-dollar booking for them, and I needed the money real bad. I was starving to death; my phone was taken out. Anyway, Horace said, "No." So I said, "If I get you this guy with a funny name—he's got the number-one record on T. Tommy's show—will you let my act off for the night?" He said, "Let me play it for Frank and see what he thinks."

Frank Page: I was actually on the air, disc-jockeying at KWKH when Elvis's first record arrived, and Horace brought it in for me to hear. I said, "Gosh, it's different. Let's give the guy a try and see what he's got." So we played the record and it got good reaction.

Tillman Franks: When Horace got back to me and said okay, I called up Sam Phillips. I told him I might be able to get his boy on the Hayride. Sam said, "He's coming by my office in the afternoon." I said, "Well, call me at Pappy Covington's [artist services manager, Louisiana Hayride]."

So he called me at Pappy's office. Elvis said, "Mr. Franks, I understand you might be able to get me on the Hayride." I said, "I can." He said, "We'd be tickled to do it. When can you get me on and how much will it pay?" I said, "Hold on just a minute." I called Horace on the other phone and said, "Horace, I got the boy on the phone. What can you pay him?" He said, "Tell him we'll give him a hundred and twenty-five dollars."

Elvis said okay, and he was scheduled to appear the next week.

HORACE LOGAN: Sam called me back and said, "No, that's the weekend he's going up to Nashville to be on the Opry." So we agreed on [October 16, 1954] for Elvis's first Hayride appearance.

:◎:◎:◎:

FARON YOUNG *(recording artist and friend)*: Elvis rented a tux and got it altered for his one-and-only appearance on the Grand Ole Opry. I visited with him in Nashville at the Andrew Jackson Hotel that day. Just before Elvis went onstage at the Opry that night, I told Jack Stapp, "Wait 'til this boy goes out there, and just watch what happens." I'd seen him on the road. I knew.

BUDDY KILLEN *(country musician)*: When Elvis came to Nashville to play the Grand Ole Opry [October 2, 1954] for the first and last time, I was a musician. I was backstage, and I saw Elvis standing over in the corner. He was shaking in his shoes, so I walked over to him and said, "Hi. I'm Buddy Killen and I work on the Opry. Who are you? And what's the matter with you?" He said, "I'm Elvis Presley and, man, I'm scared to death." I said, "No!" He said, "They are going to hate me!" And I said, "No, they're not." I stood there and talked him down. He was so nervous.

LITTLE JIMMY DICKENS *(Grand Ole Opry star)*: As best as I can recall, backstage Elvis stayed pretty close to the people he came with. 'Course at the Opry in those days—the old Ryman Auditorium—the place was so small and crowded you stayed close to everybody, whether you wanted to or not.

BUDDY KILLEN: The Opry wouldn't let Elvis do "That's All Right (Mama)," they thought it was too rock. So he did "Blue Moon of Kentucky."

The reaction wasn't as bad as they tell about it today. I remember he didn't get an encore, but he got a very, very nice hand.

LITTLE JIMMY DICKENS: "Blue Moon of Kentucky" was just barely gettin' off the ground, so hardly anyone knew who Elvis Presley was. I remember that he didn't make a big impression. Now I'm not putting Elvis down, 'cause I'm an Elvis fan. The record just hadn't been out long enough.

But I guarantee you if he'd come back a few months later, they'd a-known him.

BILL MONROE: I was on the Opry that night. He come right up to me and talked with me and made himself acquainted and everything. He told me that he was sorry that he had done "Blue Moon of Kentucky" that style and hoped I wasn't upset. He was a fine fellow.

I told Elvis, "Believe me, if it helps you and the boys get started, I'm for you one hundred percent." I said, "You done a wonderful job with it."

It seemed like the song done a lot of good for Elvis, and that's kept me feeling right about it. Later I got to where I liked it. It sold real good.

FARON YOUNG: I don't know how the hell it got started, but someone said that after Elvis appeared on the Grand Ole Opry, the guy who was the head of it, Jim Denny, said to him that he shouldn't give up truck driving.

Now Jim Denny's dead, so he's not here to deny it, but I knew Jim Denny very well. I loved him. And I'll bet you ten million dollars to a doughnut Denny never made that remark to Elvis Presley. Denny, in his heart, would never have said something like that, even if he thought it. That's a bunch of bullshit.

BILL DENNY (*son of Jim Denny, former head of the Grand Ole Opry*): I know that did not happen. I was not there, but I've had trouble with that story for years. It did not happen. Chet [Atkins] and some other people were there at the time, and I went to them and asked them specifically. Chet and the others all told me that it did not happen. My dad would never tell anybody that. He was too close to artists. He'd never hurt them.

BUDDY KILLEN: The rumor has been going around for many years that The Opry turned Elvis down. That's not true.

When rock 'n' roll started coming in, country music took a dip—it was awful. That's why they formed the Country Music Association in 1958. Country music was having a heck of a time; so why would Elvis Presley have needed the Grand Ole Opry? The Opry wasn't really what was happening back then.

:◎:◎:◎:

MERLE KILGORE (star of the Louisiana Hayride): The first time Elvis came to perform on the Louisiana Hayride radio show, I met him out back of the building when he drove up. Elvis was very polite and asked me to introduce him to Tibby Edwards, another singer on the show that night. Elvis was very impressed with a hit Tibby had out back then, "But I Do," and the two of them seemed to hit it off right away.

FRANK PAGE: I introduced Elvis his first time on the Hayride, and the reason I got to do the intro was that Horace wasn't too sure about him. Horace always introduced the big stars, and this was somebody new and un-tried, so I got to introduce him. If Horace had known how big a star Elvis would become, he probably would have been out there introducing him personally. It would have been a feather in his cap—although, it hasn't made me a penny.

HORACE LOGAN: When Elvis came in for his first show, it just so happened that I had the CBS radio network spot scheduled for that night. It was to be the first part of the evening, and because scheduling was so tight, I told all the performers there would be absolutely no encores no matter what. We had to do this so that everybody would at least have one spot on that important part of the show.

Well, no one even knew who Elvis Presley was, and when he finished his song the audience just sat there with their mouths hanging open. There wasn't any wild enthusiasm for him, and they just gave him some polite little applause. A lot of them just sat there on their hands.

MERLE KILGORE: I remember when Elvis started all that moving and a-shakin', there was a kinda fat older lady sittin' on the front row. I guess she got a little upset and just sorta pulled her dress down over her knees real good—embarrassed, I guess, like he was violating her mentally. He was pretty intense when he performed. Anyway, the crowd sorta just sat on their hands when he finished, and it upset him.

TILLMAN FRANKS: After that, Elvis and Scotty and Bill were talking in the corner. They were trying to figure out why they didn't get a big hand when they'd been getting one when he played at the Eagle's Nest. He asked me what to do when he went back out again. I said, "Go ahead and do anything you want to. Roll on the floor or do anything. They can't fire you, 'cause they haven't even hired you yet."

MERLE KILGORE: Elvis came back to the dressing room Tibby and I were sharing and said, "Y'all, what in the world did I do wrong?" And Tibby (he was a pro, and he talked in this funny Cajun accent as fast as a machine gun) told him, "Mahn, I-believe-you-come-on-too-strong." I told Elvis that there would be a totally different audience for the second part of the show and that actually the radio signal reached a lot more people later in the evening, so he had another shot at 'em. Tibby said, "Jus-go-out-der-an-kine-a-ease-into-it-dis-time. Do-it-kine-a-grajual."

HORACE LOGAN: The second part of the first show I told all of the performers: "Any encores will be strictly determined by how much applause you get." That was the whole idea of the Hayride: to let the audience run it, or at least let 'em think they were running it.

MERLE KILGORE: Man, Elvis just destroyed 'em on that next performance. They rushed the stage, and I had never seen them rush the stage like that, not even for Hank Williams. They were taking flash pictures like crazy: pop! pop! pop! And Tibby and I were over to the side of the stage giving Elvis the big "Okay" sign with our fingers.

TILLMAN FRANKS: He stopped the show completely that night, and they asked him if he could come back a couple of weeks later.

T. TOMMY CUTRER: The next day Sam Phillips brought Elvis to my house and tried to get me to manage him. He said, "T, why don't you manage this boy?" And I said, "I'm doing too well. I don't feel like I can do anything for this boy." I thought he was a white boy trying to sing black, and that ain't gonna do no good. My wife thought he needed a haircut, and she thought he needed his neck washed. But he was a good kid, and we became close friends; but at the time, I didn't think it was the thing to do. That shows you how clever I was.

FRANK PAGE: We had so many big stars on the show through the years—Hank Williams and Johnny Horton, a whole mess of 'em—I wasn't really impressed with Elvis. Not in the very beginning. It just built week after week until he just got hotter than a firecracker. Elvis developed his style there onstage. As he developed, and as he developed his wiggle, his snarl, and his mumble, I became impressed. You knew that Elvis could really draw a crowd.

HORACE LOGAN: After the first show, I invited him to come back for the next couple of weeks. Elvis brought his mother and daddy and Bob Neal with him the third week—if I'm not mistaken. Elvis was nineteen years old, and he could not legally sign a contract in the State of Louisiana. So his mother and daddy apprenticed Elvis to me—not to KWKH, but to me—for the purpose of me teaching him the music business. And they signed a year's contract for him. Elvis signed it, too.

The contract was dated November 6, 1954, and was for a year at union scale. That was eighteen dollars for Elvis and twelve dollars each for Scotty and Bill for each Saturday night they played. That contract obligated them to appear on the Hayride every Saturday night—fifty-two of them. Of course, I let the artists off some on a rotating basis, but I never did bleed my show dry.

Everybody on the Hayride was so damn good, they had to bust a gut to be outstanding. It was the hardest show in the world to work, but it created more stars than all the other shows put together. It was great training for a young Elvis Presley.

I will never forget how polite he was to people. Every woman was a "ma'am," even from young girls up to old women. Every man was "sir." All he ever called me was "Mr. Logan, Sir." How shy he was! He'd come in and say, "Mr. Logan, Sir, what do you think I ought to do?" I'd say, "Just go out there and do what you normally do." "You think they're gonna like me?" "Oh, yeah," I'd say, "I *know* they'll like you."

:◎:◎:◎:

SCOTTY MOORE: We had a 1954 Chevy Bel Air—that's what we started in. There was just three of us, but most of the time I had the bass [guitar] inside. Then we got an old Cadillac limousine; but just with the three of us and all the instruments and luggage, it was still awful crowded on those short hops to Arkansas and Mississippi. Why didn't somebody think of a bus back in those days? Seems simple now doesn't it?

PORTER WAGONER *(star of the Louisiana Hayride)*: Bill Black, the bass player, man, he was a big part of Elvis's show. He was a tremendous part of it—hell, yes, he was. He got as much applause as Elvis did because he done this mimickin' thing. Elvis would shake his leg and then Bill would just go crazy and shake his leg, ass, and everything else—really wild. People just loved it. And of course, the boy that played the guitar, Scotty Moore, he was real subdued and kinda acted like he was embarrassed about all of it, and that was a good contrast to the other two. Elvis would throw his guitar around over his shoulder, and then Bill Black would try and do that with his big stand-up bass. It was real entertainin'. People would just tear the house down!

They had this thing they did to try to get an encore. They'd leave the stage, but then Elvis would come back and stick his head and shoulders out from around the curtain and sorta shake himself. Then Bill would come back and do it even more, but he'd shake all over. I guess you'd say he kinda accented what Elvis had done, and the crowd would go nuts. I'll tell you, it was a helluva show. It was. And not taking anything away from Elvis, Bill Black was a big part of it—at least fifty percent.

BILLY JO SPEARS (*country music singer*): I was just a kid starting out about the time Elvis had that first record out on Sun. I was working with a local group and we were doing a little show at the Old Sportatorium in Beaumont, [Texas]. That was where they used to have all those old wrestling matches. That place stunk to high heaven. Anyway, Elvis was on the show. He had about forty pounds of axle grease on his head and he looked like somebody had sat him in the corner and fed him with a slingshot. He had pock marks something dreadful, and acne. Bless his heart, he was so homely looking. He had on what was supposed to be a white shirt, and it had a yellow tinge to it. It looked like nobody had done his laundry in quite a while. And he was wearing a pair of old faded black cotton britches that came up just above his ankles. He was a mess, but he was so nice, and we talked for about an hour before the show. Oh, yes, the top part of his fly had come un-sewed. It was zipped up but his zipper seam had come loose. I felt so sorry for him. I said, "We need to do something about your britches." So I gave him a safety pin, and he went into the bathroom and fixed his pants and didn't look quite so bad. I don't think he even knew what shoe polish was, but he was so nice, and he was absolutely petrified—scared to death.

We stood backstage and talked. He said, "I've worked some and sang at some places, but there's an awful lot of folks here." And the place was packed.

Elvis was almost unknown back then, but on that little show he was the headliner—the new kid on the block. The crowd just went crazy. They absolutely fell in love with him; he just knocked them out. They were all standing up and clapping and cheering. They didn't care what he looked like. He drove 'em wild. It was just him and Bill Black and Scotty

Moore. The audience just kept making them come back and do more numbers, more encores. He was amazing. I never saw him again after that.

Mac Davis *(songwriter)*: I heard him on New Year's Eve. It was my fourteenth birthday and I stayed out 'til four in the morning. I heard that record ["That's All Right (Mama)"] that night, and the next day I was looking for it all over town. But me and this buddy of mine thought his name was "Alvan Parsly." And if you think back twenty-five years ago, Elvis Presley was a real unusual name. I'd never heard of anybody named "Elvis."

Billy Walker: Me and Tillman Franks were promoting a road show. We needed work real bad and had to find a place to play. West Texas was our best bet. So Tillman and I set up a trip out that way. We called Elvis up and said, "What will you charge us to go on some dates?" He said, "A hundred and fifty dollars a day, plus ten dollars a day car expenses." (Bob Neal was booking Elvis some back then, but I remember calling Elvis directly on this 'cause I remember talking to his mother.)

Anyway, we worked Midland and Lubbock and San Angelo and maybe a couple of other dates. Little Field, Texas, was one of 'em, too, 'cause Waylon Jennings told me he put up posters for that show.

I thought I was safe in closing the show 'cause I'd had three pretty strong records, but, hey, it didn't make no difference. This guy set 'em on fire from the word "go."

I still have the ad for that Midland, Texas, show. It says: "The show will feature five stars of the Louisiana Hayride, including Elvis Presley, King of Western Bop." He had two single records out at that time. They were also calling him "The Hillbilly Cat."

The first bad notoriety he got was from that Lubbock, Texas, show we did. You might see it in some of those old 1955 *Enquirer*-kind of magazines. One of them had a picture of him at the Cotton Club—a Texas dance hall in Lubbock. We all went out there after the show because I'd played the place several times. Some gal exposed herself to Presley that night and somebody got a picture of it. Back then, that was some kind of a thing! That was the first notoriety he got.

Waylon Jennings: The first show Elvis did in Lubbock, I think he got paid some ridiculous amount—fifty or sixty dollars, something like that. I was about seventeen and I was backstage. I met Elvis and talked to him for a while. Scotty Moore was there—the guitar player—and I think Elvis had Scotty's guitar backstage, and he was singing "Tweedlee Dee." He said, "This is gonna be my next record. I'm gonna record this." And he sang us the song. I don't know if he ever recorded that or not, but I do know that on his second trip to Lubbock [a year or so later], he jumped from fifty dollars a night to four thousand. That's how hot he got, and how quick.

TILLMAN FRANKS: I booked Elvis two tours, and I traveled with him to Texas, places like Abilene and San Angelo and San Marcus. I got to know him real well 'cause I didn't drive; so he'd drive me, and I'd stay with him. Elvis was trying to distance himself from Scotty and Bill at the time 'cause they were arguing a lot. The tension of road schedules, I guess.

SCOTTY MOORE: At first Elvis was just one of the guys. We'd go out and get a hamburger, you know, just like most everybody did, 'til he became so recognizable that you couldn't even stop at a truckstop. Gradually, it got worse and worse as time went by. We finally told him, "Hey, you'd better get on a plane and let us take care of getting the equipment there, 'cause we can't even go in a restaurant and get a decent meal." That's when he started carrying a lot of his friends with him so he'd have company. Elvis didn't like to fly, and he wanted moral support. They'd go with him, and he'd have someone to pal around with when he'd be on the road.

D. J. FONTANA *(drummer, Elvis's band)*: I met Elvis, Scotty, and Bill when they first come down to do the Hayride, and I started working with them pretty soon after that.

Elvis had this charisma about him. I don't think anybody could ever put their finger on what he did or how he did it. You could just sit and talk to him for a few minutes and he would mesmerize you. This is the way Elvis related to people.

Onstage he could feel the audience out in about five or ten minutes. He knew the songs they wanted to hear for some reason, and he could work that crowd to his benefit. He was really good.

Bob Neal out of Memphis was doing some of the booking. We worked a lot of little houses, the back of trucks, and feed mills—you name it, we worked it.

MAE AXTON *(show promoter and songwriter)*: I had met Bob Neal, at the first annual disc jockey convention in Nashville, and I liked him real well. He was a disc jockey in Memphis. Well, he called me one day at my home in Jacksonville [Florida] and said, "Mae, I need your help. I want to get out of broadcasting and into management, and there's a kid here that has long hair and wears funny clothes, but he can really sing."

Bob said, "This kid made a birthday record for his mother, and Sam Phillips cut a record on him, and it's hotter than a firecracker here in Memphis. Everybody's just loving him. This kid can be a star, and I can get management on him if I can just get him some jobs. Can you help me out and put him on one of your shows down there?" Bob had also called Biff Collie in Houston, Frank Page at the Louisiana Hayride, and Bill Mack in Fort Worth. Biff and Bill were deejays who brought shows into their areas. Frank was the manager of the Hayride. Bob said, "I'm calling everybody I know and getting some shows set up for him."

I told Bob I could put Elvis on three shows: Jacksonville, Orlando, and Daytona, and I thought I could manage to pay him fifty dollars a night. He said, "Okay." I asked, "What's his name?" He answered, "Elvis—Elvis Presley." I said, "Well, send him down. Tell him when he gets into town ... is he going to be driving or flying?" He said, "He'll drive, I'm sure. That'll be cheaper." I said, "Well, when he gets to the edge of Jacksonville have him call me."

JOHNNY CASH *(country singer)*: Bob Neal had me and my band, the Tennessee Two, go on tour with Elvis in Mississippi and Texas and throughout the South. We worked three months with him, and I learned a lot about performing and projection from Elvis. I didn't have the charisma he had. I couldn't dance like he could. I wasn't as pretty as he was. But I learned a lot from him about stage presence and show business.

T. TOMMY CUTRER: Me, Tillman, and Webb Pierce, we booked Elvis in Monroe [Louisiana] and then Texarkana and Eldorado [Arkansas]. We just booked him around. He cost us a hundred and fifty dollars a night. Fifty for him, fifty for Scotty, and fifty for Bill. Elvis was splitting the money three ways. I had helped get him hot by playing his records on my radio show. (I had a real hot radio show down there.) But the way Elvis got big and stayed big in the South was by being on the Hayride; that reached a lot of people. The Hayride could be heard from California to Florida.

WANDA JACKSON *(recording artist)*: By the time I graduated from high school in June of '55. I'd already had a couple of hits on Decca and done some TV in California, but my daddy was trying to book me and he got in with Bob Neal through *Billboard* magazine. Bob was booking Elvis at the time and he said, "Well, we could use a girl on the show because we don't have a girl." So Bob started lining me up some bookings with Elvis.

I wrote and told my cousins, who lived down in Texas, that I was going to be doing a show there in Odessa, performing with a new singer I had never heard of, Elvis Presley. They wrote back to me, and they were so excited. "Golly, you're actually going to work with him?" I wrote and said, "Well, who is this guy?" "Oh," they wrote back, "He's a dream boat."

PORTER WAGONER: Fairly often way back then when Elvis was just starting, folks in the audience didn't even know who he was when he'd walk out on that stage. He wasn't yet that big a deal. But once he got out there, buddy, I mean he just stirred them people up, and women were just crazy about him.

One night we were on the same tour together, and while he was onstage doing his thing I saw this girl. She was probably maybe sixteen years old, and she was standing right over on the edge of the stage with the curtain pulled up against her body—kinda wrapped all around her. I mean, it looked like she was fixin' to climax she was so excited. I said to her, "How does he affect you?" She said, "Oh my god! All over. Just all over me." He had that effect on a lot of women.

WANDA JACKSON: The first time I actually met Elvis was in Brownwood, Texas, and I was immediately impressed with him. He was a good-looking guy, and I was really smitten. Elvis was not like anybody I had ever met. He was dressed real different. That night at the show I was back in my dressing room—my father traveled with me because I was underage. Dad came back and said, "I wish you would come out here and watch this guy. He's fantastic. Come look." I heard the yelling and hollering, and I went out to watch him work. I couldn't believe it. He was just the greatest showman—a showman deluxe. From then on I was a big fan of his. It was easy to see why the girls screamed and hollered. He wasn't called "the king" for nothing.

MAE AXTON: The first time Elvis came to Florida absolutely no one knew who he was. There was no time to get his name on the program. I had only one copy of his first record, so I gave it to one of the local deejays to play. But he never mentioned Elvis's name on the air. He'd only say, "This kid's going to be there, too."

JIMMY VELVET: Looking back, I think it was good fortune that let me meet Elvis. I was going to Paxton High [Jacksonville, Florida] at that time. I think I was fifteen. I was in the ninth grade. The first couple of weeks of school I had a substitute English teacher, Mae Axton. In fact, her husband John was my coach. Mae was promoting that first Jacksonville concert. It was kinda a combination of things that seemed like fate.

MAE AXTON: When Elvis came to Florida to perform the first time, I met him and rode to the hotel with him. I had a deal with this friend of mine who had a beautiful hotel. It was really classy looking. The deal was that if the person I brought in could not afford their own room, I would give him a signal. I would just kind of lean over on the front desk as they were checking in, and the manager would know to bill that room to me. That way, no one got embarrassed. I didn't mind helping out some of those new kids. I was making pretty good money back then teaching school and doing PR and writing stories and songs, as well as promoting shows.

Well, anyway, Elvis called and I drove out to meet him. When I got there, I was kind of shocked. I don't know how their car ever got to Jacksoneville. It didn't look driveable to me, but Elvis was proud of it. And there was not one kid, but three. Scotty and Bill were with him. Bob Neal hadn't told me Elvis was bringing musicians, and I could tell by looking at them that none of them had much money.

I said, "Elvis, you get in the car with me, and you two boys follow, and we'll go to your hotel."

When we got there, you could kind of tell they'd never been in a place that pretty. They were a little uncomfortable. I told the owner-manager friend of mine, "They'll need a couple of rooms," and he let them fill out the registration forms. You could tell they were a little nervous. When they finished, Elvis said, "How much is it, Sir?" I kind of leaned up against the counter, and the manager said, "Oh, no, it's taken care of. Don't worry about it." Of course, he billed me.

Then I told them, "I tell you what, you get some rest, and I'll pick you up in an hour or so and we'll have dinner; then we'll go out to the show."

Then I called [singers] Skeeter Davis and June Carter and got them to join us. We had dinner and went on over to the show, and Elvis opened that night. Now Elvis's name hadn't even been in the ads, so no one knew who he was. I was counting money, and from the auditorium I heard all this loud screaming. That audience was going crazy over Elvis. I just couldn't believe it. I thought, "Boy, this kid's going to be a big star!" He wasn't even on the program!

I stopped checking the money to go down to see what all the screaming was about. This student of mine was standing up watching

Elvis perform, and she was just going crazy over him—screaming, tears running down her cheeks. I tugged at her jacket, and she looked at me. I asked her, "What is it about this kid you like so much?" I think she gave the best definition of Elvis I've ever heard. She said, "Oh, Mrs. Axton, he's just a great big, beautiful hunk of forbidden fruit." I never forgot that.

We went on to Orlando the next night, and the crowds reacted much like the night before. Then the third night was in Daytona Beach. Early that morning I went out to do two radio interviews. When I got back to the motel I found Elvis sitting on the balcony staring out at the ocean. He seemed so solemn. I asked him, "Are you okay?" He said, "Oh, yes, Ma'am. I just can't believe what I'm seeing. I've been sitting here for almost an hour, and I've seen three big ships go out there and just disappear." I said, "Yes, and probably a few thousand miles out there they'll still be on water, and they'll be coming into land again." He said, "I'd give anything in the world if I had enough money to bring my mama and daddy down here to see the ocean."

:◉:◉:◉:

JUNE JUANICO *(girlfriend)*: A friend of mine had seen Elvis the previous night at the Slavonian Lodge—a night spot in Biloxi [Mississippi] where the teenagers used to go dancing. She said he was the most gorgeous man she had ever laid eyes on, and he was going to be playing at Keesler Air Force Base that night. She was only sixteen years old, and I was only seventeen. At that time Elvis was just beginning to drive the girls crazy, and they came to see him in droves. He wasn't what you'd call famous, except he became an instant star wherever he played. He was already gathering groupies, so to speak.

At Keesler when I saw him signing autographs, I had the feeling that Elvis was probably the most handsome, perfect, flawless creature that I had ever laid my eyes on.

When he was onstage, we made eye contact, and I could tell he kind of took a shine to me. When he took an intermission, I told my friend, "Let's go to the ladies room." On the way in he kinda sees me pass while he's talking to other people, and when we came out he reached through the crowd and grabbed my arm and stopped me as I passed. He put his hand on the back of my neck and said, "Are you going to stay for the rest of the show? I've only got one more set to do. I'll be through here around nine o'clock." I said, "We'll be here for the rest of the show." He said, "I'd like you to show me the town after we get through." I told him, "Biloxi's a small town. There's really nothing to see in Biloxi." He said, "Well, show me nothing."

We went out later, and our first date lasted nine hours—from nine o'clock when he finished 'til he drove me home about three o'clock that morning. And then we stayed parked in front of my house just talking and getting acquainted for three more hours. Time just passed so fast because we had so much to talk about. I mean, there's a period of time when you have to take a break from kissing and talk.

Elvis was a wonderful kisser. How do you describe soft lips, slightly parted, not too much, but just perfect? And he sometimes opened his mouth about three inches—sucked off part of my nose. Elvis was a very sensitive person, very tender—sensitive on the inside. On the outside, he was macho.

:◎:◎:◎:

MAC WISEMAN *(recording artist and record executive)*: Presley spooked the whole country with that sound he had. The word spread pretty quick that no one could follow him onstage. Once he hit that stage he did what he did naturally, and no one could follow him.

FARON YOUNG: When Presley first started, we were working out on a tour with Hank Snow, and Elvis was the bottom on the bill. We played Ladd Memorial Stadium in Mobile, Alabama [1955]. Presley wasn't no big star yet, but he was killing those people, you know, doing those two or three songs. Now I had just got back from Hollywood, doing a picture, and Elvis said, "Sir, did you have to fight in that thing?" I said, "Yeah." And he said, "I want you to teach me how to movie fight."

We were still at the hotel, and I showed him some moves I'd picked up in Hollywood. He caught on real fast. After the show at the stadium I was out there on the football field, and he come runnin' over there and started play-fighting with me. I acted like I hit him in the stomach. He doubled over, and I swung and hit him upside the head and he fell back over on the ground. Then he jumped up and grabbed me and threw me over the other way, and I'd kick him. It went on and on, all this fake fighting, and we were having a ball. But the people still up in the stands were watching us and they didn't know it was a fake fight! I got several letters from people that said, "Goddamn, Faron, that's a shame, somebody like you beating on that young boy after he done such a good job singing."

The next time I worked with Presley, I told him about it. He pissed all over himself laughing. He said, "Sir, did they really chew you out?" I said, "I'm telling you they jumped my ass 'cause they thought I'd whipped yours, and after you'd done such a damn good job! At least we put on a good show. Them sons of bitches thought we were really fightin'!" Elvis fell out laughing.

TILLMAN FRANKS: Elvis would nearly always close the Hayride show up. That was because Elvis Presley in something over a month became a star on the Louisiana Hayride. He'd done got hot when I took him out on some tours.

FARON YOUNG: Out on the road, a lot of folks still didn't really know who he was. The booker put Presley right at the top of the show—opening act. I was scheduled to come right behind him, then Hank Snow would follow me.

That's how they always did it; the bigger the star, the later in the show they'd come on. But Elvis would go out there, and he'd tear that audience's ass up. We got into Orlando, Florida, and I told them out there: "Look, I'm getting tired of this shit. I'm going on *before* Presley. That son-of-a-bitch is killing that audience." When we'd get out there, they'd holler, "Bring Elvis back! Bring Elvis back!" All he had was about three songs, and they wanted to see some more of that crazy fucker. He was so different. They'd never seen nothing like it. So I told the promoter, "I'm going on before Presley tonight. Snow, you ought to go on early, too." Snow said, "By god, I'm the star of this show, and I'll be the one who closes the damn show." I said, "All right, Snow, you just do that." He said it kind of smug like he'd won the damn argument: "Well, that's right. I'm the star."

Well, that night I went on early and did my damn part, then Elvis went out and tore their ass up. Then here come Snow onstage singing, "That big eight-wheeler rolling down the track. . . ." Well, people hollered, "Get off the fucking stage! Bring Elvis back on!" This damn announcer is rushing out there saying, "Okay, now y'all be nice, folks. Wait a minute. Y'all be nice. Hank Snow is a legend in this business. Let's show Hank Snow a little courtesy, 'cause this gentleman's been in the business for three hundred and sixty years! If y'all want to see Elvis, he's out in the parking lot behind the building signing autographs."

Well, that was like ringing a fucking fire bell. I don't mean they left one at a time; I mean they left by goddamn droves. By the time Snow got around to the end of his song, half the damn people were gone out back looking for Presley's ass. Afterwards, Snow said, "You know, by god, I might not should have followed that little bastard out there." I said, "Don't worry, Snow. You *didn't* follow him."

WANDA JACKSON: You never knew what Elvis was going to do next onstage. I would be watching him, and he would be singing along. Suddenly the band would keep going, but Elvis would stop singing and walk over to the side of the stage, and you'd see him fiddling with something on the floor. Everyone's attention would go to the floor, and there'd be a cigarette butt down there and he was trying to get it to stand on its end—just having some fun. The crowd loved it. It didn't matter what he did. He would act silly or say something silly—get the words wrong or make up words. He just couldn't do anything wrong. But it was because—I learned since—it was because he really loved his audience. He loved his fans more than anybody I've ever seen.

SLIM WHITMAN: We were in Rocky Mount, North Carolina, and Elvis and his band had driven into town in their stage clothes. When it was time for Elvis to go on, he said, "Let me borrow your coat." I said, "You got your own coat; use it." He said, "No, mine's dirty." So I said, "Okay, here's my coat." It was bigger than his, but he put it on anyway. It had rhinestones on it, and when he went on, he got a big hand. He came off stage and asked me, "How'd I do?" I said, "Fine, Elvis, but you wouldn't have done nothing without my coat!" He laughed.

FARON YOUNG: When I'd work a show date with Presley, I had to have the cops help me just because I was on the same damn show he was. Them kids would run up to me and hand me an autograph book, and I'd start to sign. Then they'd say, "No, no, no. We want you to get Elvis's autograph for us." I'd say, "Goddamn, I can't run Elvis down and get you an autograph!" They'd say, "Okay, give us back our autograph books."

MERLE KILGORE: In the early days I was on a lot of the same shows with Elvis and the guys. They were called the Hillbilly Cats back then. I remember once we were playing the NCO [Non-Commissioned Officers] club at the Red River Arsenal, an Army base near Texarkana. Elvis was hot in that Ark-La-Tex area, and the NCO club was packed and hot and smoky. After the first set we all stepped out back for some fresh air. Now the back door opened onto a narrow porch, and then a real long flight of stairs went on down to the ground—must have been equal to two flights of steps. So we're standing there, and Elvis said, "Man, it's good to get out here. That smoke in there was killing me." All at once this corporal comes busting out the back door and whams Elvis real hard in the chest with his fist. Well, Elvis goes flying down those stairs to the bottom. But they didn't call him the "Hillbilly Cat" for nothing. Just like a cat he landed on his feet and almost jumped back up those stairs and walloped that corporal real good. Then, of course, the sergeants came out and busted up the fight.

Elvis was crying 'cause he'd had to hit the guy and was saying, "Man, why'd you hit me? I don't even know you." And the guy says, "When you were singing my wife was just going crazy over you in there, and I've never seen my wife act that way over nobody. You can't do that to my wife, man."

Elvis was really upset and surprised, and he said, "That's the first time anybody's tried to fight me over the way I am onstage." I said, "Well, guess what. You'd better be prepared for it 'cause it's gonna start happening."

JIMMY VELVET: In the beginning on the road tours, the women, the girls, would want to come and see Elvis, but the boyfriends and husbands didn't want to; but they would go because they didn't want their girls to go alone. Well, they wound up being fans themselves when they saw the live shows, because Elvis was just darn good. They would feel the excitement in the theater. I have to say that he had a lot against him in the beginning, but he did all the right things.

WAYLON JENNINGS: It became impossible for Elvis to have any privacy. I had a touch of that, so I know how he felt; but I just refused to be a prisoner of who I am. You can get awful frustrated when you can't go out and have something to eat somewhere and do normal things, and you can probably get a little mean about it.

WANDA JACKSON: Elvis knew early on how hot he was getting and where he was going and how to get there. I admired it. He knew how to tease the girls in the audiences and how to make them scream. Yes, he knew just exactly what he was doing.

In the beginning when we'd go out, the fans didn't bother Elvis that much, but later on it got to be almost impossible.

I remember just after the fans had started to pull at him, he didn't have any security. He tried to sign some autographs 'cause he really loved to talk to the fans, touch them, and autograph for them. But it finally got to where he couldn't. I mean, they were really tearing at him, and he would get in the car with his shirt buttons all popped off, and his tie half off. He would just fall down in the back seat and start laughing. He'd say, "Don't that just beat all?" He never did mind. He never got mad at them. The only reason he stopped giving autographs was he was afraid that someone was going to get hurt—and their folks would blame it on him. So he just had to stop, and that was very sad because he loved the touching part of it all.

EDDIE FADAL (*friend and disc jockey*): I was a disc jockey in Waco, Texas, and Elvis came by the station promoting his early records. We struck up a conversation, and he asked if I'd like to finish the tour with him. I said, "Yeah, sure, I'd love to go." He said, "What about your job?" I said, "That's no problem. I'll just quit. I was looking for one when I found this one." So I went in and resigned right then and finished the tour with Elvis.

RED WEST (*friend and traveling companion*): I couldn't believe what had happened in such a short time. It was just hard to comprehend from what I'd known about him in high school.

JIMMY VELVET: In 1955, Elvis came to Jacksonville, Florida, with the Hank Snow Show. I had gone to see the show and gotten backstage. I was on a local TV show occasionally with Johnny Tillottson [the "Toby Dowdy Show"] and was reasonably well known in town. I was about fifteen. Of course, I wanted to meet Hank Snow, and that's why I went to the show that night. I didn't even know who Elvis Presley was. He was nineteen and just starting out. As it turned out, Elvis and I sat backstage and talked for about an hour and a half. He was so nice. I enjoyed him, but I still didn't know who he was. Nobody really bothered us, and we just sat around. He was sitting there with a guitar—strumming it—and we were drinking Cokes. We were just two guys backstage—two musicians basically. He even introduced himself to me and it didn't ring a bell. But when he went onstage, I knew him then.

   Backstage even in those days fans were trying to get to Elvis. Of course, press from all over was there. He handled it very well. Elvis was very polite, very kind to everyone, and wouldn't leave until everyone got a chance to talk to him. I admired him for that because I had seen a lot lesser stars that had been on our show from time to time that were not nearly as considerate. One thing that I noticed about Elvis through the years, no matter what, he was always very considerate of his fans. He didn't let anyone working for him mistreat his fans. They were special. They were important. He recognized that and never forgot it.

MAE AXTON: On his second trip down to Florida we had Elvis booked at the Gator Bowl along with Hank Snow, Faron Young, Mother Maybelle and the Carter Family, and some other Opry stars. I remember he had on a pink suit and a pink lace shirt and no undershirt. We were sitting at dinner early that evening, and I felt I knew him well enough to be honest. I said, "Elvis, that shirt's positively vulgar on you with no undershirt on." (You know, men wore undershirts back then, summer and winter, even with flannel shirts.) Elvis kind of grinned, and I said, "But that shirt would make me a beautiful blouse. Besides, those teenage girls are going to tear it off you tonight, anyway." June Carter said, "I want it!" and Skeeter Davis said, "No, I want it!" He just kind of grinned and didn't say anything.

Well, we went on to the show, and everything was going all right, but someone had left the big drive-in gate raised up just enough for those young girls to squeeze under. No one even noticed it being partially open until it was too late. It probably wouldn't have mattered except for something Elvis said. When he finished his set, before he left the stage, Elvis kind of jokingly said, "I'll see all you girls backstage." Then he walked off. A few minutes later I heard all this screaming backstage and knew something was going on. I grabbed a security guard and took off to the dressing room. By the time we got there, at least fifty girls were tearing at Elvis. They'd pulled off his coat and shirt and ripped them to shreds. They all wanted a souvenir. Elvis started running and climbed on top of the shower stall. They pulled his shoes and socks off and were trying to even get his pants off when I finally arrived with the security guard and got rid of the girls. Faron Young was there, too. He retrieved one of Elvis's shoes that a girl was trying to sneak out under her skirt. When it calmed down just a little, I laughed, 'cause there wasn't anything left of that pretty lace shirt. I put my hands on my hips, looked up at Elvis, and said, "I told you so. That would have made me a pretty blouse. Oh, well, I like brown better anyway."

Well, about two weeks later here came a brown lace shirt in the mail.

FARON YOUNG: I was with him at the Gator Bowl the first night he got attacked. He came off that stage, and somehow those little girls got to him and tore his clothes all up. Them girls pounced on that son-of-a-bitch like alligators.

Afterwards Elvis said, "Damn, Chief, them little girls are strong." I said, "Yeah, one of them you can whip; but fifty of 'em get a hold of your ass, and it's just like a vacuum cleaner sucking on you. You can't get away from 'em."

The next morning it was all in the damn newspaper: "Girls tear clothes off Elvis Presley!" All that sensationalism started right there in Jacksonville at the Gator Bowl. And from then on, that was the thing to do—just get to him, tear his clothes off, pull out his hair, or something. So he always had to have police and all that shit after that.

MAE AXTON: They wanted to grab him, tear him apart, but they knew they could never really have him. And that just made them want him more.

:◎:◎:◎:

TROY DERAMUS *(country performer)*: I'd heard a lot of talk about Elvis. And one night when he was on, I went to the Hayride to see some friends. I was talking to Dottie West backstage (she was doing a guest appearance that night) when they announced Elvis. The screams and yelling were so loud we couldn't hear to talk, so we moved around front and watched him. I mean, from the minute they said "Elvis Presley," the screams started, and there was so much yelling the building nearly blew apart. He started singing, but I bet I never heard ten words he sang because of the screaming. When he was on the Hayride, the young folks came in droves.

He was wearing a pink-and-black suit and he moved like a snake inside his clothes. It drove the girls wild. While he was performing, he had to pull his pants up several times. They kept slipping down from all his squirming. He performed for quite awhile, and every now and then he'd grin and the girls would scream more.

SCOTTY MOORE: It was bedlam onstage. The noise was so loud we couldn't hear him to play; we had to watch him. D. J., being an old, burlesque drummer, could follow Elvis and take cues from his body motions and get us through it. Maybe we'd hear a faint echo once in awhile bouncing back from the auditorium. It was difficult. It really was. The audience would scream and we'd get bits and pieces, but for the most part we couldn't hear him.

HORACE LOGAN: Elvis was on the Hayride one full flat-footed year, and then another six months. The only time he had off on Saturday nights, which was about five or six times a year, was when we let him off. During that time he got to be one of the most famous singers in the United States.

T. TOMMY CUTRER: It didn't surprise me at all that Elvis kept getting bigger and bigger. Then I was sorry that I hadn't said, "Yeah, I'll manage him." We did book him quite a bit though, and we used my [radio] show and the Hayride for promotion.

HORACE LOGAN: As the popularity of his records increased, pretty soon the adults could not even get into the Hayride, 'cause the kids would get there early and buy up all the tickets. Elvis was an explosion, just an absolute phenomenon.

KWKH decided we had to set up a booking agency to help support our artists if we wanted to continue. So we paid Tom Parker's expenses to come down to Shreveport to stay about three weeks and determine what it would cost to set up a functioning artist service bureau. Parker was booking Hank Snow and other stars at that time. He came up with a figure of twelve thousand dollars. The station refused to pay it, so he left. But during the time he was in Shreveport, Parker became very familiar with the growing popularity of Elvis Presley.

At the end of his first year contract, on November 12, 1955, I upped Elvis to two hundred dollars per Saturday night, and he signed a contract for another year.

He signed a second year's contract in November 1955; but after he had worked six months on the new contract, he suddenly wanted out of the remaining six months. Parker tied in with him just about the time Elvis had been on the Hayride a little over a year. By that time Elvis was already hot, hot, hot. It was ridiculous to try to keep him there for two hundred dollars per Saturday night when he could be getting twenty or thirty thousand a night somewhere else. So on April 24, 1956, we let him buy out of the remaining six months of his contract.

:◎:◎:◎:

STAN KESLER: Dewey Phillips was real powerful in Memphis, but he was the kind of person you never knew when to take seriously. Like he'd come into the studio and say, "Well, I've got to go 'cause Elvis is gonna pick me up." Elvis wouldn't show up, of course, but Dewey did a lot of kidding. He was just kind of crazy. On the air Dewey was always talking about what a great singer Elvis was and how he was "gonna make it big."

BARBARA PITTMAN: Dewey would take benzedrine to keep himself awake, but everybody else did, too. I mean you go out on the road for five days, and you get two hours of sleep. Everybody was taking those things, but they could be bought over the counter. You could buy 'em in cafes along the road. Musicians were heavy on it 'cause to make any money at all you'd have to do fifteen shows a week or something. We were traveling constantly, and you were getting two or three hours of sleep a night. Everybody was taking that stuff.

PAUL BURLISON: It wasn't uncommon to take pills in those days 'cause everybody was playing a different town seven nights a week. Most of the time you didn't get away 'til real late. By the time you'd get to the next town, well, it was almost daylight. Then you would have to go to rehearsal or sound check at three or four o'clock in the afternoon. Then you had to play a show that night and the same old routine. But, you had to get on the stage and make everybody think you were having the best time of your life—just smile and laugh and talk. Then you'd get back in the car and growl.

:◎:◎:◎:

SCOTTY MOORE: We were always really glad to go back to the studio. It was like vacation from the road. Some songs we'd do in a couple of takes; some we'd do seventy or more on. Some would get thrown out. The recording side was work, but it was a challenge. We looked forward to recording something new to play on the road shows.

JACK CLEMENT: The whole Sun Records company was housed right there in that little studio. Every once in awhile the acoustics in the room would change because the distributors would return so many unsold records, and the studio would get kind of full 'til we had a chance to shuffle them into the back of the building. When the returns piled up, the studio would sound totally different.

MAC WISEMAN: All those little-label studios would have to press thousands of records and ship them out on consignment in order to have product available in the stores, in case the record was a hit. But when the record was over and the distributors started returning all the extra unsold product, the record company would end up with warehouses full of that stuff. Not only that, the distributors wouldn't pay you for what they *had* sold until they needed another record from you, so you could literally go broke having a million-seller.

EDDIE BOND: Back then Sam Phillips was in debt real bad. Let me tell you what: Sam was going broke 'cause a little company cannot stand a hit. They press so damn many records, and they send them out, and they can't wait. They can't wait on their money.

Now take a big company like Decca, Columbia, or Capitol, or Mercury. Well, Mercury could say, "If you don't pay me for that Eddie Bond record, then I'm not going to ship you Patti Page." Decca could say, "You won't get anymore Brenda Lee," or whatever. And they wouldn't. With a little company like Sun, Sam could say, "If you don't pay me for Elvis, I'm not going to ship you anymore." The distributors would just say: "Well, don't ship no more."

STAN KESLER: Judd Phillips [Sam's brother] did most of the promotion and sales for Sun Records. He was a hard worker, and people liked him. He would go into a city and rent a hotel room and have drinks there with the radio people. If anybody was hungry, he'd order up food. Disc jockeys and promoters enjoyed being with him, and he got things played. He really did. That's how they marketed Sun Records and Elvis in the beginning.

"Crazy Mad for Me"
1955-1956

Elvis is well on his way, but is he getting too hot to handle? Insiders Owen Bradley, Mae Axton, and Mac Wiseman explain how manager Bob Neal solicits booking and promotional assistance on Elvis from former carnival showman Tom Parker long before most people even remotely suspect that the Colonel is involved.

Sun Records artist Barbara Pittman and Sun engineer Jack Clement reveal the pressure and politics involved in the selling of Elvis. Meanwhile, with the help of disc jockey Bill Randle, Elvis is positioning himself for the next big break: exposure on network television.

Then in steps the Colonel, bringing with him a vast network of connections, an uncanny ability to negotiate, and of course, a contract. RCA brings to the equation a tremendous promotional team that can transform young Elvis from a regional success story into a national recording star.

Returning to his birthplace a celebrity, Elvis seeks out relatives Christine and Annie Presley and buddy Joe Savery, who give personal accounts of the hometown celebration.

Elvis's story is fast becoming the great American fairy tale.

> "Don't let anyone tell you that I made the boy what he is today. The kids are the ones who made Elvis; without them he'd still be driving a truck."
>
> COLONEL TOM PARKER (*manager*)

WANDA JACKSON: Bob Neal and Elvis were good friends, as well as manager-artist. Bob was doing Elvis's booking, but Elvis was just getting too big, and Bob knew his own limitations. There was no problem, it was just that Bob couldn't handle it. He was getting out of his league. Bob knew Colonel Tom Parker would know what to do, so he brought Parker in as a special consultant in August of 1955.

OWEN BRADLEY (*record producer*): I went to the dog track in Daytona Beach with my family and friends, and I ran into Tom Parker. He knew I was involved with Decca Records. At the time I was assistant to Paul Cohen [artist and repertoire director of Decca's country department]. Well, Parker started working on me. He said, "Man, have you heard about this new fellow, Elvis Presley?" He started telling me that Elvis had been working somewhere out on the road with country superstar Marty Robbins and the audience didn't even want to hear Marty. They just wanted to hear Elvis. He stopped the show and did amazing things. Tom's story was just incredible, 'cause Marty was hot at the time.

Parker wanted me to go back to Nashville and tell Paul Cohen about Elvis. See, Tom wanted to get control of Presley so he could manage him, and at that time Bob Neal still had the management on Elvis. Tom said Sun was willing to sell the record contract, and he wanted Decca to buy it and let him be the manager.

Well, I relayed the message to Paul, and he called Bob Neal. Bob said he wanted eight thousand dollars, and Paul was kind of shocked. He said, "Eight thousand dollars! Are you kidding? We'll just cover you [record Elvis's hit songs with another artist] and knock you out of the charts."

At that time I was on the air playing five days a week on WSM [radio], and different country acts would come in and play—whoever was in town. The guys in those bands would tell me, "Damn, you know we were down in such-and-such a place, and so-and-so, the star of the show, was supposed to close the show, but when Elvis finished, the audience just all left! They didn't even want to see the star." Now that's pretty weird. I'd never heard of Elvis except for that one little record he had, "Blue Moon of Kentucky." I went back to Paul and said, "I tell you, Paul, these guys are coming back off the road saying this guy's really something else." So Paul said, "You know, I think I'll call Neal up again and see if I can buy that contract. He called and said, "Okay, Bob, I'll give you the eight thousand dollars." But Bob said, "Sorry, but it's twenty now!" Of course Paul got his back up again. Our company was very conservative.

JOAN DEARY *(assistant to Steve Sholes, RCA Victor)*: Early in my association with RCA, I worked for Steve Sholes. Steve felt Elvis was going to be a tremendous star, and, you know, the feeling of the other people at RCA was not all that enthusiastic. There were an awful lot of brass at RCA who felt Elvis was going to be a flash in the pan.

Steve was responsible for all country and western production, and country and western was not exactly RCA's primary interest at the time. Of course, Steve knew the Colonel because the Colonel had once managed Eddy Arnold, who was on RCA, so there was a connection there; but I think the first person who brought Elvis to Steve's attention was one of the field men. That's when Steve went to see him.

BILL GALLAGHER *(marketing director, Columbia Records)*: Now you may recall Mitch Miller was head of the artist and repertoire department of Columbia Records in the early fifties. By late '54 or early '55, he had begun to find some interest in what was going on in Nashville—what his pal Wesley Rose [owner of Acuff-Rose Music Publishing Co.] was doing. Wesley was having great success in the country music publishing field. At that point Mitch started to do country tunes with artists like Tony Bennett ["Cold, Cold Heart"] and others. We began to hear rumblings about Elvis.

I remember going to Mitch and saying, "Look, this kid in Memphis, he's making noise and there's some action there. Let's move into that scene." And Mitch said, "Aw, that's bullshit. Those cotton pickers, who the hell needs them?"

It was Wesley Rose who convinced Mitch Miller, along with Dick Link [another Columbia executive] and myself, that Elvis was a comer. We just thought. "This kid's gonna sell records. He's a good artist and he's drawing crowds."

Dick Link and I knew what the hell was going on in Nashville because we were part of that scene. We'd go down to the old WSM disc jockey convention every year and kinda look things over. That year, just before we left for the convention, we again brought up to Mitch the possibility of signing Elvis to Columbia. We said, "Look, it's going to take some money to sign him because RCA is after him." Mitch said, "You guys can offer up to forty grand—tops. That's as high as I'll go. But don't start there, and that's an advance against earnings." That was a very big advance for those days. Elvis may even have been the first Nashville-based artist to get an advance.

Well, we went down and met Colonel Tom Parker in the old Andrew Jackson Hotel lobby. I gave the Colonel the pitch that we were *the* company, we were happening, and Mitch was hot as hell then. We had the best field force, and our distribution was better than RCA's, and so forth. We gave him all that kind of crap, and he said, "Well, look, why don't you guys meet me here tomorrow? I'll have Elvis with me." Elvis wasn't a big star then, not yet. He could walk around in public just like all of us. But anyway, the following morning Link and I met the Colonel and Elvis Presley in the hotel coffee shop. We sat at a corner table, and I gave Elvis my pitch as to how great Columbia was. Everything was going well. We talked back and forth. Elvis was very pleasant.

Then, the Colonel more or less dismissed Elvis by saying, "All right, Elvis, let me talk to the boys here a little further."

I didn't screw around. I figured he was negotiating with me, but he said, "We've been offered a lot of money." And I said, "Well, look, let's cut out all the nonsense. Mitch has agreed to give you guys a forty-thousand-dollar advance." So he gave me the usual nod and laughed a little bit and said, "Well, you're way off base, but let me get back to you." That was it. He never got back to us.

OWEN BRADLEY: Next thing I knew, I was at WSM and here comes Tom Parker and Steve Sholes. As they walked by, Tom said, "Well, your guy just wouldn't get with it. We sold Elvis to [RCA] Victor." He didn't give me the details on it, but I heard later on he did a real smart thing: Tom got Hill and Range to come up with half of the money. I understand by that time it had jumped to forty grand. Tom didn't tell me that, but that was the rumor that was going around.

MAE AXTON: Steve Sholes called me and told me RCA was buying Elvis's contract from Sun and would be needing material to record on his first session. Steve had recorded a good bit of my stuff.

I used to write a lot of songs with Tommy Durden; he'd come to my house in Jacksonville every Friday. One week he came over and he had a little clipping from the Miami paper, something about a middle-aged, nicely dressed man who had torn out all his identification, wrote one line, "I walk a lonely street," and committed suicide. Anyway, for some reason the story was so sad it really caught Tommy's eye. He read it to me and I said, "Well, Tommy, everyone has someone who cares, no matter how rich or poor, good or bad, or how high or low their status in life. So if or when they find what happened, someone will be heartbroken." And just like that it hit me that this was the nucleus for a song. I said, "I'm going to put a heartbreak hotel at the end of that lonely street." Just then another friend of ours, the singer Glenn Reeves, came in, and I said, "Come on, Glenn, we're gonna write Elvis Presley's first million-seller." Glenn said, "What's the name of it?" I said, "Heartbreak Hotel." He said, "That's the silliest title I ever heard. I've got some errands to run. I'll be back in about thirty minutes." By the time Glenn came back, the song was finished. I wrote the words without hesitation, very few changes. As I wrote it, I'd read the lines to Tommy, and I told him to start working on the tune. I loved the tune, but it was a slow ballad and I felt it should have a real beat. So I went to the piano and worked out the beat to my liking. I asked Glenn to do the demo. He always played by ear and was a quick learner. It took him only a few minutes 'til he had a perfect demo. For the second time I offered to put Glenn's name on it. He refused, saying, "I don't want my name on the silly thing."

It was almost time for the annual disc jockey convention in Nashville, so I called Elvis and told him and Bob [Neal] to meet me there, that I had just written his first million-seller.

When I got to Nashville, I met Elvis and Bob at the Andrew Jackson—Colonel Tom wasn't yet [officially] in the picture—and I played them the demo. When it finished Elvis said, "Hot dog, Mae, play it again." I did, and he said, "Boy I'd like to do that." I said, "Okay, you can record it. I happen to think it will be your first million-seller." At that time RCA was buying his contract from Sun, so I told them about my conversation with Steve Sholes. I said, "If this is your first original new song released on RCA, I'll give you a third of the writers' royalties on it, and you'll make enough money to take your mom and dad to Florida to see the ocean."

Elvis was stunned. He looked at me and grinned and said, "You remembered!" I said, "Yes, I remembered."

When he got his first writer's check (he never claimed to write a word or even a note of it) he called me and asked if my children would join him and his mom in Daytona that weekend. We did, and that's when I got to know his mother and dad.

BUDDY KILLEN: I was working a little place in northern Florida called the Mellow Club, and I knew Mae Axton, who lived in Jacksonville. Somehow she knew I was working there and she came by. I asked her, "What are you doing in town?" She said, "I came to see the Colonel; I'm doing PR for him. You want to go with me tonight to the show?" I said, "Yeah." So we went over and I met Elvis again. He and I talked backstage and watched Hank Snow perform. Elvis was in awe of Hank Snow. He said, "Man, he is really something, ain't he?"

That show had Andy Griffith on it (he had a record out called "What It Was Was Football"), plus Hank, the comic singers Homer and Jethro, and a number of other people—I forget who all it was—and Elvis. Now Elvis hadn't exploded yet. He was just beginning to break out a little in all those different southern cities. That night, Mae and I were talking between sets, and I said, "You know, you've written songs for other people, and I'm working with a new publishing company, so how about writing some for me." She said, "I've got one song." I said, "What's it called?" She said, "Heartbreak Hotel." I said, "Who do you think it would be good for?" She said, "Elvis." So when I got home a couple of weeks later, there was a little five-minute reel [of tape], and on it was "Heartbreak Hotel." Glenn Reeves was singing it something like Elvis later sang it. When Elvis recorded it [the following January], he copied it note for note from Glenn Reeves. It was Elvis doing Glenn Reeves doing Elvis.

MAE AXTON: During this time Colonel Tom was trying to buy Elvis from Bob Neal. So people in the music industry began to realize that Elvis might just become something big once he went with a major record company. Word travels fast in the music business.

:◎:◎:◎:

MAC WISEMAN: Parker was smart. He got RCA to purchase all the old [Elvis] masters from Sun, so when Presley hit big they had a monopoly on his product. When Columbia signed Johnny Cash, they didn't buy up all of his old product, and it nearly killed Cash's career: Every time Columbia would release a Cash master, Sun would drag out one of his older records and release it. That damn-near killed Cash right at the height of his career. Parker prevented that happening with Presley by getting RCA to buy the old product.

JACK CLEMENT: At that time, it was the highest price anybody ever paid for an artist. It was kinda unheard of: forty thousand dollars for a singer. I know it sounds like a small amount today, but back then it astounded everybody.

BARBARA PITTMAN: From what I heard, Elvis didn't want to go. He did not want to be signed with Victor. He was scared to death of that. He was comfortable selling his few little records and doing the Louisiana Hayride. To Elvis that was a lot of money. When you have nothing, and you're making enough to buy a house; boy, you're doing all right. Elvis was scared. He thought he'd go to Victor and they'd record a couple of songs, and then he'd fade away. There he'd be without a label. Elvis did not want to leave. He actually asked Sam, "Please don't sell my contract. I don't want to leave."

JACK CLEMENT: I asked Sam point blank one time, "Did you want to sell Elvis or did Elvis want to go?" He said, "No, Elvis wanted to stay." Sam sold him to get the money.

BILL GALLAGHER: I know what RCA signed him for. They signed him for fifty [thousand dollars]. I later became a very close friend of Steve Sholes, and he told me that RCA paid fifty thousand for Elvis's contract. I don't know how they paid him the fifty—maybe it was forty plus something else. That's how Columbia Records missed getting Elvis Presley. As we later measured Elvis's position in the charts, we used to kid Mitch about how much gross billing we lost by not signing him. We'd say, "If you'd just given us another ten grand on that budget we could've had Presley in our pocket and billed forty million dollars in sales last year." It was always just a joke. You couldn't really fault Mitch in those days, he was cock of the walk—the hottest record producer in the music business.

BARBARA PITTMAN: If Elvis had stayed around Sun Records, I guarantee you he would not have made it. He was fading at the time anyway. Elvis was getting pushed back. If Parker hadn't of come along when he did, saw what he saw in the kid, and grabbed him up, Elvis would've never made it. Sam was ready to get rid of Elvis, his records weren't selling. Sam wasn't pushing them. Sam didn't want to spend any money on Elvis 'cause he was saving that for his radio station. That's all Sam wanted. Sam was not interested in music and the artist. Sam was interested in buying radio stations.

MAC WISEMAN: The Aberbachs [owners of Hill and Range Music Publishing Co.] were feeding RCA a lot of good material about that time, so they were all fairly tight with RCA. There was a lot of politicking going on then, and, boy, Parker knew where all the skeletons were.

BILLY WALKER: Do you know RCA didn't believe enough in Elvis to guarantee the money for his contract? Julian and Jean Aberbach guaranteed the money.

BARBARA PITTMAN: RCA took the money that Sam was paid from off the top of Elvis's royalties. That was front money—an advance. I asked Elvis about that, and he said, "You don't think that they just paid that money out for me. That came out of my royalties—my first record."

JACK CLEMENT: Sam got lucky. He got paid for Elvis, and then immediately he had money to put into his next hot record, "Blue Suede Shoes" by Carl Perkins. And then he had "I Walk the Line" by Johnny Cash. Sam was hot.

SONNY NEAL: Dad managed Elvis right up to and including him signing with RCA. I've got a picture of dad and the Colonel and Elvis and the RCA guys signing the contract, and I have the contract itself.

MAE AXTON: Bob Neal was a quiet, sincere, wonderful person. He told me that he was going to sell Colonel Tom Parker the management contract on Elvis. He said, "I really feel that I have taken him as far as I can go. This will give me enough money to start my own agency." And he did.

JOAN DEARY: When RCA signed Elvis, the whole company was turned upside down almost immediately. His records were so incredibly successful, and RCA was a well-oiled machine. I've heard that expression used about the Colonel and those concert tours, but it fit perfectly with what RCA Victor was able to do early in their promotion of Elvis.

DON ROBERTSON (*songwriter*): Back in '56, I was trying to come up with songs that someone, some publisher, would be interested enough in to give me an advance. I played a song I had written ["I'm Counting on

You"] for Jean Aberbach over the phone. I lived in California and he was in New York, and he liked my new song a lot, so we made a deal on it. He offered me a nice advance and said, "I'm positive I can get a big artist to record this." I said, "Great!"

But a few months down the line [Aberbach] called me and said, "Well, we didn't get you a big artist, but we got you a record by a new guy that everybody's excited about, and we think he's going to do very well. His name is Elvis Presley." I was really disappointed, and I told him so. I said, "Elvis Presley? I've never heard of him."

Of course, it wasn't long before I changed my attitude.

:◎:◎:◎:

JACK CLEMENT: In the 1950s those network TV shows had a huge audience. There weren't that many shows that exposed talent. *The Dorsey Show, The Ed Sullivan Show, The Steve Allen Show*—they were very powerful because everybody was watching, and the public didn't have all these other choices like they do today.

BILL RANDLE *(disc jockey in Cleveland and NYC, show promoter)*: We first tried to get Elvis on *The Ed Sullivan Show,* and that was impossible. We had a connection there. Marlo Lewis was the producer. But Lewis didn't like Elvis. We had gotten Elvis an audition with Arthur Godfrey [*Arthur Godfrey's Talent Scouts*], but he didn't look good—the acne was really terrible and Godfrey was kinda funny about that. Did you ever watch the Godfrey Show? Nobody had any skin problems; they were all perfect. Godfrey threw Presley out of the studio, and that's the audition that Marlo Lewis saw. So, that killed Presley for the Godfrey and Sullivan shows.

We then tried to get him on *The Perry Como Show,* but Mickey Glass, who was Como's producer and good friend and manager, looked at Elvis and said, "We'll never put anything like that on *The Perry Como Chesterfield Show.*" You have to realize, Presley was the equivalent of a punk rocker today. These kids are freaky looking, and you just didn't do that on Perry Como or Ed Sullivan.

But Jackie Gleason's *Stage Show* was a little different. We had some friends there—a man named Tina Barsea actually, who was the manager of the band. He and Tommy Dorsey had music publishing firms. We were able to cut a deal with him: in return for "x" amount of cooperation, we got Elvis Presley six shots on network TV on the Jackie Gleason *Stage Show.* I've never told that story before; I'm not sure it was legal.

They let me introduce Elvis, and I said, "This young man is going to be the biggest star in the country in a matter of weeks, and he's going to make television history." Jackie Gleason's manager, Jack Phillerman, looked at Elvis on the audition right before the show, and if he could have gotten somebody else to replace him with—and I don't think Jack will tell this story today—he would have. Sarah Vaughan was the star of the show, and George Tredwell, her trumpet-playing manager-husband, went crazy. He hated hillbillies. (Tredwell was an early black militant.) Sarah, of course, was a great black singer, and here is this redneck kid with a guitar and no arrangements and they're throwing him right in the middle of a show with Sarah Vaughan.

The only person that liked Elvis—besides the public—was Jackie Gleason.

Jackie Gleason loved Elvis Presley. Gleason was half-stoned, sitting up there watching the monitors, and he said, "That kid's pretty good. Have him do that one about 'I've got a woman.'" Gleason literally changed the show schedule right then and there. That's why Elvis did that song. Gleason was a very important figure in U.S. television at that time, so everybody listened to him. The second song wasn't scheduled, and that drove everybody crazy. "I've got a woman, she walks the streets. . . ." And let me tell you, CBS had never heard anything like that before.

:◎:◎:◎:

MAE AXTON: Elvis recorded "Heartbreak Hotel" on his first RCA session —January 10, 1956, in Nashville—and it was released by February and was a million-seller by April 21.

JIMMY VELVET: "Heartbreak Hotel" broke Elvis wide open in January of 1956. It was a smash. When I heard it, I dragged out my old pictures and said, "Hey, this is that guy!" So when he came down a little later to perform at the Florida Theater, I went back down to see him again. He remembered me and spent some time with me. I remember he had a girl [Andrea June Stephens] down there from Atlanta that had won a contest, "Win a date with Elvis."

BUDDY KILLEN: Everybody knew it was going to happen. You could tell it instantly. All you had to do was watch the crowds wherever he went. Elvis would be nothing, totally unknown, and go into a city and perform, and he would become an instant star before he even left town. It was unreal.

MAC WISEMAN: A lot of people in the industry and press were laughing at Elvis, talking about his long sideburns and him swiveling his hips and stuff, but Bing Crosby had an interview in the *Hollywood Reporter*, and I remember Bing said, "Don't underestimate this boy. This boy's here to stay. He's a talent and he can sing."

Of course, Bing being the tremendously popular singer and movie star he was, that carried a lot of weight. Up until that time, people had just never given Elvis credit for being able to sing.

D. J. FONTANA: Elvis had such a keen ear. He could listen to a song once or twice, and he knew it. But he had his own ideas. He was picking these songs, all these big monster hits, and he was always right. So after awhile what could we tell him? We couldn't tell him what to record; we'd have been crazy. He had the reins. Whatever he wanted to record, that was it. He picked "Don't Be Cruel," "Hound Dog,"—a whole string of big hits.

Hill and Range Music Publishers in New York would send demos for him, and if he didn't like 'em he'd throw 'em out, like all the artists do. But Elvis would hear about eight bars [of each song] and say, "Okay, hold that one to the side. Put that over here. I'm not sure about that one; put that over there. We'll do this first, second, third." If he had singles to do, he'd simply say, "This is the single." He just kind of had this knack for picking the hits, and everything was real simple. Elvis didn't want anything complicated, and that's why he sold records, I think. You could understand what he was doing. And there's nothing ever vulgar or suggestive in any of the records.

MAC WISEMAN: By then you couldn't have stopped Presley. He was just that hot. But Colonel Parker was smart enough to know how to control it, how to handle it, and market it. That's where he came into the picture.

I don't know if you know it or not, but Parker was my manager for a short time there, after he and [Eddy] Arnold parted ways. Parker was ahead of his time. Back when he was managing Arnold, they had a sponsorship tie-in with the Purina company, and he had gotten Purina to sponsor or underwrite those Arnold shows. It gave them a tremendous advantage. I don't know if Parker was the first to develop show-product tie-ins, but he was certainly early in doing it in the country music field. When he and Arnold split, Parker took the Purina account with him. That put him a jump ahead of other show promoters. Back then Parker did it just like those old boys do it today, with Wrangler and stuff like that. That's how far ahead of the game he was.

FARON YOUNG: Back when Eddy Arnold left [Parker's management], Parker got into some kind of business partnership with Hank Snow—a booking deal. It was called Jamboree Attractions. At that time country music had really tapered off 'cause those rockers started getting hot. It damn-near killed country music for awhile. Anyway, about that time Parker signed Snow and Minnie Pearl and some other folks; but needless to say, he couldn't hardly book nothing for Snow, 'cause at that time you couldn't hardly book a hillbilly act.

On a trip down to Florida, I think, Parker saw Presley, and later he seen Presley tearin' 'em up down on the Hayride.

Parker ended up a while later signing a side deal to manage Presley, and Snow got pissed off 'cause Presley was working and he wasn't. Snow said to Parker, "By god, what are you doing with that bastard out there working and there's no work here for me?" Parker told Snow, "Well, I'll buy you out." Snow said, "No, I'll buy you out. What do you want?" Parker was setting him up, and he said, "Anything you want to give me." Snow said, "No, I'll just sell." So they made some kind of a deal, and Parker bought the whole damn company.

Well, about a year or so later, Elvis Presley was the hottest son-of-a-bitch in the business. Snow went and got him a lawyer and was going to sue Parker. He wanted half of Presley and half of the company back. But the judge basically said, "Fuck you. You done made a deal. You got your money and run. You just made a bad goddamn deal." Parker knew he was fuckin' Snow. He knew. But Snow didn't have enough sense to know it 'cause he was still like most acts—too vain. He was thinking, "I'm the star." Snow farted around and lost out on half of Elvis Presley. That's what he did.

BILL RANDLE: Parker is a very interesting man, and he literally took over Elvis Presley. He became the person who pulled the strings. Parker didn't want anything known about anybody who had done anything with Presley in the beginning because that meant the Parker myth couldn't be created. Parker is himself, like Presley, partially a myth.

Parker came to Elvis Presley after Presley was already well on his way. He came to Presley after the deal had been made for Jackie Gleason's *Stage Show*. I made that deal in August of 1955 and presented Elvis the first time he was on national television. That was the first network TV Elvis ever did: January 28, 1956. Parker was not a party to any of that. But when Parker came into the picture, he took over Presley's life, and all the rest of it, including his past, it seems. It didn't matter to me. I had a lot of other things going for me.

First photo. Little Elvis with his parents, Gladys Love Presley and Vernon Elvis Presley. (Michael Ochs Archives)

Left: Way back when: Elvis stands in striped overalls beside his neighborhood chums. With Elvis are: (back row) Evon Farrar and James Farrar, (middle row) Guy Harris, LaVerne Farrar, and Bobbie Spencer, and (front) Odell Clark. (Guy Harris)

Opposite: Stick-'em-up! Foreshadowing his fascination with guns, blue jean-clad Elvis shows how the cowboys draw their weapons in his favorite Western movies.

Below: In 1948, at age 13, Elvis sits on the curb with his girlfriend-of-the-day. (Jimmy Velvet)

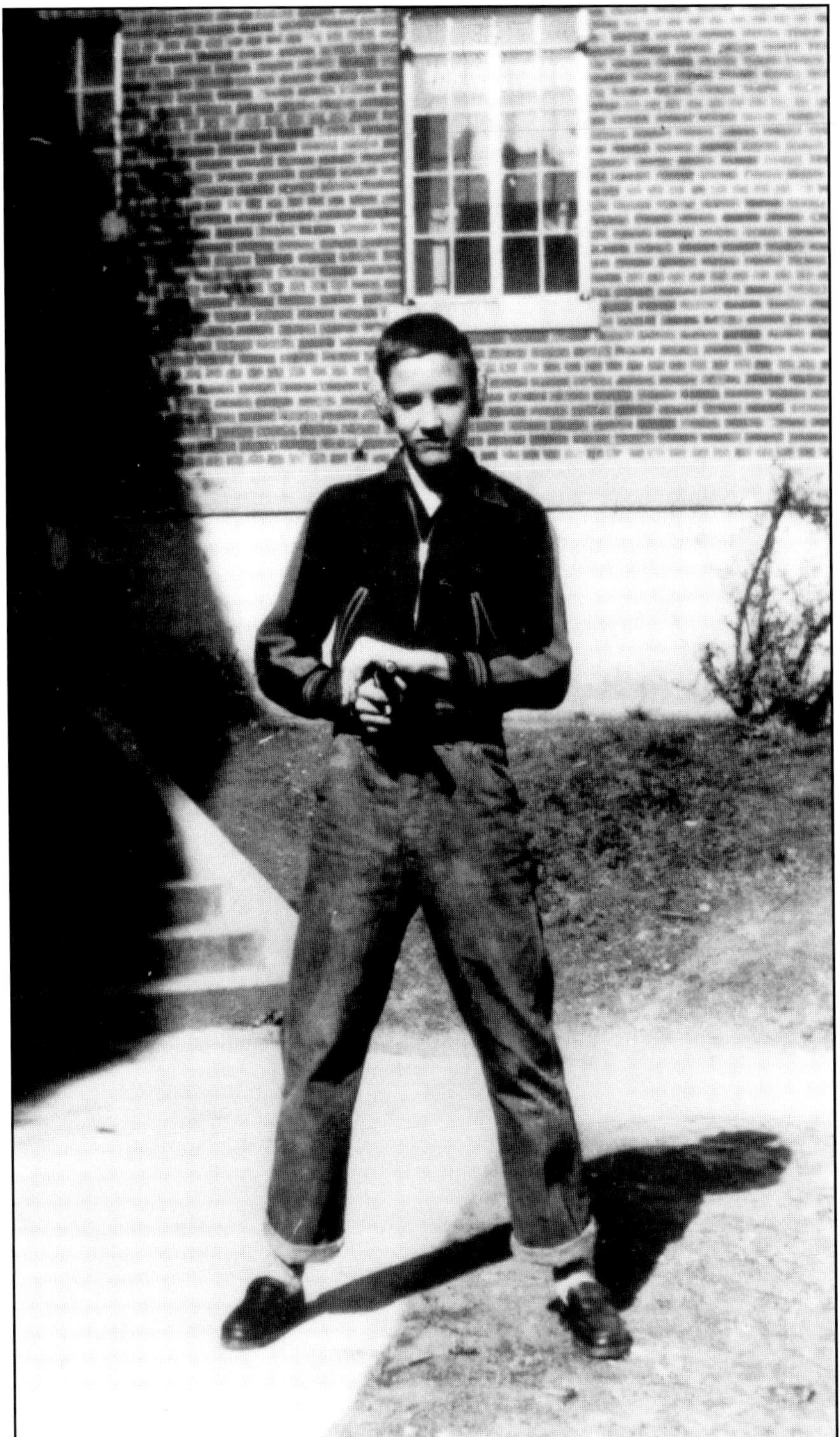

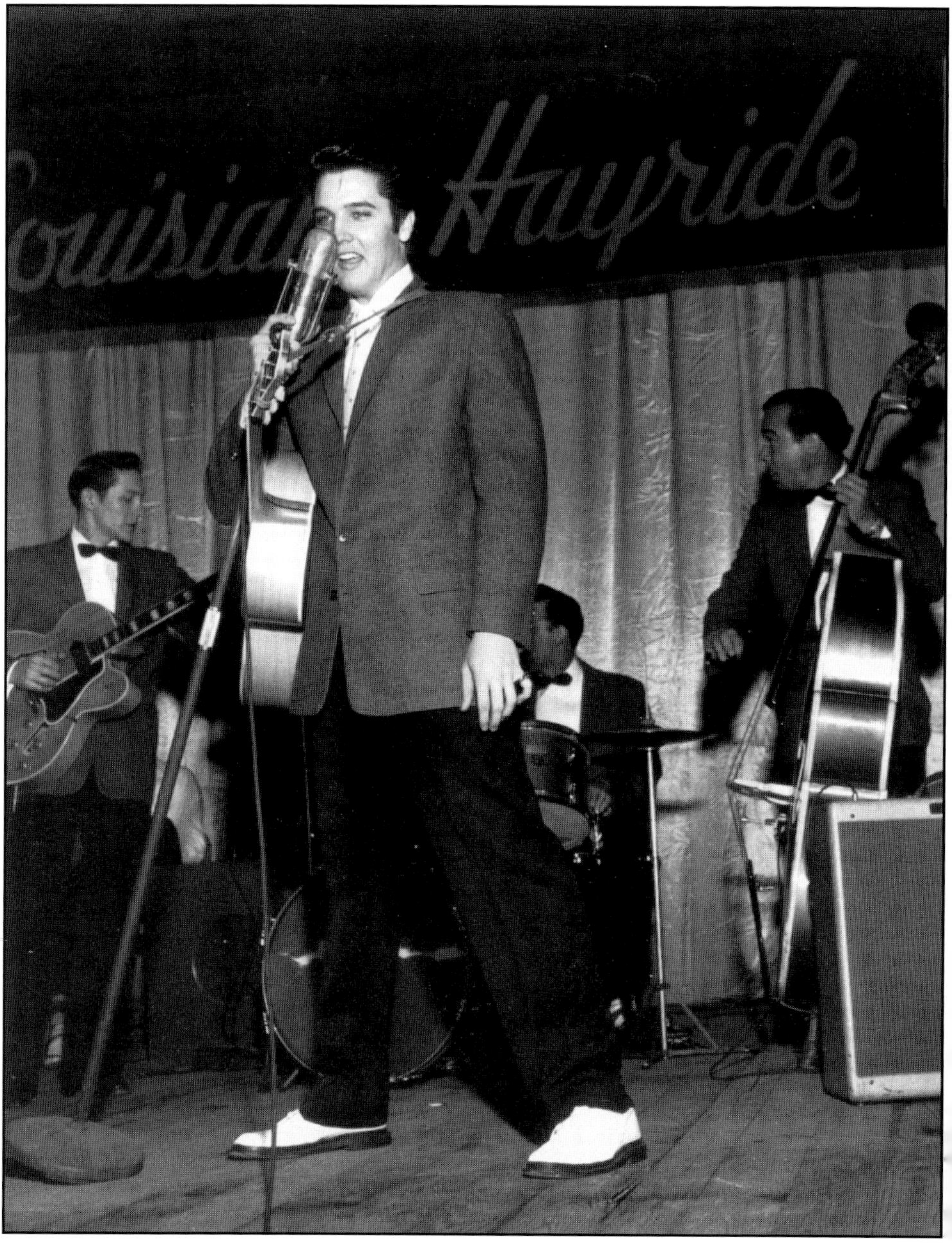
Hayride

Right: Fans hold up "Elvis for President" signs as the young singer signs autographs in 1954. (Robin C. Rosaaen)

Opposite: Headed for stardom, a youthful Elvis Presley wows 'em on the Louisiana Hayride where he appeared on many a Saturday night from October 1954 to April 1956. In the background are his band members—guitarist Scotty Moore, drummer D. J. Fontana, and bassist Bill Black.

Below: The four musketeers of Lauderdale Courts line up for Paul's birthday snapshot in 1954. Left to right, Farley Guy, Elvis, Paul Dougher (the birthday boy) and Buzzy Forbes. (Paul Dougher)

Above: A small selection of the numerous Elvis fan magazines and fan club publications. (Mark Hill)

Right: Elvis on stage in his hometown, Tupelo, is dressed in a velveteen shirt Gladys made for him, and hardly seems conscious of the news that movie producer Hal Wallis had just predicted Elvis would become the next Rudolf Valentino. (Terry Wood)

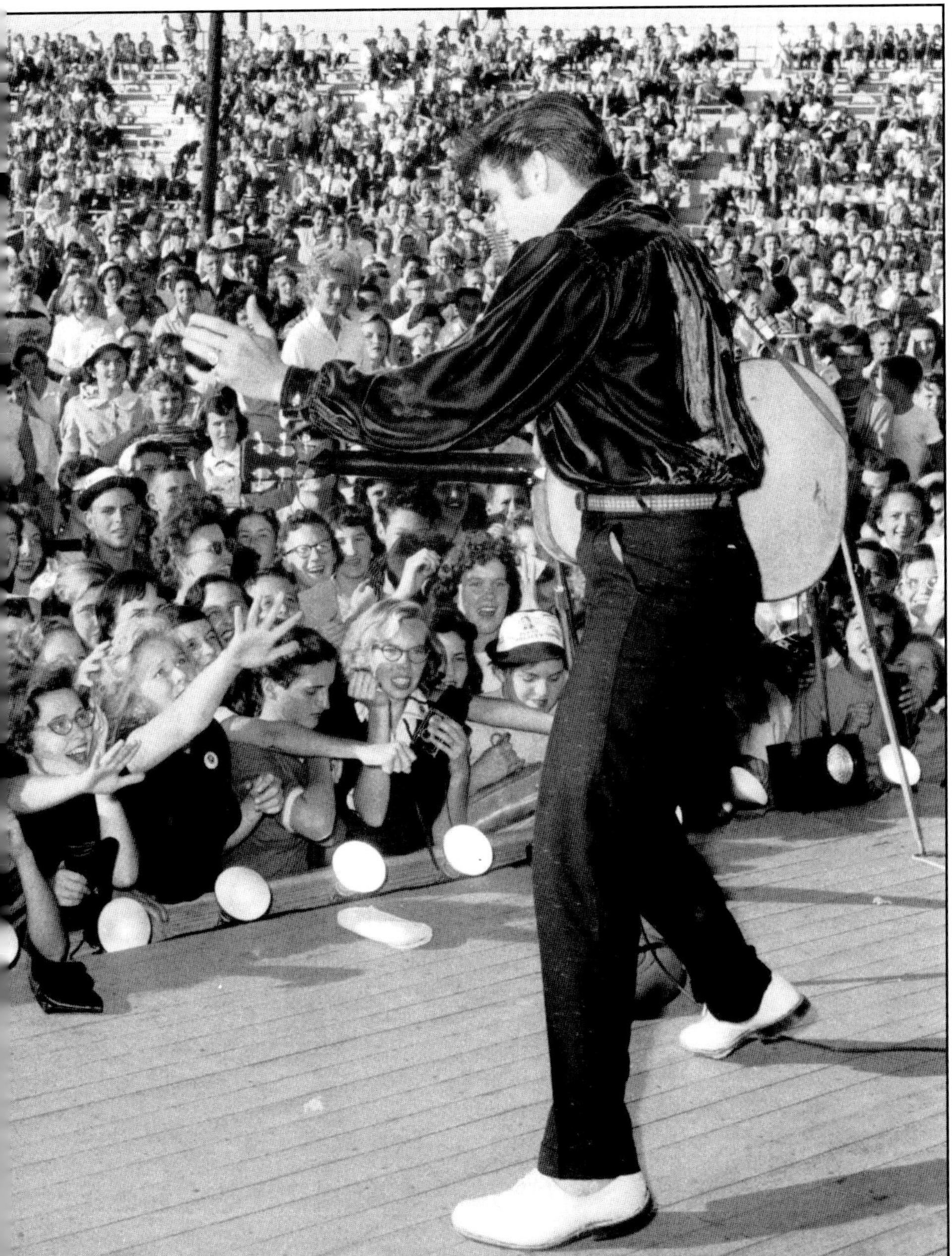

Above: Elvis, with young admirer, at the Rainbow Skating Rink, Memphis. (Robin C. Rosaaen)

Left: Gladys Presley shows friend Jimmy Velvet her pink Cadillac at Graceland shortly before she goes to Killeen, Texas, in 1958. (Jimmy Velvet)

Opposite: The face that changed the world! (Morgin Press, Inc.)

Bottom: On the afternoon of September 26, 1956, Elvis and his proud parents, Vernon and Gladys, celebrate Elvis's first hometown concert in Tupelo after he becomes a star. (Jimmy Velvet)

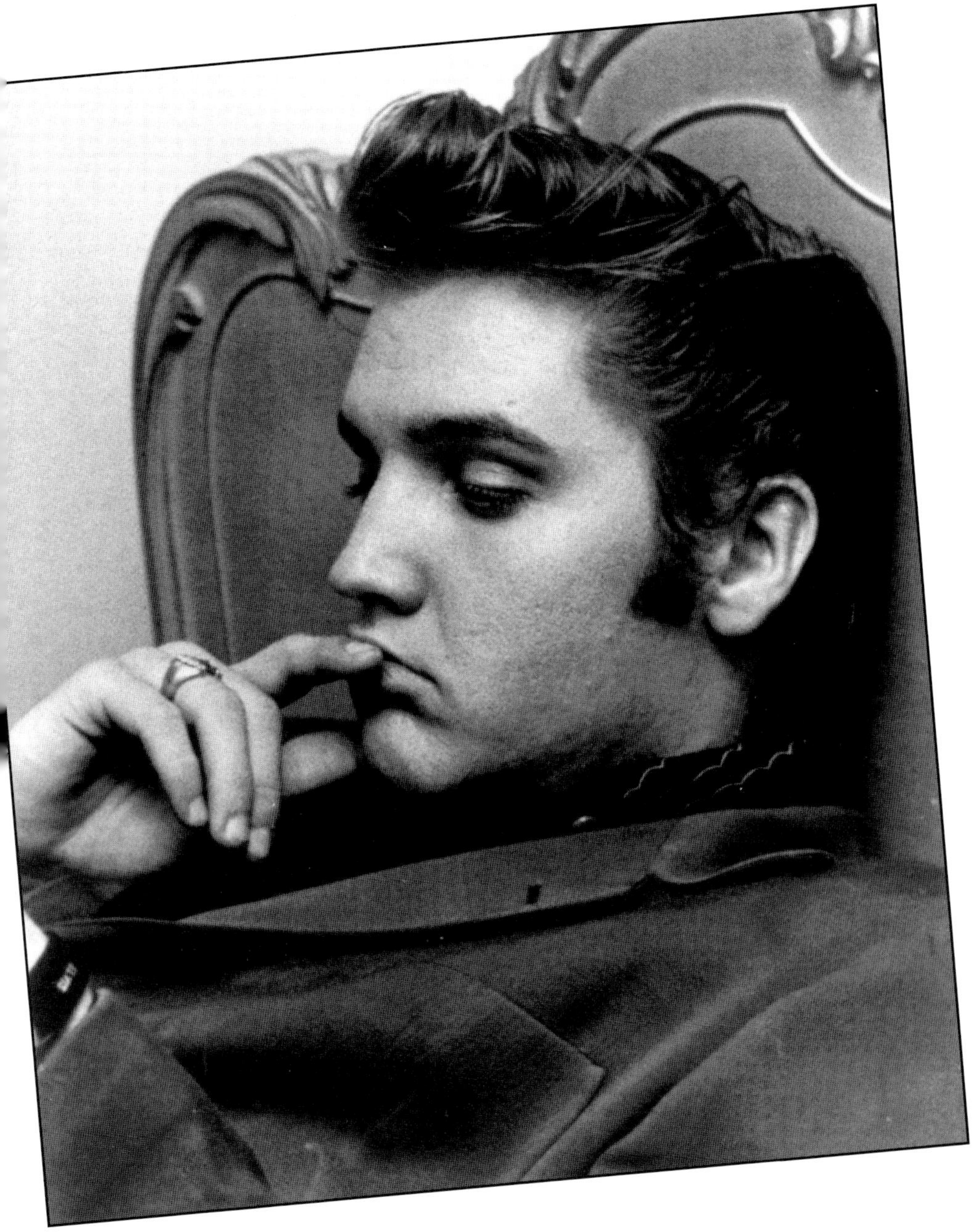

Above: A young and very talented Elvis with fan and friend Barbara Glidewell, just prior to Elvis's leaving for Hollywood to film Love Me Tender. *(Barbara Glidewell)*

Right: Captured by fans, Elvis pauses a moment before going onstage at the Mississippi-Alabama Fair and Dairy Show in 1956. (Cecilia Palmer)

Below: What a handsome couple! Anita Wood and Elvis share a late night ride on the dodge 'em cars at the Mid-South Fairgrounds in Memphis in 1957. (Jimmy Velvet)

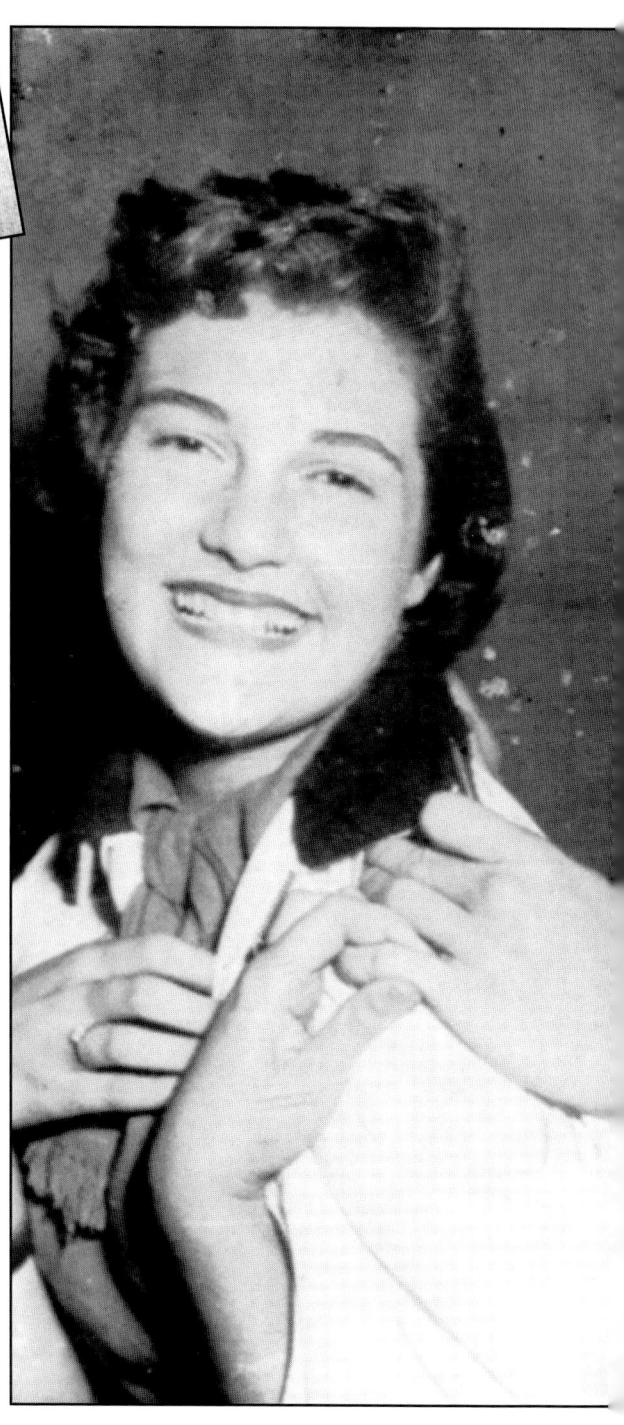

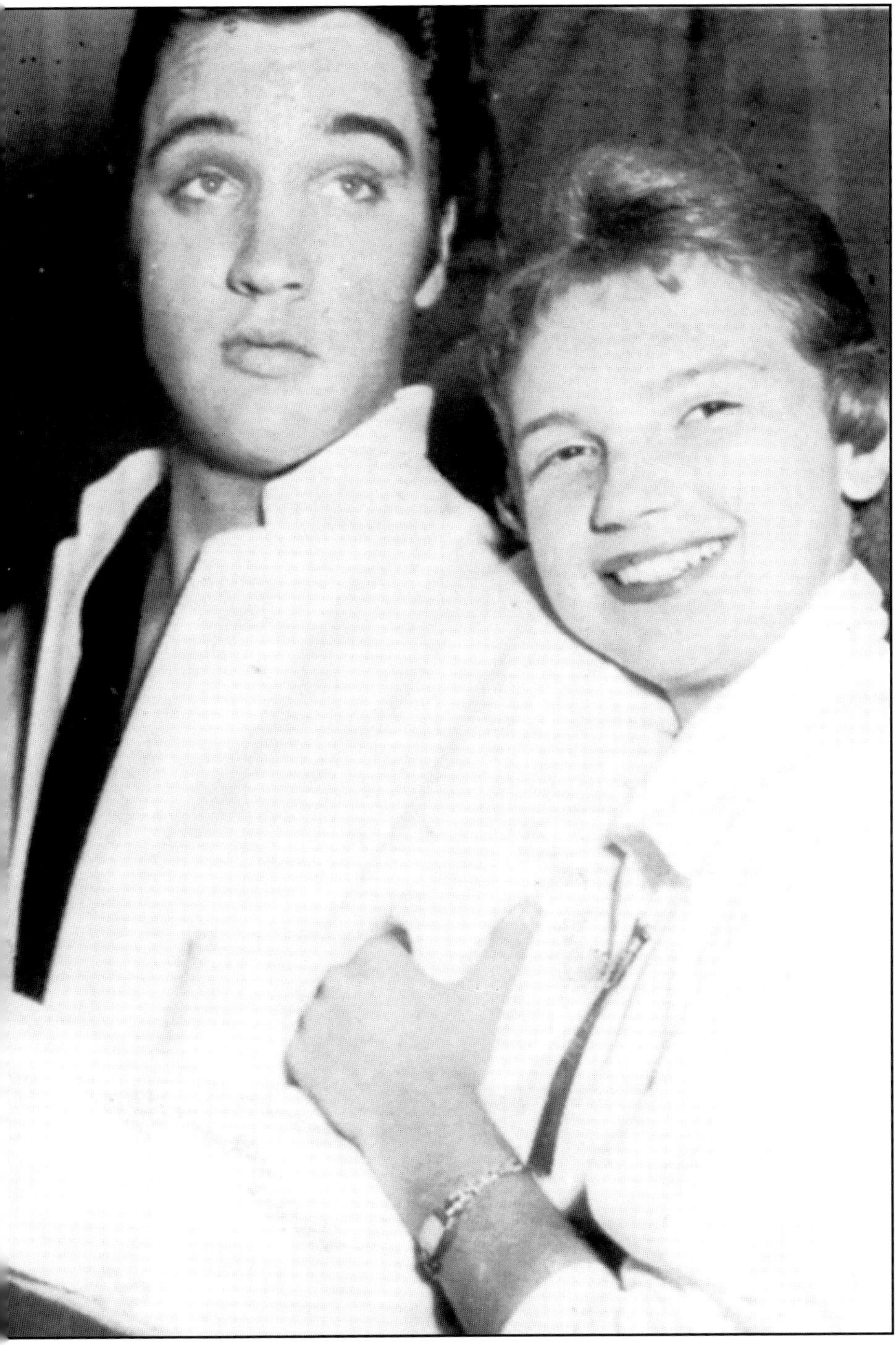

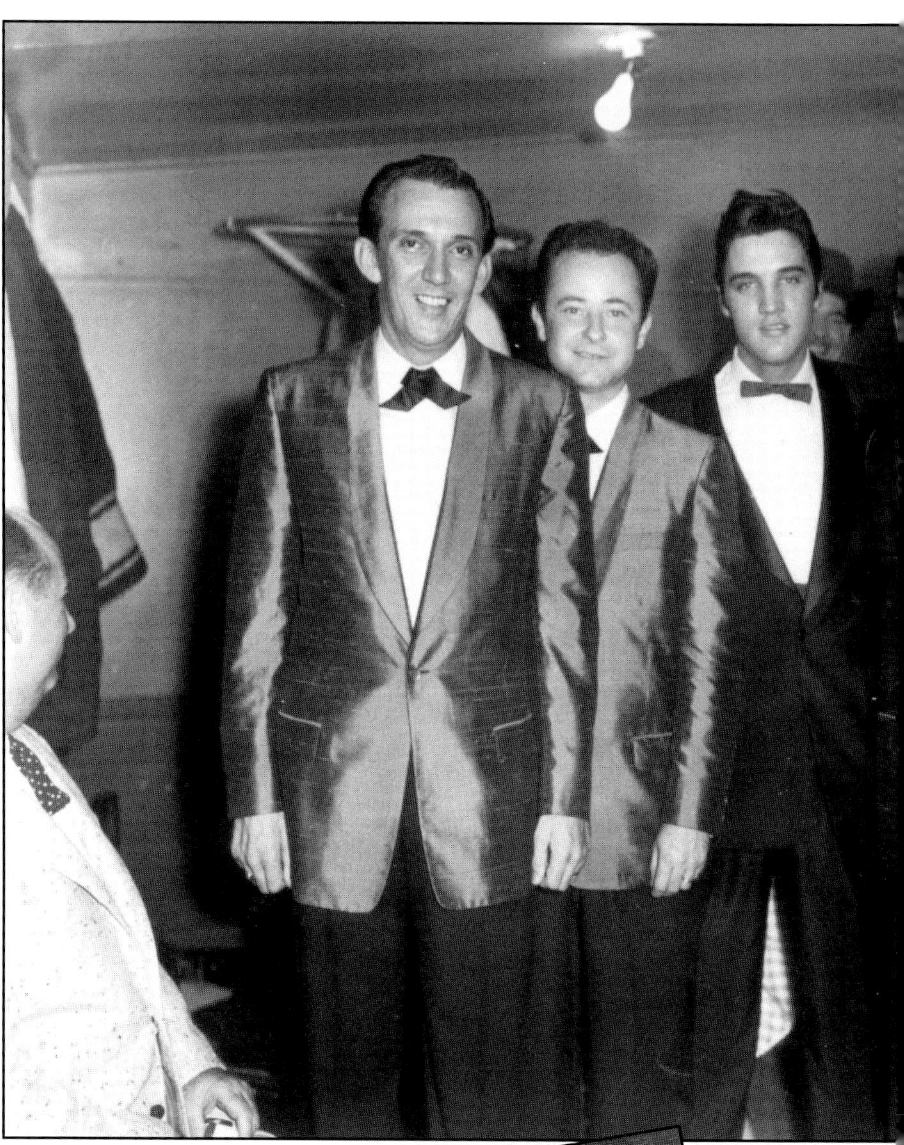

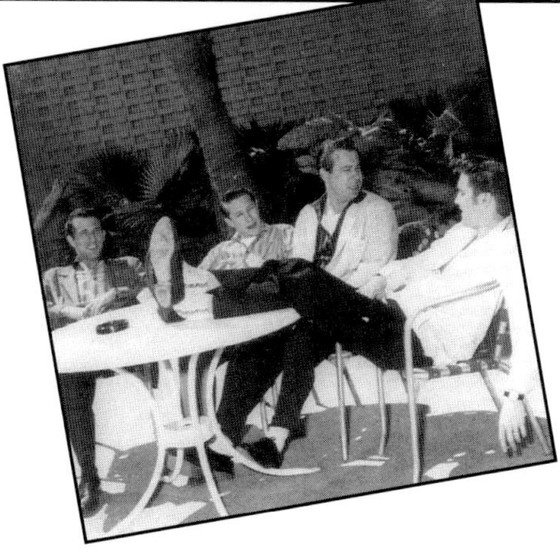

Left: Elvis bought a tux for a backstage visit with the Jordanaires at the Grand Ole Opry just before Christmas, 1957. Left to right are Hugh Jarrett (later replaced by bass singer Ray Walker), tenor Gordon Stoker, Elvis, second tenor Neal Matthews, and baritone Hoyt Hawkins. (Jimmy Velvet)

Above: Elvis backstage at the Grand Ole Opry with Colonel Tom Parker in December 1957. He didn't perform on this visit, and he left the new tux backstage when he departed. (Jimmy Velvet)

Opposite bottom: Taking a break. While in Las Vegas for his first engagement at the New Frontier Hotel in April 1956, Elvis props his feet up on a patio table alongside trusty band members D. J. Fontana (left), Scotty Moore (center), and Bill Black. (Robin C. Rosaaen)

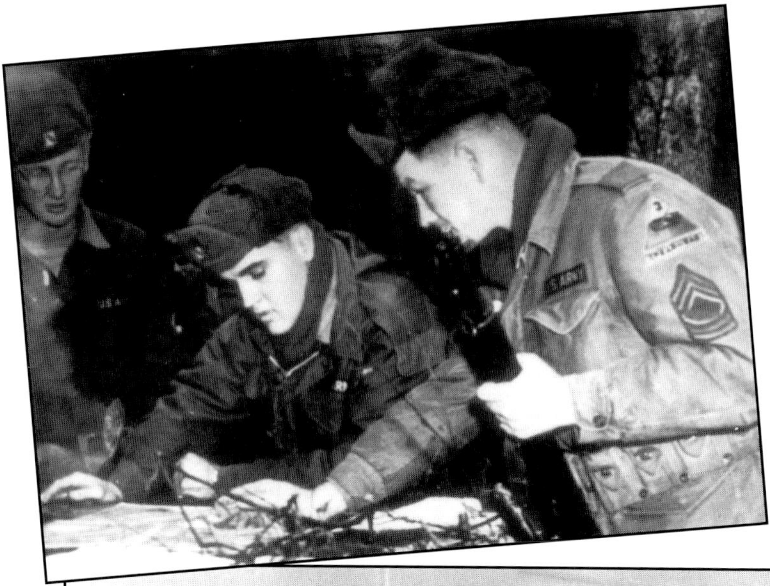

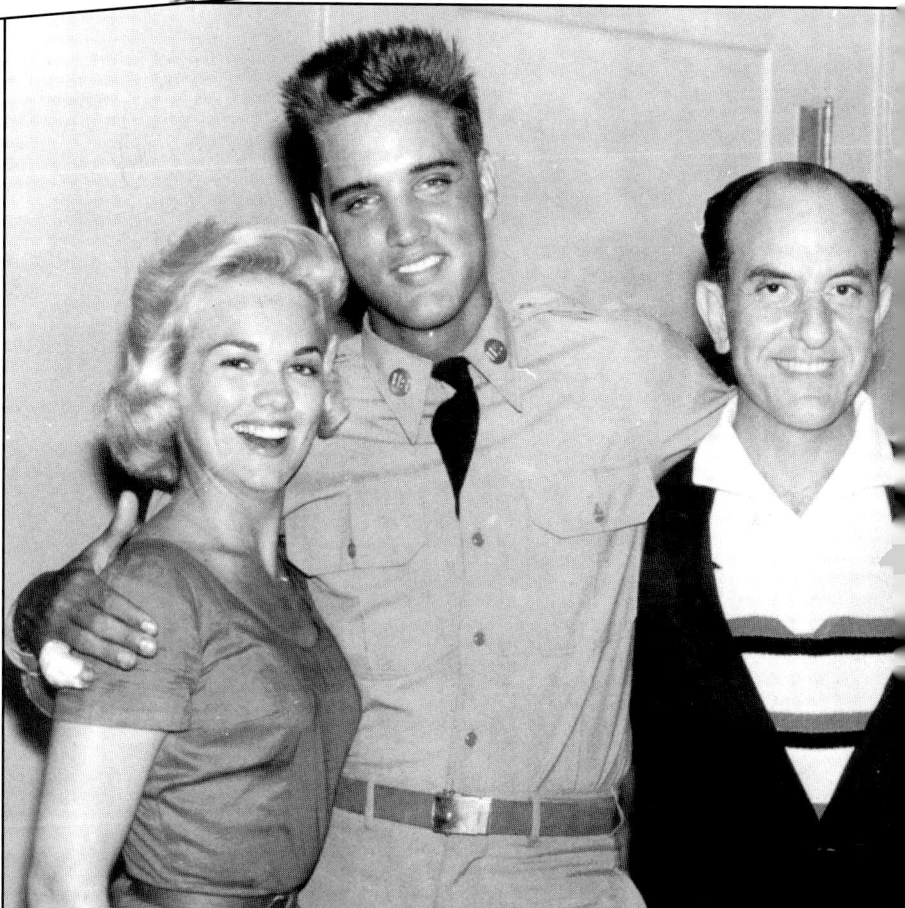

Opposite top: Elvis checks out a road map with Sergeant Ira Jones while Pat Conway looks on during Private Presley's tour of duty with the U.S. Army in Grafenwöhr, Germany, spring of 1959. (Ira Jones)

Above: Farewell, soldier boy! Elvis poses for one last picture with friends at his rented house in Killeen, Texas, before departing for Germany, September 22, 1958. Left to right: Kate Wheeler, Gene Smith, Dotty Ayers, Arlene Cogan, Earl Greenwood, Eddie Fadal, Elvis, Vernon Presley, Junior Smith, Lamar Fike, Red West and Jo Osuna. (Eddie Fadal)

Left: Pretty blonde Anita Wood and nearly blonde draftee Elvis Presley visit the home of friends Eddie and LaNelle Fadal in Waco, Texas, in 1958. (Eddie Fadal)

Below: Elvis relaxing in the barracks at Friedberg, Germany, spring of 1959. (Ira Jones)

Lovebirds Priscilla, age 14, and Elvis, age 25, spend a little quiet time together in 1959, shortly before Elvis's tour of duty with the U.S. Army in Germany ends and he returns home to Graceland.

OWEN BRADLEY: Tom Parker was a shrewd negotiator. He really negotiated for his client and, of course, for himself. I think they respected him for that. You might not agree with him. You might sort of wonder how the hell he's gonna get that much money for this guy, but he'd get it, and more too: it'd be double!

BARBARA PITTMAN: Gladys [Presley] thought Parker was just the biggest crook that ever lived. She couldn't stand him. Parker was always coming in trying to order her around, telling her how to dress, how to act in front of people, and the image that he was creating for her, and all of that. That just infuriated her. Gladys didn't like the Colonel at all.

Colonel Parker always wanted Elvis's mama to look like this little religious, church-going lady. Man, Gladys was stoned 'til Sunday morning. She couldn't even get up to go to church. (I shouldn't say that about Gladys. I loved her very much.)

Vernon just sat back quiet and sort of took it all in. He was a pretty heavy drinker, too, you know. He just enjoyed having all that free booze and free life, 'cause, you know, he never worked anyway. He always had "a bad back."

JAMES BLACKWOOD: In Elvis's early performing days, before Colonel Tom became his manager, we had singings every month—gospel music singings at Ellis Auditorium [in Memphis]. If he was in town, Elvis always came and sat backstage and enjoyed himself. I remember at those singings, I would introduce him, and he would come out and sing a number. We would sing with him—back him up on it. He usually did "Peace in the Valley," or something like that.

Colonel Tom found out about it and told Elvis that he couldn't sing out in public anymore if he wasn't getting paid. So from then on, when Elvis would be at the singings, I would just introduce him. He would come onstage and take a bow and that was it.

:◉:◉:◉:

HAL KANTER (*director and cowriter of* Loving You): The producer of *Loving You*, Hal Wallis, called me one day and said, "I'd like you to come over and look at a test of a new young actor." I asked, "What's his name?" He said, "Elvis Presley." I said, "You mean the kid who's been singing on television that's caused such a furor?" He said, "Yes." I said, "You're gonna make a film with that man?" He said, "Yes. So would you come over and look at the test?"

So I went over to Paramount Studios and they showed me the test that Elvis had made, a scene from *The Rainmaker*. I was absolutely astonished at how adroit the man was in handling the scene, and the animal magnetism of the man just jumped off the screen. I went back to Hal's office and said, "I can see what you mean. There's really something about the man that nobody has seen before." Mr. Wallis handed me a first-draft screenplay. I forget what the title was, but he said, "Go to work on it."

Wallis hired me to write and direct, but while I was doing that, he had already (unknown to me) loaned Elvis out to Fox to find out if indeed his instinct was right, and if indeed the boy could carry a film, or even come off in film.

So Elvis's first picture [*Love Me Tender*] was done at Fox. I understand it was a role that they expanded just to accommodate him. Originally it was a very small, four- or five-line role, but they made it a little larger and threw in a song called "Love Me Tender." Of course, Elvis took off, and by the time I got around to meeting him, he was, in effect, established as a movie star.

The only thing Mr. Wallis insisted on for our film was that there be ample opportunity for songs, because, quite obviously, songs helped sell the picture.

We set out with our first draft of the screenplay [for *Loving You*] to develop a vehicle to which could be attached any number of songs—enough for an album.

JUNE JUANICO: Elvis was tickled to death when he knew he was going to Hollywood. This was his dream—"If my friends could only see me now." He was very excited. He had already had his screen test. In *Love Me Tender*, his character got killed in the end, and that upset him. We were together when he first got the script and read maybe twenty pages from the beginning and then skipped to the back. He said he wasn't going to do the movie, because the character dies at the end. I said, "Well, I think you ought to reconsider, because when I go to the movies I always remember the character that does not necessarily have the happy ending and the character that dies. That stays on my mind much longer than a happy ending." Elvis thought about that and said, "You know, I think you might have a point there. Maybe I ought to look at it that way."

Of course, Colonel Parker had to have his way and throw songs into the movie, and that was completely against Elvis's wishes. You see, the movie had no songs in it in the beginning. Then the Colonel called and said they did have one song, "Love Me Tender," and that Elvis was going to sing it in the background. You wouldn't actually see him singing it. The Colonel told him the song would just be played instrumentally as the theme throughout the movie. That's what Elvis's understanding was.

Later Elvis sang "Love Me Tender" to me on the phone. He said, "How do you like it? What do you think?" I said, "I love it." Wouldn't I have given anything to have had a little record button on my telephone? I could have kept that record forever as a memory.

WANDA JACKSON: I worked with Elvis off and on from the summer of '55 to January of '57. He was already recording for [RCA] Victor, having huge hits, and he left in August of 1956 to go to California to make a movie—Love Me Tender. Eventually, our careers took totally different directions. He was already a big star by then, but I was still getting to work with him some. We still liked each other. He phoned me almost every day from wherever he was. He just usually called me "Baby," and we dated some when we were together.

:◎:◎:◎:

RICHARD EGAN (star of Love Me Tender): In Love Me Tender [filmed August 23–October 8, 1956] Elvis had a dramatic part, and he showed extraordinary ability to catch on. I think they should have been aware of that. Instead, they seemed to put him in front of a backdrop and have him sing a song. Of course, he could do that easily, but he had much more depth than that.

I liked him. When Elvis came to the set he was very modest. He realized he hadn't had any experience as an actor and he wasn't afraid to ask for help. And he remained very direct, very straightforward.

BEN WEISMAN (songwriter): The music for Elvis's first movie, Love Me Tender, was controlled in Hollywood, but for the second movie, Loving You, Freddy Bienstock from the New York office of Hill and Range Music Publishers oversaw the collection of the songs. The way it all worked was that the Hill and Range writers were sent scripts from Hollywood, and we were told where the songs would fall in the movie. There might be six to ten different songwriting teams writing songs to fit all those spots in the script. It was a free-for-all, a battle. Everybody competed, tried to come up with the best songs for the most spots in the film.

Freddy was in charge of listening to the songs and approving or not approving them. If he approved one of your songs, you would go in and make a demonstration record (we called 'em "demos") so Elvis and the film people would be able to hear the song. Before you knew it, there might be thirty or forty or fifty demos in the competition for the ten song spots they needed in the movie.

After the first batch of songs were written, they would send them out to Hollywood before the movie was shot. All of us writers, the whole gang there, would stand by to find out if anything we had written had been selected for the movie. Freddy would come back from California and say, "Well, Ben, you got spot number three; so-and-so, you got spot number eight"; and so forth. That's the way it worked throughout the years. They never came back and said, "Well, Elvis likes this song but he wants you to rewrite the third and fourth lines," or anything like that. He either liked it, or he didn't. I don't ever recall having had to change a song at his request.

Elvis and the Colonel got one-third of the writers' royalties on songs Elvis recorded, even though he didn't write the songs. That was on all royalties from the sale of records, not the air-play royalties. That was the deal; I could either take it or say I don't want to do it.

Writers knew if Elvis recorded a song, and they were lucky enough to get a single, it would be a smash. And it wasn't just Elvis, it was a very common thing back then for hot artists to get what they called "cut-in" on the action. When you're struggling as a writer you're willing to do things like that to get a hit.

:◎:◎:◎:

BECKY MARTIN: When Elvis moved to the house on Audubon Drive [May 5, 1956], it was about two blocks from where my father lived. I would go over on Audubon in the afternoons and nights and talk to Gladys and Vernon. Sometimes Elvis would be at home and he would take us to dinner, and then we'd all go home and sing.

PAUL DOUGHER: I went out to his new house not long after he bought it, and he was so proud of it. Elvis was beginning to make some money then, and he wanted to show me everything he had: "Look here what I bought Mama," he'd say. "Look here what I got her." He took me all through the house. He was just like a kid with a new toy—so excited. As he made more money, he kept getting Mrs. Presley more things. It was just something that he wanted to do, and if it had been his last dime, he would have done it.

RONNIE SMITH: Elvis had a bumper pool table at that house. He kept laughing about it, saying, "I wanted a [regulation size] pool table but ain't got room for it." His house looked like a furniture store, 'cause everything he liked he'd buy, and if he liked it real well he'd buy two of 'em.

JIM ORWOOD (fan): After Elvis got popular, we used to go by Audubon Drive on Sunday afternoons and just look at his house. One afternoon we took my daughter out there. She had been born with a birthmark on her right cheek. As she got older it turned pinkish-red and wouldn't go away. We talked to the doctors about having it removed, and they said it would leave a worse scar than the birthmark. She was about eighteen months old then. [Movie stars] Natalie Wood and Nick Adams were visiting Elvis, and Elvis was the only one signing autographs. So when Elvis signed an autograph for me, I asked him if he'd kiss my daughter Cheryl on the cheek—on the birthmark. He did.

Later, when she was growing up, kids would make fun and ask her about her birthmark. So she'd tell them, that was where Elvis kissed her.

HORACE LOGAN: I visited Elvis at his house once, not Graceland, but the first big one he bought. Johnny Horton and I stopped by there one day on our way to Nashville. We went out to the garage so Elvis could show me his Lincoln Continental and his mama's Cadillac and his daddy's pickup truck.

Elvis said, "Mr. Logan, Sir, did you see that story in the *Confidential* that said I was in bed with three girls?" I said, "Yep. How many was it?" He said, "Six!" His daddy just beamed.

:◎:◎:◎:

BARBARA GLIDEWELL (friend): My girlfriend and I went to a concert in Russwood Park [Memphis]. We had seats in the third row. When Elvis came on, girls started running toward the stage screaming and hollering. I turned around and told my friend, "You can't even hear him sing. You don't even know if he has a voice. You're just screaming." Well, she got so mad she said, "Who do you think you are, the Queen of Sheba?" I'll never forget it. She slapped me with her camera, and I went flat out on the ground.

A policeman wanted to help me get out of the crowd, but I told him, "You're not going to take me away. I came here to see Elvis, and I'm going to see him." He said, "Well, if you don't come with me, you're just going to die right here, 'cause these girls will trample you to pieces." He carried me backstage and sat me down right on the back of the stage. Then, I thought, "How lucky! Elvis is right where I can see him!"

After the show, Elvis walked by, and his mother was just standing there with me waiting for him. We started talking. Mrs. Presley said, "You poor thing, you got hit over the head with a camera? You didn't have to go through all that. All you had to do was come by our house." She gave me her address, 1034 Audubon Drive. "Come out there and I'll introduce you to Elvis. He'll give you his autograph." Elvis walked past again and I thought, "God, he looks a lot different." He'd gone from pimples [the first time she saw him in 1953] to absolutely beautiful.

Mrs. Presley said, "Elvis, this poor girl got hit over the head with a camera just 'cause she wanted to see you and get your autograph." He kissed me on the cheek, and they jumped into a police car and rushed away.

BILL PERRY: At Russwood Park, Elvis was the primary entertainer. He got out there and he wiggled and did all that crazy stuff. That was the only time I saw his hair messed up, he worked so hard. His hair was so long 'til it was hanging down. He was soaking wet.

The girls threw apartment keys to him. I'm not lying to you. They were screaming, and they would actually pull out their own hair. They probably weren't even aware of what they were doing. One girl got so excited she scratched her arm and drew blood, and she didn't even know she had done it.

BARBARA GLIDEWELL: The day after the Russwood Park show, I went to Elvis's house, but he wasn't home. I waited a long time, but his mother said, "You just never know when Elvis is coming back. He gets in that car and he goes downtown. You just don't know when he's coming back."

The following day I went back, but they had the gates closed. I bet there was fifty people out there. I waited and waited, and about six o'clock Elvis pulled up in his Lincoln Continental. Naturally, I was the first one over to the car. When he drove into that driveway, I just thought I would die. He was the most gorgeous person I had ever seen, and he acted like he had known me forever. He said, "Barbara, I knew you would be here." And I thought, how did he know my name? He said, "I knew you'd be here 'cause my mama told me."

After he parked his car he came right back to the gate and talked to all of us. He told me, "Some of these kids have got to get away from here, because there's just too many." Then he went in the house to eat. We waited a long time, and when he came back he was eating a candy bar; he had taken one bite out of it. He handed it to me and asked me if I wanted it. Well, I still have that candy bar. It's in my mom's deep freeze right now—it's a Milky Way. He used to laugh at me about it.

The police finally came and said that some of us would have to leave if we weren't invited guests, because people in the neighborhood were complaining. Well, I felt like I was invited, so I wasn't going anywhere. A friend and I just drove around a little while and came back when everybody had gone.

Elvis was a friend from then on. We went into the house, and we sat in the back room listening to records and talking. After that night, we did that a lot.

:◎:◎:◎:

JUNE JUANICO: Parker was afraid of me in a way. I had met the Colonel in August of '56 when Elvis was on the Florida tour. I was on the tour with him, and I was in Elvis's room. The Colonel didn't knock or anything—he just burst in.

He said something had to be done about "these rumors going around about your engagement here." My mother, bless her heart, she didn't really know how to keep things a secret. Some reporters from Miami called me and my mother, and I wouldn't give 'em any kind of straight answers about how serious our relationship was. But when they called my mother they made it sound like, "Shame on you for allowing your young daughter to go out of state with Elvis Presley." At that point in time he was getting bad press about his swiveling hips and that sort of thing. Some preachers and newspapers and magazines were calling him "the devil." Naturally, Elvis denied the engagement publicly. A New Orleans radio station came out saying he hadn't popped the question to me yet.

But he did pop the question in late July that year. He proposed on the front lawn by the house that he had leased for the summer in Ocean Springs, Mississippi. He told me he couldn't get married right away. But he said, "I'd like for you to wait for me, and maybe in three years. . . . I promised the Colonel I wouldn't do anything stupid, but I want you to wait for me." I said, "Okay."

It was Colonel Parker's fear that the fans wouldn't love Elvis anymore if he got married. Elvis felt that the Colonel had made a big star out of him. He really believed that with all his heart. So he was following the Colonel's advice, and we didn't get married.

While he was in Hollywood working on *Love Me Tender* Elvis sent me a telegram, and all at once I was the celebrity of Biloxi. Western Union's local Biloxi guys called me "Little Bitty" for months after that, because that's how Elvis started his telegram. It said, "Hi, Little Bitty. Miss you, baby. Haven't had you out of my mind for a second. I'll always be yours and yours alone to love. Dreamed about you last night." Signed, E.P. I read it a million times. It was better than a phone call because I had something I could hold in my hands and kind of squeeze tight. I was just tickled about my telegram.

:◎:◎:◎:

DOTTY AYERS *(friend)*: Elvis was getting a lot of flack then about how he wiggled and how he was a bad influence on teenagers. I would write to Elvis's mother and tell her it was not so, that his fans didn't look at him that way. Gladys would write back and say that she was glad to hear it, 'cause people was really giving him a bad time. It really upset Elvis.

MAE AXTON: The third time Elvis came to Florida—he had already signed the management agreement with the Colonel—he was booked at a theater, and some judge came down and told him he was not to swivel his hips and all that stuff. They held up the show for a long time. It was a problem. I was doing PR for the show, but I didn't go down there. The Colonel finally talked them into letting the show go on.

ANNIE CLOYD PRESLEY: We all backed Elvis when the preachers were attacking him. We were proud of him. I didn't see no harm in what he was doing.

JAMES BLACKWOOD: In the very beginning there were some in the church world that did not accept Elvis because of some of his body movements. But many of his fans were devout church people, and they loved Elvis as well as the rock 'n' roll fans. Elvis had such a wide appeal.

I remember one night he was appearing in Texas: we had a gospel music school every year south of Fort Worth at the Assembly of God college. We used their facilities to teach our gospel music school, and Elvis was at the auditorium in Fort Worth. We wanted to go, and we had J. D. [Sumner] get tickets for us. Elvis's greatest ovation of the evening was for "How Great Thou Art."

After the show J. D. took me over to the hotel across the street and up to

Elvis's suite. There were several people in this one room just sitting around, and Elvis was in an adjoining room taking a shower. When he came out, he came right over to me and sat down. We started talking and visiting.

I complimented him that night on a note—a high A-flat, which is a rather high note. He had really belted an A-flat out that night on "How Great Thou Art." "Well, I've been working on that," he said. But we had a good visit, and finally I said, "Elvis, I know you've got people to see and things to do, I just wanted a chance to visit with you." He said, "Oh, no, I'm in no hurry."

:◎:◎:◎:

JIMMY VELVET: The Colonel wasn't around [Elvis] a lot. He was always one or two steps ahead, doing what he did; but, from what I could see, the Colonel was really great for Elvis. The Colonel could get him in the right doors. The Colonel could make anything happen—just had a way about him. He had a magic.

I've heard lots of stories about the Colonel booking Elvis back in '56. You know, Elvis was between five and ten thousand dollars a night even back then, and everyone was trying to book him; but the Colonel would turn down bookings right and left, saying, "He's booked solid. There's not a date open for another year-and-a-half." But, what the Colonel would do is, he would turn around and get those same people to pay double to get Elvis. "I can move his bookings around, and give you the date; but you will have to pay Elvis ten thousand dollars, plus the ten it will take to get him out of the other booking." Stuff like that. Elvis wound up booked as often as he wanted to be and at a high price.

BUZZY FORBES: Elvis had gone to Las Vegas [New Frontier Hotel's Venus Room, April 23–May 6, 1956] for the first time in his career. He didn't get a very good response; so when he came back home, he came over to see me. We talked about it. He said it hurt him bad. He had a week's engagement that first time [actually a month's engagement that was canceled after two weeks]. Of course, a totally different type of music was popular out there, and there's not very many teenagers in Vegas.

The first night there was a really bad response, but the second night it was kinda like warming up the coffee pot. It got to going a little bit better, but not great.

I think Elvis learned a lot about how to respond to the negative and turn it around. I'm so proud of him for how far he got just using his own judgment and senses. He responded to things and learned for himself what worked.

June Juanico: Elvis's popularity wasn't a threat to our relationship. Colonel Parker was the threat, and I was a threat because Elvis was so crazy mad for me.

I really didn't care for Parker that much. You could smell the Colonel around the block, you know—with his cigar. I thought the Colonel was a manipulative shyster of a man.

Becky Martin: I didn't know whether [Elvis] would recognize me or even speak to me when I first went to Memphis to see him after he got popular, but he did. He came to see me in that first pink Cadillac he bought for his mother. He just never was any different. I think it was just because he was Elvis. It was just the way he was.

Fred Fredrick: Elvis's first Cadillac burned, I think. The next Cadillac he bought was the one he gave Gladys, the blue Cadillac that he eventually had Dick Moore paint. Well, Dick Moore got the paint, and then Jimmy Sanders painted it pink. It's still out at Graceland.

Dick "Bucky" Moore *(automobile salesman)*: I was working at the Studebaker warehouse at the parts counter, and Elvis came in. We had a '54 Studebaker Commander up on the showroom floor that was pink with a black top. Elvis had seen that car from the street, and he wheeled into the store in this brand-new, blue, four-door Cadillac that he had just bought. He said he wanted to paint that blue Cadillac pink, and he wanted to buy paint in the exact pink color that was on that Studebaker.

June Juanico: Elvis tried many times to give me gifts, but I would never accept any. This is part of being raised in the old school that you do not accept gifts from gentlemen, because when a gentleman gives you gifts they want something in return. Isn't that dumb? Think of all the Cadillacs I passed up!

:◎:◎:◎:

Bernard Lansky: Lansky's was big in Memphis in cut and trim, making shirts, and pants and jackets to match. People from as far away as St. Louis and Nashville used to come in for us to make their clothes. Gamblers and pimps used to drive down in big Cadillacs. We'd dress 'em up, put the big hats and zoot suits on them. It really was sharp at that time.

Elvis used to come in. He was a dynamite young man; not only was he a good customer, but he was a PR man for us all over the country. People would ask him where he got his clothes and he'd say that he got them down at Lansky's on Beale Street in Memphis. We started doing a fantastic business.

Elvis came in one day and had to have some outfits to go on the Ed Sullivan Show. I said, "Well, we'll get something for you."

STEVE ALLEN *(TV personality)*: *The Milton Berle Show* had presented a number of performers that night [June 5, 1956], and one of them was this lanky, ungainly, slightly amateurish kid. He wasn't a great singer, but he had something about him—star quality. I just dictated a note at that moment, "Let's book this kid."

When Elvis appeared on our show, Ed Sullivan was watching. He called Elvis's manager, and Colonel Parker told me, "Sullivan says he'll offer five confirmed appearances at ten thousand dollars each." In those days you got seventy-five hundred no matter whose show you were on. That was it. Colonel Parker said, "If you can meet this offer, you can have Elvis as often as you want him. You can have him every week if you want him." So we said, "No thank you. We do a comedy show, and we send you to Ed Sullivan with our blessings."

DINAH DODD *(fan)*: When I was about fifteen years old, [we] figured out that whenever Elvis went to New York to be on *The Ed Sullivan Show*, he would come through our town [Greenville, Tennessee] on the train. So four of us went down to the station on what [we] figured would be the right day. When the train pulled in, sure enough, Elvis was on it. We hollered and asked him if he would come out of the train to see us, and he did. He talked to us and gave all four of us a little kiss on the cheek. We were just thrilled. But the next time the train came through with him on it, there was a big crowd at the station, and we didn't get to see him. I guess we had blabbed it all over Greenville.

MARLO LEWIS *(director,* The Ed Sullivan Show*)*: Ed said to us just before Elvis was to do the show, "We're in trouble. Elvis is doing something in those concerts that can no way be shown on television. He's hangin' some kind of device in the crotch of his pants so that when he moves his knee back and forth, it looks like his personal organ." Ed used a little better language than that. "It's waving back and forth just above the knee. We can't have that on Sunday night. That's a church night."

So when we shot the show, I took camera two and I said, "Dolly into a chest shot and stay there." And for that entire six minutes we only saw Elvis from his chest to his head. We never revealed the rest of him, nor did anyone ever see this "implement" between his legs. And I'll tell you a secret: it wasn't there.

BETTY COCKERELL *(fan)*: I was about fifteen when Elvis started out. I remember hearing him back before he was ever on Ed Sullivan. And when I did see him on that TV show that night, I just thought he was the cutest thing I ever saw. Some folks didn't want to see him wiggle, but I didn't see anything wrong with that.

ANITA WOOD *(girlfriend)*: When Elvis came on *The Ed Sullivan Show* the first time I ever saw him, Mother called me to the living room and said, "Anita, this is that young boy from Memphis. He's so good. Come look." I remember going and watching him, and I said, "Oh, Mother, he *is* cute." I thought he was very attractive, but that was it [at the time].

:◎:◎:◎:

JOE SAVERY: The biggest thing that impressed me about Elvis Presley when he came back home to Tupelo [for the Mississippi–Alabama Fair and Dairy Show, September 26, 1956] was when he came to our house for dinner. My mother had fixed this big dinner for him, and Vernon and Gladys were coming, too. Elvis pulls up in a big Lincoln. He wasn't driving; some man was driving. Elvis had a blonde on one side of him and a brunette on the other. That made the biggest impression on me. This guy has two dates! (And they seemed to get along.) I said, "I cannot believe this."

JOHN W. MCAFEE, SR. *(newsreel cameraman)*: When Elvis was appearing in Tupelo, I had an assignment for Theatrical Newsreel and went down to cover the concert. We were the only news covering it. I asked where Elvis was, and somebody said: "You can't see him, but Colonel Parker is back in the tent there off of the field." So I walked back there, and there was the Colonel, open-collar shirt, sitting on one of those regular tables with a cigar stub in his mouth. I told him who I was, and he said, "Well, you want to photograph my boy? Have you ever been to one of these things before?" I told him, "No, it's the first time."

The Colonel said, "Well, let me give you a little information. When we appear on the stage we have to have a way to get out, because the mob will rush the stage—the young girls." Naturally I listened.

We go down where the stage is, and they have it roped off. The National Guard was there. I thought, "Hey, the Colonel must have been telling the truth."

The Colonel told me they had a trapdoor on the stage. In case of any riot or rushing of the stage, they would just drop through the trapdoor and go get in the car and leave. I decided to stand beside the National Guard, between the stage and the crowd.

Elvis comes out and starts singing. I'm making close-up pictures of the crowd. The girls were just going crazy, hollering and carrying on. All of a sudden I noticed two of the girls: their eyes just rolled back into their heads, and suddenly they dropped to the ground. I thought they were putting on, but they were out; they were gone! Two or three more did the same thing. Then the crowd started pushing. The National Guard couldn't hold them. They pushed just like the Colonel said. When I turned around to get a picture of Elvis, he was gone. He had gone through the trapdoor and got out. I bent down and walked under the stage back to the tent. Elvis was already in the car, pulling out. So, that was it. The crowd surged up onto the stage and Elvis was gone. This was no put on; it amazed me. This was for real.

CHRISTINE ROBERTS PRESLEY: Elvis came down to Tupelo once with Natalie Wood. She just hollered and waved at me, but they couldn't neither of 'em get out of the car. I'll tell you the truth, there was too many people. Finally Elvis got out of the car, ran real fast across the yard to the house. He kept watching up and down the street 'til he could beat it back to the car.

PAUL BURLISON: Elvis called Johnny and Dorsey [Burnette] and me, when we was recording as the Rock 'N Roll Trio, and told us to come out to his house and see if we could find some songs that we wanted to record. He was really hot then and everybody was sending him songs. We didn't stay long because Elvis had Nick Adams and Natalie Wood out there. I took one look at her and I thought, "Boy, she's good-looking." Yeah, she was. I thought to myself, "That's when you know you've arrived."

:◉:◉:◉:

1955-1956

JACK CLEMENT: Elvis was always loyal to Sam, always called him "Mr. Phillips." He had kind of a homing instinct, and Sun was kinda centrally located if you were on your way downtown or somewhere. So Elvis [even after he signed with RCA] would sometimes just drop by 706 Union [the studio] to say hello and maybe go to Taylor's Restaurant next door.

In December of 1956, I had been working at Sun Records for about six months and had already recorded with Jerry Lee Lewis (I was kinda using him as my studio piano player); an interesting thing happened one day.

It was just before Jerry Lee got on the road with that first record of his. We had him in the studio playing piano with Carl Perkins. Carl had invited Johnny Cash by, and Elvis was there just hanging out. So all four of them guys—these stars—were there at one time, and they started singing. I was in the control room, and I looked over at that tape machine. It was just sittin' there waiting to be turned on. So I cued up a seven-inch reel that gave me thirty minute's worth of recording time. I thought to myself, this is a historic moment. I went out in the studio and set up a few microphones and started recording all this stuff these guys were doing. When the tape would end, I would stick another one on. That was all there was to it. It was basically sort of a party. Today these tapes are treasures.

:◎:◎:◎:

HORACE LOGAN: It was not all that big a thing when Elvis left the Hayride. Bear in mind that we had started the show in 1948, and in '49 Hank Williams popped big, then left. That's when the thoughts disturbed me that the Hayride might fail. But suddenly Webb Pierce popped big for us. We found out real quick that when one hot star would leave, somebody else would take their place. That's how it was when Elvis left us—no big deal.

I was going to agree to just let him go, but the manager of the station, Henry Clay, insisted that since we were paying Elvis two hundred dollars per Saturday night he was going to have to pay us four hundred not to appear. Since Elvis's [Hayride] contract was with me, Elvis made out a check to me for ten thousand dollars to cover the twenty-five weeks remaining on his contract. By that point, Elvis could demand almost any damn thing he wanted. That was a drop in the bucket. He also had to come back to Shreveport and do one final show for us. We had it at the Hursh Coliseum. The money went to the YMCA to build them a swimming pool at Forbing, Louisiana.

FRANK PAGE: We held a farewell concert for Elvis at the Hayride in December of 1956—on the sixteenth. Horace Logan did the introduction at Hursh Coliseum [Shreveport, Louisiana], and he did all the emceeing of the Elvis portion. I was scared to death. There were nine thousand screaming teenagers with their Brownie reflexes flashing off out there.

HORACE LOGAN: For a long time Elvis thought I got the ten thousand he paid to get out of his contract. Finally, I had a chance to see him again, and I told him, "Hell, I didn't get that money; the station got every bit of it. It wasn't me. I was gonna let you go free 'cause I knew you had outgrown the Hayride."

BILLY WALKER: Actually, in one respect, Elvis helped kill the Louisiana Hayride. He got so hot so fast with so many young kids that the older people couldn't get tickets, and the true country music crowd down there didn't really like Elvis Presley. It was those young, fifteen-to-twenty-year-olds that were wild about him, and they'd come early when Elvis was on and buy up all the tickets. The Hayride audience began to be like thirty percent kids, forty percent, then seventy percent. Then all of the sudden when Elvis exploded and left the Hayride, the kids left, and it really did hurt. It really hurt.

"On a Rocket Ride"
1957

Once women see on national television the face that goes with the voice, Elvis Presley's life takes a dramatic turn. When he comes to life on the big screen, there is no turning back; Elvis belongs to his fans. Long-time friends Ronnie Smith and Paul Dougher note how Elvis reacts to his newfound success, as movie producer Hal Kanter and songwriter Ben Weisman marvel at the genuine humility of America's hottest new movie star.

While fan Janice Pennington recounts Elvis's fun-loving flair for entertaining, girlfriend Anita Wood reveals what it is like to date the teen idol. Two members of Elvis's gang, Arlene Cogan and Frances Forbes, join Dotty Ayers and Barbara Glidewell, two youngsters befriended by Gladys Presley, in sharing insights into the unique relationship of Elvis and his mother.

As a result of his success, Elvis buys Graceland. It was a symbol of dreams come true. For a short while, the spacious house is a haven for the Presley family, but with more room comes more people. Strangers swarm outside the gates. Inside there is music and laughter, fun and games; but, there is also a proud mother whose heart is torn by uncertainty and fear.

> "Elvis Presley was the beginning of Youth Culture, basically—definitely in this country—and without that there wouldn't have been a Beatles, there wouldn't have been WHAM! for sure. Up until then, music was created by adults, and then Elvis really created the first youth music."
>
> GEORGE MICHAEL, *(recording artist)*

JOAN PRICE *(fan)*: The third time Elvis passed through Greenville, Tennessee, on the train [to perform on *The Ed Sullivan Show*, in New York City, January 1957], the crowd at the station was just huge, and we couldn't even get anywhere near him. We were very upset, so my mother bought tickets for the four of us girls to ride down to the next town. We got right on the train with him. After the conductor punched our tickets, we went and sat in the dining car right across from him, and we ordered Coca-Colas. Back then Cokes normally cost a nickel, but on that train those Cokes were a dollar-and-a-half a piece! We were just horrified at how expensive they were.

Elvis remembered us and was very charming and polite. So there we were sitting across from him and we're loaded down with movie magazines and records and all kinds of stuff for him to autograph.

DINAH DODD: He asked us where we went to school, how old we were—things like that. I'm sure we were so silly, giggling and all that kind of stuff. The other guys with Elvis were kind of teasing him about us. You could see them cutting their eyes at him, then back to us, grinning.

JOAN PRICE: We were on the train with him about thirty minutes. Don't ask me what we talked about. We were just making sure we got lots and lots of things signed.

DINAH DODD: Elvis was very nice and cordial and pleasant. He was just a little country boy, not at that point full of himself. We were having such a great time, but we had to get off at the next stop, Morristown. When we did, we carried off the napkins from his table, and the placemats, the pen he signed with—just about everything we could grab.

JOAN PRICE: One of the other girls even took some crumbs from his table. I wonder if she still has them. I've still got that napkin in my scrapbook.

DINAH DODD: And I still have his autograph.

JOAN PRICE: There was a big article in the Greenville paper about us meeting him and about our little trip.

:◎:◎:◎:

PAUL DOUGHER: Naturally success changed Elvis, but not with me as far as our friendship went. It changed him as far as being unable to do the things he wanted to do at the times he wanted to do them. He couldn't get out and go like he wanted to.

BARBARA GLIDEWELL: Elvis's house on Audubon Drive was just a small ranch kind of house. It was kinda gaudy inside, with awful wallpaper. There was a big den in the back where Elvis used to hang out, and the kitchen was up toward the front. The house had three bedrooms. I hardly ever saw Mr. and Mrs. Presley—seems like they stayed in their bedroom most of the time.

There was a carport to the side of the house and a swimming pool in back. Nothing elaborate.

RONNIE SMITH: One day Elvis was showing me his seven new gold records. He said, "I don't know what I'm worth [financially]. All I know is there's people supposed to be taking care of that. What I know is I ought to be able to write a check for anything I want, and the money better be there."

HAROLD LOYD: When it come to money, even Elvis's money, Vernon was really tight. Back in the early days, when Elvis would come off his tours and be home for a few days, him and the guys would sometimes go out to record stores at night to check the record charts and things like that.

Well, I was sitting in the dinin' room one night with Grandma, Gladys, and Elvis. Vernon had been doin' somethin' in the other room, but pretty soon he came to the door of the dinin' room and said, "Hey, Elvis..."

and Elvis looked around and said, "Yeah, Daddy?" Vernon had this brown paper bag that was over half full of [guitar] picks, and Vernon opened the sack up and said, "Just look here, you done went and got a bunch more picks, Son. What's the matter with you? You're spendin' your money like it grows on trees. You got a fruit bowl full of 'em just sittin' on the coffee table, and that little candy dish is full, too. Now you done went out last night and got some more."

Elvis looked at him and said, "Daddy, I want to tell you somethin'. I buy them guitar picks 'cause I'm always breakin' them, throwin' them out in the audience for the people, losing them and everything. And that's just a habit. It don't cost that much." Vernon came back with, "It's just a-wastin' money, Son, just a-wastin' money."

You could see that Elvis was beginnin' to get a little annoyed. He said, "Come here a minute, Daddy, I want to ask you a few questions." Vernon walked into the room. Elvis looked at him and said, "First of all, Daddy, are you hungry? Do you have plenty to eat in the refrigerator over there?" Vernon said, "Well, yeah, why?" Elvis said, "Wait a minute, I'm not through. You've got nice clothes, right? Plenty of clothes?" Vernon nodded. "A brand-new car sittin' out there in the driveway you can drive anytime you want, and you got money in the bank?" Vernon said, "Yeah." Elvis looked him straight in the eye and said, "Well, Daddy, you took care of me. You worked and fed me and took care of me, and, of course, took care of mama when I was growin' up; and I appreciate it. Now I'm tryin' to take care of you. But if I want to buy a damn guitar pick, I will. I'll buy them by the goddamn truckload if I want to. Matter of fact, I might even buy the goddamn factory that makes 'em, and that ain't none of your goddamn business. It's my damn money, so I don't want to hear another damn word out of you about no damn guitar picks!" Vernon just kind of mumbled somethin' and walked out of the room.

Have you ever heard that old expression about someone being so tight they could squeeze a nickel 'til the buffalo falls off? Vernon was pretty much like that.

:◎:◎:◎:

HAL KANTER: Elvis was a great movie buff long before he appeared in films. I'm sure he never thought that he'd ever be in the movies. We got together at his home in Memphis—and it wasn't the Graceland mansion that we talk about today, it's what he considered to be a mansion at that time: a comfortable, small, middle-class home. We had eaten dinner and gone into what he called his playroom, a den in which all of his gold records were mounted on the wall. He had a pool table there, and a few of the accoutrements of a successful truck driver were evident in that room.

I had been told by Mr. Wallis not to bring a copy of the script [*Loving You*] along. Elvis was not to read the script, because we still had work to do on it. Elvis knew just the general, vague outline of what the picture was about, but he said to me at one point, "Do I have to smile much in the movie?" And I said, "What do you mean, smile?" He said, "Well, I mean, are you gonna make me smile in the movie? You're gonna direct it, aren't you?" I said, "Yeah." He said, "Well, am I gonna smile?" I said, "Well, I don't recall off hand whether you smile. Why do you ask a question like that?" He said, "Well, I've been studying the actors the girls like—Jimmy Dean, Humphrey Bogart, Marlon Brando—and they don't never smile. When they do smile, it becomes an event. If I don't smile, I'm gonna get 'em."

Pretty interesting observation, right? There was more to him than just a country boy, and more to him than just a musician. He was a real student of motion pictures.

I thought he was a charming, amusing, young man with a great deal of natural ability. I thought, given the opportunity and given enough time, he could develop into an excellent screen actor. I don't know about an actor—but a screen actor. There's a difference, you know.

FARON YOUNG: For a long time Elvis was afraid what everybody was saying about him was true—that he was going to be a flash-in-the-pan. And some people told him, "You're gonna do good, but you won't be around long." He talked to me about it once. He said, "You know, they're telling me I won't last long, so I'm gonna try to make all the money I can and save it 'cause at least I can get me a house, and a car, and stuff like that."

I said, "Presley, don't listen to these sons-of-bitches. They don't know what you're gonna do. They don't even know if you're gonna be a big star or not. You show me somebody who can tell you what a hit record is, and who is gonna be a star, and I'll show you a fuckin' billionaire. Nobody can tell you that. Now don't you listen to that shit. Just do your thing. You see that audience out there going crazy, tearing your ass up? Well, they don't even know who you are yet. Just hang in there."

GORDON STOKER *(backup singer, member of the Jordanaires)*: Elvis did his first recording session for RCA in January, 1956. I started working with him then at that session. We did "I Got a Woman," "Money Honey," and "Heartbreak Hotel."

At that time, there was not a good singer on every corner as there is now. There's worlds of great singers now, and I think Elvis inspired guys to pick up a guitar and start singing. He inspired me to stay in the business. He made me want to sing more, and sing better, and try to do a good job at everything I did.

FARON YOUNG: I knew Elvis liked the Ink Spots, so one day I said to him, "I'm gonna write you a song." He said, "Great!" So I wrote a song that went: "If you tell a lie, you know that I'll forgive you. . . ." I tried to sing it on the demo tape like that Ink Spot he loved so much, and I played it for him. The song was called "Is It So Strange." Elvis said, "Hey, that's good. Who wrote that?" I said, "I did, you little fucker. I wrote it for you." He said, "Give me a copy of that." I did, and damned if he didn't record it. He called me one day and said, "Little Chief, I cut your song. I'm sorry it ain't gonna be a single, but I put it in my album." I said, "Man, I'm honored you even cut the damn thing. I appreciate it."

Hell, that song's been in a bunch of albums. I probably made fifty or sixty thousand dollars off that damn song. I've had people come up to me and say, "I just found out Elvis Presley recorded one of your songs . . . and I didn't even know you wrote." I say, "Yeah, I'm a helluva writer."

HAL KANTER: The *Loving You* script was designed for Elvis. We began production January 21, 1957. It was Delores Hart's first film, and we had signed Lizabeth Scott and Wendell Corey.

On set Elvis was not cocky at all. He didn't say, "I'm a star and I know what I'm doing." Never. He always asked, "What is the challenge?" Once he was told what to do, he did it, and did it very well. If we said, "Cut, let's try that again, and don't be so broad," or "do less," or whatever the direction was, he accommodated that.

He also had the great advantage of working with a seasoned film star in Wendell Corey, and he liked Wendell very much. There was a mutual attraction there. Wendell did not like just every young player with whom he worked, but he really was devoted to Elvis.

I thought Elvis was a first-class citizen, and I really enjoyed working with him. He was very playful in between setups. When we said, "Okay, Elvis, let's get to work," he buckled down and went to work. He came on the set knowing his lines. He was very open to suggestion, not only from me as his director but from his fellow players, his makeup man, from prop men. If anybody had a suggestion, he would entertain it. Then he would always check with me. He always referred to me as "Mr. Kanter." Right up through the last time I saw him, it was still "Mr. Kanter." He was a delight to work with, an absolute delight, very knowledgeable, very intuitive, and prompt. He showed up. That's a big step in anybody's movie career—just showing up on time.

DON ROBERTSON: If you didn't write songs for Hill and Range, it was hard to get material to Elvis. Once the Aberbachs got their [music publishing] companies going with Elvis and the Colonel, I got the impression that they tried to prevent him from even seeing material unless they had already made a deal for it. I don't know how much he was even aware of that.

BEN WEISMAN: Elvis was usually in control of his own recording sessions, and he usually didn't have much trouble getting a good vocal performance. But once in a great while he would have trouble hooking it—like on the "Loving You" session. I remember he sang that song "Loving You" over and over. Freddy Bienstock was in the control room watching, and Elvis just couldn't seem to get it good enough to satisfy himself. He must have had thirty-two takes before he finally accepted one of them. The rest is history.

:◎:◎:◎:

BARBARA GLIDEWELL: Elvis had to leave Audubon Drive because of the fans. The other people who lived on the street got up a petition to get him to move because fans and other people's cars were there day and night—going up and down the street—honking. Guys would be yelling, "Elvis, do you have any extra girlfriends?" You know, it was really just a hard place for him to live. It kinda made him mad 'cause he said, "I ought to be able to live wherever I want to." But there was always somebody standing outside the gate waiting.

JUNE JUANICO: In March of 1957, I think on the eighteenth—the day before Elvis signed the papers to buy Graceland—I got a telegram from him. He was coming from Hollywood, changing trains in New Orleans, and he asked me to meet him there at Union Station. I had been going out with the guy I later married, and Elvis had been seeing Las Vegas show girls. Regardless, I drove to New Orleans to meet him.

He wanted me to go back to Memphis with him. I made all sorts of excuses, but he had an answer for all of them. Finally, I said, "I can't go with you. I'm engaged to be married." He was stunned and said, "You're kidding!" I told him, "No, I'm not kidding." Meanwhile, the train whistle gave five warning toots, three shorts and two longs, and the train made that jolting motion that proved it was leaving, and I ran through the door to get off the train. I just left him sitting there with his mouth hanging open. I found myself crying and looked back at the train as it pulled away. Elvis was hanging out of the doorway waving. That was it. That was goodbye.

Elvis had become a big star. He was on a rocket ride.

:◎:◎:◎:

BARBARA GLIDEWELL: Elvis carried me on his motorcycle to see Graceland when he bought it. I think he had paid a hundred thousand dollars for the house and thirteen acres. He bought it from Mrs. Ruth Brown Moore. It was kind of run down.

JERRY BAXTER: When Elvis bought Graceland it was still considered to be out in the country. When you went to Whitehaven, which is where Graceland is, it was a trip. There was nothing on the highway but maybe the Bellevue Drive-In. No lights. No nothing. I'd say Graceland was about three miles outside the city limits on Highway 51 [now Elvis Presley Boulevard].

FARON YOUNG: Graceland was just an old house teenagers had used to have parties in. Kids would go out and have weenie roasts there. The people just moved out and left it, and the teenagers had knocked out all the windows and put holes in the walls. For some reason, Elvis bought it, and he completely gutted it and rebuilt the damn thing.

I went down there after he first moved in [April 10, 1957], and he put that little den downstairs and had him a projector and an ice cream bar in the basement, and all that shit. After that he went on and built a lot more to it.

The swimming pool was in full view of the street back then, and I remember telling him, "Elvis, that pool ain't gonna work. See them kids down there looking over the fence. They can see y'all up here." He said, "Yeah, I know it." Later he put up a row of hedges all alongside the pool for privacy. But that day he had a whole bunch of diving stuff by the pool. I said, "What are you doing with all that scuba gear laying over there?" (Must have been three or four thousand dollars worth of it.) He said, "I bought that damn stuff 'cause I was gonna learn how to scuba, but I got in the damn water and liked to have drowned." He said, "Little Chief, why don't you just take that stuff home with you?" I said, "What do you want me to do, drown, too?" I said, "Hell, if you're trying to give me something, I'll just take that Harley-Davidson [motorcycle] sitting over there." He said, "Here's the keys." I said, "See, you son of a bitch, you're still trying to get me killed!" I didn't even know how to crank that damn thing. He said, "If you can drive it out of here, it's yours."

That's the way it was with Elvis. You never told that fucker you liked something or he'd hand it to you.

ARLENE COGAN *(friend)*: Gladys loved Graceland. There was a lot for her to get used to. Everything was happening so fast for Elvis, and her and Vernon, too. I've heard them all say that. You know, "Things are happening so fast; everything has happened so fast." And his mother really didn't get a chance to adjust to the sudden change in their lives, you know.

Gladys and Vernon would go for a walk around the back part of Graceland. They would go for long walks early in the morning, and they had Alberta [Holman] to cook, but Gladys would cook for Elvis most of the time.

One night when I was at Graceland, Elvis asked me if I would make him a peanut butter and banana sandwich and bring him a glass of milk. I said, "Okay," and went upstairs to the kitchen. I spread the peanut butter over the bread, sliced the bananas, placed the slices neatly on the bread, and cut the sandwich in half. Then I took it downstairs where Elvis was talking with some people. Elvis looked up and said, "Thanks, Honey." He picked up half the sandwich, and here's all these slices of banana rolling out all over his shirt and into his lap. He didn't get mad. He just sat there and laughed at the mess. Elvis took me to the kitchen and showed me the proper way to make a peanut butter and banana sandwich—mash it all up together and spread it on the bread real thick.

:◎:◎:◎:

JOHN W. MCAFEE, SR.: Elvis was a big movie fan. He liked motion pictures. So to keep from causing any trouble with crowds at the theater, Elvis would call the owner, and they would be glad to let Elvis use the theater after hours. (This was, of course, before movies were on tape, before you could rent them to watch in your home.) Elvis usually requested movies that had not yet run in the local theaters.

DOTTY AYERS: Elvis always liked to practice fighting; this was just before he got into karate. One night we were waiting to go to the Memphian theater, and Red West or somebody had brought a pair of boxing gloves in. They were all boxing and hitting around. Elvis had a pair of gloves on and Vernon walked in. Vernon told Red, "Let me try those." So Vernon took the boxing gloves, and he and Elvis faced off with each other. They kept going around and around in a circle, but neither one of them would try and hit the other. Finally Elvis took the gloves off and said, "Daddy, I can't hit you." And Vernon said, "I can't hit you, either." They just sorta hugged each other, took the boxing gloves off, and went on doing something else.

ARLENE COGAN: The first Christmas at Graceland they had a Christmas tree that revolved when music played. Elvis recorded four gospel songs earlier in the year, and they played 'em throughout the house during the holidays. It was just beautiful.

Gladys talked about "Peace in the Valley." It was her favorite. She talked about what a beautiful job Elvis did on it.

MACK GURLEY: We had a ball at Graceland having the firecracker battles. It usually happened on New Year's Eve. Elvis would say, "Wear your leather jackets because we're going to have a war." We'd choose up sides—late at night—and we'd wear our leather jackets. We'd shoot Roman candles at the jackets, never any other part of us, of course. Sometimes there'd be misfires—little black burned spots—but it was a ball.

One night Elvis tossed the keys to the limo to me to go buy all the Roman candles I could find. He signed a blank check, and when I got over to West Memphis, [Arkansas], they didn't want to take the check. "Aw, you don't know him!" I said, "That's his car. Check it out if you want to." Finally, we loaded the entire back of that limousine full of Roman candles. It was just another one of those fun things—something original.

BARBARA GLIDEWELL: Elvis lived at night; he slept all day. So if you had to go to school during the day and tried to keep up with him at night, you prayed he would go away and make a movie or something so you could get some rest. It was pitiful. But you kept trying to make every minute count.

Elvis called my school one time to say I wasn't going to be in class that day. It was a very strict Catholic school. A bunch of us had stayed up all night at Graceland. He called and told them he was my daddy; and, lord, that got me in real trouble 'cause my daddy had left us when I was five, and they knew I didn't have a daddy. I didn't know he said he was my father 'til the next day. Elvis told them that I was very sick; I had a rare disease. It was very comical. But I really got into trouble. The principal said I was going to the devil for liking Elvis. They tried to send me to confession.

JACK CLEMENT: One time me and some guys were shooting craps on the floor back in the control room at Sun Records, and I looked up and there was this cop walking in; but it wasn't a cop at all, it was just Elvis in his motorcycle suit!

Elvis was a very fun guy to be around. Everything with him was just kind of a party, more or less.

WILL "BARDAHL" MCDANIEL *(friend)*: He'd call and invite Jerry Lee [Lewis] up to the house. Elvis would grab the guitar and Jerry Lee would hit the piano, and we'd all sit back there and sing and clown and have a ball. Contrary to a lot of stories, Jerry Lee and Elvis were great friends. They were like night and day—their personalities and all. Jerry was really enjoying his fame and the fans and the crowds, but Elvis, he was a shy person.

ALAN FORTAS *(friend)*: One night we were at Elvis's house when Jerry Lee Lewis happened to come up there. Both of them were sitting at the piano, and they were each playing their own version of "Heartbreak Hotel," "All Shook Up," and different songs they had recorded. This went on 'til the wee hours of the morning—two, three, four in the morning. Elvis loved it.

JIMMY VELVET: After meeting Elvis again in '56, I wound up joining the Air Force. Sometime after basic training, I was stationed at Mitchell Air Force Base on Long Island when Elvis was playing in Philadelphia at the Arena. I took the train over, and I wore a jacket he had given me—a plaid jacket. I was trying real hard to get backstage, and they wouldn't let me, even though I had a backstage pass Elvis had signed. It said: "This will admit bearer backstage at any time, Elvis Presley Show," signed by Elvis. I think the message was rubber-stamped or something. It wasn't very official-looking. They wouldn't let me in, but I kept trying. Finally, I got a guy to take back to Elvis some pictures of him and me together and the pass he had given me. Elvis sent for me, and I went back.

BEN WEISMAN: Elvis gave a concert in Philadelphia and I went to see it. I just watched the crowd; the place was mobbed: girls with their feet dangling down from the balconies—everybody going crazy. I sat there and said, "Look at this! This is a phenomenon!" As a matter of fact, while I was sitting there, a tomato went hurling through the air—Elvis was onstage—and it hit and broke the strap on his guitar. He was furious! He stopped his show and said, "Hey, wait a minute! If somebody's got a problem up there, why don't you just come down here and we'll work it out." Elvis was going to take the guy on, but whoever threw it wouldn't come down from the balcony. He sure got booed.

JIMMY VELVET: Elvis's show was unbelievable. I had never seen anything like it. I mean, Jacksonville wasn't anything like this. There were so many kids there climbing over each other it was amazing. The screaming—you never heard anything; the screaming never stopped. But he didn't have to hear very much, he felt it.

I took pictures that night with Elvis. I don't know whatever happened to those pictures, but I do have some of Elvis's band members, Bill Black, D. J. Fontana, Scotty Moore, and myself standing in front of Elvis's Cadillac, the pink one with the white top—the one he had given to his mother. We went over to the hotel that night after the show, and I had a great time. Of course, I had to get back to the base for the next morning, so I couldn't stay.

I remember it well. Before I left for the concert, everybody at the base was kidding me: "No, you're not going to go over there. You're not going to get in." I went back with some fresh pictures, and everybody went crazy over them. It was fun.

GEORGE KLEIN: The word had got out that some guys were gonna "get us." They were gonna cut Elvis's hair or kidnap him or something. Gladys was real concerned about that. When we got home, she said, "Elvis, what happened in Philadelphia? What happened in Cleveland? Chicago? He said, "Mama, I can't remember anything. It's all a blur. All these places look alike to me. George knows everything about every show in every city. Ask him." At that time he kidded me 'cause I would collect hotel keys, thinking they would bring back a memory. So I would sit down with my keys spread out in front of us and tell her what happened—how we got to the coliseum, what the kids did, and so forth. She wanted all the details.

:◎:◎:◎:

JANICE PENNINGTON *(fan)*: I snuck onto the set of *Jailhouse Rock* in [May] '57 when they were filming. I knew Himey Rogers who was a choreographer on that set.

Elvis never had formal dance training. That wasn't his thing, but he had that natural rhythm and he had a passion for whatever he was doing. Elvis didn't have to go to singing coaches and dance coaches; as I remember, there was nothing he could do wrong. Elvis had it naturally. Sometimes he'd joke around and he'd always have fun with everyone. He couldn't seem to make a mistake; even if it was wrong, it was right.

GEORGE KLEIN: One time (the only time I was on his payroll was 1957 when he was making *Jailhouse Rock*), Elvis came to us and said, "Guys, I'll give you anything you want, but the Colonel says we got to put you on the payroll for tax purposes while we're making this movie; otherwise I can't write you off." So he gave us fifty bucks a week or something. In '57 that was like maybe two hundred dollars a week now, and we said, "Elvis, we don't need it." He paid for everything.

JANICE PENNINGTON: Actually my motivation for coming to Hollywood was to meet and marry Elvis Presley. I was all of fourteen, and I was a great fan of his. I had all his 45s and I would spend hours in my room singing and watching myself in the mirror, trying to get all his moves down. I would skip school, get off the bus on Hollywood Boulevard, and stand out in front of the Knickerbocker Hotel when I knew he was in town. My girlfriend Andrea and I became friends with the doorman. He would tell us when Elvis would be driving out on his way to the studio. One day Elvis pulled his long Caddie out of the Knickerbocker, stopped, and waved us over. He was with all his cronies. He said, "I'll see you girls tonight." He had arranged with the manager of the hotel that he would let us come up and meet him in his suite.

So we came back that night; got all dressed up in our Springalater heels and teetered up Hollywood Boulevard. We stopped at the Hollywood Ranch Market for jelly doughnuts, then teetered on up to the Knickerbocker. Gene Smith, Elvis's cousin, came down to meet us and took us up to his suite. It was like the thrill of our lives. There were hundreds of girls out in front, and for us to be able to just walk right through the crowd was too much to take. So we went up. I remember sitting in the hotel room waiting with Gene and one other person I can't remember. I could see Elvis down the hallway, standing in front of a mirror, combing his hair. I felt like I was going to faint.

He came in. He was very nice, very friendly, and he ordered up a case of Cokes. I remember there was a glass-top coffee table in the room. He wrote his name in lighter fluid on the glass-top table and set it on fire. It was real strange. I guess he was putting on his own little private show for us.

"Teddy Bear" hadn't come out yet (this was in '57). But he put on a demo record of the song and said, "You want to hear my new single that's about to be released?" Of course we said, "Yes!" I think we sat there stiff as boards, you know; we were so paralyzed just being there in his presence. He put on "Teddy Bear" and proceeded to sing along with it using the floor lamp like it was a microphone. It was so exciting. Of course, we peeked out the window to show all the girls down in front of the hotel that we were up on the eleventh floor with Elvis. They were all screaming.

I just thought anything that Elvis did was fantastic. But I was so intimidated by being in his presence that I think I just sat there in awe and let him put on his show. We were there maybe forty-five minutes or an hour. Then he walked us to the elevator and there was a girl hiding in the corner by the fire escape. She had climbed up eleven flights of stairs on the fire escape! And she was just standing there shaking when she saw Elvis walking us to the elevator. He was very nice to her. He first said, "Hello," and then, "Come on, it's okay." Later, I think he let her go down the elevator instead of going back down the fire escape. He kissed each one of us at the elevator.

First he kissed my girlfriend, and I thought, "What kind of a girl does he think I am?" I was very self-righteous at fourteen. But I still let Elvis go ahead and give me a kiss, too, just on the lips, a little light kiss. Then we went down on the elevator and left.

I had a pink diary with a little rhinestone on the front, and that night I wrote in my diary all about my little experience at the Knickerbocker Hotel. The last thing I wrote was, "Boy, can he kiss!"

ANITA WOOD: I was hostess on *Top Ten Dance Party* with Wink Martindale in Memphis, and a friend of Elvis's worked there. Elvis watched the [TV] show on Saturday afternoon. One day after the show, I had a phone call from one of his cronies, Lamar Fike. He said, "Elvis would like to meet you." He wanted to know, "Can you see him tonight?" I said, "No, I'm sorry. I have a date with someone else." He said, "What? You can't break the date to go out with Elvis Presley?" I said, "No, I'm sorry. You know, Elvis wouldn't like it if I broke a date with him to go out with someone else. I can't do that. I'm sorry. Please call again." I thought, "Well, that's it. I'll never hear from him again, ever. I've blown it." I went on the date that night with Jimmy Omar. I never will forget, and, of course, I was miserable. Every time an Elvis song would come on the air, I thought, "Oh, I could be with him."

About a week later Lamar called again; this time I told him, okay. So they came to my home. I lived with Miss Patty, an elderly lady there in Memphis. Elvis came by, and the boy that worked at the TV station came in with him and introduced him to Miss Patty and to me—very proper.

MARTY LACKER: Not long after Elvis moved into Graceland, George Klein called me one night and said, "Hey, you want to go out to Elvis Presley's house this weekend?" I said, "Sure, I would love to." I didn't think that Elvis remembered me really, 'cause so much had happened to him and to me in the couple of years that had passed. But I remember that night like a picture. 'Course I know now why George had asked me: George didn't drive. I had a car and George didn't. You just couldn't bring somebody out there unannounced, so George had to ask Elvis first.

We drove up to Graceland. That's when there was no jungle room, nothing but a patio out back. Elvis had a garage; it hadn't yet been turned into an apartment. George and I got out of my car in the back, and we were walking into the backyard toward the house when we spotted Elvis coming across the back of the property (from where the barn is) with Anita Wood. He had on this white polka-dot shirt. I hadn't seen him since school, and for some reason he looked bigger. He was a little bit more open. By the time he got up to the fence, we were standing there waiting for him.

George said, "Elvis, you remember Marty Lacker don't you?" He shocked me, 'cause he said, "Sure I do. You just got out of the Army, didn't you?" I looked at him and said, "How in the hell do you know where I've been? I mean, I know where you've been, but . . ." "I keep up with things," he said. But I'm pretty sure George had told him when he had asked about bringing me. Well, he introduced me to Anita, and we went into the basement and we shot pool and talked all afternoon long. Before I left, he said, "Hey, man, anytime you want to come back, come on. I'd like to have you." So I was going up there almost every night, you know, except when Elvis went to California to do movies.

MACK GURLEY: When I was discharged from the Air Force, I moved back to Memphis. I was lost. I could not find anybody I knew. I started going by Graceland and had the time of my life.

Elvis treated me better and with more respect than anyone else I had ever met. He would take the time. He would listen intently. He would even drop his head down and look at the floor so he would have no distraction. Anything I would ask for, he'd give it to me.

FRED FREDRICK: When Elvis hit number one with "(Let Me Be Your) Teddy Bear" [in July of 1957], he had this crazy idea about having his own candy bar. He wanted me to try it. I took a bite of it, and I was trying to talk to him and not chew. It was funny as hell; it didn't taste very good. I asked Vernon, "Who's idea was this?" He said, "It's Elvis's idea." The package was silver and black and the size of a Baby Ruth. It was called a "Teddy Bar," after the song. He was gonna have it manufactured.

WILL "BARDAHL" MCDANIEL: One evening Billy Fletcher, who was a quarterback from Memphis State, come up and brought three girls with him—the first time they'd ever been inside Graceland. Elvis had teddy bears down both sides of the hallway. Not small ones—the large ones. Well, when those girls got ready to leave that night, each one grabbed a couple of teddy bears and walked out with them.

A little while later, Elvis come walking by and saw some of the teddy bears were missing. He started yelling at everybody about what happened to his teddy bears? I told him, "The three girls that were with Billy Fletcher picked 'em up, two apiece, and walked out with 'em." He said, "Bardahl, you get ahold of Billy Fletcher and tell him I want my teddy bears back tonight!" I did, and about an hour later, Billy gets there, and one of the girls came back, too. She come in and sat all six teddy bears back where they'd been and apologized to Elvis. Elvis said, "Thank you. Now get you a couple of them and take them home with you."

Elvis would give you just about anything, but you didn't steal from him. If all three of the girls had come back and apologized, he would have give 'em all the teddy bears they wanted. That's just how he was.

:◎:◎:◎:

MARTY LACKER: When I started coming up to Graceland, the house was quite a bit different from what it became. The room off the kitchen was a breakfast nook. It had a small table covered with an oilcloth tablecover, and it was kinda homey and nice. We used that room a lot. Gladys started staying away from lots of people about then, 'cause, you know, she drank some and took pills to try and get thin. So I hardly ever saw her. She was a nice lady, but she was tough.

ARLENE COGAN: I saw Gladys quite a bit, and I never seen her even tipsy. She was always in control when I saw her. So I don't know when she was supposed to be doing this drinking. Maybe it was the time of day when people weren't around, I don't know, but I never saw her drunk—never.

DOTTY AYERS: Gladys would tell me to come up to the house during the day while Elvis was asleep. Gladys said she couldn't get out much. She was very shy, and the people would just mob her if she went out anywhere—just like they did Elvis. So, she stayed in.

ALAN FORTAS: Gladys didn't drive. She was a very quiet-type person. Her everyday life was to just sit at the table in the kitchen and watch people who came and went in the house. She was unaffected by all the glamor and glory that Elvis attained, but she enjoyed speaking to people. She enjoyed life, and she was a wonderful woman. There wasn't a day that'd go by that I wouldn't come in there and she'd be sitting in the kitchen. She'd be dipping her snuff, and we'd sit there and talk. She'd say, "Take care of my son for me, will you? You guys are supposed to take care of him." That's all she wanted in life was for people to take care of Elvis.

BARBARA GLIDEWELL: Gladys would get upset with all those fans always around—and I mean always. She wouldn't get a minute's rest. It was either somebody calling on the phone or waiting around outside. I remember one time Elvis gave me his new telephone number, and he said, "Now this can't go out to too many people because my mama gets so mad when the phone rings night and day. We've had the number changed so many times the phone company says they're not going to change it anymore."
Elvis would say, "Mama, when they don't come around is when you have to worry." At that point, I think she still didn't really realize how popular Elvis was.

ARLENE COGAN: One night just as we were walking out to go somewhere, Gladys called Elvis into the bedroom. I happened to be standing there and overheard her asking, "What time are you going to be home? You know you don't have to leave so late and come in so late." Elvis said, "Oh, Mama, don't worry. Everything is going to be all right. I'm with five hundred people!"

HAROLD LOYD: Elvis depended on his mother for advice on everything. Whenever he had a problem he couldn't seem to handle himself, he always went to her. He never went to Vernon. Many times I've heard him talkin' to her about somethin' that would be a minor thing for us, but to him it was major. She'd listen real close and say, "Well, Son, I don't know the answer to that, but I'm gonna tell you what: you go in there and get the Bible, and you sit down and start readin' it. You read it from front to back and you'll find your answer." He'd say, "You're right, Mama."

ARLENE COGAN: One time Elvis kept putting off going to the dentist, and he came down to breakfast one afternoon, and I was sitting with them. Gladys said, "Son, you've got to call the dentist. You need to do it now." The next thing I heard was, "Hi, Doc. This is Elvis." He was making an appointment. He always did anything his mother asked him to do.

GEORGE KLEIN: There wasn't any discussion when Gladys told Elvis to do something. He did it. As an example, she said, "Elvis, I wish you wouldn't fly. Please, Son, don't fly. It scares me." So he didn't fly.

Gladys had a tremendous influence on Elvis, and she was really more than just a mother. She was a good friend, an advisor, and a confidante.

LAMAR FIKE *(friend and Elvis employee)*: Let me tell you, Gladys ran the house. When Gladys said, "Rabbit," you saw a lot of people jump. She was a very strong lady, and Vernon would talk very low to her. When Vernon would argue with her, you could hear her in Cleveland, Ohio, but you could hardly hear Vernon argue at all. Once she started she was likely to just pick up a pot and crack you right in the head. Elvis's temper was her temper. Elvis would get mad and go bananas. His mother was the same way. Gladys would pick up whatever was near and she'd cold-cock you with it.

Elvis told me a story one time: They were sharecropping when Gladys grew up, and the guy that owned the farm they were sharecropping on made her mad. Well, she picked up a plowshare—they must weigh nearly a hundred pounds! She picked it up and hit this man in the head and almost killed him.

ARLENE COGAN: Elvis was completely wrapped up in seeing Gladys happy. He bought her a mink coat, a very expensive thing. She told me it was so hard for her to adjust to their new life. It was such a drastic change. She said to me, "You know, Arlene, where am I going to wear a mink coat?"

How often am I going to need it?" But Elvis wanted her to have it, so she had a mink coat.

MACK GURLEY: His mother never realized that what he was doing was really a career. Gladys would say, "I think you ought to buy you a furniture store and we could be happy." Isn't that something? She thought he should go get a real job. And his father never realized they had money. Vernon would say, "We're gonna buy another car and go broke!" It was comical to me at the time, but it could be a little pathetic, too. They never really accepted the fact that Elvis had wealth.

GEORGE KLEIN: Gladys was very protective. She told me, "Watch out for some of those girls." In San Diego, early on, a girl knocked on the dressing room door and we opened it. "Is Elvis here . . . ?" She was a gorgeous girl and naturally we let her in. But she jumped right into the room and grabbed Elvis around the neck, and suddenly here comes a photographer around the corner trying to get a picture. That was the stuff Gladys wanted us to guard against.

ARLENE COGAN: It wasn't Elvis's fame that scared Gladys. She was proud of Elvis and what he had accomplished. Gladys would look out the windows at Graceland at the mobs of people waiting for a glimpse of Elvis, and she'd tell me she was afraid they would hurt him. She said, "What scares me the most is there's only one of him." The way she talked, Gladys had an understanding of the love these people had for Elvis, and she truly wished that each and every one of them could meet him, but she knew it was impossible.

When Elvis went to make a movie or record, Gladys would never touch his room until he returned home. That was a known fact. Gladys just had this fear that something was going to happen to him.

LAMAR FIKE: The more Elvis worked, and the more he became famous, the more concerned Gladys became because he was away from her. For someone who had only a third-grade education, someone who grew up on the rough side of life, you know, from poverty, it was all like an onslaught of people and fans coming at her. She never really (and I can think back and see Gladys because I was very close to her), she never ever was comfortable with Elvis's fame. It really bothered her; like Gladys would make the statement to Elvis, "I really hope that I die before you do because I could never look at you in a casket."

:◎:◎:◎:

MACK GURLEY: Elvis finally started realizing that he was who they said he was—instead of, "I guess I'm gonna pinch myself and wake up."

Elvis's love for people was his greatest quality. He tried to help everyone. He had to be way above the average person. He could have anything, and he shared it beautifully.

BARBARA GLIDEWELL: We were driving down Bellevue [now Elvis Presley Boulevard] in a hurry, trying to go some place, and Elvis sees an old man trying to change a flat tire, obviously having a hard time of it. So he drives around the block and pulls up beside him. This old man did not even know who Elvis was, but we stopped and Elvis changed the man's tire for him. Elvis was like that—and he was already a star.

BILL E. BURK *(newspaper columnist)*: When actor Nick Adams was visiting at Graceland, he and Elvis and some others went to a movie downtown. They were driving back home and they turned onto what is now Elvis Presley Boulevard. Elvis saw this old man—what we'd call a homeless man today—with a beard, tattered coat, and everything. Elvis wanted to get his car over to the curb to give this man some money, but traffic wouldn't allow it. Elvis drove around the block, but then he couldn't find the man. Nick said he drove around the block several times and even looked into stores, driving very slowly, trying to find the man. Finally they drove on home to Graceland, and Nick said Elvis actually started crying because he was not able to find the guy, and he was so obviously in need. I've always felt that of all the stories written about his generosity, that was the story that really typified the man himself.

ANITA WOOD: Elvis was also the jealous type. One day while we were carrying Nick Adams to the airport, Elvis thought I was staring at Nick too long. As soon as we dropped Nick off, Elvis told me he did not like that. Isn't that funny? I mean, Elvis and Nick Adams!

:◎:◎:◎:

NEAL MATTHEWS *(backup singer, member of the Jordanaires)*: Elvis was more relaxed in the studio than any place that we've ever seen him. That was his domain—the recording studio. He was very much at home in that studio. That was his security blanket.

GORDON STOKER: Elvis put a lot of feeling into a song. Of all the great artists—and the Jordanaires have worked with many great artists, and still do—he was the only artist that we've ever worked with that listened to a demo a few times and got up and sang it by memory—never missed a word. He put his heart into every song; felt what he was singing. Every word of every song meant something to him, and I think that's the reason his music has continued to live on.

BEN WEISMAN: Elvis would get a batch of demos and he would take them to his own private place and make his decisions as to what he wanted to record. I would never have invaded that area.

When he came into the studio, he was always prepared, very prepared. He was a perfectionist. He was totally in control of everything except the engineering. He left that to a technician, but he was boss over all the rest.

:◎:◎:◎:

NAOMIA STIERS *(fan club organizer)*: The first Elvis movie I ever saw was *Loving You*. When it opened at the Majestic theater in Houston [July, 1957] at ten o'clock that first morning, I went down there and I sat there until it was time for me to go to work at two-thirty. I loved it, and I went every day 'til they changed movies at the theater.

JIMMY VELVET: I liked *Loving You* because I thought it portrayed him a lot like he was. Elvis could easily get into a fight with someone if they embarrassed him or if they were trying to cause a problem. He wasn't afraid of anything.

HAL KANTER: It has been said by critics, and by reviewers, and historians, and trivia buffs who go in for that sort of thing, that *Loving You* was probably a more realistic view of the Elvis persona, his life and his style, than any film that he made after that. I choose to believe that.

Now, don't misunderstand me, *Loving You* was no documentary, no great analytical evaluation of the man's life, nor his style, nor his philosophy; it was just closer to the way he operated at that time in his career than anything he had done before, and closer than anything he did subsequent to that.

BRENDA FIELDER *(fan)*: I remember going to see Elvis in *Loving You*. He had the sweetest little face, and the most beautiful eyes, and when he looked at the camera, it looked like he was looking right at you. It would just melt you. He seemed very vulnerable and very accessible in a way. He was not intimidating to women. I think that's one reason women found him so attractive and so adorable at the same time.

ALAN FORTAS: Elvis was attracted to the younger girls because he felt, in that day and time in Memphis, the younger girls had not been around as much as the older women had. So I guess he felt they were more pure than a woman of an older age.

FRANCES FORBES *(friend)*: I first met Elvis when I was thirteen and he lived on Audubon Drive. I was a fan—a fan that went down to the gate one night. I think he met lots of girls that way. A lot of them stayed with him for a long time, and a lot of them just faded away. He didn't pay any attention to me then, but when I was fourteen he noticed me. Fourteen was a magical age with Elvis; it really was.

ARLENE COGAN: Elvis was crazy about females. I mean, he said that in interviews himself. He really liked all women. He loved to flirt. There was certainly a lot of different women in his life.

ANITA WOOD: I was little—five feet two—about 105 pounds. I had tiny little bitty feet, and Elvis had a fetish about tiny feet. He called me "Little" from the first time I met him. You know, he had pet names for everybody.

FRANCES FORBES: Have you ever heard the song "Love the One You're With"? I think Elvis really did. Truly, at the time he was with someone, he really loved them if he cared for them at all. There were a lot of women in and out of his life that he didn't love; but for the ones that were with him several years, when he was with that specific person, he loved them, or he thought he did.

DOTTY AYERS: I don't think Elvis really ever got over Dixie Locke [whom he dated 1953–1955]. He took her to the senior prom. They were going to be married, and then he got this hit record out. He went out on the road and he was gone all the time. For almost two years Elvis was just traveling constantly. He came back one night and went over to her house, and she told him that she was in love with this other guy and didn't want to see him anymore.

FRANCES FORBES: Back then if you were madly in love with Elvis like I was, when he hugged you, it was like you had the whole world, and nothing could hurt you. He was a nice kisser; he really was.

He didn't want any of the girls he was seeing to be with anybody else. He was very possessive in that respect.

WANDA JACKSON: My fondest memories of him were those little very intimate moments: him looking at me, his eyes were so captivating; him reaching over and brushing his hand against my cheek, or gently pushing my hair back and saying something personal to me. I remember that.

FRANCES FORBES: I never thought of Elvis as a big superstar—just a great-looking guy and a lot of fun. I was never around any of his concerts or his recording sessions.

It was special to be with him, because if you were out somewhere people would say, "Looky there. Who's that with Elvis?" That was great!

When I was fourteen or fifteen years old, I wasn't dating anybody else. I'd never known any other men. I wasn't interested in any of the guys at school 'cause I knew Elvis Presley. That was my whole life!

Now you didn't date any of the guys that worked for him, I'll tell you that, because that would probably be the last time you saw Elvis. A lot of the guys that were running around with Elvis would meet girls down at the gates at Graceland, and the girls would date the guys thinking they'd get up there to Elvis. They might get up there, but that wasn't the way to do it. You had to be all for Elvis or nothing at all. I didn't mind. Back then I didn't mind at all. I just figured you had to share, you know; he belonged to everybody.

ANITA WOOD: He had real pretty lips, and he was very handsome. Elvis was my first love. You never forget that. I was very naive and very protected. I had never even gone steady with anyone, so when I was nineteen years old and met Elvis, I immediately fell in love with him. He made a big impression on my life.

FRANCES FORBES: Elvis was king of the mountain. That's exactly what he was. It was like he had his own little kingdom, and he wanted fun people around him. He was very loving, and these people that were around him, he loved. He really did. And they loved him.

ANITA WOOD: He had a magnetism about him. People wanted to follow him and be around him. He was so fun-loving that you just wanted to be a part of that. It was fun living and being with him. You don't see talent like his very often.

FRANCES FORBES: I don't think Elvis treated everybody the same. I think he treated everyone individually. I knew Elvis real well from the time I was fourteen until the time I was nineteen. Every time he came home, I would be with Elvis at least once or twice myself without other people. And I'm sure it was the same with many other girls. He always made time for each one.

ANITA WOOD: When Elvis was in California and I was back in Memphis, many times I knew he was probably dating his leading lady. I wasn't stupid; I was very naive—I must admit that. I knew he dated some, but he did not want me to date. He would have been very angry; but he was also very respectful. Yes, he was very respectful of me all the time I knew him. But, we weren't engaged to be married; so he went out. I know that he did. He was bound to. He was a normal young man. I would not say that I was the only one—no, no, no—during our period of years, but I think I was an important one. His letters prove it.

FRANCES FORBES: Elvis was always kissing, and it was a good kiss, a real good one. He might be doing anything—playing pool, anything—he'd walk up and kiss you, or he might turn his cheek for you to kiss him. He did that in the car a lot.

Elvis was especially romantic when it was just you and him. He could have a nice conversation. He might talk to you about things that bothered him, and just like teenagers you'd neck a little bit. Elvis was like a teenager somewhat—the things we did were things that kids do; they really were all very innocent. A lot of people didn't think so, but it was. It was a different day and time.

BARBARA PITTMAN: Elvis was like a kid in a candy store trying to make up for all those lost years when he couldn't get a girl.

ANITA WOOD: Elvis wanted everyone to be completely loyal to him. Once in California when I was visiting him and he was making a movie, he gave me a ring. One of the guys in the entourage came up to me from behind and was looking over my shoulder. He said, "Oh, that ring is just gorgeous." Elvis came into the room and saw him leaning over me and just threw a fit. That young man was on the train back to Memphis that day. Nothing had happened— absolutely nothing; but Elvis was so upset over it he never had anything to do with that guy again. It absolutely blew my mind. It was strange, but that was him.

BARBARA GLIDEWELL: Yeah, I loved him. I only left because when I got older and out of high school, I didn't want to share him with all those other people. He'd say, "Okay, we're going to the movies." You thought maybe it was going to be just a few people, but he would invite the whole world. And you just didn't want to share him.

:◎:◎:◎:

JACK CLEMENT: I think I'm the first one that knew Elvis got drafted. He came by Sun, and I was the only one there. He came into the control room and he seemed kinda happy about it—or relieved. It didn't seem like it was distressing to him at all. He just wanted to come by and tell somebody.

"Everything I Have Is Gone."
1958-1959

While sharing the rewards of his success with friends Mack Gurley, Fred Fredrick, and the girls in his gang, Elvis receives notice that his presence is requested in the U.S. Army. The notice of separation, as sad as it initially seems, is only a foreshadowing of what is to come: the shattering of a dream, the breaking of a heart, and the realization that life as Elvis Presley has known it will never again be the same.

Leaving behind his beloved mother, Elvis trades his fancy stage clothes for Army fatigues. Texas disc jockey Eddie Fadal offers the new recruit a weekend home away from home, where Elvis attempts to re-create his happy life in Memphis. Lamar Fike and Alan Fortas bring Elvis's loved ones from Graceland, but tragedy strikes, and Elvis must rush back to Memphis for a final farewell...

Returning to Texas to complete basic training, Elvis Presley soon sails for Germany as a regular soldier, leaving behind a flourishing career and facing an uncertain future. Sergeant Ira Jones and soldiers Ed Hart, John Callender, and Keith Gibson help Elvis make the best of Army life just miles away from the tense border with Eastern Europe.

As the rock 'n' roll controversy continues to rage back stateside, loyal fans, the Colonel, and RCA keep the home fires burning.

> "When we started working with Presley, everyone said, 'You better get it while you can because he ain't gonna be around long.' All the record officials and the heads of the large publishing companies in Nashville said that."
>
> GORDON STOKER

BARBARA GLIDEWELL: I remember Elvis's twenty-third birthday. They gave him a party at the hotel downtown, and he sang. Elvis, George Klein, the whole group—maybe fifty people—was there. He had a birthday cake, hamburgers, Pepsi Colas (he loved Pepsi Colas), and then afterwards we all went roller-skating.

MACK GURLEY: We had fantastic times at the skating rink. Elvis would rent the whole rink for all night.

FRANCES FORBES: One game we played was called "knock down," I believe. There was two teams—one at one end and one at the other end of the room. Someone would blow a whistle, and we'd skate toward each other to see how many people you could knock down. The ones that were left standing were the winners.

WILL "BARDAHL" MCDANIEL: When I first met Elvis, I was only seventeen. I used to roller-skate at Rainbow and worked there a lot. One night, a friend of mine was sick and asked me to take his place and work a private party. He forgot to tell me whose party it was. He said, "All you have to do is come in and give out the skates, pick 'em up when it's over, and lock up the place. There'll be a couple of guys come in. They'll let in the people they want; you'll have nothing to do with that." That night, about an hour after we locked up, two guys come in. I didn't know who they were, but they let in about a hundred people.

After I gave out all the skates. I put mine on and got out there with them. 'Bout thirty minutes later, Elvis Presley comes walking in. He'd been next door at the Terrace Room eating. Then I knew whose party it was. A little while later somebody blew a whistle and all the females got off the floor. The guys—half went to one end, and half went to the other end. It was gonna be a war. I'm standing down at the one end looking at Elvis at the far end of the rink, and I tell some guy, "I sure would like to get ahold of Elvis." He yelled, "Elvis, this guy wants you." Elvis just kind of nodded and grinned. When they blew the whistle, we'd skate straight to the middle and have a free-for-all.

Well, they blew the whistle and the two sides collided. About five minutes later I woke up; they had me in a chair, a rag on my head, and Elvis was standing over me apologizing. I said, "Hey man, this is your party. Let's go play some more." I have to admit, I'd done got a little irritated. They blew the whistle the second time and down the floor he came—same thing. But by then I'd done got damn irritated; that is, when I'd woke up again. The third time they blew the whistle only two people come out on the floor: Elvis and me. We collided in the middle. I stood up, looked down. Here's Elvis laid out on the floor.

He had a little arm move that would slap you hard upside the head as he went sailin' past you. That's how he'd got me, and that's the way I finally got him—with the same move. I just made it before he did. But I was sure he'd be mad, and I thought, "I'm gonna die!" So I went and hid under a table.

A few minutes later a guy comes looking under the table—it was Red West. He yells, "Elvis, he's over here!" At seventeen years old, your life flashes in front of your eyes; you know you're fixin' to die. Elvis came over and motioned for me to get up. I crawled out, stood up, and faced him. Red West was off to my right. I had no idea what to expect. Elvis, he looks at me, and then he looks at my T-shirt (I was wearing a Bardahl motor oil shirt). He says, "Bardahl, huh? I like you. Red, give him the phone number to the house, and he can come up any time he wants." To my surprise, Elvis just turned around and skated away.

FRANCES FORBES: If you went somewhere like the skating rink, you had to be a pretty good skater, let me tell you. Several nights I'd come home looking like I'd been in a car wreck. It was a rough game that you played. You had to be able to stand your ground.

BARBARA GLIDEWELL: We all had to wear knee pads because they played rough. They played crack-the-whip, where you form a long line of skaters. Someone would be the center anchor, and everyone else would go spinning around. They would spin faster and faster until the ones on the end were really going fast—so fast eventually they'd have to let go and go flying into the railing. Pow! Pretty rough, but you usually had knee pads—and sometimes "happy pills." Elvis would get the pills at the dentist. He'd take one, and so he didn't mind how rough the game got. He was immune to the pain, so we would all want one.

DOTTY AYERS: I believe that the only drugs Elvis took back then was when he was having a lot of dental work done before he left for the Army. They capped his teeth, done a lot of bridge work, and he had some pain pills, and he would take those.

ARLENE COGAN: Sometimes when he was back home in Memphis, Elvis would rent the amusement park at the fairgrounds, and a whole gang of us would go over late at night to ride the rides and play.

FRED FREDRICK: There was this nice guy named Whimpy Adams. Whimpy would open up the gates to the fairgrounds and turn on all the rides. The first thing we'd do, we'd always go to the dodge 'em cars—choose up sides, you know, Elvis and Red [West] and me, and whoever the other groupies were hanging around out there.

BARBARA GLIDEWELL: Elvis always felt like he should be the center of attraction. If you brought a date to the amusement park, he would keep the guy on a ride until he got sick to teach you a lesson. One time I brought this boy who was the captain of the football team at Treadwell High School. The boy really wanted to meet Elvis. But Elvis got him on that Tilt-a-Whirl thing that went around-and-around and kept him on there forever! I said, "Elvis, he has been on there forty minutes. Don't you think it's time he got off?" Elvis just laughed. Finally the guy got sick. Elvis had a mean streak in him, you know. Afterward the guy said, "I don't ever want to see Elvis Presley again! Never!" And I never did bring another date to the fairgrounds.

WILL "BARDAHL" McDANIEL: Elvis loved the roller coaster. That was usually one of the first things we went on at night at the park, and we'd finish up with the dodge 'em cars. One night as we're getting on the roller coaster, the guy that was running it for the amusement park stopped Elvis. Being kind of cocky, he said, "I bet you fifty bucks you won't ride this any way I will." Elvis said, "No, I won't, but I got somebody else who will." He hollered out, "Hey, Bardahl!" I went over to see what he wanted and he said, "This guy bet me you won't ride this thing any way he will." I said, "Let's go!"

We rode that thing every way you can think of except sitting down. There was a headlight on the front of the roller coaster, and there was just enough room to put one foot on each side of the headlight and hold on to the bar of the front seat; so I told Elvis, "I'm gonna ride it on the front." He said, "Can you do it?" I said, "Yeah, I can do it." He said, "Okay." He had Anita Wood with him that night. So Anita got in first, Elvis got in, and my little sister sat next to him. I got on the front and stood there holding onto the bar, looking at Elvis straight in the face. When we got started, if we were gonna turn one way, Elvis would just point the way we would turn so I could lean against it. What a ride!

We got off and told the guy, "It's your turn." The guy just turned around and paid Elvis the fifty dollars they had bet. He handed me the money and said, "You know, it was worth it to shut him up."

:◎:◎:◎:

ARLENE COGAN: Elvis got a sixty-day deferment (or whatever you call it) from the draft so he could finish filming *King Creole*. He was not looking forward to going into the Army at all, but he knew he had to do it.

BEN WEISMAN: *King Creole* was originally called *A Stone for Danny Fisher*. As a matter of fact, my song "Danny" was recorded by Elvis, and it was supposed to be the title song of the movie. It was all set to go, and, all of a sudden, they decided to change the title of the movie to *King Creole*. They took the song "Danny" out and put it in the can. A few months later, I was told that Conway Twitty was coming up for a session. He had just had a big hit with "It's Only Make Believe." I remembered "Danny." We changed the title, and Conway recorded it and had a huge hit under the title "Lonely Blue Boy." It was a number-one record.

JIMMY VELVET: I thought *King Creole* was one of Elvis's best pictures. I wished it had been in color. They were rushing to get the film done in time because of the Army. He had already been signed to do it when he was drafted, and I think he had six weeks or so before he went to basic training. They worked around the clock to get at least Elvis's parts in.

During the filming, we were staying at the Roosevelt Hotel in New Orleans. The streets were blocked and people couldn't get by. They stood back in crowds, and, of course, the director had to shoot over and over. A lot of scenes had to be reshot because even though they would try very hard to keep the crowd quiet, some girl would scream out or something wrong would happen over and over again. The staff would be trying to get something done, and Elvis would just grin; the girls would scream all the more. Everyone else was in a hurry, but Elvis would just stop and grin about it. It was amusing to him.

:◎:◎:◎:

JOAN DEARY: Before Elvis went into the Army, they did a tremendous amount of recording. Steve Sholes was still involved at that time, and he had those releases planned for enough time to keep the product flowing, and to keep Elvis hot. There was a great deal of concern that the two years he was going to be gone were really going to affect his popularity. Would he still have that appeal, or would the music have passed him by?

GORDON STOKER: You couldn't push Elvis. If we were told to do three or four numbers each night for the soundtracks or the albums, or whatever we might have been doing, he would not push himself. He always took his time to do everything, and do the best he could do.

D. J. FONTANA: In California, Elvis was always concerned about us making enough money from the time we worked in the studio. He'd sometimes ask us, "Are you guys making any money?" We'd say, "No, Elvis, you're recording too fast." So he'd take us out for a two- or three-hour lunch break, and then we'd come back to the studio. We got paid for all that time.

ARLENE COGAN: Elvis mentioned on more than one occasion when some of us were sitting around, that his mother didn't really trust Colonel Parker and didn't like him. Elvis would dread it when Colonel Parker would come to Memphis—absolutely dread it. Colonel Parker would just take over the house. He would bring in some of his men, and they would man the telephones. I mean, all the calls were screened by his people. Elvis detested this. Vernon would tell us that when Colonel Parker would come to the house and get Elvis locked up for a meeting, that he couldn't even talk to his own son until Parker left.

MARTY LACKER: Gladys was a pretty good judge of people, and if she didn't like you, you had a problem. She didn't like Colonel Parker. She really didn't want Elvis to go [sign the management contract] with him to begin with. She was one of those people that had a sixth sense about others.

I was like that with Parker the first time I ever met him. He was brusque. He was brusque because he didn't care about anybody else, including Elvis. Parker's a hustler and a con artist, and he's out for Parker. Always has been, and the ol' fucker will probably be 'til he dies.

FRED FREDRICK: Back when Elvis was drafted they had a buddy plan. Everybody was going to go with Elvis—five hundred people were going to join the Army with him. Well, when the time came to go, only two or three went, I think Farley Guy went. Lamar Fike was going but didn't pass the physical.

BARBARA PITTMAN: Elvis cried in my lap because he had to go into the service. Parker had said, "Look, son, you're going in. You play the hero. If you start battling it and try to get out of it to support your mother like some of them did, it's going to make you look bad. Just be the good ol' boy, the All-American-kid type."

:◎:◎:◎:

CHARLES HOLMES *(Army draftee)*: Elvis was inducted in March 1958 and went to Fort Chaffee, Arkansas, for processing. Then we were sent to Fort Hood, Texas, for basic training and advanced training with the Second Armored Division. I didn't know it, but that unit, with three or four thousand people, was being trained to replace the Third Armored Division that was serving in Europe.

EDDIE FADAL: I hadn't seen Elvis for a year-and-a-half; then one day I read in the paper that he would be coming in to Fort Hood, which is near my hometown, Waco, and would be there for Army basic training. I said to myself, "I think I'll go out there and see if he remembers me." I had a hard time getting on base. The security was very tight, but I finally talked my way through. I had a picture of Elvis and me together, and I showed this to all the guards so they would let me go through. They told me where to go to look for him. I finally got to the dayroom for Elvis's division. He had just gotten in from the field and was there shining his boots, and he remembered me immediately.

He yelled "Eddie!" and hugged me and said, "Let's go somewhere and talk." "Where?" I asked. "I don't know anything about this base." He said, "There's a Dairy Queen down the way, and we'll go over there and chat." So we did. I asked him if he'd like to come to our home on weekends and have some family cooking, and he said, "I'd love that, but it'll be two weeks before I can do it. I have to stay on base." I said, "Fine. You just give me a call and come on to Waco when you're ready. I'll give you directions on how to get to the house."

I left the base after a couple of hours, and in two weeks, true to his word, my telephone rang. He says, "I'm out here at the circle. How do I get to your house?" I said, "You stay right where you are and I'll come after you." He was in a black Cadillac—alone. This was his first trip after he was inducted into the service. He followed me to our house, and that was the first of many weekends he spent with us. We built a room onto our home and decorated it in the colors he liked—pink and black—just for him. I had a customized hi-fi—it wasn't stereo in those days, it was hi-fi—and he played it all the time.

When he came to our home the first weekend, he wanted to call his mother 'cause he hadn't been able to call her from the base, and he'd been in Texas two weeks. He did, and all he said was, "Mama..." and apparently she said, "Elvis..." or "Son..." or whatever. From then on, for a solid hour, they were crying, weeping, moaning on the telephone—not hardly a word was spoken. He was very sad, very low, very depressed at that time.

Awhile later Gladys and Vernon came down, and then Grandma and the rest of his relatives. They came down to try and cheer him up. That was our goal in those days: to try to keep him happy and get his mind off things, 'cause he really thought it was the end. He thought his career was over.

ANITA WOOD: A sergeant who lived on base, and his wife, invited me to stay with them while Elvis was in six-week training. After-hours and on weekends Elvis would come over and visit. He was just so normal. He would drive a regular Army vehicle over, and we'd sit and talk with the family. We'd go out in the backyard and look at the sunset and really just have a good time doing nothing. I loved that early period in Texas and, yes, I loved him.

EDDIE FADAL: I think Anita Wood was always his number-one girl. In fact, Elvis told us that many times. He would drive by our house with Anita some afternoons and say, "Let's go to Dallas and see what's going on." And we'd all go to Dallas. I would sit in the front seat with Anita in the middle and Elvis driving. We did this many times, just drive up there and see the sights and drive back to Waco. He wanted to get away from the base. One time on the way back we stopped and got some gas at a service station, and while Anita went into the restroom he called me over to the front bumper of the car. He put his foot on the bumper and said, "Eddie, I want to tell you something. When old E here gets ready to get married (he pointed to himself as "E"), it's gonna be to that girl, Anita Wood, and no one else. She's the one."

I think his relationship with Anita was very smooth. He brought her to our house every weekend, and he called her "Little Bitty." It was "Little Bitty this" and "Little Bitty that." One day she was not feeling well. Elvis was very concerned about her health, and we called the doctor. The doctor gave her an aspirin and told her she'd be all right in the morning. That was just it. But he had to have a doctor tell him that.

ANITA WOOD: When he was in basic training, Elvis looked great. The dye had grown off his hair—his real hair was light brown. He couldn't wear the lifts in his shoes. He had a nice tan. He was so handsome and down-to-earth. That was the time when he was really himself. It's what I would have loved for him to be like all the time, but that could not be.

EDDIE FADAL: Elvis had his own key to the door. He liked to see us when we weren't prepared for him. When we knew he was coming, our best china would be out and our best silver and the tablecloths and the linen napkins. He didn't want to see us like that. One time I was in some shorts out mowing the lawn with a push mower—not a power mower—and he got out of the car and bent over double laughing. He got a big kick out of that and yelled, "Now I see you as you really are." He'd say, "If you want me to come back, I want to eat in the kitchen." He didn't want any airs put on around him, and I think that tells a lot about the man.

He brought his mother and his dad to our house, too—and his grandmother. There was always a caravan of cars when Elvis would come, seven or eight cars, and we'd hustle around real quick to get a meal ready for them—big job. Gladys would go shopping with my wife to buy a few things that Elvis liked. And she would go into the kitchen and put her little apron on and help cook the food. It was always a big meal. To my wife, Elvis represented work. When she saw him coming she'd say, "Oh, man, I've got to go to work." There'd be food to cook, dishes to wash, pots and pans. People ask her today, "What do you remember most about Elvis?" and she says, "One four-letter word: W-O-R-K!"

CHARLES HOLMES: I recall the Army issued you a set of underwear, socks, uniforms, helmets, and whatever, including two sets of fatigues. You wore one, and the other you kept clean in your locker for the sergeant to inspect them day or night. It was awkward. You took off your clothes at the end of the day; they were dirty, and you had to get some clean ones somewhere. Elvis bought everybody in his outfit an extra set of fatigues. Later I began to learn that that was the type of guy Elvis was.

EDDIE FADAL: He hated pulling KP [kitchen police] on the base. He would pay somebody to pull KP for him. He hated it. He did it one time and said "Never again!" But there was always a willing taker of whatever he would give them—sometimes it was ten dollars, sometimes it was twenty dollars. If they played hard to get, he said, "Okay, I'll give you twenty dollars."

Army pay meant nothing to Elvis. He didn't accept it. He never accepted his Army checks. He gave them to charity or bought whatever was needed on the base. He had bought every television set that was on the base at that time. He bought them and put them in the dayrooms all over the base.

:◎:◎:◎:

RAY WALKER *(member of the Jordanaires)*: We worked with Presley in June of 1958 while he was on a two-week leave from basic training. He came to Nashville and recorded "Now and Then There's a Fool Such As I."

D. J. FONTANA: Elvis was comfortable recording in Nashville. He knew all his regular musicians. If he wasn't comfortable doing something—a session, a movie—he'd just "get sick" and go home.

He liked to record late at night, but he wouldn't push himself. If he wasn't in the right mood, he'd stall or sing gospel [music] or talk. Sometimes he'd just say, "I ain't singing good. Let's go home. The hell with it." We'd all come back the next night and everything would go great.

JOAN DEARY: RCA paid Elvis's recording costs. But compared to other artists of his caliber who went into the studio and recorded for us, his costs were very cheap. He could go into the studio, work all night, and in three sessions you might get six or seven hit songs. With most artists you were lucky if you got one hit.

FRANCES FORBES: A few days before Elvis returned to Army duty in Texas, we watched *King Creole* with him. He was sitting between me and Arlene. It was really strange to be sitting there beside Elvis and looking at this big character of Elvis up there on the screen. It felt funny. I was watching the movie star up there, and in reality I've got him sitting right next to me. I'd never really put the two together.

ARLENE COGAN: Elvis loved *King Creole* because it was more of a dramatic role, even though it did have songs in it. He said he was very pleased with it. He liked the fact that he had the chance to act a little bit.

MACK GURLEY: Elvis used to say, "I still can't believe it's happening to me. I think I'm gonna wake up, but I hope I don't."

ALAN FORTAS: After his two-week leave in June, Elvis wanted Gladys to go back to Fort Hood with him because he was worried about her health. Gladys and Vernon and Grandma Minnie Mae and Lamar drove four hundred miles to Fort Hood. I think the trip really tired Gladys out.

Elvis rented a trailer and parked it outside the base for the Presleys to stay in. The fans just hung around all the time, day and night. Gladys couldn't get any rest. Finally Elvis rented a house in Killeen that had three bedrooms.

EDDIE FADAL: A lot of Elvis's friends visited him before he went overseas. I'm not sure, but I think they paid for their own tickets and he would pay for the motel rooms. I've seen him do that, and I've seen him send Vernon out to pay so-and-so's motel bill.

Food was always there at the house. Grandma was the cook. They always ate there and sat around the table with Elvis. He loved having his friends around the table with him, and he liked eating very simple food. Lots of times it was distasteful food, but, boy, people ate it just to be around Elvis. One of the dishes I just couldn't eat was sauerkraut and wieners. To me it was obnoxious—just the scent of it.

One day I had gotten to Elvis's house early, and when he came in nothing would do but I had to have dinner with them. I had just finished dinner at home and I said, "Elvis, I'm full. I couldn't eat another bite. I'm way up to here [to my neck] with food." Elvis said, "Oh, come on. You've got to eat with us." Then Gladys and Vernon would chime in. Red West was there; and finally after about seven or eight attempts to get me into the kitchen, Elvis sends Red West into the living room. Red picks me up, throws me over his shoulder, and takes me and sits me right next to Elvis at the table. Elvis said, "Now, eat. I've eaten at your house; you've got to eat with me." And what was it but sauerkraut and wieners!

DOTTY AYERS: Grandma Presley was fun. She was a little firecracker. She was as tall as Elvis, you know, but real slim—real skinny. She cooked for Elvis. She wouldn't let nobody else cook for him down in Texas when she was there. She spoiled him. Elvis loved Grandma Presley just like he did Gladys. He would kiss on her and hug her. She would slap him when he would get carried away, jumping around and playing tricks on her and everything. She would just slap the devil out of him.

LAMAR FIKE: Gladys was going through menopause. Back then they would give you mood elevators, and she would drink a beer or something in the evening. One thing led to another. What led to the disease of the liver, I had no idea. It could have been family history, I don't know. Her side of the family had a very short life expectancy.

BARBARA PITTMAN: Gladys had been sick a long time. The doctors had warned her that her liver was bad and that she had to quit drinking. This was long before she got so terribly sick. I saw it happening. Gladys never even came out of her robe. She'd walk very slow. She was sick. She was pale and looked so much older than her forties—like she was in her late fifties.

ALAN FORTAS: Gladys's condition really sank. She got to where she was suffering and in constant pain, so she finally went to the doctor in Texas, who said she should come back to her own doctor in Memphis for treatment. Elvis couldn't get leave from the Army, so Gladys and Vernon got on a train and went home.

EDDIE FADAL: Vernon and Gladys went all the way from Killeen to Memphis on the Santa Fe Railroad. She was immediately hospitalized. Elvis stayed in Killeen because of the Army, but the very next day Vernon called and said, "She's in critical condition. Come home." Elvis got a three- or four-day leave.

On August 13, Elvis came through Waco and went to Dallas and caught a plane and flew to Memphis.

DOTTY AYERS: I saw Gladys the day that she died; in fact, I was up at the hospital. They had told her that she was getting better and that Elvis was coming home. Vernon was there. He stayed at the hospital with Gladys. We were in the room talking, and they brought in some flowers and asked Gladys to sign for them. Her hands were swelled; she was swelled all over, and she asked me if I would sign for her. I signed, "Mrs. Presley," and laughed and said, "I didn't think I would ever be signing this name." She said, "Don't ever give up hope, honey."

Gladys looked at me, and she must have had a premonition or something. She said, "Dotty, I don't think I'll ever see Graceland again." I said, "Gladys, you know the doctors said that you're better." She said, "I know, but I just got this awful feeling." She said, "Will you promise me something? Will you watch after my boy, 'cause there's just so many people that don't care about him."

We were out at the gate waiting for Elvis when he came home. He came in a cab from the airport. Then he got into his car and drove up to the hospital. He stayed until they ran him out. They told him that his mother could come home tomorrow if she kept improving.

BILL E. BURK: Vernon told me he was asleep that night and woke up when he heard Gladys struggling for breath. He said, "I got to her as quick as I could. I raised her head." Then Vernon called for a nurse and told her "to do something quick—to call the doctor." They called the doctor and put her in an oxygen tent, but it was too late.

DOTTY AYERS: They called Elvis real early in the morning and told him that she had died. Elvis went completely to pieces.

BILL E. BURK: On the day Gladys Presley died, Elvis told me his mother's death broke his heart. He cried throughout the interview, saying, "She's all I lived for. She was always my best girl."

Elvis told me that he had spent the day with his mother at the [Methodist] hospital. He said, "I kissed her good night and told her I'd come back early this morning and take some of the flowers home. She was talking good and feeling so much better. I was home asleep when the phone rang about 3:00 A.M. I knew what it was before I answered it."

EDDIE FADAL: Early in the morning of August 14, I got a telephone call. Someone was crying on the phone. I said, "Elvis?" and he said, "Eddie, Mama passed away. Can you come?" I said, "Sure. I'll be on the first flight out of here." And I was. Junior Smith, his cousin, was dispatched to the airport to meet me and bring me to Graceland, where I stayed for thirty days.

Elvis was devastated. When I walked into the living room after we first got there, Elvis and Vernon were at the casket. Elvis was touching Gladys's hands and her forehead and crying and talking baby talk, him and Vernon both. Only they knew what they were saying. Then Elvis said, "Mama, you never would dress up for me, and now here you are dressed up in the most beautiful gown. I never saw you dressed up like this." And he would cry, "Look at those hands, those beautiful hands. They worked so hard to raise me." And he would sob, he and Vernon together. I just stood back and watched. Then he turned around and saw me, and he beckoned me over to the casket. He had his arm around me and he said, "Mama, here's Eddie. You know Eddie. You met him in Killeen." It was very sad. I'm having cold chills just telling that story.

BARBARA PITTMAN: After Mrs. Presley died and we were all out at Graceland, they had her coffin in the white room. We were all there with Elvis. Colonel Parker came in and tried to run us all off. "Get all of these people out of here. I want them out of here, now." It was just Elvis's close friends, you know. Elvis told Parker, "Look, these are my friends. Don't you come in my house and tell me to run my friends out of here."

HAROLD LOYD: I didn't even know Gladys had been sick until I heard it on the radio in Mississippi, where I was livin' at the time. I went to Memphis as soon as I could and spent the week. When I got there, there must have been two or three thousand people hangin' 'round in front of the house —fans and such. Gladys's body was laid out in a coffin with a glass top.

Elvis and Vernon were sittin' there when I walked in. Elvis said (and it kind of shocked me), "Lord have mercy, Harold, where did you come from?" Gladys used to say those very words to me whenever I'd walk into her house in Tupelo without knockin'.

Elvis was in pitiful shape. His eyes were all swollen and red. He would walk over to the casket and say, "Wake up, Mama. Wake up, Mama. Wake up, Baby, and talk to Elvis."

As they were takin' the casket out to the hearse, Elvis was followin' right behind 'em. He was cryin', "Please don't take my baby away. Bring her back. She's not dead. She's just sleepin'. Oh God, please don't take her away."

He said, "Everything I have is gone—everything I've ever worked for. I got all this for her and now she's gone. I don't want any of it now." It was real sad.

JAMES BLACKWOOD: The Blackwood Brothers Quartet sang at Gladys's funeral. Elvis called and asked us if we would. He said that we were his mother's favorite group. And so we did. I have a very vivid memory of the funeral service. It was at the Memphis Funeral Home. After the service was over, we had sung several songs, including "Take My Hand, Precious Lord" and "Precious Memories." Everyone had gone out of the chapel except Vernon and a police officer and Elvis. I remember Elvis went over to his mother's casket and leaned over and kissed her. He was weeping and said, "Mother, I would give every dime I have and even dig ditches just to have you back."

MAE AXTON: I was in the hospital and couldn't go to Memphis. The Colonel called me and asked if there was anything at all I could do. Elvis was so distraught. I asked, "What if I write him a letter? I'll get it on the plane as soon as possible." I did, and Tom Diskin [Colonel Parker's business associate] went out to the airport and got it. They called back and said later that Elvis took the letter and went back by himself and read it with tears rolling down his face. I wish I had kept a copy. I didn't, but I remember that I told him about how very sorry I was that I couldn't be there, 'cause I loved Gladys, too. I said for him to just remember that she would be with him always, and that where she is now she is happy, because she's with God.

BARBARA PITTMAN: Elvis stayed at the cemetery while they lowered the coffin. I think it was tradition for the family to throw a shovel of dirt— the ashes-to-ashes-type ceremonial thing. It was most heart-wrenching. God! Elvis tried to jump in the ground with his mother. They were holding him back and he was screaming. It was horrible. It was really just the worst thing I had ever seen.

ARLENE COGAN: Elvis was just inconsolable. He walked around carrying Gladys's nightgown for days. He wouldn't put it down. He had no sleep—hadn't slept in days. He refused to go to sleep. He would sit there, and, I mean, he was totally exhausted, and he would sit there holding his mother's nightgown. It went with him everywhere he went. He would be sitting in the chair (you could see how tired he was) nearly falling asleep, and he would fight it. He fought sleep.

BARBARA PITTMAN: Elvis was in so much grief and hysteria that the doctor was brought in to help him. People were screaming, "Help him!

Somebody please help him!" This doctor went upstairs with him, and when he came down Elvis was feeling no pain.

I saw Elvis come down from his bedroom at Graceland so stoned out of his mind he didn't know where he was. He had a line of mirrors that ran along the stairs in the hallway. Elvis came down the stairs and said, "Hey, look at all them little Elvises! A thousand little Elvises here!" and that kind of thing. The doctor that took care of Elvis when his mother died was giving him tranquilizers, and he liked 'em.

GEORGE KLEIN: The stories about his love for Gladys are not exaggerated. When she died, he was in mourning for a long time—extreme mourning, physically crying all the time. He was completely destroyed.

ARLENE COGAN: Elvis was in pretty bad shape over his mother—mentally, I mean. He really wasn't ready to go back to Fort Hood when he did. Actually, he had the opportunity then to get out of the service. I was there in Killeen when two high-ranking officers gave Elvis the opportunity to get out if he wanted to. Elvis's friend Earl Greenwood was there; he heard it, too.

Now Elvis would have given anything to have gotten out of the Army at that point. However, there was no way he could do it because of who he was. Every mother in the United States would have been saying, "Elvis Presley can get out, but my son has to serve his time." Elvis said he couldn't do that; he was going to do what he had to do and serve his country.

ANITA WOOD: After Mrs. Presley died, when Elvis returned to Killeen, it was just bedlam, just wild. People everywhere coming out of the woodwork. Strangers taking over. I think it was a weak moment in Elvis's life. He allowed these people to come into his life to keep him busy—to keep his mind occupied.

Elvis and his father had rented a home in Killeen, and I went there. At that particular time, it was not a lot of fun. It was so crazy. There were strangers there that I did not know. They were getting close to Elvis, and so intimate with him, it appeared to me. When we were playing the piano or sitting around watching TV, I found myself among strangers, and I didn't like that. I thought they were taking advantage of him. That was his choice. You couldn't tell Elvis what to do—what not to do—he did what he wanted.

DOTTY AYERS: I think what happened in Texas had to do with the remark that Elvis made to me down there. Elvis was very lonely. He had to go by the rules of the base, even though he was living off base. He had to go to bed early, and he had to stay at the house. He wanted the guys to come down there and be with him 'cause he needed them right after Gladys died. But they didn't come. The only guys that went down with him was his cousin Junior, and Lamar Fike. That's it. And Red was there. Elvis said, "Yeah, when it's partying in Memphis, or when I go to Nashville to record, or out to Hollywood to make movies, they could always get away. But when it's down here, and there's no parties, and its just the hard times, they can't get away." They all had something they had to do.

ARLENE COGAN: We felt that it would help if we went down to Fort Hood to be with Elvis before he left for Germany. He planned on renting a Greyhound bus so the whole gang—all the guys and girls—could come to Texas, but I understand Colonel Parker had got wind of it and had a fit. So Elvis had to forget that idea.

EDDIE FADAL: You couldn't keep up with life in Killeen. There was somebody coming in all the time. There was not much bus service from Waco to Killeen in those days, so Elvis would call me to go to the bus station and pick someone up and bring 'em. I did this many times—girls I didn't know. I'd say, "Describe her. What does she look like?" He'd say, "Oh, she's a brunette and she's short," or "She's tall and weighs about a hundred and ten pounds." This happened a whole lot. There was always a house full of people. Besides the people he desired to have around him, there were the fans in the Killeen area and the soldiers' families. That was a huge Army base—one of the largest in the world—and a lot of those folks would come to the house in the afternoons and just wait in the yard to see him come in. There was always a mess of people he had to wade through to get to the front door.

DOTTY AYERS: In Texas, Elvis really told me a lot. We had some long heart-to-heart talks in the middle of the night when he couldn't sleep and Anita wasn't there. She was off in New York doing some talk show deal; I can't remember which one it was. Anita just walked across the stage one night—the mystery girl. Then the next night she would stay a little bit longer, and they built it up. Then when the show was broadcast, we were watching it one night and they mentioned that [national television] wouldn't show Elvis from the waist down. Anita said, "Oh, that's the best part!" Elvis said, "Oh, my god, Anita. You have ruined me!" Elvis just kinda grabbed his face and slid down in his seat.

ARLENE COGAN: After Elvis came back to Killeen, we would think everything was okay, that he was doing better 'cause he would sing and play his guitar and try to joke. I mean, Elvis was such a clown. But you know, the joking around was not near as consistent as it was prior to Gladys's death.

EDDIE FADAL: Elvis loved putting on a record and playing the piano along with the record and changing the style of the singer to the way he would do it. He did that hours upon hours.

He dearly loved "Happy, Happy Birthday, Baby" by the Tune Weavers. I bought seven of those records, and, believe it or not, we wore out all of 'em. He played 'em and played 'em and sang with it over and over. Then he'd say, "If I was doing it, I'd do it this way." And he'd say, "Start it over, Eddie." We'd start it over, and he'd do it the way he wanted to do it. If it wasn't just right—to show what a perfectionist he was—he'd say, "Play it again, Eddie." All of this kind of thing is on a tape we made in our home.

ARLENE COGAN: One time I was going to get something to drink in the kitchen, and I didn't realize Vernon and Elvis were in there. As I started in, I saw Elvis and his father hugging each other. They were both crying —just hugging and crying and talking about Gladys.

EDDIE FADAL: Elvis and I talked a lot about the effect the Army might have on his career. He said, "It's all over, Eddie. There's no way I can come back and they're gonna remember me." He said, "It's over." And he really believed that. I kept assuring him, "No way. You've got four or five records in the can. The Colonel will release them periodically, and the disc jockeys will be playing them. How can they forget you? It's not over!" I did my best to keep his chin up, but I think he really believed it was over. He said, "In two years they're not going to even know me."

ARLENE COGAN: When Elvis left Fort Hood [for Germany] it was like a death. It was that solemn. Elvis was worried. He didn't want to break down in front of all those [soldiers] that he was going to Germany with. He told me that, and we were trying real hard on the way to the base not to cry. It was terrible.

There were eleven of us staying in the house just before he left. Anita was there that weekend, his father, his grandmother, Lamar, Red, his cousin Junior, and Earl.

On his way to Germany, Elvis had an interview in New York. Well, you can buy the record, *Elvis Sails*—that's the interview. There's film footage of it, too, and you can look right in his eyes. I admired him so much for being able to do that interview, because they talked about his mother's death. He said his mother had always been there for him. He could get up at any hour of the night if anything was troubling him, and she was there to talk to him.

:◎:◎:◎:

IRA JONES *(master sergeant, First Medium Tank Battalion, 32nd Armor, 3rd Armored Division)*: Elvis came by ship [the U.S.S. *General Randall*] from the States. I was sent to the port of Bremerhaven in northern West Germany to escort some troops back on the train to the tank battalion base at Friedberg. One of those troops was Elvis Presley.

The troop train I was in charge of was the closest one to the ship, and we were all ready for Elvis to climb aboard. By the time he came off the ship, a crowd had gathered outside the barricade the MPs [military police] had set up, and they were yelling, "Elvis! Elvis! Elvis!" There must have been thousands of people there waiting. This was all a little bit strange to me because I didn't know much about Elvis Presley or who he was. When Elvis got there and come off the ship, for some reason, someone took the barricades away and let the people run through the unloading area. Well, there was a big MP on each side of Elvis, so that was one of the ways I was sure I would recognize him. He didn't get bothered much, but those MPs took a lot of shoving from people trying to get close to Elvis.

I felt sure that when I saluted my colonel back at the base and told him my mission was accomplished—Elvis was delivered to the base—that that would be the end of Elvis Presley and Sergeant Ira Jones.

CHARLES HOLMES: When Elvis first got to Germany and settled in, the commanding general called him in for an audience. Now, here's a private with a general. The general is very impressed about being around a star, but he's also impressed with being a general. He said he was going to put Elvis in Special Services. Elvis could appear in concerts around Europe to boost morale and bolster the image of the Army, help with recruitment and such. Elvis Presley told him (I heard through the grapevine), with all due respect, that he chose to serve as a regular soldier and not go into Special Services.

ED HART *(first lieutenant, platoon leader of the scout platoon, First Medium Tank Battalion of the 32nd Armor)*: Elvis was one of a group of replacements for our tank battalion that came in October of '58. I remember being in on a meeting as to what to do with him. The vivid thing I recall is that not only was he not to get any special treatment, but we were supposed to avoid even the perception that he was getting special treatment. At that meeting we went through a laborious exercise of what to do with him. Most of the guys in our company were specialists. There were also some jeep drivers, but most of the men who rode in the jeeps were officers. The Army didn't want Elvis to drive a jeep for an officer, 'cause then it would look like he had a big daddy looking after him. The decision was finally made to put him in the scout platoon, which had fourteen jeeps. If Elvis became a scout driver, he would probably drive for a sergeant. Ended up, he drove for Ira Jones.

IRA JONES: A week after I had met Elvis at the ship, my company commander asked me, "Sergeant Jones, what are you going to do with Elvis?" I said, "I already did, sir. I went to Bremerhaven, got him, and brought him back." He said, "Well, orders have changed. He's going to report to you tomorrow morning." Sure enough, next morning Elvis showed up for first formation of my reconnaissance platoon.

JOHN CALLENDER *(platoon sergeant)*: Because the headquarters jeep drivers slept with my platoon, the sergeant major called me up one day and introduced me to Elvis. Until he moved off, he fell under my command.

IRA JONES: Elvis was sharp, very determined, very quiet—didn't have much to say. When I gave him my "new soldier" speech, he asked a few questions and paid attention.

KEITH GIBSON *(Army buddy)*: When we heard Elvis was being assigned to our platoon, we weren't really all that impressed; we didn't have any idea how popular the guy really was. But gradually, as we heard more about him, and when his movies came out over there, it kinda sunk in. I told Elvis I admired him for not getting into Special Services but staying a regular soldier and getting in the mud and the snow just like everybody else did. He asked for no favors and got none.

JOHN CALLENDER: I had the job of taking Elvis around, gathering all his field equipment, getting him his military driver's license, and all that. Then when we went into the field, he was sometimes driving my jeep along with my regular driver. He really got a kick out of driving the jeep. Elvis was like a kid himself, in a way.

IRA JONES: I sent a couple of sergeants and Elvis and another driver out on a patrol. When they came back, they acted like they were the best of friends. That seemed unusual to me, because normally it takes at least a few days for new soldiers to relax with each other.

When he first arrived, Elvis was living in a hotel in town. Since he didn't have a car, I offered to give him a ride. All of a sudden I became more acquainted with what Elvis Presley was all about: As we drove up to his hotel, there were mobs of people all over the place, waiting for him!

LAMAR FIKE: Just after Elvis went over to Germany (about five days later), I flew over with Red West, Vernon, and Grandma on an eighteen-hour flight from New York to Frankfurt. We stayed in hotels at the beginning. Then we lived in a house at 14 Goethestrasse. Frau Pieper owned the house.

ED HART: Elvis settled right in. I didn't detect any difference in attitude from that of any of the other guys. He did have one privilege that most of his other bachelor contemporaries didn't. He was allowed to live off post. This was because his father and his grandmother, who were over there, were his dependents. The strict wording of the regulation was that if your dependents were in theater [area], then you were allowed to live off post. He lived in downtown Bad Nauheim, which was about a ten-minute drive from the kaserne, or base.

ANITA WOOD: After he got to Germany and rented a house, Elvis wanted me to come over. I had gotten my passport and everything, but Colonel Parker said, "No! There's no way she can go. [The press] will have you married, and it will just ruin you. You can't afford to do anything like that, because you'll need the good publicity when you come back from Germany to get back on track." So, I didn't get to go to Germany, but I took all the shots and got my passport. I was ready to go, and Elvis wanted me to come.

ED HART: Maybe we were paranoid, but I do recall that we were very, very concerned about the Russians. Our attitude in the fifties was that if we turned our backs for a minute, all the Russians in the world were going to come across that border. We had a very strong sense of mission.

KEITH GIBSON: Things were tense over there. In fact, we thought a couple of times that things were headed for war. Thank god they wasn't. When you've had supplies on order for two years and you can't get 'em, then all of a sudden they deliver 'em overnight; that's pretty serious. They were having trouble in Hungary; the people were trying to rebel against Communism. The president of the United States said on the radio that the Russians were getting ready to invade Hungary, and all [the Hungarians] have to do is ask for our help and they've got it. That would've been us, the troops stationed in Germany. Thankfully, that never happened.

ED HART: We were only say fifty, sixty miles from the East German border —not all that far back. We had a fifteen percent rule—no more than fifteen percent of any unit could be away from the base at any given time. It even applied at night. You had to have eighty-five percent of the troops on post at all times. The battalion had to be ready to roll out in two hours, but for our [Elvis's] platoon the notice was thirty minutes, 'cause we had to get on the road ahead of the battalion to mark the route for the tanks.

IRA JONES: Our platoon was responsible for checking the bridges and roads throughout a large area of Germany. Elvis was very quiet, but I noticed that when he went out with a crew or something, pretty quick they'd all be real friendly with him.

One day we headed out on a trip to Kitzengen, and there's a little snack bar there; so we always had a vote as to whether we'd stop for sandwiches. Of course the guys voted to stop. I knew they would. But Elvis kind of froze. He didn't want to go in. I asked him, "What's wrong?" He said, "Back in the States I get in trouble going out in public where there are a lot of people—restaurants and places like that." So the guys in the platoon kind of gathered around and said, "Oh, come on. We can protect you."

Well, we went in and had sandwiches. There wasn't anybody seemed to pay any attention. I said kind of joking, "Elvis, you may be in more trouble than you think. You may be in an area where no one knows who you are or cares." But when we finished our sandwiches and started to leave, I opened the door, and I guess there were one hundred to one hundred-fifty people outside. I was sort of shocked. He autographed for awhile, then we got in our jeep and went on about our business.

KEITH GIBSON: He was just as common as an old shoe. I felt really sorry for him. Elvis couldn't go nowhere, to a movie, out to eat, or nowhere. He was so popular; everybody knew him. He had to stay confined just to survive. Be nice to have his money, but all that fame'd be kinda hard to live with.

Anywhere he went there was a crowd. I thought, "Man, how do you put up with that?" I think he loved the fame, but everybody needs a way to escape to themselves every once in awhile.

IRA JONES: If I had to rate Elvis as a soldier, I'd rate him very high—the highest. He really knew the basics, and they say he'd done well in basic training at Fort Hood—caught on fast. He was good with vehicles. Even though there were a lot of guys who tried to help him, he maintained that vehicle very well by himself.

ED HART: I would characterize Elvis's attitude as good but realistic. He was a typical draftee for those days: he wasn't extremely crazy about being there, but as long as he had to be there, he was going to do a good job. In those days, the late fifties, being drafted was just looked on by most young Americans as a thing you had to do before you could get into your life. Most young men got drafted. They did their two years in the Army, and then they went on to whatever it was they were going to do.

:◎:◎:◎:

MARY LOU POPE *(fan, daughter of Naomia Stiers)*: Mom and Mildred [Eden] formed a fan club in Texas in order to keep Elvis on top while he was overseas. They would buy up every new Elvis record that was put out, and they would ask all of the other fan club members to buy every record. Mom and Mildred would go around town on days off and put dimes (that's when it just cost a dime) in all the jukeboxes and play his records over and over.

When they would go on trips out of town, Mom and Mildred would buy stacks of penny postcards. We would write radio stations in different styles and sign different names and mail them from all over, requesting Elvis's records. We had all the fan club members do the same thing. We'd send them to local radio stations and to [Dick Clark's] *American Bandstand* [television show].

MAE AXTON: While Elvis was in Germany, we had a thing back in Jacksonville—a get together just to remember him and let him know that everybody still cared. It was held out in a big open field. All we did was play Elvis records. Do you know, eight thousand people showed up!

:◉:◉:◉:

ED HART: I had a friend who was an adjutant of a unit up in Bad Hersfeld, and when we had to go there, he used to let my guys stay in the barracks with the troops in the cavalry. Of course, back in those days the haircut regulations were very, very stringent. You generally had to get a haircut every week to comply with regulations. We came rolling in on a Saturday, and we took care of our equipment and our vehicles, but we hadn't had a chance to get a haircut that week.

So on Monday we all lined up for morning formation, and the first sergeant announced that a German Red Cross team would be on post that day and they were having a blood drive. Anybody that gave blood would get the rest of the day off. 'Course, the whole dang company took one step forward!

They picked a certain number of guys from each platoon. Presley was one of the guys from scout platoon that went to give blood, and while he was there, somebody from the press took his picture—it was good "copy." First thing in the morning the commanding general from Frankfurt called our first sergeant and says, "I saw Presley's picture in the paper this morning! Sergeant, you take him out and get him a haircut!" 'Course, none of our guys had a haircut. They were shaggy, too. But it was Elvis's picture they took.

IRA JONES: I told Elvis once, "You know you look a lot better without those sideburns." He said, "I feel better, too, but they're worth a million bucks apiece."

JOHN CALLENDER: Elvis used to sing with Jones a lot. They'd sing little songs and hymns. Elvis would think nothing of buying a case or two of Cokes and bring 'em out and just let all the guys help themselves.

IRA JONES: I whistle and hum whatever I'm doing, and Elvis said one day as we were driving along, "Sergeant Jones, I know that song you're whistling." He said, "In fact, I know every song there is." I kinda laughed and said, "That's pretty hard to believe, Elvis. I'm older than you and I know a whole lot of old songs." He said, "Try me." We had this kind of a game; we done it all the time. Sure enough, I don't think I ever stumped him at all.

JOHN CALLENDER: The Germans adored Elvis and, you know, just him going home from the base at night was always a hassle. Lots of times one of us would take him home. He'd get in the back seat of the car and lay down, and we'd drive out through the gate. The Germans would be crowded around in front of the gate just waiting to see him; they all wanted to holler at him or touch him. It was a real problem for Elvis, but he handled it; he didn't have much choice being who he was and everything. When we'd be out in smaller towns, we usually moved the jeeps out in front of the tanks and posted road guards at intersections, but we couldn't use Elvis for anything like that, 'cause as soon as the Germans recognized him they'd just block the roads. They had a hell of a communication system there in Germany! If he was spotted, it didn't take long for a crowd to gather. They just all wanted to get around him.

Jones usually had Elvis park his jeep out on a hill during maneuvers. He had the radios to use for a relay in case we needed one. That way, Elvis was out in the woods someplace and didn't cause crowd problems.

ED HART: When we went to a training area, Elvis would stay in the barracks with all the other troops. Occasionally when my driver wasn't available, he'd drive my jeep. Ira Jones was the number-two guy in the platoon; although, in reality, he ran the damn thing. Most all sergeants do, you know.

I didn't think Elvis was that big a deal back in those days. I was not a real big fan of his. And even though I knew he was a celebrity, I was well prepared to just treat him like one of the troops. But at platoon level you're close to your guys. You talk to 'em a lot. You're not like Moses handing down the tablets. When you're out in the field you're up to your neck in the same slop your troops are.

It didn't take long to realize that Elvis was an outstanding soldier. He never asked for anything because of his status. He got along outstandingly with the other young troops; they were basically close to his age. It was never, you know, "Well I'm a big shot and you're just little people." He got right in with everybody.

JOHN CALLENDER: Once we went into a German tavern late at night to eat. It was wintertime and we all put our parka hoods up when we went in so the Germans wouldn't recognize Elvis, because we weren't supposed to be in a place like that. We hadn't got fed that night, so we went in to get what they call *schnitzel*. Everything went good until we were getting ready to leave. I had collected the money from everybody and I was going up to pay for it, and Elvis came walking up behind me to go out the door. The owner's daughter was standing in the kitchen, and she saw Elvis and just screamed, "Der Presley!" Of course all the other GIs took off out the door; we had a contingency plan for that. We jumped in the jeep and took off out of town with him. We all laughed about it, 'til it came out in a German paper; then Ira and I had to go down and explain it all to the battalion staff officer—explain that we weren't in there partying; we had just stopped in to eat.

IRA JONES: I wanted to go somewhere one day, and the chow line was real long; so I said, "Come on, Elvis, I'll put you at the head of the line so we can leave." Right quick Elvis said, "Sergeant Jones, I can't do that." I asked him, "Why not?" He said, "It would look like I was getting special treatment."

I could have done the same thing with some other driver and there wouldn't have been anything said, but since it was Elvis and he didn't want to look bad to the other guys, I waited until he got through eating, and then we left. He was very sensitive about the feelings of the other soldiers.

JOHN CALLENDER: A lot of the Germans I knew would ask me to get his autograph, and they'd bring in pictures of him to be signed. I'd find out what their name was and I'd ask him, "Can you sign this?" I'd show him the name in German, and he'd spell it out and sign his name. Then I'd give it back to the Germans. He never said, "No, I don't have any time," or "I'm too busy," or anything like that.

IRA JONES: Sometimes when we were out in the field or somewhere and we weren't too busy, we'd have kind of group singing things. This is not unusual for an Army platoon, but in this case the guys had a kind of little motivation. They wanted to get in on the act, I suppose. Anyway, when everyone would be singing, Elvis would not distinguish himself from the other singers. I noticed this out on patrol one day. He didn't sound any better or worse or louder than all the rest of us. That was, of course, on purpose, so he'd fit in and make everybody feel equal.

One day when we had coffee call, Elvis asked me, "Sergeant Jones, is there a piano in the NCO club?" "Yeah," I told him. "There's an old one in there." He asked, "Can we take our coffee and go in there?" I said we could, and I could tell by the way he looked at me that this time the rest of us weren't supposed to put our two-bits worth in by singing with him. Well, he sat down behind the piano and poured it on. I mean he went from rock 'n' roll to gospel to country and back to rock 'n' roll again. The guys loved it.

There was a cleaning lady in there. She was in her mid-fifties, I'd say. At first she was trying not to pay any attention to Elvis, but it wasn't long before she was froze right in her tracks. When our break was up and he was finished, he stood up and started to go back to work, but he seen her standing over there. She had a piece of paper in her hand. So he went over and signed her an autograph, got out his handkerchief, wiped her tears, and kissed her on the cheek—then went back to work.

JOHN CALLENDER: We were out on maneuvers one time, and, jeez, it was cold that night! There was an old latrine out on this hill. I guess it was about a six- or ten-seater. It was a big one, and everybody piled in there and put ponchos up around the walls to keep the wind out. We lit a couple of mountain cooksets—little one-burner Coleman stoves—to get some heat. As we each pulled guard that night, we kept a jeep running, and the guy on guard would get in his sleeping bag and get up on the hood of the jeep to get whatever heat he could off of it. Winter in Germany got really cold; but Elvis was right in there with the rest of 'em. That was probably the first time something like that ever happened to him. He probably got a kick out of it. If Elvis ever did any complaining about Army life, he did it at home; he never complained around us.

ARLENE COGAN: Elvis talked on the phone about how bitter cold it was out on maneuvers, and how he had to do all kinds of things just to keep warm. Of course, he talked a great deal about how much he missed home and missed us. He always knew exactly to the month and week, how much time he had left to serve. Every time I talked to him he told me.

DOTTY AYERS: While Elvis was in the Army, Earl Greenwood and I did his fan club and answered all the mail. Elvis wrote us some short, handwritten letters when he was out on maneuvers. I guess all the boys were writing home and Elvis wanted to be one of the boys. He always talked about how much he missed Graceland.

FRANCES FORBES: Oh, gosh, I never expected a letter from Elvis. I thought it was a joke when I first saw the envelope. What was so funny was a little later that day Alan Fortas called and said, "You'll never believe this, but I got a letter from Elvis." I said, "So what? I got one, too."

It's a treasure. The highlight of my letter is at the bottom where Elvis signed, "All my love."

PAUL BURLISON: While he was overseas, Elvis was always calling home. Every time he talked with somebody he would say, "What's Orbison got out? What's Orbison doing?" If Orbison had the looks that Elvis had, oh, man!

FRED FREDRICK: Roy Orbison was Elvis's favorite singer of all time. Elvis said that his was the most perfect voice.

ARLENE COGAN: One time when I was talking to Elvis on the phone while he was in Germany, he said, "Arlene, will you please, please send me a box of Reese's peanut butter cups? I can't get them over here and I'm dying to have some." Well, I went out and bought several boxes of them, went to the post office, and sent 'em off to him. The next time I talked to him I said, "Oh, Elvis, did you get the peanut butter cups?" And he says, "Yes, honey, I did. Thank you so much! They were all melted but I ate them anyway."

:◎:◎:◎:

JOHN CALLENDER: When our unit would go to Grafenwöhr for training for a month—that's down northeast of Nuremberg about fifty miles—Elvis would have to stay in the barracks at night. He was always clowning around with the guys there 'cause we couldn't go anyplace but the movies, and he'd sing a little bit.

But when he was off duty in Bad Nauheim, he'd go to the villa he had rented. He had his family and friends there. Some of the platoon would go over there, and they'd horse around, play football, and stuff like that.

LAMAR FIKE: It was pretty normal at night; we'd sing around the piano 'cause we had no TV. In a way, it was humdrum. On holidays we'd drive to Munich or Paris or somewhere like that.

In Paris we stayed at the Hotel Prince de Galles and we went to all the shows—the Moulin Rouge, the Lido, the Folies Bergère. That's when Elvis felt once again like the star he was, 'cause everyone mobbed him.

KEITH GIBSON: Heck, you couldn't even go in a restaurant to eat dinner 'cause Elvis would always draw a crowd. Lots of times we'd go in to eat and it'd just be me and him. I'd tell him to pull his hat down over his eyes, and he would; but instead of sitting in the shadows where you might have a hard time recognizing him, he'd find the lightest place in the restaurant to sit. Later, I'd try to get him out of there quietly. I'd tell him to go on out to the jeep and I would pay the bill, but he'd just kinda stand there by the register and shake his head 'til his hat would fall off. I'm sure he did it on purpose so people could recognize him. I kidded him lots about it, and we had a lot of fun.

One day we were in Grafenwöhr and I was just piddling around working. He said, "Why don't you come go with me? I gotta go to Friedberg. There are some papers I have to sign." I just smiled and said, "Well, have a good time." He said, "Aw, come go with me." I said, "E. P., man, I can't get off duty, and besides, how are you going?" He said, "I'm gonna hire a taxi." I thought he was kidding, but he wasn't. He took a cab a hundred and fifty miles and had the cab wait for him and bring him all the way back. Must have cost him a fortune. Elvis traveled first class.

LAMAR FIKE: The first time Priscilla [Beaulieu] came to visit, we were living at the house in Bad Nauheim. Elvis's friend Currie Grant brought her. She was fourteen years old and living in Germany with her mom and dad. Her dad was in the Army and was stationed there. She came into the living room and she had on a little sailor blouse. Her hair was in ringlets. Elvis came in the living room to meet her, and I introduced her to him. She sat over there on the couch most of the afternoon, and she went home about six-thirty or seven that night. A week or two later she came back again, and after that she was there a lot. She was smitten. Goddamn, she wouldn't have been human if she hadn't been. He started dating her. The queasy thing about it was that she was fourteen years old!

Most of the time I had to drive to Weisbaden to pick her up, and then take her home late at night. Sometimes the fog would be so thick you couldn't tell where the road started and ended. One night I was driving her home and the fog was horrible. We couldn't see where we were going, and I had to get her home. I said, "Look, why don't you get out and just walk in front of the car. She said, "I'll do that." She got about four or five yards in front of the car, and I was just creeping along behind her. She walked to the top of the hill and the fog got a little better, so she got back in the car and we creeped to her house.

CHARLES HOLMES: In 1959, Elvis Presley's time was winding down, so they did the background shooting for *G.I. Blues* in the little German town of Idstein, which is on the Rhine River south of Frankfurt. Idstein is a beautiful little town with castles and such. They were shooting a couple of scenes there, and I had a bit part as a jeep driver—drove past a restaurant. Elvis, of course, didn't do anything on the movie until he got out of the Army. A fellow named Tom Creel from Mississippi was Elvis Presley's stand-in. A lot of the German girls thought Tom was Elvis Presley, and Tom signed autographs for them. I signed as "Tab Holmes."

LAMAR FIKE: The time in Germany was kind of a reprieve of sorts for Elvis. He just did his job, and that's all he really wanted to do. It was a two-year relief, really.

:◎:◎:◎:

DOTTY AYERS: After Elvis sent Vernon home from Germany I went to Graceland to spend some time with him. Vernon said, "I got sent home from school!" and kinda laughed.

Vernon was telling us about this woman that he had met, and about how much trouble he was in with Elvis. Vernon said, "I don't think that it's this woman in particular; I think it would be any woman right now that Elvis thinks was taking his mother's place." Vernon said that he really thought he was going to get married and that she had these three boys. Her name was Dee Stanley.

CHRISTINE ROBERTS PRESLEY: I heard about Vernon and that woman he was with. Them Presleys were bad about such as that.

"Where He Left Off"
1960

When Elvis returns from his stint in Germany, Memphis extends a hero's welcome to its favorite son. Happy to be home, Elvis flings open the gates of Graceland in an attempt to recapture his glory days. Collecting new recruits like Jim Crowe and Bill Browder for his faithful group, Elvis and his Graceland troops resume their all-night excursions to his much-missed local amusements.

Soon, with his eager entourage at his side, Elvis travels to Nashville and begins again making music with the Jordanaires. Then it's off to Hollywood and the silver screen, where buddies Red West and Alan Fortas get into the act. A dazzling schedule of soundtrack recording follows, winning Elvis a bevy of new fans.

Gradually, however, friends realize that Elvis has changed amid rumors that a young girl named Priscilla Beaulieu has caught the fancy of the man destined to become known as the king of rock 'n' roll.

> "Now the Army changes 'em. It sure does. It makes a different person out of 'em."
>
> Annie Cloyd Presley

Bill E. Burk: When Elvis was scheduled to come back home to Memphis after his tour of duty in Germany, there was a big cash-prize contest for who could get the first interview with him. Well, I heard that the train Elvis was gonna be on would stop for a moment at Grand Junction, east of Memphis. My photographer and I sneaked aboard at that stop, but Lamar Fike, a member of Elvis's entourage, intercepted us on the train in Elvis's car. We were scuffling with Lamar in the hallway, and Elvis was in the latrine area at the other end of the hallway. He heard the noise and stuck his head out the door, standing there in just his skivvies. He had his toothbrush in his hand and toothpaste all over his mouth, and he asked, "What's going on?" I said, "Lamar don't want us on the train." Elvis told Lamar it was okay to let us stay, and at that moment I thought, "We're sitting on a gold mine!" I said to my photographer, "Every time he breathes in, take a picture, and every time he breathes out, take a picture."

From Grand Junction to Memphis was just under an hour, and my photographer took three hundred sixty photographs in that period of time, and I got my interview.

As the train was heading toward Memphis, Elvis put on his Army dress uniform—a navy blue coat and light blue pants. When he put on his jacket, I noticed he was showing four stripes—the stripes of a staff sergeant. I said, "Hey, man, wait a minute. You just made sergeant; you're not a staff sergeant." He said, "The tailor made a mistake." To this day I still believe the man with the flair—Tom Parker—knowing all those pictures were going to be taken, had that fourth stripe put on because it had more prestige.

We pulled into the station just at the deadline for the first edition of the paper, so I had to dash down and turn the story in. It took up about three-quarters of page one and all of page two, so it was a very exciting moment.

Arlene Cogan: I was right there at the station when Elvis got off that train. He came and hugged me the minute he saw me. We let him go home by himself first. He told us all, "Come on up by eight o'clock."

The only major change at Graceland when Elvis came home was, obviously, that his mother was no longer there. I think it must have been hard for Elvis. Still, he was ecstatic about being home. Elvis was not a person of change. He basically always remained the same. The only difference I noticed about him was that he was maybe a little more mature.

GEORGE KLEIN: When Elvis came back from Germany, I saw a much more mature guy—a guy who was ready to take care of business. He had a little harder side at first, but then he softened up. The Army will put an edge on you. He had that Army hardness to him, but it disappeared after awhile, and he became Elvis again.

At first we thought the Army situation was a bad deal for him, but now I look back on it and think it kind of brought him back down to earth. He kind of settled down a little and saw another side of life. You know, he went from poor to rich—boom, like that! There wasn't any in-between. Then the Army brought him back down to earth. I think that was good.

ARLENE COGAN: Elvis didn't mention Priscilla 'til after he came home, at least not to me. When he did, I felt he was just infatuated with her beauty, because he never talked about anything else but her beauty. He said she had the most beautiful eyes he'd ever seen. He never even talked about how nice she was, or what a wonderful personality she had. I thought he was infatuated with how she looked more than anything.

FRANCES FORBES: Before Elvis went to Germany it had been just the elite little group. Elvis didn't see too many strangers. When he came home from Germany, especially the first few months, it was like he just opened the gates and anybody who wanted to could come in. It was a big party then. There were so many people, I can't remember all their names . . . just people that he surrounded himself with the whole time. I don't know if Elvis missed the activity and the things that he did before he went into the Army, or if he was grateful that people remembered him.

DOTTY AYERS: Elvis brought a lot of boys back with him [from Germany] that we didn't know. He brought Joe Esposito and Charlie Hodge. He had a different crowd. He picked up that Richard Davis and a few others. It ceased being a hometown crowd where everybody was just friends and hung out.

They came girl-hunting, if you know what I mean. The guys would canvas the gate down there and the theater and every place and look over the girls that they might like to go with. The Memphis guys seemed to get along with the new crowd okay, but eventually a lot of the older friends were kinda pushed out.

BUZZY FORBES: It was always hard to get time with Elvis with so many people around. He and Paul [Dougher] and I went and got inside a broom closet one night, turned the little ol' light on with the switch (nothing but us and the mops and the brooms) to get away from everybody where we could spend some time and go over the old days and talk.

FRANCES FORBES: After Elvis first came home from Germany, I met Joe Esposito for the first time. Joe was always one of my favorite people. We were in the living room, just cutting up, and Elvis came in there, and he threatened to throw us both out if we didn't stay away from each other. He was kidding—and he wasn't kidding. Elvis was very possessive, very jealous.

:◉:◉:◉:

MACK GURLEY: Elvis had only been home for about two weeks when he went to record for the first time in two years. The session [March 20, 21, and 30, 1960] was at RCA Studios in Nashville.

RAY WALKER: We were all at RCA Victor getting ready to do a session, and we didn't know whether to expect Elvis at seven o'clock, eight o'clock, or nine o'clock. We were facing the control room, listening to that lousy record player (Presley had said it looked like they could afford to get him one that would work after all the records he'd sold). No one was facing that back entrance door, and Presley had never come in any way except through the side or the front door and through the control room. So we were kind of watching for him there.

Well, we were listening to demos that Freddy Bienstock [manager of Hill and Range Music Publishers] was hoping Presley would record. The record player was playing loud, people were talking to each other; some were taking notes. Even with the record player going, everybody—there were twenty-three of us in that room—everybody turned around at one time when Presley just had walked in the back door. He hadn't made a sound—you couldn't have heard it if he had—but everybody, just like we were on pivots, turned, and there he was.

It was a strange feeling. It's much like if you have children or something, you sense something about your child, or you sense something about your wife or your mother. Presley walked into that room, and everybody turned. Now that really made me think, "What a burden this boy's got to carry!" Because if you have that mystique about you, and you affect people that way with just a physical presence, it's hard to have any privacy at all.

NEAL MATTHEWS: Yeah, when Elvis walked into a room, everybody there just knew his presence. He just had it. Some people do and some people don't. That sort of appeal made him dynamic.

RAY WALKER: In and out of the studio, Presley had a great sense of humor. I've seen Presley laugh until it was unbelievable. He would laugh over some silly little something that was happening until he couldn't even sing.

One time at a recording session they'd been getting some interference on the recording. There had been a tall, blonde-haired woman in there, probably in her middle fifties, dressed in bright red with a chiffon stole and real high, pointed heels. I had no idea who she was. Bill Porter [engineer for RCA] was doing the session, and he said, "I guess we're just going to have to go out there and kick that box." The woman walked out into the studio and kicked the transformer box clear across the studio.

They told Presley about that and it struck him funny. He laughed 'til he couldn't sing. He laughed and then he couldn't keep from making remarks like, "Man, I can't afford to shed any tears or my mascara will run." Then he'd get tickled all over again, and we might laugh for thirty minutes.

JOAN DEARY: After Steve Sholes turned over the production of Elvis's records to Chet Atkins, Chet guided the sessions musically and technically but did not interfere with the creativity. He just complemented it, reinforced it. When he'd hear something that wasn't working, he'd say, "Well, let's try the chorus doing this," or something like that. He was gentle, but knowledgeable and firm.

EDDIE FADAL: Elvis didn't think he could do something as operatic or classical as "It's Now or Never," and I think that record gave him a bit of confidence in himself, confidence that he could do anything he really wanted to.

MACK GURLEY: After that thirteen-hour session at RCA, Elvis and I were sitting in regular fold-up chairs in front of these large speakers, listening to the tapes he had just done. He would turn to me and say, "Does that sound okay? How do you like that? Anything you'd change on this?" I thought, "Who am I to know or be able to advise him on anything?" I would just say, "It still just baffles me that you're able to do this and do it so well."

JOAN DEARY: RCA went gung ho—went all out—for Elvis after he got back to the States. I think by serving in the Army he had added another faction of society to his fan base. We released "Are You Lonesome Tonight?" and "It's Now or Never."

EDDIE FADAL: The record shot up to number one on the charts and stayed there for five weeks in a row.

JOAN DEARY: These records were not at all based on the same appeal as "That's All Right (Mama)" and "Hound Dog" and "Don't Be Cruel." Suddenly Elvis was not just for kids.

RCA had a musical director by the name of Hugo Winterhalter—he was one of our top musical directors and he did big orchestra stuff. His wife called one day and asked for a copy of "Are You Lonesome Tonight?" I thought, "There you are. That just shows how widespread Elvis's appeal is."

MAE AXTON: Shortly after Elvis came back from Germany, he and the Colonel invited me down to Miami where he was taping a big TV special with Frank Sinatra [March 26, 1960]. Elvis was excited about being there, but he was almost in awe of Sinatra—and Sinatra was almost in awe of him. They just got along great. Elvis had gooey stuff in his hair, and it was poofed up real big. It was all black and shiny. Rehearsal was actually the fun part. They cut up a lot and did silly things. Too bad they didn't put the rehearsal on TV—outtakes, you know.

The Colonel had given people tickets on the condition they would really scream and yell 'cause I think he was fearful that folks wouldn't really remember Elvis that well. But he needn't have bothered. When Elvis walked out, the whole place went wild!

While we were there, the Jordanaires and I went back to the hotel and got on the elevator up to the floor where Elvis and all his guests were staying. It was a modern, automated elevator, but when we got on, this little girl was there all dressed up in a bell captain's uniform and a little cap. She said, "Which floor, please?" Well, we knew right away that she wasn't legit, and I looked at the Jordanaires and smiled, but we told her the floor and she pressed the button. When we got to the floor, she jumped out right in front of us and took off down the hall trying to find Elvis's suite! A guard stopped her, of course, and she began to say she was carrying an important message for Elvis, and all sorts of other reasons why they should let her in. She tried everything. We watched all this and really got a kick out of it. 'Course, she never got into the room.

:◎:◎:◎:

NAOMIA STIERS: I finally got to meet Elvis in April 1960, and he really surprised me. We were sitting in his living room there at Graceland, several other fan club people and myself. I was talking to someone, and Mildred walked up behind me and said, "Mrs. Stiers, I want you to meet somebody." I turned around and looked up at this tall, gorgeous man! He was the most beautiful creature I ever saw in my life. He had the most beautiful blue eyes, beautiful complexion. It was Elvis, of course. I couldn't believe it. I had seen him on the screen and thought he was beautiful, but unless you saw him in person, you couldn't understand how much more beautiful he really was. He took hold of my hand and held hands with me and asked me where I was from. "Houston, Texas," I said. "That's my old stomping ground," he told me. We were just standing there chatting. He was still holding my hand when Mildred walked back up and said, "Are you gonna hold his hand all night?" He just laid his other hand over our clasped hands and said, "I just might do that. This is a nice little hand."

He was one of the most polite people I ever met. I had him sign an autograph for me, and he asked me how to spell my name. I told him, and later, much, much later, I took another photograph up there that I wanted signed, and he didn't even ask my name. He just wrote it down—and spelled it right, too. He always knew me when he saw me.

MARY LOU POPE: When Mom [Naomia Stiers] came home, she was on cloud nine. She really did love meeting him. She said he was even more than what she had thought he would be. She said he was even more handsome, too, but I think it was something more than that.

NAOMIA STIERS: We had gotten pretty well acquainted with Travis and Loraine [Smith, Elvis's uncle and aunt] while Elvis was away in Germany, so the first time we went back to Graceland after Elvis came home, we didn't have any problem getting in whenever we wanted to see him. There was always a large crowd of people out front. My friend Mildred's husband had given her a black-and-pink custom-built Lincoln Continental for Christmas. (Pink was Elvis's color then.) Any time that black-and-pink Continental drove up, if Travis (who worked at the gate) was there, he let us go through. We got out and went in at the front door. There were usually other fans in there with us.

CHERYLE JOHNSON *(fan)*: I went to Graceland with Mildred and Naomia and some others when I was about twelve or thirteen. Elvis was just back from the Army. I met him then. He got us all together and thanked us all for what we'd done—all the work of the fan clubs, all the support.

Naomia and Elvis had a real special relationship. They really did. He kind of treated Naomia like a mom. He always called her "sweet lady." Naomia really related to him like a son. She was with Elvis a lot and she stayed a loyal fan for many, many years—still is.

NAOMIA STIERS: I only heard Elvis sing one time in person, and that was in his home. It was just before "Such a Night" was released, and he kept singing a few words to it over and over. Finally he asked me, "You like that?" and I said, "Yes." Then he sang two or three more words; then finally he played it on his piano and sang it all the way through.

Elvis didn't like for us to play his records at Graceland. If someone put a record [by Elvis] on [the turntable], they'd have to turn it off. I never put one on, but one of the other girls did it a time or two just to see what he'd do. The minute it started playing, he started down the stairs. He gave the girl a kind of a look, so she shut it off. He didn't like to hear himself sing, I guess. I don't know.

One night we were all in the dining room, and Elvis and one of his cousins started practicing karate and breaking those big boards—you know how they do it. They had practiced for quite some time and they had a big pile of boards. I said, "Loraine, could I have one of them for a souvenir?" Loraine said, "Sure." Well, I went and picked up a board, and when I did, everybody else picked up one. Before you knew it all the boards disappeared.

Later on, after everybody else had gone home (see, Mildred and I always stayed around longer than anybody else), I went into the kitchen for something, and Elvis was sitting at his little dinette eating out of a bowl of banana pudding. I waited a little while and then I asked, "Elvis, when you get through with that, would you do something for me?" He said, "Yes, Ma'am." I said, "Would you autograph this board for me?" He laughed and shook his head. "I've been asked to autograph an awful lot of things, but never an old board! I laid the board down there and said, "Now put something else on there besides just your name." So he wrote up at the top of it, "Thanks. Elvis Presley." Mildred had got two boards, and she had come in and wanted him to autograph hers; but he only put "Elvis Presley" on her boards. So mine is one of a kind.

A fellow offered me fifteen hundred dollars for that board, but I wouldn't take it. I told him I intend to keep it as long as I live.

WILL "BARDAHL" MCDANIEL: I'd pick the boards up and throw 'em in the garbage—never saved 'em, never thought about it. We could have gone out of the house with truckloads full of junk—junk then, it would be priceless now. We never thought about souvenirs back then.

ARLENE COGAN: All Elvis wanted while he was in Germany was to come back home, and contrary to what people say, Elvis picked right up where he left off with the parties at home, going to the fairgrounds, the movies, and wherever. None of that changed.

NAOMIA STIERS: We were at the show one night. Elvis had invited a bunch of us to go to the movies with him. We were still out in the lobby waiting for it to get started. I wasn't standing very near to Elvis, but there was a little girl about five years old standing there by me and she started crying. When I asked her what was wrong, she told me she had a card she wanted Elvis to sign, but she'd lost it. A woman took a little piece of paper out of her purse and handed it to the little girl. She walked over to Elvis and wanted him to sign her little piece of paper. After he signed it, she held that paper, just held it in her little hand, and was smiling real big. Her father walked up and told Elvis, "If I hadn't been a fan of yours before, I certainly would be now because you have made my little girl happier than anyone else possibly could have." There were tears in the man's eyes, he was so touched. Elvis told him, "It was my great pleasure to do it."

JIM CROWE *(friend)*: There was many nights we'd leave the house and go to the show, sit there and watch two or three shows, all go back to the house, and sit around for a little while. Then Elvis would say, "Shoot, let's go skating."

So they'd make arrangements, and we'd take off and go skating. We'd be there 'til the sun come up. It was hard on the ones that had regular jobs.

Me and Jim Kingsley worked at the same cotton company uptown, just right before Kingsley went to work for Elvis. We spent many a night out at Graceland 'til daylight. We'd go home, change clothes, go to work, come back home, lay down, get back up, get ready, go out to the house, party all night long again; then we'd do the same thing and go back to work.

JEAN CROWE *(Jim's wife)*: Jim got fired for falling asleep on his lunch break!

JIM CROWE: Jean and I would go to the fairgrounds with Elvis. He would rent it maybe one or two nights a week. We'd go out there between eleven and twelve o'clock—it just depended on what time he felt like going—and we'd be there 'til daylight.

One night we were at the fairgrounds and all the guys were standing around talking. Kingsley happened to notice the watch Elvis had on. He told Elvis, "That's a nice-looking watch. Pretty watch you got on there." Elvis said, "You like that?" Of course, we all looked. About a minute or two later we was talking, and Elvis raised his arm up and he took the watch off and handed it to Kingsley. Kingsley said, "What are you doing?" Elvis said, "Well, that's something about me. If somebody sees something that I have that they admire, I can't help myself. I've just got to give it to 'em."

So right at that time the rest of the guys learned never to comment on anything Elvis was wearing, 'cause we found out how quick you'd end up owning it. That's the way Elvis was. It caught us all off guard when he done that.

BILL BROWDER *(later known by his stage name,* T. G. Sheppard): I met Elvis back in the early sixties, probably '61 or '62. I was a sixteen-year-old kid, a runaway at fifteen from Humbolt, Tennessee, my hometown. I guess like any kid that age I wanted to do something in music, and my father was dead-set against that. I wanted to be a singer, so I hitchhiked to Memphis, lived there for a while on the streets and in doorways. Then I sucked up my pride and went and called on my mother; she had moved to Memphis, so I lived with her for awhile.

I'd go skating at night out at the Rainbow Skating Rink, and one night I was walking out of the skating rink as they were closing it up. Two big pink Cadillacs pulled up, and Elvis gets out of one of them and starts talking to me! I was kind of flabbergasted! He asked me if I would come inside and skate with them. Of course I did. After we got through skating, we all went back to Graceland. We ate some sandwiches, shot some pool, and hung around the house 'til daylight; then I went home. I felt like that would be it, but I left my phone number with Elvis's people just in case.

I even went back to the skating rink several times, but they never showed up. I thought, "Well, that's it." But a week or two later, I was sitting at home in the afternoon and the phone rang. It was Elvis. He called direct. He said, "I met you. Do you remember?" The question should have been mine, "Do you remember me?" He said, "We're going skating tonight if you'd like to go, and afterwards we're going to the movies. If you wanna come, meet us out there about midnight." Well, that was the start. I kept going to his parties and we became friends.

:◎:◎:◎:

JIM CROWE: Vernon was always around [Graceland] somewhere. Before he married Dee [Stanley], he would wander downstairs and stand around and talk to the guys a lot of times. Sometimes he'd come down there and play pool with them. Mostly he'd come in, see Elvis, and he'd be gone.

DOTTY AYERS: Vernon had been totally devoted to Gladys when she was still alive. He had lived such a quiet life, and I saw how upset he was at her funeral. I knew that Vernon needed somebody.

ARLENE COGAN: Alan Fortas, Earl Greenwood, Elvis, and I had been out boat-riding on McKellar Lake [in south Memphis] one afternoon, and when we returned to Graceland, Elvis asked Alberta, his maid, to prepare dinner for three extra.

We were all sitting in the small dining room off the kitchen having pork chops and potatoes. It was the evening that Vernon and Dee were getting married down in Alabama. Elvis had refused to attend the wedding. Instead, he talked about his dislike for Dee. He said he didn't trust her, and he said that there was no way that he could ever think to call her "mother;" that would never in his life happen.

He was not liking the fact that she was going to be married to his father, but he said if she would make his father happy, then that's all he really cared about. He said that up 'til then, he'd had all his property and money in his dad's name, but he told us he had put everything back in his own name 'cause he didn't trust Dee.

BILLY STANLEY *(stepbrother)*: I was seven when Mom and Vernon got married. My brother David was four and my brother Rick was five. When we first drove up to Graceland I thought it was the biggest house I'd ever seen. It was like driving through the pearly gates, almost. Elvis seemed larger than life when I first met him, and it kind of scared me. But I got over it quick.

Elvis was shooting pool and he came up to us and said to Vernon, "Daddy, I always wanted a little brother, and now I have three." The love I felt for him that day—that is my single greatest memory of him.

The next morning we woke up and found three of every kind of toy you could imagine in the backyard. I thought Elvis was Santa Claus for a long time. We'd been in a boarding school and that was probably the first time in nine months that we'd seen love.

ARLENE COGAN: Vernon and Dee were sleeping in Gladys's old bedroom on the first floor, and Elvis was not liking that at all.

JIM CROWE: There was always maybe twenty or thirty people around the house, something like that. There was Sonny West and Jerry Schilling, and, of course, Joe Esposito, Alan Fortas, Lamar Fike, and a guy we called Chief—his name was Ray Sitton—and lots of others.

ALAN FORTAS: The press started calling Elvis's group of guys the Memphis Mafia. That's how it originated. Elvis hated it, but most of the guys kinda enjoyed it. They thought it was funny.

GEORGE KLEIN: Elvis tried to hire me several times and I very graciously bowed out. I said, "Elvis, I like to do my own thing, but I'd still like to keep the doors open so I could go on the road with you sometime." He said, "Anytime. You've got an open invitation."

PAUL DOUGHER: Elvis was always wanting me to travel with him. I told him once, "Look, I see these other guys you have around you and the way they have to do things for you all the time. You would probably tell me to do such and such and I wouldn't want to do it. Then we would get into an argument. I'd rather just be friends. If I went with you and worked for you, it wouldn't be the same. Somewhere down the line we would disagree, and I don't want that." He said, "No, we won't. You could do whatever you wanted to." He tried to convince me it would be just like it always was, but, you know, I didn't want to take that chance 'cause we were friends.

ALAN FORTAS: Mainly all the guys around Elvis had jobs to do—not originally—but as time went on. We were really just traveling companions in the beginning. The number in the group varied depending on what Elvis was doing. Sometimes there would be four or five of us with him, sometimes as many as eight. All together, through the years, the Mafia must have numbered forty to fifty different guys.

I never liked the term "mafia." We were there to help him and protect him, but we weren't officially bodyguards. Yet there were some who probably would have given their life to protect him—Red, for example.

LAMAR FIKE: I was just with Elvis. We didn't all have specified jobs back then because all of us weren't being paid. We were like a buffer zone around him.

WILL "BARDAHL" MCDANIEL: Why did Elvis take me to California? He was just the type that thought if somebody would enjoy something, you know, he would do it on the spur of the moment. So I went out to California with him for a year, and things out there were completely different than Memphis. At Graceland there was no drinking. Every once in awhile someone might slip in a bottle, but we didn't need to drink; Elvis had a natural high. In California, Elvis pointed out the bar and told me, "You just let me know what kind of booze you want to drink and I'll keep it stocked for you." I asked him once, "Elvis, do you ever drink?" He said, "The only time I ever drink at all is in Las Vegas. If you don't drink out there they think there's something wrong with you."

:◎:◎:◎:

RED WEST: Elvis was so glad to be out of the Army, he hated to even get back into uniform; but he had to for the movie *G.I. Blues*. Juliet Prowse was his costar. They were close. How close, I don't know; she was dating Frank Sinatra at that time. One day Elvis and Juliet were in her dressing room—in those days they had the little dressing rooms on the sound stage so they wouldn't have to go outside. They were in there rehearsing, I guess. All of us were sitting outside.

Now Elvis and I, we were always playing practical jokes on each other, so I ran up and knocked on the door real hard and hollered, "Elvis, Frank's coming!" Well, the door flew open, they both looked around for Frank, and finally they saw it was a joke. Elvis said a few choice words and went back inside.

Sure enough, it wasn't two minutes 'til we look up and see the big stage door opening, and here comes Frank and that bodyguard that was always with him. It really was! From where he was coming in, Sinatra could see us. He was walking straight toward us. I kind of slowly stood up and eased over to the door and tapped on it and said, "Elvis, no shit, here comes Frank." Well, Elvis yelled something like, "Fuck you!" from inside the dressing room. I said, "Oh well." Just then, Sinatra came up and knocked on the door. It was unbelievable. Luckily they were studying their scripts. It was like when the little boy cried "wolf" too many times; that's exactly what happened.

NAOMIA STIERS: When *G.I. Blues* was about ready to open at the Majestic theater in Houston, we went to the theater owner and asked him if we could have a special midnight premiere and sell tickets to it.

He said, "Okay." That night, before the movie, a bunch of us had a big parade. We got everybody that we knew who had a car and we decorated 'em up and drove all over town blowing our horns and attracting attention to *G.I. Blues*. At twelve o'clock there wasn't a seat vacant in the whole theater!

CHERYLE JOHNSON: I liked *G.I. Blues* because I got to see Elvis in his uniform. The music was good and I thought that it had a pretty good story. Back then, everybody would go to see his movies because that was the only way we could really see Elvis; he wasn't doing concerts, so we just waited for his movies. If the first movie started at one o'clock, we would stay until six o'clock, and we'd see it over and over again. Back then all of the fan club members would take tablets and write all the dialogue down.

:◎:◎:◎:

RED WEST: Elvis and I did a couple of fight scenes in *G.I. Blues*, and then in a lot of pictures after that I was either doubling for Elvis fighting or actually fighting him.

I broke my elbow while we were filming *Flaming Star*. My arm still won't straighten out. We were doing a fight scene; Elvis was playing an Indian, and I had to jump him. Well, I jumped off of the side of a gully down on Elvis, but I did a flip and hit on a rock and it broke my elbow. I couldn't put any pads on my elbows because I was naked from the waist up. I had to keep going. I did that fight scene; then I did another fight scene doubling the guy that was trying to kill Elvis in the movie. Elvis was playing a half-breed, and everybody was against him. I was playing an Indian in one scene, and in the next one I was doubling the white guy that was trying to shoot his mother. I was lucky. I could still stand in with that broken elbow, but I didn't have to do any more stunts.

One day after we wrapped, I jumped on an old horse and was galloping past Elvis, acting like I was going to run him down. Elvis happened to have a rope—and he had never thrown a lasso in his life. Just as I galloped past him, he threw out that rope and it caught me right around the neck. The damn horse was going full speed! I just yanked hard on the reins and the horse reared up and stopped dead in his tracks! Elvis never even let go of the rope; he was so shocked that he'd got me.

:◎:◎:◎:

LANCE LeGAULT *(choreographer)*: I met Elvis one day at a hotel he was staying in while he was doing a movie. I told him I was a musician. He said, "What are you doing tonight? Where are you playing?" And I told him and he said, "Well, I'd like to come out." And I'll be a son of a bitch if he didn't come out that same night. I didn't think he'd come that quickly, but he did. I think he had Tuesday Weld with him that first time he came; he was filming *Wild in the Country* with her. Later, he brought different ladies, whoever he was dating. He always came in the back door and sat in the balcony of the club. We became good friends, and I worked with him on a lot of his movies 'til 1968.

RED WEST: I played Elvis's brother, Hank Tyler, in *Wild in the Country*. Elvis was pretty close to Tuesday Weld; he dated her for a while. She used to come out to the house. Millie Perkins was kind of shy, but Hope Lange and Tuesday and everybody got along fabulously. Elvis respected all those people. Philip Dunn, the director, was a real nice man. He added something for me as Elvis's brother in the courtroom scene.

I had my first film line in that movie. I'd rehearsed and rehearsed all weekend, but when they said, "Roll 'em" and Hope Lange stepped in front of me, I couldn't think of my name. Elvis laughed like hell.

He was always looking for something to laugh at, some way to make fun of you. We had a real great fight scene. It had kind of got 'round that Elvis was doing some great fight scenes without using a double. It was always him and me, so it got to the point that everywhere we went they were ready for him and me to do a fight scene. Luckily we used to do a lot of karate demonstrations together, so we didn't have to think too much, just kind of knew what each other was going to do.

:◎:◎:◎:

ANITA WOOD: While Elvis was shooting the movie *Wild in the Country*, I was at the California house and I came across a book that caught my interest. As I was opening the book, I discovered a letter from Germany from Priscilla. In the letter there was something to the effect of—"You need to call my daddy and talk him into letting me come over. I want to come really bad."

When Elvis came home from the studio, I confronted him with the letter, and we had a terrible argument. He said, "She's just a young, fourteen-year-old child, and she just has a bad crush on me. She wants to come over. We're family friends, Army buddies, her daddy's a good friend of mine." He just tried to smooth it over that way. Well, I did not understand because I had seen pictures of Priscilla waving "goodbye." She was waving "goodbye" like I was waving "goodbye" when he left Memphis. Elvis kept saying, "She's just so young. It means nothing." But I was still perturbed. So, I went back to Memphis, and I understand she came in shortly thereafter.

MARTY LACKER: I've always known Anita to tell the truth. If she said that's what happened, probably that's what happened. Elvis flew Priscilla to the States for a visit in 1960. That was two years before she came here to live.

FRANCES FORBES: To tell you how secretive Elvis could be, I never knew back then that Priscilla spent Christmas of 1960 at Graceland.

"Just Having a Ball"
1961-1963

Making movies, making music, making love, Elvis is living the life that will one day produce its own fantasy movie script. Costar Angela Lansbury describes the shy, polite personality beneath the movie star image. Memphis Mafia members Alan Fortas and Marty Lacker share tales of Elvis's offscreen antics in both Memphis and Hollywood, while producer Hal Kanter and songwriter Don Robertson give reminders that big business hides behind the madness of entertainment.

Elvis continues to crank out movies at an astonishing pace. But *Girls! Girls! Girls!*, *Girl Happy*, and *Follow That Dream* are more than simply his movie titles; they reflect the whirlwind of fun-loving activities consuming his life, and in 1962 Elvis earns a new title: Top Box Office Draw of the Year.

Elvis's personal life, however, gets complicated as he continues juggling lovers. Vying for Elvis's attention are Anita Wood, Tuesday Weld, Anne Helm, Priscilla Beaulieu, Ann-Margret, Ursula Andress, and many others. Meanwhile, back at home Elvis's stepbrothers Billy and David Stanley, friends Jerry and Geraldine Kyle, and secretary Becky Hartley disclose the changes that occur in Memphis once young Priscilla arrives from Germany and places her stake in Graceland.

> "Elvis had a libido that would make Jerry Lee Lewis look like a monk."
>
> BARBARA PITTMAN

ARLENE COGAN: While Elvis had been in California making *Wild in the Country*, Dee had been making some changes in the decoration of Graceland. I believe she had changed some draperies. Well, when Elvis came back and found things different than he'd left them, he blew his top! I mean, he really got mad. He said, "If she thinks she is going to just take over Graceland, she has another think coming." Elvis believed Dee had overstepped her boundaries.

JIMMY VELVET: Elvis actually went to see *Wild in the Country* himself. They say it was the only one of his movies he ever went to the premiere of. The premiere was held in Memphis, and if I remember right, it was at the Loew's theater where he had been an usher and gotten fired years before. I was staying with Aunt Loraine and Uncle Travis and Billy and Bobby Smith, and Elvis invited us all to go. It was fun to watch the movie with him being there. He would get embarrassed and would yell out, "Oh, no!" or something. Everyone would laugh. He made it real funny.

:◎:◎:◎:

HAL KANTER: Mr. Wallis [Hal B. Wallis, producer] wanted to do a picture that featured a returning veteran, which, indeed, Elvis was at that time.

Elvis was a very thoughtful young man. He had a riotous sense of humor—loved to play. Unlike a lot of people who said that his whole career was a happy accident, I don't think it was an accident at all. I think he was very much aware of everything he did. He knew exactly what to do to turn an audience on.

The cast of *Blue Hawaii* included Joan Blackman, who was cast opposite Elvis, and Roland Winters, who played Elvis's dad. Angela Lansbury played his mother. I remember it was only the second time she had played comedy, and she was wonderful.

ANGELA LANSBURY *(actress)*: I've had a lot of fun through the years with the Mother's Day card story, which was that in the film I played Elvis's mother, and for years after I would receive a Mother's Day card from him. But in truth, I've never believed those cards came from Elvis. They came from Colonel Parker. I have no way of knowing if Elvis even knew they were being mailed. But it was fun to receive them, and they did make for a fun story.

Elvis was essentially a one-take actor. He liked to get his scenes in one take. It wasn't the kind of material that allowed him to show signs of unusual talent. What I do remember is that he was experienced with karate. During free time on the set, he broke bricks with his hand.

RED WEST: When he wasn't filming, Elvis would kick back and get rid of his tension by doing karate demonstrations. In Hawaii we left broken boards all over the beach. At that time, in Hawaii, karate was just getting big, maybe in part because of him. That's when all the karate stuff really took off. A lot of people are making karate movies now and they can partly thank Elvis for making it popular back then. He would do a karate demonstration anywhere for anybody. I've got the bruises to show for it. He was good.

HAL KANTER: In a typical Elvis movie, everything was tailored specifically for him. As far as *Blue Hawaii* was concerned, a screenplay had been written, but Mr. Wallis was not satisfied with it. I rewrote it to incorporate those elements that he wanted. He wanted the film to bring a boy back from the Army and show how he was now dissatisfied with his life as a result of his Army experience. Whether or not that comes through in *Blue Hawaii*, I don't recall. It was an enormously successful picture, probably one of Elvis's biggest grossers.

BRENDA FIELDER: My mother took me to see Elvis's movies five and six times apiece. *Blue Hawaii* was my all-time favorite—the scenery, the songs. I was probably thirteen, fourteen, at the time, and you could just picture yourself being there in Hawaii with Elvis and him marrying you. It was a very romantic movie and the best soundtrack he ever had.

CHERYLE JOHNSON: I think the last movie that I really liked of Elvis's was *Blue Hawaii*. After that I thought it didn't look like he was enjoying what he was doing. I thought he was miscast in a lot of the later movies. A lot of them didn't really even have a story.

ANGELA LANSBURY: I never gave Elvis any advice. I would only say that in the scenes with his parents, he knew that he was acting with two experienced professionals. He in turn was professional with me and with Roland Winters, who played his father. We didn't spend a lot of time with him socially. He had his own coterie around him. But being with him was always a pleasant experience. He was a nice young man.

HAL KANTER: It is my contention that Elvis could have been really a very good dramatic actor, or a good light comedian. There was a great deal more to the man than what appeared, particularly in his later films.

:◎:◎:◎:

GORDON STOKER: I had the joy of being in the studio with Elvis and working across the mike from him doing several duets like, "All Shook Up." He would try to break me up, punch me when we were singing.

In those days everything was on one track. I had to sing with him on the same microphone, and he picked at me the entire time we were doing "All Shook Up." On the end, I kind of goofed on "yeah, yeah," and I said, "Let's do the whole thing over."

Elvis said, "Man, if it isn't sold by that time, it isn't gonna sell anyway."

DON ROBERTSON: By 1961 Elvis had already recorded several of my songs, and someone sent word to me that he wanted to meet me. He was working on a project at Radio Recorders on Santa Monica Boulevard in L.A. and I went over to the studio. I remember it very vividly because Elvis was already a hot star by the time I met him. He was standing there in his little captain's hat at the microphone, and I waited in the control room. After a bit he took a break and came in. We just sat, the two of us, and talked for five or ten minutes.

Elvis sort of sketched in his background, like he just assumed I didn't know anything about him. He never just assumed that everybody in the world knew who he was. That impressed me because he was a such hot new name even then. After a short visit he went back into the studio, and before he started his next song he stepped up to the microphone and did a little parody of my song; he sang, "When the evening shadows fall and you're wondering who to ball. There's always me." He looked at me and kind of smiled and winked.

GORDON STOKER: One night Elvis was telling us about this pretty little black-haired girl he'd met in Germany: Priscilla. He told us, "I want to record this song next, and while I'm doing it I guess I'll have my mind on Priscilla." The song was "Can't Help Falling in Love."

DON ROBERTSON: You hear rumors that everybody who wrote songs for Elvis's movies made a fortune, but when the moment of truth came and you got your songwriter royalty statements from Hill and Range, your actual royalty check, you would certainly not have a fortune. I would say two hundred thousand or three hundred thousand copies was about average for sales of those soundtracks, except for *Blue Hawaii*. I think the writers involved in *Blue Hawaii* got paid on over a million sales.

At that time writers were getting about a penny per reported sale, so that would be about twenty-five hundred dollars total to the writer. Of course, if I had a cowriter, he'd get half of that—and remember, the royalties were all being reduced by a third, the kick-back to Hill and Range for "Elvis and the Colonel." So it was not very much, not considering your song was being recorded by Elvis Presley. It took a lot of work to get it, too. It wasn't enough to live on, for sure.

Oh yeah, when Elvis would record one of your songs for his movies, you'd get a whopping big synchronization fee for the use of your song in the movie. Yeah, a whole dollar! But half of that buck went to the publisher and half to the writer, or writers. If there were two writers on a song, you'd each make twenty-five cents for having your song used in an Elvis Presley movie! What a joke. People thought you were getting rich. But you did it for the opportunity to be on the soundtrack album, and maybe the remote possibility that your song might get to be a single [record] release.

:◎:◎:◎:

RED WEST: *Follow That Dream* was a real fun movie. Joanna Moore and Anne Helm were in it. That was the movie I got married on—married for real—and I spent my working honeymoon down in Florida getting paid and having a ball. We all had a real good time on that one. Elvis could kind of relax and play a character for a change—a slow, dumb, ol' country boy.

BILLY STANLEY: We were down in Florida when Elvis was making *Follow That Dream*, and we went to the hotel after shooting that day. I was about eight years old, too young to know any difference, but I came into the room and Elvis and Anne [Anne Helm, costar of the film] were sitting together, hugging and holding hands and kissing and this and that, and I just walked up and bluntly said, "Oh, by the way, Anita wants me to tell you hello." Well, Elvis looked at me with a very, very dark look and said, "Okay, boy, it's time to go to bed." I knew I was in trouble.

DON ROBERTSON: I was sort of embarrassed for Elvis in some of the movies because of the poor quality of the stories and everything. But, god, at the same time, the guy was so electrifying. I mean, you couldn't watch him on the screen without being riveted.

ANN MARIE MCCLAIN *(fan)*: On my tenth birthday my dad made me stay in and watch an Elvis movie—*Follow That Dream*—and he's been kicking himself for twenty-nine years now.

I became an Elvis fan through his movies. Most of Elvis's fans were the fans from the fifties or from his stage shows or the TV shows. I was only exposed to the movies, *Follow That Dream*, *Girl Happy*, *The Trouble With Girls*, and things like that.

What I liked about Elvis first was his sense of humor. He was so deadpan. I just got a kick out of watching him and listening to him. I mean, I went out and bought—with my birthday money—a couple of 45s and an album, and we didn't even have a record player!

:◎:◎:◎:

HAROLD LOYD: Elvis hired me to work security at the gate at Graceland in September of 1961, and I just retired a while back. (I'd been at Graceland a little over thirty-one years.) When Elvis would be at home, if the weather was suitable, he would come down to the gate late in the evenin' and have me open the gates and let all these hundreds and hundreds of fans come in. He would shake hands with 'em, give autographs, kiss the women, just have a ball. I enjoyed that, although it was pretty rough on me tryin' to keep an eye on everybody. I wish to god I could have had a video, just filmed some of that.

There were funny things that happened at the gates, and sad and touchin' things, too.

A lot of handicapped people, or people with serious illnesses, would come to the gates, but they'd act just like everyone else; they didn't ask me for special privileges. You could just look at some of them and tell they were sick, dyin' with cancer or somethin'. But they didn't ask me if I would call up there and try and set up an appointment to see Elvis. I did that on my own. I'd do it on my own 'cause I knew how Elvis felt. Man, he would bend over backwards for little kids, handicaps, older people. He loved 'em, man, he loved 'em (I'll get to crying in a minute now). He was very tender-hearted, very tender-hearted.

:◎:◎:◎:

MARTY LACKER: After Elvis had already done a few movies, we were shooting pool one night, and I was getting ready to take a shower. Elvis said, "Hold up a minute, I want to ask you something. Why don't you go with us tomorrow?" I looked at him like he was crazy and said, "Go with you tomorrow? You're going to California to do *Kid Galahad*!" He said, "I know where I'm going! I'd like for you to go with me."

Well, at the time I had a wife and a child. Nobody else with Elvis had that kind of responsibility. Naturally, anybody that age would just jump at that kind of opportunity, but I said, "Well, yeah, I would like to, but I need to think about it." Do you know, Elvis got pissed off! He walked out of the poolroom and went to the other room in the basement. A couple of guys that was around us said, "Man, you shouldn't have said that. He was wanting you to go."

I went to the other room, and Elvis was sittin' there; he's got the newspaper up in front of his face, so you can't see his eyes. I said, "Elvis, you got to understand that it's not that I don't want to go, but I've got to think about it; you know I've got a wife and a child." See, first of all, he just didn't like anybody saying "no" to him, and he didn't take into consideration anybody else's situation. It was just basically what Elvis wanted, and he couldn't figure out why a twenty-four-year-old guy would have to think twice about something like that. Well, it finally dawned on him, but he still covered up. He put the newspaper down and said, "Well, all right, damn it, but don't think about it too long. We're leaving at two o'clock tomorrow afternoon, and if you're going, be here." That was it.

I was so caught up in it, I didn't even ask what he was going to pay me. I went home to my wife. Of course, she just broke down, 'cause, quite frankly, I was a son of a bitch as far as my marriage was concerned. That's the one thing in my life that I really feel bad about. I trusted her to bring my kids up well, and she did an excellent job. The way I convinced my wife to let me go was to say to her, "Look at all the contacts I'll be able to make," 'cause I was in the radio and music business.

It tore my ass up to leave the next day. I didn't even consider how much I was going to make or anything like that. It turned out to be forty-five dollars a week—and I was one of the higher-paid guys!

RED WEST: Most of *Kid Galahad* was filmed on location near Los Angeles at Idlewild. Gig Young costarred, and Lola Albright, Joan Blackman, and Charles Bronson. That was before Bronson really hit it big.

Gig Young was married to Elizabeth Montgomery at that time. I remember, on the set there at the studio, that Elizabeth came over to visit Gig. Elvis saw her (she was quite an attractive lady) and walked over to Gig and said, "I've just bought a new Rolls Royce. I'll trade you for her." Gig Young thought for a minute and said, "Well, let's see . . . it's not used?"

BEN WEISMAN: Some people today mock his movies, but I say that his movies were much healthier than a lot of the movies of today. Today's movies are often violent, full of murder, rape, incest. Elvis's movies were fun. They were healthy. And his movies always made money.

ALAN FORTAS: In May 1962, the movie industry named Elvis the Top Box Office Draw of the Year. It was ironic because Elvis was more and more beginning to hate the movies he was making.

ARLENE COGAN: Elvis hated Hollywood; he hated it with a passion. If Elvis had not been such a great talent I would have said he was in the wrong business. He was not meant to be away from home. He always told us [in Memphis] that his California gang [of girls] were good people but they didn't mean to him what we did. I thought it was sweet of him to say, but I never really believed it.

:◉:◉:◉:

ALAN FORTAS: Elvis had a huge two-way mirror installed in the ladies dressing room of the cabana by the pool at his Bellagio Road house. The only trouble was, to get to it, you had to crawl up under the cabana.

The first time we had female guests who were changing out there, Elvis crawled up under there and surprised me. He had dirt all over him. I said, "God almighty, Elvis, what the hell you doing under here? You're all dirty. You don't have to do this. Hell, they'll let you look!"

He kind of grinned and said, "Yeah, but it's a lot more fun this way."

DON ROBERTSON: Elvis had a chimp. They called him Scatter 'cause if he got mad he'd scatter his feces around, and he had a mean temper. Elvis kept him some place; I think in a room down in the basement. He was a cute little chimp. They let me hold him one evening, and it was like holding a child, really. He'd put his arms around your neck, a very affectionate little beast. He liked to look up girls' dresses! Elvis thought it was very funny.

ALAN FORTAS: Scatter was what you might call a party animal. He'd been something of a Memphis TV star. Elvis bought him from Bill Killebrew, who was a cartoonist for a local TV station. Sometimes we'd dress Scatter up and he'd sit at the bar next to us.

One time a former stripper friend of ours named Brandy came over to a party, and she got down on the floor and jokingly simulated sex with Scatter. Elvis and everyone thought it was so hilarious; they nearly choked to death, laughing.

I used to put a chauffeur's cap on Scatter and drive the Rolls Royce with him on my lap. When a car would go by, I'd duck down in the seat so it looked like Elvis's chimp was actually driving. It shocked a lot of drivers, almost caused some drivers to go off the road. Elvis thought it was hilarious.

:◉:◉:◉:

LANCE LeGAULT: *Girls! Girls! Girls!* was the first movie I did with Elvis. I played bass and sang "Return to Sender" with him, and I did some choreography. Everything in a movie has to be choreographed, and what I choreographed was not dancing per se, or what most people think of as dancing. In a movie you can't just walk out and wing it; you'll be out of focus or you'll wind up in the shadows. So, when you say choreography, it was more like movement in and around key marks. To do it, it helps to have a musical background and a little movement background. What I always tried to do was just make all the on-camera moves as natural and comfortable for Elvis as possible.

ARLENE COGAN: I was visiting Elvis in California when he was finishing up *Girls! Girls! Girls!* He brought home his new record, "Return to Sender" (which was in that movie), and he told us all, "You've got to hear this. Listen to the words. I just love this song." And he played it over and over for us. We loved it, too, and, of course, it went on to become one of his biggest hits.

ALAN FORTAS: Elvis especially hated the movie *Girls! Girls! Girls!* He disliked the plot and couldn't stand some of the music; most of all, he hated having to sing "Song of the Shrimp." He complained to the Colonel, but the Colonel wouldn't listen. In a strange way, maybe the Colonel was right, again. The soundtrack went "gold," and "Return to Sender" from the movie became a huge hit.

JUNE JUANICO: The problem had always been those damn silly songs and the silly scripts. I mean you put James Dean or Marlon Brando in a musical drama and what have you got? You've got a joke. But they just would not take Elvis seriously as an actor, and that's a damn shame. That was his desire.

ARLENE COGAN: When he would finish a movie and come back to Graceland, everything was happy there. Everything was up. It was nothing but hugging, kissing, and warmth.

ANITA WOOD: Elvis was never the same after his mother died. I think possibly that's when he began taking some medication, and you could tell there was a change there. After the Army he was not quite as into the more childish things, like the skating and the fairground. I noticed after he came home he started taking all this medicine—the pills, the tranquilizers, and sleeping medications like the doctor had him on and prescribed to him immediately following Gladys's death.

:◉:◉:◉:

MACK GURLEY: I know something I was personally involved in, and if Anita finds it out she'll never have anything to do with me again. Anita was one of the first ones Elvis thought about marrying. He made the statement one time, that if, and that's *if*, he ever got married it would be to Anita. That was a long time back.

In those days Elvis avoided the press, but every time we'd go somewhere the press was there, and no one could figure out why. He enlisted the people he really trusted to help figure it out, and one night I ran back into the house as we were about to leave Graceland for a movie. Everyone had already gotten into the cars but Anita. She was on the hall phone to the newspaper telling them where we were going. Her and Elvis's relationship had been deteriorating somewhat, and that was the final straw. Of course, I told Elvis; so if you're looking for a guilty party on Elvis's breakup with Anita, I guess I was the one.

ANITA WOOD: I was going downstairs to the kitchen area, and Elvis was sitting at the bar with some guys. I heard him say, "I'm having a terrible time. I cannot make up my mind. I'm so confused." I knew he was talking about Priscilla and myself. I have a lot of pride. So, I came in and I said, "I'm going to relieve you of that problem." So, we went into the dining room; his dad was there eating breakfast. I just told Elvis that I had decided to leave so he wouldn't have to make that decision [between Priscilla and Anita]; I had made that decision for him. He cried. I cried. His daddy cried. Elvis said, "I pray to God I'm doing the right thing here by letting you go." I said, "Well, you have no other choice."

FRANCES FORBES: Prior to Priscilla's coming to Graceland, I'd already sort of eased my way out somewhat. I was beginning to think, "Did I miss something by not being at school all the time or dating?" Out there [at Graceland] you led a very sheltered life—you really did. You were protected from the whole world.

ANITA WOOD: Elvis was not a normal person, and there would have never been a normal life there. There were never many times when you were alone. There were people everywhere—all over the house. You could not call it your house—everyone was there; all the time; in every room. No, there could never have been a normal life there.

BECKY HARTLEY *(Graceland secretary)*: Back in the sixties if you knew somebody that knew somebody that knew somebody, it was not hard to get into Graceland. They had parties, and Elvis was very kind and didn't want to say no to anybody. The parties weren't anything wild; they were just people sitting around. There was guys playing pool, they had a jukebox on the patio, and they played records.

One particular night during a party at Graceland, I was in the room across from the poolroom downstairs. I was sitting on the couch. Somehow I just managed to sit by Elvis that night.

At that particular time I had heard on the radio, like maybe three weeks before, that Sandy Hill, who had worked for Elvis, was no longer working for him. I thought, "That would be neat. If I'm ever around him, I'm going to ask him for a job." But I did it the other way, I asked him, "Do you need a maid?" Elvis said, "No, I don't need a maid, but I might need a secretary."

JIM CROWE: If you got hungry, you could go up to the kitchen. The cook usually had some sandwiches made up, or if you wanted something special, you could ask her and she'd fix you something. Downstairs in the den Elvis had a soda fountain and you could have all the Cokes (Pepsi, I think it was, back then) you could drink.

FRED FREDRICK: I remember Elvis drinking milkshakes. He loved strawberry milkshakes. At least that's what we always had in the basement [at Graceland]. I never even saw him eating anything other than snacks down in the basement (the dungeon I used to call it). We'd go down there and watch movies [on TV] or listen to records. There was always some kind of snacks in little bowls, and different things.

JIM CROWE: Down there in the basement den, many times Elvis would be sitting over in a corner with a bunch of girls sitting around him. They'd be talking about fifteen or twenty minutes, and two or three of them would get up with tears in their eyes and go to the bathroom. They'd be so touched 'cause Elvis would get to talking about his mother.

BECKY HARTLEY: About two weeks after I met Elvis, they called me to come to work for him. I was really shocked. I couldn't believe that first day going up to Graceland; I thought they wouldn't let me through the gates. I was just in awe. The office wasn't anything fancy. I remember they had an old green Army desk in there and an old gas heater, but it didn't matter to me whatsoever what that office looked like, because I was up on that hill, right behind Elvis's house! That was in March of 1962. Vernon and Dee had already moved out. They had their own place.

JERRY KYLE *(friend of Rick Stanley)*: In 1962 my mom [Geraldine Kyle] met Dee while she was getting her hair fixed at a beauty shop right across the street from Elvis's house. I started going up to Graceland with mom, and then I met Dee's boys, Ricky, Billy, and David. Ricky and I hit it off real well 'cause we were the same age. I just started spending the night with them almost all the time. Dee and Vernon had a house over on Dolan Street, which was adjacent to Graceland's backyard. All the Stanley brothers did was hang around Elvis. I mean, he was their life when they were growing up. He bought them motorcycles and just about anything they wanted.

GERALDINE KYLE *(friend of Dee Presley)*: Dee was a wonderful cook—a good Southern cook. She knows how to put the finishing touches on anything. I always said the best thing that ever happened to that family after Gladys died was Dee Presley, because she gave it all the class it ever had. And I still say that.

Vernon was down-home, good people, as far as I'm concerned, and I always respected him. But, as far as having the kind of class that went with the man Elvis became, I don't think Graceland had any of that until Dee married Vernon.

JIM CROWE: When we first started going out to Graceland, Elvis was dating Anita Wood. Then after that Priscilla came for two weeks in December 1960. Anita and Elvis broke up, and Priscilla came to stay a couple of years after that.

BECKY HARTLEY: I had only worked at Graceland for a few months when Priscilla came to stay. She was wonderful, just great. She was beautiful and sweet and shy. We used to have a lot of fun together. We would go out to lunch or she would just come out to the office and visit.

FRANCES FORBES: Priscilla was very pretty and sweet and probably very innocent; that would attract Elvis. One thing Priscilla had going for her over there in Germany was that she didn't have to share Elvis. It was probably a big transition for her when she came to Memphis.

ARLENE COGAN: I think Anita had been good for Elvis in that she liked all the fun and excitement that Elvis liked. She liked to do the same things he loved to do. Elvis would date some women that didn't really care for the things he liked to do.

JIM CROWE: Priscilla was more, what you might say, laid-back. She sort of held back more. When she came into town and Elvis started bringing her out, he quit renting the fairgrounds so much, and we would just mostly go to movies.

DOTTY AYERS: Priscilla was a spoiled little girl. At the Rainbow skating rink she would sit on the sidelines while we skated. She didn't want to get messed up, I guess. That's exactly what I thought of her.

BECKY HARTLEY: Priscilla was very shy in the beginning. I think anybody would be. You've got to take into account her age, too. She was probably overwhelmed, you know. But things began to slowly change. I don't think it could have kept on anyway. Elvis couldn't continually keep on letting that many people into his house. You know what I mean? 'Cause I remember it was just people sitting all around the room, and then in the next room there would be people, and in the next room there would be people lined up. When Elvis would walk in, they would get just really quiet.

JIMMY VELVET: Elvis had a charisma—I don't even know if you would call it charisma—maybe it was magnetism. He could walk into a room where you were looking the other way, and automatically you would turn, even at Graceland. Elvis could come down those stairs, very quietly, and folks would be sitting in the living room talking, and heads would turn because they would just know he was there. He was always the center of attention.

BILLY STANLEY: We caught on very soon at school that sometimes when the kids were being extra nice to us, what they really wanted was to come to our house so we could take them up to Graceland and they could meet Elvis—girls and boys. But it was pretty strict around our house, and we couldn't just bring anybody home that we wanted to.

BECKY HARTLEY: People would sit around and talk, play pool, or just wait for Elvis to come down, you know, just to look at him. I can imagine what Priscilla must have thought. When you are in love with somebody and you are going with somebody, you don't want all those other people around all the time.

But again, if Elvis and Priscilla wanted to get away, they just went upstairs to Elvis's bedroom. It wasn't like just a little-bitty bedroom; I mean, he had his office up there, too. He had a refrigerator up there. They could get away from the crowds and be comfortable.

DOTTY AYERS: Priscilla was very young when she started going with Elvis, and he was such a big star. He filled her life so much that she didn't know anything else. When we were around Elvis, everything was focused on him: how he felt, what he wanted to do, when he wanted to go to bed, when he wanted to get up, if he was in a good mood, if he was in a bad mood. Elvis was the total center of attention. Everyone else was secondary, including Priscilla. Around Elvis she had no life of her own.

WILL "BARDAHL" McDANIEL: Whenever we could, we'd go to the movies. The movies Elvis wanted to see would mostly be movies that hadn't made it to the local screen yet—new ones, but one night we saw *Gone*

With the Wind. It had been out for years, but Elvis wanted to see it again, so we all watched that.

JUNE JUANICO: I went back to Memphis with a group of girlfriends for a bowling tournament, and we found out one night that Elvis was at a local movie theater. We went over, and someone recognized me and let me in. I said, "Don't tell Elvis I'm here. Let me surprise him."

Elvis was sitting in the center section alone with his date, who happened to be Priscilla Beaulieu. She looked like she was maybe fourteen or fifteen [Priscilla was actually seventeen in 1962]. I went in one row behind him and tapped him on the shoulder. He gave me this, "Who is annoying me?" type of look, and then he did a double take. He stood up and kneeled down in his seat, and he was giving me a bear hug. Joe Esposito came running from the front of the theater to see who had Elvis in a headlock. It was real funny. Priscilla, bless her heart, she just sat there, keeping her eyes on the screen. She just took it all in stride.

Later that night, I cattily remarked to my girlfriends that all the drugstores in Memphis must have sold out of mascara, 'cause Priscilla had it all on her eyes.

DAVID STANLEY *(stepbrother)*: Priscilla used to put on that black mascara and tell me and Billy and Ricky that she was a vampire and chase us through Graceland. We used to play hide-and-seek all the time at Graceland. We were pretty close. That's the times I miss. That's back when we were a family. That was when it was fun.

FRANCES FORBES: I don't think Priscilla knew about all the other girls at that time. If she did, she didn't know what they meant to him. I'm only guessing. I don't know for sure.

GERALDINE KYLE: When I first met Priscilla, she had just come over from Germany. My husband and I were Catholic and she was, too. We ended up taking her to Mass with us every Sunday. We'd go by and pick her up. We felt sorry for her.

DAVID STANLEY: When she first came to Memphis, Priscilla lived with Vernon and Dee and Billy, Ricky, and myself on Hermitage Drive (she did when she first came, at least for a week or two). She was almost like a big sister.

I remember when I turned nine years old she took me out shopping.

She bought me a skateboard, a Jetbell helicopter, and a goldfish. She spoiled me rotten, and we were real close at that time. Then when she moved to Graceland, whenever Elvis was gone I used to go over and spend the night with her. It was almost like a slumber party. Of course, I was just a little boy. We would stay downstairs in either Grandma's room or the other room where Aunt Delta later lived. Sometimes I stayed upstairs with her, and we'd sleep in Elvis's room on his big bed.

JERRY KYLE: Everybody knew Priscilla was upstairs there, staying and sleeping in the same room with Elvis. That was common knowledge. Priscilla moved up to Elvis's room pretty quick, 'cause, I mean, I know she didn't live with Dee and Vernon. She just moved right in [with Elvis] with Vernon's permission, I guess, because it was not really legal; she was so young.

BECKY HARTLEY: Graceland was pretty private. There would be times that you almost felt like you were a prisoner working there, because nobody got in but the postman or whoever was supposed to. At night, when Elvis was home, anybody that came up would be whoever he chose to come up. As far as stories getting out about what went on, they just never got out.

I can remember now how drugs were back in the early sixties when I started working [at Graceland]. There was uppers and downers. I remember one guy (he didn't work there but about a year); I remember his little case. It would be full of Dexedrine, and that other drug they had in the early days before the quaaludes. You got to remember that this was before the government really tightened down on the diet pills—that's what I call them.

:◎:◎:◎:

EDDIE FADAL: There are things about Elvis a lot of people don't know. A lot of things he didn't do for publicity; he did them from his heart.

For instance, once we were driving around the streets of Memphis. He wanted to show me the city because I'd never been there before. There was a blind man sitting on a corner with a tin cup in his hand—you know the scene, you've probably seen it a thousand times. Well, Elvis couldn't get over to him because of the traffic, so we drove way out of the way to get back to this guy. Elvis put five one-hundred-dollar bills in his cup. The man probably never knew who put them there. These are the wonderful little things about Elvis people don't know.

MACK GURLEY: If there was anything we could do to please him we would do it, because he was always doing all he could do to make us happy.

BECKY HARTLEY: Elvis would get mad at some of the guys sometimes and have his little temper tantrums, and he might fire them, but he would turn around and hire them again. I would imagine, probably, when you work that close with somebody, you're going to get mad sometimes anyway.

:◉:◉:◉:

LAMAR FIKE: In 1962 I moved from Memphis to Nashville and went to work for Hill and Range [Music Publishers], which was actually the company that administered the two fifty/fifty publishing companies with Elvis: Elvis Presley Music and Gladys Music. I became, along with Freddy Bienstock, the liaison between Hill and Range and Elvis. We would find material out of Nashville and out of New York. Between the two of us, we would pitch most of the songs to Elvis that he eventually recorded.

JOAN DEARY: I was not an Elvis fan when I first heard his records. I couldn't understand the lyrics, but he worked so hard on himself through the years. When you compare those early records from the fifties with later ones after he came out of the service, there's a big difference. After the Army you had a totally polished performer. A lot of people have criticized the loss of that raw (what would you call it?), that raw rock 'n' roll sound, but I think he developed as an artist tremendously. Having worked with so many artists, I don't know of any other artist who had that kind of flexibility.

DON ROBERTSON: It was tough to come up with really great songs to fit all those movie script situations. And it was kind of sad to me to see Elvis involved in less than top quality, first-rate things. I would have thought he'd have been unhappy with a lot of the stuff he had to record. However, all of us staff writers were just spitting out songs to fit specific situations and to help move those movie plots along.

JOAN DEARY: The movie albums drove me up the wall. I hated them. And the fact that they were handled in the strange way they were, with no particular person in charge, caused me a tremendous number of problems later on when I was doing the cataloging. Many of those tapes never made it to the tape vaults 'cause no one ever asked if there were any other takes of the songs. Some of them have turned up on bootleg albums. The amount of bootlegging on Elvis—even today—is phenomenal.

Don Robertson: Elvis was beautiful in the studio. He was great. He very rarely made mistakes, and even when we did five, or six, or seven takes on something, he usually did a good performance every time. Musicians or someone else made a lot of the mistakes. I don't know how he kept his patience, but he was always, like, "Well, let's try it again."

:◎:◎:◎:

Arlene Cogan: When Elvis would leave for Hollywood to do a movie, I'd go up to Graceland and visit his cousin Patsy [Presley]. She was one of Elvis's secretaries. We loved to read the fan mail that came in for Elvis. Boy, did it come in. They brought it up in a truck.

Becky Hartley: We had people that wrote Elvis every week and a girl out of Canada that wrote Elvis every day. She wrote like she was writing a diary. We would love to read her letters because she would tell all about her boyfriends.

Even men wrote to him. Elvis got letters from Yugoslavia, Romania, Czechoslovakia, the Philippines, and there were even a few from Russia and from Cuba. The Japanese would send a lot of those little paper good luck necklaces. It was just unbelievable.

Cheryle Johnson: We wrote to Elvis all the time. Believe it or not, somebody answered all our letters. I got Christmas cards from Elvis every year that Naomia told me he really did personally sign, and I have an Easter card he signed. They were also doing some kind of a newsletter that came out of Graceland that they would send to all the fan clubs, you know, telling them what Elvis was going to be doing next, what movie he was working on, and so forth.

Arlene Cogan: People would send him jewelry. Sometimes, expensive jewelry. I remember some really beautiful crosses he got from fans.

Becky Hartley: We would get, you name it, just about everything in the mail.

Sometimes Elvis even got dirty letters. Women would send in their nude pictures. They'd write a letter and tell who they were, their measurements, and everything. I mean, some of them were pretty bad. They were like homemade pictures. I had a special drawer that I kept them in. Usually it was the guys that wanted to see them. Elvis wasn't that turned on by them.

We didn't put the naked ones in the photo album we kept at Graceland, but there would be, like, grandmothers, young kids, male or female, every age, that would send their pictures in—school pictures—from all over the country. Elvis enjoyed looking at them, and he kept every one.

ARLENE COGAN: There was this one woman who wrote Elvis a love letter once a week. She'd write it on, of all things, a roll of toilet tissue. We would roll it out all across the living room and into the dining room and read it and laugh. She would tell Elvis all this stuff. He said, "She probably lives in a mental institution." And, you know what? We found out she did!

:◎:◎:◎:

RED WEST: We filmed *It Happened at the World's Fair* right in the middle of the real Seattle World's Fair. And we had a great fight scene in that film: Elvis fighting me and a couple of other guys. Joan O'Brien was in the movie with him, and there was a little girl, Vicky Tiu. Gary Lockwood was in it. He and Elvis played crop dusters.

When we were back in L.A., we had a football team. Most of us had played football in high school and college, and Gary also had played football at U.C.L.A., I believe. Sometimes he came out and played football with us.

Elvis had broken his finger playing football one time, and the studio asked him not to play, but that didn't make him quit playing. Anyway, Gary Lockwood told Elvis maybe he ought to wear a helmet since he was filming at that time. Elvis said, "No, I'll be okay." Well, I'll be damn if Elvis didn't get his eye split open. He had to go in Monday and shoot a scene, and they did the best they could with the makeup. When you are making a movie, they don't want you to get out of bed, you know.

The next time we played, Elvis told the guys, "I hope you don't think I'm a sissy for wearing this helmet, but if I get a bad cut on my face, or something, production could stop."

JIM CROWE: Elvis would come back to Memphis for the holidays—sometime during November or the first part of December—and he might be home 'til the middle of January or February before he'd have to go back to California.

BECKY HARTLEY: There was just something magic about the holidays at Graceland, especially just before Christmas. You always knew Elvis was coming home. Mr. Presley would send somebody to cut down the biggest live Christmas tree they could find. There were lots of decorations and all that. The whole house would be lit up. It was homey and wonderful.

I think Elvis was sensitive and appreciative. He even opened all the gifts from the fans at Christmas; but he was hard to buy for, which is not uncommon among wealthy people. He could go buy everything he wanted, and he did.

PAUL DOUGHER: Only thing Elvis ever gave me was a gift one Christmas when we were at Graceland. It was a travel clock of some kind—a nice leather thing, you know. I'm sure he didn't really know I was going to be there, and he probably had bought several of them for unexpected people. But I never asked him for nothing and he never said, "Hey, would you like for me to buy you something?" or "Let me give you a car," or anything like that. I think he knew it might insult me as far as our friendship went. Anyway, he knew I wasn't looking for a dime from him—just his friendship.

BECKY HARTLEY: The New Year's Eve parties we went to were great. A lot of times Elvis would rent the Manhattan Club here in Memphis. The first year Priscilla was here he rented it, and they went there with a bunch of people.

CHERYLE JOHNSON: Somehow the Colonel controlled a lot of what the press said about Elvis, and his relationship with Priscilla was kept out of the gossip columns. I don't think anybody really had any indication that Priscilla was living at Graceland at that time. The fans thought Priscilla was just in the States going to school—living with Vernon and Dee.

BECKY HARTLEY: Priscilla finished her senior year at I. C. [Immaculate Conception High School] in June 1963. Elvis went to the school for the graduation ceremony but was afraid to go in and cause a commotion, so he waited outside in the car.

Two weeks later he left to start work on another movie.

ALAN FORTAS: In July of 1963 we went back to the coast to start shooting *Viva Las Vegas*. We were living on Bellagio Drive. That's when we met Ann-Margret. I loved Ann-Margret. She was fun to be around and great to me. She played Rusty Martin in the movie (Elvis nicknamed her "Rusty Ammo"). They were together night and day during the making of the movie, and she was telling the press in California they were engaged. It was a pretty hot affair. I don't know how he managed to hang on to Ann-Margret in California and Priscilla back in Memphis, but he did.

LANCE LEGAULT: Ann-Margret and Elvis got along great—two good-looking people just having a ball. They both sang. That broke the ice right there. They both liked to move. When they did those numbers together, it was great; they were playing and having fun. They dated, and you could just tell they really liked each other. It was all up on the screen.

RED WEST: The director of *Viva Las Vegas* was also very fascinated with Ann-Margret. Sure was. That was the only time I ever knew Elvis not to complain but just kinda joke about not getting great close-ups. He said, "Damn, all the close-ups are of Ann, and I'm just over the shoulder."

LANCE LEGAULT: In *Viva Las Vegas* we went to work about six in the morning, and we quit about two-thirty when it got too hot. Then the sun would set, and we'd go back on a second call.

I did a lot of things in *Viva Las Vegas*—bit parts, choreography. I doubled Elvis in that fall off the diving board at the Flamingo Hotel when Ann-Margret pushes him. That's not Elvis, that's me. The insurance companies would not let Elvis do a fall like that. That was about a twenty-foot fall with a suit on and a guitar around your neck, going off backwards. That's a good way to lose your face. It had nothing to do with whether he could, would, or wanted to do it. If Elvis had done the fall and gotten hurt, he could have shut production down on a picture for two or three weeks while his broken nose or black-eye cleared up at a cost of one hundred thousand dollars a week minimum, even in those days!

CHERYLE JOHNSON: I remember there were a lot of rumors about Elvis and Ann-Margret going together. The fan clubs were talking about the fact that she and Elvis were dating . . . but I didn't think Elvis was any more serious about Ann-Margret than anyone else. Elvis and the people around him really guarded all of that.

RED WEST: Elvis cared about all the women he was with. Ann-Margret was a nice lady and we all loved her, but there were others—so many others. He liked all of them. Whoever he was with at the time, he loved.

Sometimes, he'd have one leaving and another one coming in the door. He was busy. I don't know what to say. He got around. It was fun to watch.

JIM CROWE: Elvis had Ann-Margret here [in Memphis] one time—one weekend. I didn't meet her. She was introduced to everybody and spoke to everybody. I don't know where Priscilla was.

BECKY HARTLEY: It was kinda tough on Priscilla when Elvis would go off to California to make a movie; there she was by herself at Graceland. Elvis would leave money for her, but when she needed more she would have to go to Mr. Presley. Priscilla had a good relationship with Dee and Vernon, but she absolutely dreaded worse than anything to have to ask Vernon for money. This was when she first came over to stay.

GERALDINE KYLE: I will say one thing, Dee was really good to that girl. I don't know what Priscilla would have done without her, because Priscilla was terribly lonely as it was. Dee would take her out—take her anywhere she wanted to go—and spend lots of time with her.

BECKY HARTLEY: Priscilla took modeling and she took dancing. I don't know what she told people about where she was staying. She might have told them she was living with Dee.

:◎:◎:◎:

ALAN FORTAS: Ursula Andress starred with Elvis in *Fun in Acapulco*. I don't know which was worse, the plot or the music. Elvis played a seagoing trapeze artist who was afraid of heights. And worse, Elvis's manager was a nine-year-old Mexican kid. The kid gets Elvis a job singing in a hotel and demands a management fee of fifty percent. Strangely enough, a few years later Colonel Parker and Elvis signed a new deal: for fifty percent!

BUZZY FORBES: You hear an awful lot about, "If it wasn't for Colonel Tom Parker, Elvis wouldn't have become such a big star." I don't think Elvis could have hid his candle under a bed. He would have made it with or without Parker. And if Sun hadn't been there, I really believe that Elvis would have found another studio to cut a record for his mother, and that would have started it all.

HORACE LOGAN: Parker takes credit for everything. He takes credit for discovering Elvis. He takes credit for molding Elvis. He takes credit for building Elvis's career. The son of a bitch ought to be hung up by his balls. He practically destroyed one of the greatest talents that ever lived. You know that? No, it wasn't all Parker's fault, no; but those lousy, stinking horrible, terrible songs Elvis did in those movies! And those movies! My God, a lesser talent would have been destroyed by that crap!

"While the Iron Is Hot"
1963-1967

As Elvis's success increases, so does the pressure. He jumps from movie studio to movie studio, from soundtrack to soundtrack. The Colonel handles the business; Elvis handles the art and craft of being a star. Director Gene Nelson tells about Elvis the actor, and his talent; actress Mary Ann Mobley tells about Elvis the man, and his charisma. Cronies Alan Fortas, George Klein, and Marty Lacker are on the scene to explain what it takes to keep it all together.

Musician Chip Young and songwriter Ben Weisman reveal Elvis's attitude toward his movie soundtracks, and Red West and Jimmy Velvet discuss his distaste for many of his later movie scripts. Meanwhile, the Jordanaires are among those who recall the recording of a magnificent song that twice wins Elvis a Grammy Award.

His life continuing to bounce back and forth between the surprising and the too predictable, Elvis buys a getaway ranch in Mississippi. Longtime newspaper columnist and friend Bill E. Burk, and Doctor E. O. Franklin give insight into Elvis's reason for the move.

While there are still plenty of good times to be had by all, it is indeed evident that the times they are a-changing.

> **"Elvis is a tremendous entertainer; certainly he would have made it without me, but I know that like all good things, too much can be harmful. I make sure Elvis isn't exploited and over-promoted."**
>
> COLONEL TOM PARKER

GENE NELSON *(movie director, screenplay writer)*: Every movie studio in town was submitting possible pictures to Elvis. In fact, some of us had to wait in line. Someone would come up with a project and submit it to Colonel Parker. The Colonel always said, "I don't care what the script is. If you can pay the money up front and twenty-five percent [or whatever] we'll do it."

Sam [Katzman, the producer] hired a writer named Joe Grayson Adams to write *Kissin' Cousins*. Sam hired me to direct, but when I read the first draft I came up with loads of complaints, so Sam got me to rewrite it. When I finished the script I was very pleased with it, so I got a messenger and sent a copy of the script over to the Colonel along with a note, "Dear Colonel: Here's the finished script. I hope you like it. And if you have any suggestions, I'll be very happy to entertain them." The next day I got a note back by special messenger from the Colonel. It said, "Thank you for the script. It's okay with me. As far as offering suggestions is concerned, I get twenty-five thousand dollars for consultation." He was such a joker. I know a lot of it with him was tongue-in-cheek.

I didn't know what to expect or how I would handle Elvis, but when I finally met him, all of my concern was dispelled. He was fun and congenial, and just as nice as could be.

ALAN FORTAS: The Colonel was somewhere between a practical joker and a con artist. One time we were at MGM, and Elvis and the Colonel came out of a big meeting. Elvis was laughing. He told us he'd just signed a huge deal with the studio—five pictures at a million dollars a picture—but the Colonel had refused to sign the deal unless the studio threw in this cheap glass ashtray that was sitting there on the table. Of course they gave it to him. The Colonel did crazy things like that, and Elvis thought it was so funny.

GENE NELSON: When I was rewriting the script for *Kissin' Cousins* and I came to a scene that I thought would be an ideal musical situation, I would write down two or three, maybe four, suggested titles. The Hill and Range music writers would [write the songs and] make demos of all the songs that were to be considered for a movie. They would send three, maybe four songs for each title we told them we needed. I would listen to the demos and make my choice. Then I would package them up and send them with a letter to Elvis. I told him my recommendations on which songs I thought fit the script best, and I guess I was just blessed 'cause he agreed with all of my suggestions.

JOAN DEARY: Steve Sholes felt the songs Elvis was recording for those later movies were not at all strong or commercial.

DON ROBERTSON: I often thought, "God, he could have great songs by Johnny Mercer and all kinds of tremendous writers—except a lot of those writers were too established and too successful to give up a share of their writer royalties just to get Elvis to record one of their songs.

BEN WEISMAN: How many beach party things can you write about? I don't know, but there's an old saying that when something's going well, you stay with it; when it stops going well, do something else. We're talking business now. That must have been the Colonel's attitude.

LANCE LEGAULT: In *Kissin' Cousins* Elvis played both cousins, but when you shoot like that, someone stands in for the second part, so I was "the other cousin." We shot every scene twice, and that was almost a continual laugh thing. They made two wigs for me to match Elvis's hair and two wigs for Elvis to match my hair. We'd shoot something and then change wigs and clothes and shoot the damn scene again. We'd laugh shooting it the first time and then come out and look at each other and crack up laughing again. Elvis said if he'd known how much of a pain in the ass that movie was going to be, he might not have agreed to do it. But check the figures on that picture. We shot the picture in a little over two weeks; it was a quickie. It came out, jumped up there, and Sam Katzman got a bigger office and made a lot of money.

GENE NELSON: Even with the trivial kind of dialogue we had in *Kissin' Cousins*—and other Elvis films I've seen—there were moments where he obviously incorporated a great deal of thoughtfulness into his delivery. I think he would have been terrific in something a little heavier. Whether his fans would have bought him or not, I don't know.

The typical Elvis movie was ten or eleven musical numbers, frivolous, and sex-oriented in a very nice, mild way. Pretty girls were mandatory, lots of them. In *Kissin' Cousins* we had a bevy of them.

Elvis played two parts, himself and his country cousin. We made him a blonde wig for the cousin role. He is just a fine-looking little ol' hillbilly boy having a good time, playing his guitar and running around with the girls. Elvis's other character was an officer in the Army Air Corps. When the Army comes to build a missile base on top of the mountain, that's where everything gets involved, and it goes on from there.

:◎:◎:◎:

RED WEST: On set Elvis never threw temper tantrums, not in front of any of those people. Now, let's face it, sometimes a scene just don't always go well, and at least he was professional enough not to show it out there in front of people. He would go off to his dressing room or be on the way home, and he'd raise hell about something—but not very often.

GENE NELSON: Elvis did pretty much whatever project the Colonel devised for him. Wherever the money was, that's where they would go. An experiment into the more dramatic area, though, might have been a great deal of fun for Elvis, but the Colonel stayed away from that. See, they owned a lot of their pictures. They also controlled the music, and they had the soundtrack albums. On *Kissin' Cousins* the whole budget was 1.3 million dollars. We made the picture—excluding Elvis—for six hundred fifty thousand dollars, actually. Elvis and the Colonel got seven hundred fifty thousand dollars.

:◎:◎:◎:

LARRY GELLER: On April 30, 1964, I received a phone call from Alan Fortas, one of Elvis's aides. He asked me to come up to the house to prepare Elvis's hair for a film he was doing, *Roustabout* with Barbara Stanwyck. So I went up to Elvis's house. I drove up to the Bel Air gates where I was met by another one of Elvis's aides, and he showed me the route up to the house. I walked in the door, and Elvis was sitting there having some lunch. Elvis was twenty-eight-years old at that time, and yet he was not even into his prime. Well, I expected a barber's chair and all the fine accoutrements of success, but I ended up washing his hair with him leaning over the bathroom sink!

The appointment lasted four hours! And for some reason Elvis felt he could just bare his soul to me. He literally came unglued and told me his life story. Within an hour-and-a-half, he's crying to me, telling me about his mother, about poverty, how lonely he was, and how he really was inwardly, secretly searching for meaning in his life, which kept eluding him.

Elvis asked me, "What are you into?" He gave me a very intense look. I said to him, "Obviously, I do hair, but what I'm really more interested in than anything else is trying to discover things like where we come from, why we are here, and where we are going." As I'm saying this I'm thinking he might think I'm some kind of a kook, but while I was talking, I noticed Elvis's eyes were lighting up like light bulbs. He said, "Man, just keep talking, just keep talking." I said, "Now I realize what my purpose is." When I said that, he leaned forward in his chair, and asked, "What do you realize? What is your purpose?" I said, "My purpose is to devote my life to discovering my purpose. It could take me a year; it could take me a lifetime. It doesn't matter. The pursuit of finding the answers is what's going to enhance our lives." Elvis said, "Oh man, this is unbelievable, unbelievable. Larry, this is what I secretly think about, too. I have no one to talk to about this." He said, "You know, I've always felt an unseen hand on my shoulder, guiding my life. There had to be a reason why I was plucked out of millions and millions of lives to be Elvis." I told him right then and there, "Look Elvis, if you want, I can introduce you to a whole array of books. I study them myself, and I meditate." He said, "All right!"

By the time I left his house that night, I was working for him.

ALAN FORTAS: Larry Geller came to cut Elvis's hair one day and ended up getting hired. He led Elvis into parapsychology, some of the Eastern religions, mysticism, a number of things. Elvis called him his "guru." It wasn't long after that when Elvis started referring to himself as the "divine messenger." We never really knew if he was kidding or not. For some reason, I thought he was being very serious.

LARRY GELLER: There was a lot of jealousy and tension when I came on the scene because I was taking too much of his time, and Elvis started to change. He started to get very serious about himself, and a new maturity started to manifest itself. It was seen by everyone in the group and everyone at the studios. Of course, it really ticked off the Colonel, because all the Colonel wanted was for Elvis to be Elvis and do his work and do these movies. That's where the money was. For Elvis to become independent and to start thinking for himself was something I don't think the Colonel really appreciated.

:◎:◎:◎:

LANCE LeGAULT: Elvis was great on taking advice and instruction, and quick. Bing, bang, boom! Yeah! We were always on budget with his pictures and on schedule. There was never a problem with Elvis. I'd set up a mock-up of the set on a big rehearsal stage and teach it all to him—once it was okayed by the director. Working with Elvis was quite an education.

RED WEST: Barbara Stanwyck and Elvis hit it off real well on *Roustabout*. They did. She's a very professional lady and was nice to everybody. If anybody could have been a prima donna, she could've; but she got right in there with everybody—not just Elvis, but everybody. Elvis had a great respect for her.

LANCE LeGAULT: Elvis had a lot of conversations with Barbara Stanwyck on the set because he respected things that she'd done before. As a matter of fact, he asked me on the set one day if I had seen her in *Cattle Queen of Montana*. Barbara was standing right there chatting with us. It had played on television the night before. I said, "No, I didn't see it," and he went on telling how great she was in it. He really liked her.

:◎:◎:◎:

MARY ANN MOBLEY *(actress, former Miss America)*: I filmed *Girl Happy* with Elvis and Shelley Fabares during June and July of '64. It was my first movie.

Elvis had a great sense of humor, a good attitude, and he was a perfect gentleman. When I entered, he stood up and said, "Where's Mary Ann's chair?" I think Elvis was, in a way, proud of me, if I can say that. I think he was proud because someone from his home state of Mississippi had won the Miss America title. I never dated him, but I did two movies with him, and we became friends. Elvis and Shelley Fabares got along well, too. She's a lovely lady as well as being a good actress. She didn't have any hidden agendas with Elvis, either.

LANCE LeGAULT: There was always a lot of pressure on set to stay on schedule because it was costing money, but Elvis didn't seem to have any trouble. He put in a full day's work, but it was done fairly easily. We hit it at eight o'clock in the morning and we would get out of there at six.

:◉:◉:◉:

GENE NELSON: The second picture I directed for Elvis was *Harum Scarum*. We made it for a total of 1.9 million dollars—Elvis and the Colonel got a million. I think Elvis would have liked to have switched from musicals to drama, but of course, their company controlled the music, too, and the merchandising, so they had a lot to consider and a lot to lose in switching directions. The Colonel was reluctant. He wasn't interested in Elvis's latent dramatic abilities. I had come up with an idea for Elvis that could've been a serious film with music—not as much music—but the Colonel's stock answer was just, "You come up with the money; we'll do the picture." That's the way he worked. The Colonel was a real character.

MARY ANN MOBLEY: I was sitting in Colonel Tom's office [on the MGM lot] one day signing a contract and the phone rang. It was *Time* magazine calling, and they were offering to put Elvis on the cover. Colonel Tom said, "Well, that will be twenty-five thousand dollars." Yes! That's what he said. And the *Time* guy said, "You don't understand, this is *Time* magazine." And Colonel Parker said, "You don't understand. We don't need you." That's a true story.

JOHN W. MCAFEE, SR.: Now I've been in the entertainment business for more than sixty years, and you've got to realize one thing—do like they say: "Strike while the iron is hot." All Elvis's movies were money-makers.

GEORGE KLEIN: Remember the old cliché "if it ain't broke, don't fix it." The Colonel said, "Look, we're making a lot of money. Let's not mess with it until it runs out." Through the years Elvis was offered *Midnight Cowboy*—the movie that Jon Voight did. He was offered *West Side Story*. He was offered a lot.

I was there when Robert Mitchum came up to the hotel and offered him *Thunder Road*. That ain't no bull. I was there, opened the door, and Mitchum walks in. Later, I went to Mitchum's house with Elvis to talk about it. But there again was Colonel Parker: money and percentages!

Elvis missed a lot of good roles. But still, on the other side of the coin, the Colonel kept Elvis on top for so many years; it's hard to fault him.

JIMMY VELVET: Elvis wanted better roles, but his movies were always planned and picked based on how much money he and the Colonel would be getting. Maybe Elvis would rather have taken no money and done a better picture, I don't know. It's a shame that he didn't take some of the really good roles that were offered.

LANCE LEGAULT: I never heard Elvis talking about wanting to do more serious roles. I think it might be a myth that's grown up over the years. I don't know how it started, but I am curious.

BEN WEISMAN: Every artist wants to do something of a serious nature, but still, Elvis is going to be remembered for all the fun movies he made. People forget that a lot of folks loved his movies. The critics can say whatever they want, but the bottom line is: the public loved his movies!

GENE NELSON: To hold down the budget on *Harum Scarum* we just borrowed, begged, or stole whatever we needed. We got [director Cecil B.] DeMille's old sets from *King Of Kings* and used those. It was a modern story set in a period situation. It was supposed to be this long, lost, forgotten country in Persia. The idea was that they go back two thousand years in time.

We had a lot of costume designers, but we also got old costumes from *Kismet*. When I worked with the designer for Elvis's costumes, I said, "I want him to look like Rudolph Valentino." Elvis loved that. He always thought Valentino was great. Valentino was one of his idols. Elvis had that same suave kind of "sheik" look.

While we were making *Harum Scarum*, production was running behind, and Sam [Katzman] had had a mild heart attack. I loved him; I hated him at the same time. He was on my ass, really giving me a rough time. I was behind a couple of pages [of script], and when Sam left the set one day we took a lunch break. We turned the lights out, and I walked over and sat down on a bundle of straw in one of the horse stalls. I was just sitting there when Elvis came over and said, "Can I talk to you for a minute?" I said, "You bet. Sit down." He said, "It's getting a little rough out there, isn't it?" I said, "Yeah, but nothing for you to worry about. This is my problem. I don't want this to affect you or your performance in any way at all. I'll take care of it." Elvis was such an aware and considerate person. He said, "I just wanted you to know, if they're not giving you enough time to do this picture right, I can get sick in such a hurry you'd be surprised."

CHARLIE MCCOY *(Nashville musician)*: I was hired to pick guitar on the "Harum Scarum" album in 1965. I was sixteen years old. I had a bit of a mixed emotion because, number one, when I first got the call I was thrilled, but then as you know, most of the movie music wasn't so hot, and I was disappointed.

I noticed the producer from L.A. [Freddie Karger] cut everything completely dry [with no echo]. We said something about it, and he said, "Don't worry about it, we'll add echo later." I don't think they ever did.

When they did the next movie soundtrack album, "Frankie and Johnny," they got their old team of musicians back. But Scotty talked them into keeping me on. So I ended up doing the soundtracks for seven of Elvis's movies.

JOAN DEARY: Those soundtrack songs drove me up a wall. They just seemed to get worse and worse. It was to Elvis's credit that he was even able to perform those songs—I mean, "Queenie Wahini's Papaya"! Give me a break!

:◉:◉:◉:

TOM JONES *(recording artist)*: In 1965 I was on my first trip to the United States. At that time I had had two hit records on one hit album and I was excited about being in America. Everything was happening so fast for me. I was in California doing a song for a movie, and Elvis was shooting on the [movie] lot. Someone told me Elvis had heard that I was there, and would I like to go and say hello? I thought to myself, "Elvis Presley doesn't know who I am!" But I went onto the set where he was filming. I can't remember the name of the movie. He was sitting in a helicopter. He sorta waved over in my direction, and I thought, "Is he waving at me?" Just in case he was, I waved back! It was strange, you know, because I had never seen the man before. Then he came over and said hello and said he knew every track on my album! We chatted for a while and I asked him, "Any chance I can get a photograph together with you for the British newspapers?" He said, "Of course." Then, as we were doing the photographs, he started singing songs off my album! I was really dumbfounded. I was thrilled that he even knew who I was. Our friendship started right then.

:◎:◎:◎:

LANCE LEGAULT: If you check the records you'll see that when someone came in and did a good job on an Elvis film and got along well with Elvis, they probably did another picture with him. Bill Bixby did a couple. Arthur O'Connell did a couple. Shelley Fabares did three: *Girl Happy*, *Clambake*, and *Spinout*.

CHERYLE JOHNSON: During the time Elvis was filming *Spinout*, he designed the "TCB" insignia his crew wore on chains around their necks and as patches on their jackets. TCB stood for "taking care of business," which was something that Elvis would say to his bodyguards: "Take care of business!" He scribbled out TCB and then drew a lightning bolt on it. That signified taking care of business in a flash. Then Elvis came up with the TLC insignia for the wives and girlfriends—it stood for "tender loving care." He gave these insignias to people he especially cared about.

SONNY WEST *(bodyguard)*: Elvis was always giving someone something. When he gave me my first car in 1965, it was a Cadillac convertible. He'd given me and some of the guys motorcycles just a few months earlier—bought ten or twelve of them, and he'd bought Marty Lacker a car because Marty was scared of motorcycles. I had a bad accident on the motorcycle he'd given me, so he decided to buy me a car. First, he said he wanted to buy himself a car, and would I just go with him to look. Then he decided to buy me one at the same time. When he tried to present the keys to me, I backed away and said, "Naw, I'm not taking that." I said, "Thank you, Elvis, but no."

 I went and got back in Elvis's Rolls Royce. He came over to me and got in the car and said, "What's wrong with you?" "Nothing," I told him. "You know, you always seem to be giving, and we always seem to be taking." Elvis said, "Sonny, you're giving when you don't know you're giving. I put a lot on you guys, and I know it; but you handle it, and you take care of things and you get it done. This is just a little way of mine that I can show you how much I appreciate it. I also know that when you were younger you stood on the corner and watched those Cadillac convertibles go by and you'd say, 'One of these days, I'm gonna have one of those.' Well, that day is here. You've got yours. Now, let's go get mine."

:◎:◎:◎:

JOAN DEARY: In the very beginning the Colonel was like a lightning rod, and I think that got Elvis most all the things that he got. The Colonel brought him to the attention of the whole country, the whole world as a matter of fact. I don't think Elvis could have moved that quickly by himself. The Colonel got him a movie contract; but later on, I think that Elvis could have done a great deal more creatively under different management or direction. Let me put it this way, I think Elvis could have been a great actor.

MAE AXTON: The Colonel and Elvis's early relationship was wonderful—except, the only thing Elvis said to me was that he hated doing those movies, grinding them out. He'd already done about eight or ten films by then. He said to me, "I can act, but I don't get into this. This is not real acting. I can do this in a breeze." But Elvis loved the Colonel, and he trusted him implicitly. After all, the Colonel got him the screen test and helped take him right to the top.

RED WEST: The Colonel treated all of Elvis's friends hot and cold, hot and cold. He was friendly, but he always kept his distance. I never did care for the Colonel. I'd like to know who says he's the greatest manager. It couldn't have been anybody that was around Elvis.

MARTY LACKER: Colonel Parker would never start anything with me if Elvis was around, but one time the Colonel and me had a real clash in Hawaii, during the filming of *Paradise Hawaiian Style*.

We were over there about three weeks, and what I would do every Monday was go out to the location and have Elvis sign an expense check—something like fifteen-hundred bucks. (We had about eight or nine guys with us, sometimes more.) I would go back to the hotel in the limo with the driver to get the check cashed, and then I would come back to the set with a wad of money.

So, I'm out there on the beach. It was about 10:00 or 10:30 in the morning, and the Colonel came walking over with his cane that he carried (he really didn't need it) and he sees me. Alan Fortas was standing there with Richard Davis, and as I was counting out their money the Colonel said, "Let me have three hundred dollars." I looked at him and said, "Well, I can't do that, Colonel." And he said, "What do you mean, you can't do that." I said, "Well, I have to give this money to the guys so they will have money to eat on." And he asked me, "Whose money is that?" "It's Elvis's money," I said, "to give to the guys so they can eat this week. This is their weekly per diem." He knew what it was, but he said, "Are you telling me," and his voice was getting a little louder (the crew was standing around and the Colonel's going to put on a show) "I can't have three hundred dollars of Mr. Presley's money?"

I said, "Colonel, if it was my money, you could have it. It's not my money. I have this money for . . ." And I'm repeating all this shit again. Well, he starts fucking yelling! Everybody could hear him. Elvis was farther down the beach, rehearsing a shot, and now the Colonel's putting on a show. I said, "Let me put it this way, Colonel," and by now I'm shouting, "You go over and talk to Elvis. If Elvis comes to me and tells me to give the Colonel three hundred dollars, I'll give it to you. Until then, I can't give it to you!" Well, he raised his cane up in the air and said, "Goddamn you. Don't ever ask me for anything!" And I looked him straight in the face and said, "Colonel, I never have, and guess what—I never will!" And I turned around and put the money in my pocket. If I could have, I would have taken that cane and wrapped it around the Colonel's fat ass. I really would have.

Elvis comes running over and he's saying, "What the hell is going on here?" I just turned around and started walking up the beach. Elvis came running after me, put his arm on my shoulder. He was chuckling. He said, "Let me tell you what that old son of a bitch said to me." "What?" I asked, even though I really didn't want to hear it. Elvis said, "He told me to hang on to you, 'cause you were looking out for me." I said, "Bullshit!" Parker probably said it, but Parker said it to cover his own ass. He needed three hundred bucks like I needed two cents. He just tried to put me in that little bag of his, and I wasn't going to allow him to do it.

GEORGE KLEIN: Colonel Parker was a genius. He made a lot of mistakes, but he made fewer mistakes than a lot of other managers might have made. Nobody in the world could negotiate contracts like Colonel Parker. He was the best.

:◎:◎:◎:

BECKY HARTLEY: I talked to the Colonel on the telephone. The Colonel would call a lot and talk to Elvis's daddy. If the Colonel didn't like something that Elvis was doing, he would discuss it with his daddy. The Colonel was not at Graceland all the time. When Elvis came to Graceland, he wasn't making movies, and he was there at his home resting and having fun and doing what he wanted to do.

Graceland was Elvis's own personal place.

LARRY GELLER: Back in the mid-sixties people were experimenting in so many different ways. Elvis wanted to try acid and so did Priscilla. So the four of us—us and a friend—went upstairs to Elvis's room and dropped acid. As it turned out, it was, thank god, not a detrimental experience. It didn't harm anyone. I think everyone learned something from it.

Priscilla went through quite an experience. All of a sudden she came into the room with a little hand mirror and she kept looking at herself. She said, "I'm ugly! I'm ugly!" Apparently, she was seeing herself that way. She came up to me and said the same thing. Afterwards when the drug subsided, we all walked outside, around the gardens, and had a wonderful conversation. We were all glad we took it, and we felt connected to one another like a special family. In terms of Elvis's experience, he didn't need to take it. Elvis was imbued with an energy that was so potent, so dynamic he didn't need acid, and he knew it. I don't think he ever tried it again.

JIM CROWE: It seemed like when Elvis and Priscilla were getting real serious about each other, everything started getting more laid-back and more subdued. You could just feel the mood changing. Everything started getting more like a "couple" deal. Some of the guys that worked for him married their girlfriends and it got to be couples going here and there, doing this and that. Seems like we went to more movies then, and the skating rink and the fairgrounds kind of went by the wayside.

FRED FREDRICK: Elvis and Priscilla were together privately a lot. The guys kind of got shoved aside a little bit. There weren't any more big parties, and if you went to the movies, it was a smaller group. I think there was a lot more family-type stuff at that time.

:◉:◉:◉:

GERALDINE KYLE: Priscilla was a natural beauty, but it wasn't a glamorous beauty. Here Elvis was, out in Hollywood where women wear all this makeup and all these high styles; he wanted Priscilla to have the same glamor and the look of Hollywood.

My husband Charles and I went to the funeral when Elvis's uncle died, and when we went over to the family side to offer our condolences, to my shock, there sat Elvis and Priscilla, looking like twins! Elvis had blue eyes; Priscilla had blue eyes. Elvis had his hair dyed coal-black; Priscilla had her hair dyed coal-black. I just wasn't expecting it. I told Charles when we sat down, "Dear Lord, they look like twins!" And they did.

BECKY HARTLEY: Naturally, Elvis being Elvis, he had gone with so many women; and of course, it was rumored he was going with Ann-Margret during and after the making of *Viva Las Vegas*. Well, Priscilla was here in Memphis then. Ann-Margret called the house for Elvis one time and Priscilla answered the phone. Priscilla didn't like it at all. I think it had been written up in some of the magazines about him and Ann-Margret, but, of course, Elvis told Priscilla it was all just publicity. He did the same thing when he went with Ursula Andress.

JIM CROWE: At that time Elvis's schedule might be to be back in California on a certain date, but whenever he got in the mood to go they'd leave at a split moment. A lot of times the guys just had to grab what clothes they could as they ran out the door, 'cause if Elvis would come down and say, "Let's go to California," they'd all just load up in cars and go.

LARRY GELLER: We'd go back to L.A. for a few months at a time to make a movie. When we'd leave, Elvis would keep Priscilla back in Memphis—simple as that.

BECKY HARTLEY: I remember one time Priscilla came out to the office, and there were letters in this one file cabinet that Priscilla had written to Elvis when she was still in Germany. She wondered if they had ever gotten to him because they were there in the file cabinet.

There were some letters from other girls, too. So you know, I watched out for Mr. Presley [Vernon] while Priscilla read them.

GERALDINE KYLE: Sometimes Priscilla would come over to my house with Dee. She liked to go through my closet and trade clothes with me. She started out by telling me what she wanted—it was a crushed gold-and-white short dinner dress, sleeveless. Priscilla wanted that dress and I didn't much want to trade. She said, "Well, if you'll trade me that dress, I'll trade you two dresses that Elvis bought me at LaCledes, which was an expensive dress shop in Memphis, very ultra at that time.

Later, we were both at a wedding reception in Memphis. I was at the buffet table and Priscilla came over. I had on this little one-piece dress. It was shocking pink, and it had this pretty white, silk-shantung jacket to it. It was an A-line skirt, which was popular at that time.

Priscilla came over and said, "Oh, Gerry, I just love your suit. Where did you get it?" I said, "Sears and Roebuck." You ought to have seen her little face fall. She said, "Sears?" Then she turned around and walked away. She didn't want to trade for that one.

:◎:◎:◎:

MARY JARVIS *(RCA Nashville secretary and wife of Elvis's record producer)*: Felton [Jarvis] was a big Elvis fan, and when Felton came to work at RCA, Chet turned the production of Elvis's sessions over to him. Felton could not have been happier. He thought Elvis was great.

Elvis always had final control over his record sessions, but the two of them actually did all the producing together from that point on. Elvis trusted Felton, and most of the time Elvis would just leave the overdubbing of instruments and the mixing of the finished masters up to Felton.

FELTON JARVIS *(record producer)*: Elvis had to sing a song the way he felt like singing it at the moment he was recording it. I couldn't tell him how or when to do a song. He might come in to record a rock 'n' roll album, but first he'd spend several hours just singing gospel songs. That was how he warmed up. Sometimes he'd get down to business very quickly; other times he just wanted to sit around playing gospel and singing for hours. When he'd actually start working, though, he was fast and efficient. Elvis didn't make very many mistakes.

CHIP YOUNG *(session musician)*: Elvis, if he didn't want to record something, he didn't. I've seen Elvis take demo records and sling them all the way across that little RCA studio. He'd say, "Piece of shit!" Boy, that song demo would go flying across the studio!

SHAUN NIELSEN *(backup singer)*: When Elvis got ready to do his *How Great Thou Art* album, he had Felton call us [The Imperials] and ask us if we would be interested in singing with him on the album. That was probably one of our quickest career decisions.

We recorded in RCA's little Studio B, which now is a museum in Nashville. I must have been nineteen or twenty at the time, and I remember standing in the studio thinking, "Boy, if mama could only see me now!" I remember standing over in the corner feeling somewhat intimidated because of all the great musicians who were there. Then Elvis walked in!

As I recall, he was dressed in a "superfly" outfit and had a black hat on, straight from Beale Street. Now if I'd been wearing it, they would have run me out of town, but it looked like it was made for him. He had that incredible ability to look good in whatever he wore. He walked through the door and kind of looked around and began to walk straight over to me. I was thinking, "I wonder what he's got to say to me?" He stuck out his hand and said, "Hi, I'm Elvis Presley," like I hadn't figured it out for myself.

Elvis said, "I just want you to know I've got all your records and you're one of my favorite singers." That was *his* opening statement to me! He said, "There's a song you have on one of your albums that I'd like to record. Would you sit down here at the piano with me and kind of run through it? I really admire the way you sing it." It was "Where No One Stands Alone."

RAY WALKER: The Jordanaires taught Elvis "How Great Thou Art" on the actual recording session. He was looking for songs to do [for a new gospel album], and I said, "You ought to record 'How Great Thou Art.'" Presley said, "I don't know that song." I said, "Well, I'll teach it to you." So I went out and got a song book for him. He rehearsed it three-and-a-half or four hours—playing the piano, singing it over and over—and then he got up and recorded it. It was beautiful.

SHAUN NIELSEN: I was asked once why did Elvis have so many backup singers on the "How Great Thou Art" session. He hired three groups to sing backup for that. At the time they were his three favorite gospel groups and, knowing Elvis, I suppose he just didn't want to hurt anybody's feelings by leaving some of them out.

CHARLIE MCCOY: We recorded the "How Great Thou Art" sessions in Nashville in May of '66 and "If Every Day Was Christmas" about a month later. Then Elvis flew us out to Hollywood to record the movie soundtrack for *Double Trouble*. I played on a lot of those soundtrack albums with Elvis and I totally understood the game. I thought, "Gee it's a shame. This is the greatest recording artist in the world and he's got this bad material to work with. Obviously, either, number one, he doesn't have a choice, or number two, he's just so easygoing that he doesn't want to create any flack. You never really understand the total thing unless you're on the inside; but for his sake, I felt disappointed in the sound track material he was recording.

CHERYLE JOHNSON: After the early movies, somehow things changed, and the new movies didn't appeal to me as much. Maybe I was just growing up, but it seemed to me even back then that Elvis deserved better roles than that. I really felt that those movies were insulting to him. But I was still a fan of his, even though I stopped going to see his movies.

RED WEST: Elvis just hated most of those later films. I mean, in *Stay Away, Joe* they had him singing to a bull!
 They kept throwing these bad stories at him. Hal Wallis even said in an interview one time, something like, "Well, we know exactly how much we are going to make off each Presley picture, and we don't want to change because profit's the nature of the business."
 The money was all that mattered. They didn't give a damn about the person that had to bear the burden of being in them: Elvis.

BRENDA FIELDER: When I was very young, I would imagine Elvis sitting up on that horse, singing to me, and it was just incredible. Then, as I got older, the whole musical thing was not as wonderful as it had been back in the late fifties and early sixties. Elvis couldn't just break into song in the middle of a scene and look very real.

LANCE LEGAULT: The interesting thing about Elvis as an actor was I never saw him look at a script on set. He came in superprepared to work and he knew all his lines. Elvis had a great memory, developed from memorizing all those songs, maybe. On one hand a simple script wasn't a great challenge; on the other hand, sometimes a lesser script is a hell of a lot more of a challenge. You have to work hard to make it happen. He was always affable; he was on time, and he knew his stuff. Elvis would come in and knock it off quickly.

GEORGE KLEIN: You could tell toward the end of his movie career he had become less and less interested in the roles he was playing. I asked him, "Elvis, what's *Easy Come, Easy Go* about?" He said, "Same story, different location." He was real quick about it.

:◉:◉:◉:

DR. E. O. FRANKLIN *(veterinarian)*: Elvis kept some horses at Graceland and I took care of them for him, but as Memphis grew, the city kind of closed in on Graceland. Graceland was no longer "out in the country." At this time Elvis was becoming more and more interested in horses, so he was kinda locked in at Graceland. Also, by the late sixties Elvis was more and more interested in finding some place where he could get away from all the people. He was needing more time to himself, so he bought a small ranch down in Mississippi, not far from Memphis.

BILL E. BURK: When I wrote in one of my columns an open letter to Elvis, "You've got more money than the Lord allows," I didn't know he was getting rid of it as fast as he was making it. I had no idea that through the years he had been spending money at breakneck speed. The Circle G Ranch [aka, The Flying Circle G], for instance, cost him a bundle of money.

I happened to be in Chicago at the White Sox stadium [Comiskey Park] when Elvis committed to buying that ranch—and for far too much money!

Shortly before this, Elvis had been on a motorcycle driving down into rural Mississippi, DeSoto County, and he passed a farm that had a sixteen-foot white cross erected out by a little private lake. He immediately fell in love with the place. He didn't know who owned it, or if the owner even wanted to sell, but he tracked down the information. Well, turns out the owner was Jack Adams, who, at that time, was one of the biggest used-aircraft salesmen in the world. I was flying Jack around from time to time, and we had just taken Johnny Sane up to rejoin the Detroit Tigers in a game against the White Sox. While we were up there, Johnny said, "Why don't the two of you come to the game tonight?"

He got us into the press box. Well, we're sitting around and the phone's ringing off the wall; finally a young sportswriter picked up the phone and looked at me and asked, "Is there a Mr. Adams here?" I said, "Yeah, I'll take the call." I picked up the phone and a very familiar voice said "Hello, is Mr. Adams there?" I said, "Elvis? This is Bill. What the hell are you calling for?" He said, "I need to talk to Mr. Adams." So I called Adams to the phone.

Both Elvis and Mr. Adams were the superpolite, "Yes, sir; No, sir," type of people, and I overheard part of the conversation. I heard Adams say, "Well, Mr. Presley, as far as I'm concerned, we have a handshake agreement." After the conversation, I asked Jack, "What was that all about?" He said, "Well, Elvis came down to the ranch awhile back and asked me if I would sell it to him. I figured, you know, this is Elvis Presley, so I jacked the price up real good and he said 'Okay, we'll send you the check.' But when Elvis went back to his father and told him to cut a check for 'x' amount of money, his father just went through the ceiling!" Vernon, you know, went through the ceiling if he had to write a check for two cents.

Vernon apparently told Elvis, "You're paying way too much for that." So Elvis had called Chicago the night we were up there and wanted to back out of the deal. But—this is so Southern, so "Elvis Presley," too: Mr. Adams said, "You know, Mr. Presley, all I can say is we shook hands on it." So Elvis immediately honored the agreement and bought the ranch. He actually paid four hundred and fifty thousand dollars for the ranch, some equipment, and some cattle, according to Adams.

The house on that property was a very small place. When fans go down to Walls [Mississippi] and look at that house, they're expecting to see a mansion, but they find it's just a little house sitting right on the road. They are usually surprised.

Anyway, once Elvis bought the ranch, he went gung-ho.

DR. E. O. FRANKLIN: It was a walkout deal. Elvis bought cows, tractors, the whole works. I think at first Elvis just kept the cattle 'cause they came with the place. Then all the horse purchasing began.

That was quite an affair. What Elvis did to the horse market in northern Mississippi was unbelievable. We would go out and look at a horse that was a three hundred dollar horse, but when the people found out it was maybe for Elvis it became a three thousand dollar horse!

I also went through the pickup truck-buying stage with him. One day we bought eight pickup trucks—something ridiculous—for all the guys in his entourage.

Then he bought house trailers so the guys could have some place to stay. The money he must have gone through!

DR. GEORGE NICHOPOULOS (*personal physician*): I got called to go to the ranch one day because Elvis's regular doctor was not available. It looked like a carnival with all those trailers.

Klein took me to Elvis's trailer, and Priscilla and Elvis were there. Elvis and I went to another room and he told me he had some saddle sores from the excessive riding he'd done that week. He didn't feel like he was going to be able to start his movie (the next Monday) because it was, apparently, a very physical movie. He wanted to get treatment, and he wanted me to get in touch with the producers [in Hollywood] to put things off 'til he got himself back together. That was the beginning of our friendship.

PAUL BURLISON: I saw Elvis one day after he bought that ranch. I lived right down the road. I came around the corner one morning, it was kinda early, and Elvis was sitting up on the picnic table out in the yard with his feet on the seat—just sitting there by himself. When I pulled in the driveway, he got up and shook my hand and patted me on the shoulder. I told him, "You've come a long way since the old Crown Electric days." He said, "Yeah, man, I might have been an electrician by now."

BECKY HARTLEY: The bills from the ranch would get unbelievably high because you had the guys that worked for Elvis living there, eating there, using the phone. I know because I used to have to check all the phone bills. There would be months when Elvis's bills would be sixty thousand dollars! Of course, we're not talking about today; we're talking about in the late sixties and early seventies. Sixty thousand dollars was a lot of money then. Well, that would be a lot of money even today, but back then it was a small fortune going out every month.

RAY WALKER: The best I ever saw Presley look was in 1967 at the Circle G. His hair was back to blonde, like it was naturally, the color of a fawn, just as shiny as could be. He'd had a suit made the very same color as his hair, and shoes that matched exactly with the color of his suit. He walked in and we [the Jordanaires] were stunned. He'd been out riding his horses. He was tanned and his eyes—they just shone like diamonds. We couldn't believe it. We just stood there and looked at him. Finally, he said, "Shall we dance?"

MIKE MCGREGOR *(employee)*: I started working horses for Elvis in about February of '67. At the ranch, Elvis'd come out to the barn, and if he wanted to ride—which he usually did—I'd saddle his horse. He liked to run his big yellow horse, Sun. He would go out and just run and play.

LAMAR FIKE: Priscilla and Elvis had a lot of fun at the ranch, rode horses together all the time. They got along real well; of course, they'd already been living together for several years.

MIKE MCGREGOR: I was probably one of the lower guys on the totem pole of pay scale. I'm pretty sure the guys who were traveling with him and had to stay with him made far more money than I did, and on top of that he was constantly giving them things: cars, mink coats and jewelry for their wives and all that kind of stuff. He didn't give me all that kind of stuff, but I think one of the things was he felt, "Well, Mike is a little bit on the independent side and he makes his own living." I think he liked that.

MARTY LACKER: Believe it or not, at that time Elvis was paying me forty-five or fifty dollars a week and, of course, picking up the expenses. But expenses don't help support your family back home. I couldn't just go to him and say, "Elvis, I can't survive on forty-five dollars a week." He just couldn't relate to that—he never worried all that much about money, but he would go and talk to his father [about giving us a raise]. Vernon would burn you in a minute. "Goddamn!" he'd shout; "You give them this, you give them that. What in the hell more do they want?" Elvis would come back and say, "Can't do it."

BECKY HARTLEY: Considering that all the expenses were picked up, that wasn't really bad pay back in those days. I really didn't make that much, but I would have paid Elvis to work for him.

DR. E. O. FRANKLIN: Naturally, my opinion of the people around Elvis was, "Why do they do this?" I couldn't [even] understand what they did. I knew in essence that he paid them all, that somehow or another they were making a living there. In my own right, I didn't like them 'cause I thought they were taking advantage of Elvis; but I'm sure that my mind was partially formed by Aunt Delta, [Biggs, Vernon's sister], who was very derogatory toward them. She didn't like them worth a darn.

BECKY HARTLEY: I don't remember the guys who worked for Elvis ever hurting for anything. You know, they were given cars, they were given nice Christmas bonuses, their wives were given jewelry, and they were given money to gamble with when they went to Vegas.

Then again, I think the main strain on Elvis and Vernon's relationship was maybe when Elvis bought the ranch. Vernon would have me make up lists of all the money being spent so he could show it to Elvis. It didn't do any good, but Mr. Presley would worry about it.

MARTY LACKER: Elvis loved his father. The problem was Vernon, not Elvis. Early on, Vernon was basically jealous of Elvis. As the years went by, the normal father-son roles reversed. Elvis became the provider.

Vernon loved Elvis, too, but the only thing really that Vernon was concerned about was whether he was going to be poor again—whether Vernon was going to be poor. That clouded some of his thinking.

FELTON JARVIS: We were in Nashville cutting the soundtrack for *Clambake* in 1967 with the Jordanaires, and Elvis told them, "Y'all sing on the chorus with me." Well, the director of the picture was there, and he said, "Elvis, I don't think you understand where the song's going to be used in the picture. In this particular scene, you're riding down the highway on a motorcycle singing this song. The voices can't sing along with you. Where would we put the singers?"

Elvis thought a second and said, "Put 'em the same damn place you put the band." That was the end of that.

"Eye of the Tiger"
1967-1971

Just when the public grows accustomed to expecting nothing extraordinary from America's most eligible bachelor, the Colonel releases shocking news: Elvis is married. Best men Marty Lacker and Joe Esposito, together with Judge David Zenoff, who officiates at the wedding ceremony, give eyewitness accounts of the year's surprise event. Afterwards, Elvis and his young bride Priscilla set up housekeeping—not in his beloved Graceland mansion but in a double-wide trailer at the Circle G ranch. Elvis does his own version of settling down.

As his movie commitments draw to a close, Elvis returns to television. This time he's host of his very own network special, giving a much younger audience a brand-new look at Elvis being "Elvis." A captivating jam session that includes two of his original Hayride band members, Scotty Moore and D. J. Fontana, not only wins the king of rock 'n' roll rave reviews but a solid position in entertainment history as well.

Returning to Memphis to record for the first time in more than a decade, Elvis performs masterfully with the backing of American Studio's Chips Moman and his studio musicians. They describe what goes on behind the scenes at these sessions—sessions that produce some of the most successful recordings of Elvis's career.

Then he returns victoriously to Las Vegas, and backup singer Myrna Smith and drummer Ronnie Tutt describe Elvis's undefinable musical magic.

But, just as Elvis's phenomenal career appears to be soaring out of reach, his private life falls to pieces.

> "It's all in the timing. Everything in life is supposed to be when it's supposed to happen. You can't force it, and you can't make it happen when it's not time; you can't turn your back on it when it *is* time."
>
> — T. G. Sheppard [Bill Browder]

MARTY LACKER: Elvis wasn't even thinking about marrying anybody. By rights Elvis shouldn't have married; he really didn't want to be married. He wanted to have a child—he wanted a son—but he didn't really want everything else that went along with it.

LAMAR FIKE: I think of all the women he went with, it was Ann-Margret he liked best of all. She was a sweetheart. They got along real well. But the relationship was doomed from the beginning 'cause Ann wasn't gonna quit the business, and Elvis had those old-fashioned Southern values, you know, "a woman's place is in the home." Ann was gonna stay in the business regardless of whether he wanted her to or not, so it just wasn't meant to happen.

JOE ESPOSITO *(employee)*: Elvis decided in December of 1966 he was going to marry Priscilla.

MARTY LACKER: Elvis didn't have to marry Priscilla in the sense that some people might think, that she was pregnant. He told me that there was some pressure being exerted on him. To be quite frank, he cared a lot about Ann-Margret, but because of pressure, marrying Priscilla was the decision he made.

LAMAR FIKE: Between Priscilla's family and the Colonel, there was a lot of stuff that went on there regarding them getting married. I think there were a lot of promises Elvis had made, and I think the markers were called.

MARTY LACKER: Well, you know, basically, in order to get Priscilla over here, Elvis had made promises to her stepfather and her mother—like, it's not just a one-night stand, I'm really serious about her—and they called him on it. He really didn't want to marry anybody.

GERALDINE KYLE: I think it was her innocence that attracted Elvis to Priscilla.

I was coming out of Grandma's room one day and Vernon was on the phone to somebody. As I passed by, I heard him say; "Well, Elvis told me the reason he was going to marry her was that Priscilla was one girl he knew no man had ever been with." I never told anybody I overheard that conversation.

JOE ESPOSITO: Elvis and the Colonel talked about the wedding, and the Colonel set it all up. The Colonel told everybody where to go and where to be; that's how it went. His friend Milt Prell helped organize it.

JUDGE DAVID ZENOFF *(officiated at Elvis and Priscilla's wedding)*: It was not unusual to be called once in awhile to perform a wedding for somebody favorite to one of the Las Vegas hotel owners. In this case I was already on the Supreme Court of Nevada, which was in Carson City—five hundred miles from Las Vegas. Milton [Prell] called me and said, "I've got to keep something secret. I would like for you to perform a wedding, but I don't want to tell you who it is. Would you just take my word for it?" I said, "Sure." So he told me the date [May 1, 1967] and down I came. I was taken to a room—Milton Prell's penthouse. There were a few flowers, but nothing else that was special.

MARTY LACKER: I was to be one of the best men at Elvis's wedding, along with Joe. Everything was going fine, but just a few minutes before the ceremony I was told there wouldn't be enough room at the actual ceremony for all of Elvis's guys. They were really upset.

JOE ESPOSITO: There were a lot of curious people around the hotel, I guess, but I really didn't pay any attention to what was going on outside the small room where the actual wedding ceremony was to take place. The periphery of the room was surrounded by press, but I blocked everything else out of my mind because I knew security was taking care of all that. All I was concerned about was having a nice wedding ceremony, and I think everybody in the immediate party felt the same way.

JUDGE DAVID ZENOFF: Before the wedding, I remember saying I wanted to meet separately with the bride and groom in advance of the ceremony.

Colonel Parker brought Elvis off to the side of the room to meet me, and I chatted with him a few moments. My pre-ceremony meeting with Elvis was probably the most impressive part of the whole experience. I was simply amazed at the boy's modesty. He was low key, handsome as a picture, very respectful, and very intense. I just sort of tried to put him at ease: "Now, I know you're nervous. You're expected to be nervous, but don't be. I'll have you in and out of here in two minutes. Just listen to me and answer my questions and that'll be it. You'll know it's over when I say, 'You may kiss your bride.'"

He understood I had come quite some distance and he thanked me for it. I said, "I have prepared some thoughts which I will impart to you and your bride and I hope you'll hear them and pay heed to them." He was most respectful and so nervous he was almost bawling.

Then I was taken over to meet Priscilla. She was absolutely petrified. She couldn't open her mouth—just stood there staring at me and nodding a little bit when I explained things to her. I think she nodded when I indicated to her, "Do you understand? Is there anything you want to ask me?" She shook her head a little bit.

JOE ESPOSITO: The ceremony itself wasn't written especially for them like people do these days for their vows. I think it was pretty much just whatever the vows were for Nevada.

JUDGE DAVID ZENOFF: Everybody was properly respectful, solemn, scared. I said, "Elvis, you stand here." I don't remember if I said, "Priscilla, you stand here"; I pointed anyway, and they just lined up. When I saw they were in place, we went right to it. Elvis was tied up in knots by this time, and I think he was memorizing every word I was saying. Elvis towered over Priscilla and at the end of the ceremony he leaned over and kissed her.

JOE ESPOSITO: They were Mr. and Mrs. Elvis Presley. Priscilla was thrilled; she was grinning from ear to ear, but still she was sorta in shock, to tell you the truth. I think she was really nervous. It was probably a big relief to her when it was over.

They had a very small reception. There were some friends there, but we didn't know a lot of people in Vegas. When we walked into the reception, there was big applause. It was like Elvis walking onstage, but with his wife now. Elvis and Priscilla sat down at the table, and people would come by and congratulate them.

MARTY LACKER: The wedding cake was decorated with pink-and-white roses, and it was six tiers and five feet high.

GERALDINE KYLE: When Priscilla and Elvis got back to Memphis, they had a second wedding reception at Graceland for all the friends and family who couldn't go to Las Vegas. I was impressed because Elvis and Priscilla wore their wedding clothes. It was just very uptown, very classy.

JOE ESPOSITO: In those days, they all thought it would affect a star's popularity if they got married, or even had a steady girlfriend. But then we realized it didn't matter—a lot of people didn't care if he was married or not. They just loved Elvis.

Elvis and Priscilla spent their honeymoon at the Circle G Ranch—in a trailer; yes, in a house trailer! Let's face it; Elvis was not a normal human being. He liked unusual things, and staying in a trailer was exciting to him.

BECKY HARTLEY: Elvis seemed very happy when he was at the ranch, and Priscilla did, too. They had the house down there, but Elvis's cousin Billy [Smith] and his wife Jo lived in the house; Elvis and Priscilla stayed in a trailer. She loved living in that. They had picked out a double-wide and they were both real proud of it.

LAMAR FIKE: Life at Graceland never really changed that much after the marriage. Elvis just went out beyond the boundaries of Graceland more because he still wanted to roar.

JERRY KYLE: I didn't see a whole lot of love in that family. There wasn't the closeness that I was used to at my house. I mean, I never saw any hand-holding.

BECKY HARTLEY: Priscilla came to my office one day and told me that she was pregnant. She told me, "I did exactly like you said, Becky, but we were counting the rhythm wrong." She must have gotten pregnant on her wedding night, or right after that. She didn't get pregnant before [the wedding]; I mean, she probably was not in a hurry to get pregnant because she was probably still worried about her figure then.

As it turned out, Priscilla never really had to worry about her figure because she never even wore maternity clothes—never, never. She did not gain that much. You couldn't even tell she was pregnant.

GERALDINE KYLE: I gave Priscilla a baby shower at the LaRonde Restaurant [Memphis], which is on top of a building near the Methodist Hospital. LaRonde is supposed to be French for "the round," and, of course, it was a revolving restaurant. It was one of *the* places to go at the time in Memphis. There were all kinds of reporters there. I remember we played baby bingo. I forgot what I had as prizes or who won; I cannot even remember what I gave Priscilla for the baby, but I still remember what I gave Elvis and Priscilla for a wedding present. It was Vincent Price's cookbook, because in the sixties I knew that Priscilla couldn't cook water. She seemed to be thrilled with it.

FRED FREDRICK: When Priscilla had Lisa Marie [February 1, 1968], Elvis was just ecstatic.

BECKY HARTLEY: Elvis was all smiles after Lisa Marie was born. He was just very excited.

JAMES BLACKWOOD: One Christmas Eve my younger son Billy and I were driving around. I said, "I haven't seen Elvis in some time; let's drive in and see if he is home." So we drove in, and Charlie Hodge took us to the living room and we sat down. Elvis came down in a few minutes and we visited. He said, "I want you to see Lisa." He went back upstairs and brought her down and showed her off. He was real proud of her.

GERALDINE KYLE: They would keep Lisa Marie in a crib downstairs right between the kitchen and the back den. Sometimes I'd pick her up and hold her. I felt kinda sad for that little girl because Dee wouldn't even be in there, and Elvis hadn't come down yet, and, I guess, Priscilla had to be upstairs, too. The only person in there was whoever was doing the cooking. She was just a baby, but I just thought that she was going to have a lonely life. I guess she got a lot of perks with it, though.

:◎:◎:◎:

DON WARDELL *(disc jockey, Radio Luxembourg)*: Radio Luxembourg was, at that time, the most powerful radio station in Europe. You could always pull great programming ratings on that station by programming Presley. The demand was so great we even had to put on our own weekly Elvis show.

    The fans in England were very dedicated. They kept sending the message back to Elvis that they wanted him to get back to live performing and get away from those movies. The message began to get through.

Tom Jones: In '68 while Elvis was still making movies, I went to Las Vegas to perform and they told me that Elvis was going to drive up from Los Angeles to see my show. He wouldn't fly in those days; he was terrified to fly. They said he would come up in a limousine, and I thought, "Sounds a little strange," but all at once, there he was. I didn't really know it then, but he was actually studying me onstage because he wanted to come back into live stage work himself. He told me later that watching me reassured him that an audience was still there for him. He was nervous about going back, especially after being off so long.

:◎:◎:◎:

D. J. Fontana: Elvis was a little worried about the '68 Comeback Special [*Elvis*, NBC-TV]. He said, "What do you think, guys? You think they'll like me?" He hadn't been in front of a crowd in eight or ten years. I said, "Elvis, all you can do is go out and do the best you can, and you'll find out in about twenty-four hours."

Bill Belew *(costume designer)*: When we had the first production meeting for the TV special, it was decided that his concert outfit was going to be very important. We were sitting around talking and I said, "You know, the one thing everybody used to think was that Elvis wore leather. He did wear leather jackets—motorcycle jackets—but he never really wore total black, a total black leather outfit."

At that time, denim was the big thing among the hippies. I was doing embroidering and all kinds of things to jeans to make 'em look different. I said, "Why don't I take a jean jacket and a pair of jeans and duplicate those in black leather?" That's how the black leather outfit came about.

Elvis liked the idea from the start, but he said, "I want something to wear around my neck. I don't want to wear a lot of jewelry." What was in vogue at that point was to wear a scarf with a little clip you ran the ends through like a ring; it held the scarf at the neck. That's actually where the legendary Elvis scarves began.

Scotty Moore: The 1968 *Elvis* special was a real fun time. We had a ball getting ready for the show. Looking at it now, it's obvious Elvis had a good time, too. We weren't trying to pick up any music awards or anything—just went out and had fun. And that's the way it came off.

LANCE LeGAULT: I remember Elvis was a little concerned about doing a live performance. He hadn't done a live performance in many years.

When we did that in-the-round sit-down thing—the jam—they told us just do whatever Elvis wants to do; they were only going to use ten minutes of it. So we just had a great time jamming, and later on they used that whole thing, uncut, unedited, and with no musical overdub. We didn't even have a bass player! D. J.'s beating on a guitar case. Elvis took Scotty's guitar and gave him the acoustic, so Elvis had the electric. It was fun, and that's the real Elvis.

MARY ANN MOBLEY: I thought that was Elvis at his best in that 1968 Comeback Special. We really saw a relaxed Elvis in that. Elvis natural, doing what he enjoyed most, just sittin' around and singing and talking. He wasn't trying to be anything but himself. That was the best of Elvis Presley. He looked great and he sang great and he seemed so relaxed.

JOAN DEARY: The '68 Special brought Elvis back visually into the real world, and it was very much acclaimed.

T. G. SHEPPARD [Bill Browder]: When I saw him on the Special, I was amazed at how up-to-date he was, how he'd been around so long but was still so hip in the leather suit. That was more of a rock 'n' roll Elvis than a movie-star Elvis. It set the persona. It set the mood for the music that came in the years following. That was the jump-start for Elvis's career again—that special. I was amazed by how great he looked and how he still had that magnetism.

:◎:◎:◎:

TOM JONES: I was told by Priscilla that when I was around Elvis he seemed to be a different person. We spent some time in Hawaii together. He went up and got two guitars and brought them back to the house. We sat down like two kids, really, when they first meet and want to play together. Priscilla said, "I've never really seen this side of Elvis before. He's so thrilled to have somebody around that really understands what he's doing musically."

LANCE LeGAULT: The last picture I did with Elvis was *Speedway*, with Nancy Sinatra. Elvis liked her a lot. He came to me one time and he said,

"You know what Nancy just told me? She said the two men she respected most in her life were her dad and me." Elvis was real proud of that.

BILLY STANLEY: We went to the set of *Speedway* when Elvis and Nancy Sinatra were filming it. They looked like sweethearts to me on the set. It was almost like it was awkward for Elvis that day because my mom was there. Now he didn't mind doing things in front of me, Ricky, or David, but in front of my mom, that was a different story. Nancy and Elvis were holding hands and talking and cutting up with each other in between sets.

ALAN FORTAS: Elvis made twenty-eight movies in a span of eight years. All of his movies made money, but by the time he got to *Charro* and *The Trouble with Girls*, there was a noticeable decline in profits, and an even more noticeable decline in Elvis's interest in movies.

The '68 TV Special had proved what a great performer he still was, and so it was time for a change.

LANCE LEGAULT: That sensation and excitement of playing for a live audience is something that you can't replace with a camera. That's why so many actors do theater from time to time and personal appearances. Singers like Elvis need to sing, you know, and they need that rapport with the audience—that feeling you get in live entertainment.

:◎:◎:◎:

CHIPS MOMAN *(record producer and co-owner, American Sound Studio)*: Marty [Lacker] was working for American Sound at the time, and George Klein and I—we had been talking about "When's Elvis gonna get some good songs, man? When's he gonna quit cuttin' that crap?"

MARTY LACKER: There used to be a television set in the den in front of the waterfall [in the jungle room at Graceland]. We used to sit there and watch TV. One night Elvis was there and Klein was there and Felton Jarvis. Felton said, "Well, okay, the sessions will start Monday."

I had really gotten involved over at American Sound and I knew how many hit records they were cutting over there. Elvis and Felton were talking about going back to Nashville to record, and it was just pissing me off. I just knew he'd go back there and just cut the same old shit and probably the same old shitty songs. Nothing against Nashville. I like Nashville, but the timing seemed bad to me.

I was basically talking to myself and I was upset—and Elvis looked over at me and said, "What the hell is wrong with you?" I said, "I don't know, Elvis, I just wish you would try Chips's musicians just once."

Elvis said, "Well, maybe someday I will." And boy, I could just feel myself burning inside. Just then the maid came out of the kitchen and said, "Dinner's ready." Normally I would be the first one at the table, but I just sat there. They all got up and said, "Come on, let's go eat." I said, "No, I ain't hungry." Elvis looked at me and turned around and went into the dining room. I sat there and I was just cussing under my breath.

Felton comes out about five minutes later, and said, "Elvis wants to talk to you. He wants to cut in Memphis!" I said, "Are you shitting me? Is that the truth?" Felton said, "No, he really wants to cut in Memphis." I didn't walk in there; I ran in there.

CHIPS MOMAN: When Felton called, we worked out the deal for Elvis to record in my studio. We started looking for material, asking around, pulling together some songs we already had.

BOBBY WOOD *(musician)*: The first night Elvis actually came into the studio, I had psyched myself out. We were the hottest recording group in the country at that point, and I said, "Well, Elvis is coming here to get our sound, no need of me getting butterflies when he gets here." But, man, I knew when he was in the back parking lot! I just felt his presence. I felt him. It was almost like Christ was out there or something. There was no doubt about it. I tell you what, I got chill bumps when he came in. I couldn't help it. It just happened. You knew he was there.

CHIPS MOMAN: Mac Davis brought in "In the Ghetto," and when I first heard it I just loved the song. I think anyone would have loved that demo; it was great. But you kinda have to remember the time. It was the sixties (racial tension and all that) and Presley had never done a song like that before. There was a discussion about what people might think about a white guy singing about life in the ghetto.

BOBBY WOOD: Mac Davis, who wrote "In the Ghetto," played it in person for Elvis. He was scared to death. We were all in the control room. Mac was shaking like a leaf 'cause he was performing for Elvis. Elvis told him "That's a hit!" He said it right there, "That's a smash!" And almost everybody in the control room agreed.

GEORGE KLEIN: "In the Ghetto" kind of bothered me. I thought it might be too risky for Elvis, and he was too big to need to take risks. I said, "God, Elvis, I don't know if that's right for you or not." Chips agreed.

After Elvis left, Chips turned to me and said, "Holy shit! What a great song for Roy Hamilton!" He was producing Roy at the time. And it's true: Roy Hamilton would have sung the devil out of "In the Ghetto." But that night I went home and I thought, "Man, I made a mistake!"

I went out to Graceland the next day before Elvis went to the studio. I walked in the backdoor and he was sitting on the couch. I said, "Elvis, I made a damn big mistake." He said, "What?" I said, "I made a statement last night about 'In the Ghetto.' I was wrong. I think that's a number-one song for you." He laughed and said, "No shit! I'm cutting it tonight!"

CHIPS MOMAN: Elvis had a good ear for music, and if he didn't think he could do a song he'd toss it out. However, when it came time to do the sessions, there was a lot of them old Hill and Range songs that it seems like some of the people around him wanted him to cut real bad, and they kept pushing for 'em. I don't even want to tell you what I thought of some of those songs! Truth is, the trouble wasn't really with Elvis but with some of those publishers.

BOBBY WOOD: The whole thing started out on a bad note—a disagreement over publishing rights. It looked like the whole thing was going to be called off.

I think Elvis was honestly looking for a hit. He wasn't selling but about two hundred thousand on a release at that time. He hadn't had a million-seller in several years.

CHIPS MOMAN: Hill and Range wanted the publishing rights to "In the Ghetto" and "Suspicious Minds." I just blew up! I said, "Hey, there ain't no more session!" We had already done some sides, and I said, "You can take everything we've done so far, be my guest, and just get out of my studio, 'cause there ain't no more sessions!" That's when Harry Jenkins—he was with RCA at the time—stood up for me. Harry said, "Hey, speaking for RCA, we haven't ever said anything about what Elvis has been recording since he's been with us, but I'm gonna tell you right now, this boy's right" (talking about me), "so we're gonna stay here and we're gonna do these sessions his way."

BOBBY WOOD: Suddenly something like a miracle happened: Elvis asked Chips personally, "How can we work without all these problems?" Chips told him, "Leave those [publishing] cronies out of the studio. I don't want to see 'em no more." Elvis said, "You got it." That's exactly how we started cutting all the hits. We got the riff-raff out of there and got down to business and only had Elvis's key people around.

CHIPS MOMAN: There was just too many people, and it was aggravating, I guess, on all sides. But I think they were kind of shocked when I stood up to them. They probably had never had anyone ask them to leave the studio before—but I did, and it turned out better for Elvis.

The thing I enjoyed most was when I got just him and me in the studio, two or three times. There was no hassles, no problems with anybody. The only time it got really hectic was when all those guys were around, and it would be almost like he thought he had to perform for them, you know, say something cute, do something funny, make 'em laugh. When it was just him and me, one-on-one, he was just one of the easiest people to work with.

WAYNE JACKSON (*musician*): I'll say this, when he was singing "In the Ghetto," and I was sitting there playing horn, I knew that it was going to be a big, big record, and probably one of the most important records of his life.

This was after Martin Luther King's assassination in Memphis. Over at American Sound they had dogs around—one dog in the studio. Sometimes they would have a guy on the roof with a shotgun just watching over the parking lot. It was tense, especially in the parts of town that were mainly black. That's where Stax [Records] was. That's where Hi [Records] was. And that's where American Sound was.

So we were actually in the ghetto, and here was Elvis singing a pertinent song about the South and about the social climate of the day. He's singing and chills went all over me. I thought, "Yeah, that's the one."

MIKE LEECH (*musician*): Elvis seemed to be excited during the whole thing. Of course, I didn't have any way to judge that because I'd never seen him in any other studio or recording situation. The only thing I remember is that he worked just as hard as the rest of us and his concentration was up.

Really the only thing us musicians were told was what song Elvis wanted to do next. We would all listen to the demonstration record, and then our job was to put the arrangement together in the studio. There wasn't a whole lot of direction given. We did it ourselves, us musicians. We worked it up. And we usually went the opposite direction from the demos they would play.

WAYNE JACKSON: I loved Elvis's singing. He was a powerful soul singer. Elvis had a real love affair with his voice. That's what it takes. You have to really love your own voice.

CHIPS MOMAN: "Suspicious Minds" was a song that Mark James had written. I had recorded it with Mark, but nothing was happening with his record 'cause I don't think Mark had really got the vocals on it the way Presley did later. I played it for Elvis and he loved it. We did the arrangements about the same as on Mark's record—but we had that Presley voice! Presley was a great singer, man. He could sell a song! And the rest is history. It was one of the biggest records Elvis had had in years, a great song for him.

BOBBY WOOD: We worked a lot differently at American from what Elvis was used to. It usually took Chips and the other engineers a good long while to get "a sound." That was rough on the singers. They'd have to stand there and sing the same song over and over for an hour, before we'd even record a take. After about the third night, Elvis lost his voice. He had bad laryngitis, so we had to just record music tracks for a couple of nights without him.

MIKE LEECH: By the time we had the arrangement ready on a song, Elvis was usually ready to record. "Suspicious Minds" has that slow-down part in the middle of it. I think we had to run over that a couple of times for everybody to get real comfortable, but Elvis nailed it.

BOBBY WOOD: You can tell the songs Elvis really liked. Like any artist, he sang the heck out of 'em.
  Elvis cried when he heard a Johnny Christopher song called "Mama Liked the Roses." We really debated on whether to play that for him because they didn't know how he was going to take it. But Elvis said, "I've got to do it." We all knew he was thinking about Gladys.

CHIPS MOMAN: "Kentucky Rain" [written by Eddie Rabbitt and Dick Heard] was one of the few songs that came out of the Hill and Range catalog in New York that I really liked. Elvis loved the song and said yes to it the first time he heard it. Lamar Fike brought that one in. It turned out to be Elvis's fiftieth gold record.

MIKE LEECH: We did twenty-six songs in a period of about three-and-a-half weeks. The titles all started running together after awhile.

JOAN DEARY: When I first heard the tapes from the American sessions, I called Chet Atkins and asked, "Who did Elvis's recording of 'In the Ghetto'? Who was the engineer?" Right off the bat he said, "Chips Moman," and he said, "Why do you ask?" I told him, "Because the sound is so superior to what I've been hearing on Elvis, I can't believe my ears! There's such a big difference between this and his old stuff." That whole Memphis recording collection was incredible, and yet Elvis never went back and recorded with Chips again. I'm not sure why. Maybe it was the influence of Hill and Range, which had always had a big piece of the publishing on other Presley records. They lost their total control when Chips entered the picture.

FRED FREDRICK: Everybody in the whole recording industry had these huge speakers and big amplifiers and everything. All Chips had on his desk was a six-inch car speaker. He said, "Nobody that I know's got that kind of big equipment [stereo systems]. I'm gonna play my music back through a car speaker 'cause that's how people are gonna hear it." That's how it started right there. How's it gonna sound on your car radio? That's all he wanted to know.

CHIPS MOMAN: Hindsight's 20/20 I guess, but I didn't really think anything so special about getting the chance to record Elvis—not when it happened. Oh, it was okay, but to tell you the truth, we were so busy producing records in Memphis back then (and a lot of 'em were hits 'cause we were hot at the time with Neil Diamond and a lot of other stars) that we had to actually work a double shift and cut Roy Hamilton during the day and Elvis at night in order to do those albums. He only had so much open time on his schedule. Now don't get me wrong. I had always liked Elvis. I always loved his music, especially the early years of his career, but I just went in to work on it like any other project—no big deal. You see, most everybody in Memphis kind of took Elvis for granted—didn't pay any attention to how big a star he really was. Remember, he was a hometown boy. He's bigger now in Memphis than he ever was in his best days when he was alive.

Later I thought to myself, "It sure was a privilege to have worked with him. I wish I had realized that at the time we were recording, 'cause there's a lot of things that I would have liked to have said to him."

DON WARDELL: When Elvis returned to cutting non-soundtrack records, the response was immediate; it was extraordinary, and that wasn't just in America; it was worldwide.

WAYNE JACKSON: I think Elvis was very happy at that period, and why not? He had a beautiful wife and a new baby. His life was clicking.

GEORGE KLEIN: Elvis had one more movie to make under his contract, so he went back to the coast to film it. It was *Change of Habit*. It was a cute little picture with Mary Tyler Moore. Elvis played a doctor and looked like a Greek god.

DICK "BUCKY" MOORE: When Elvis was out in California making that last movie, for some reason or another they decided to sell the mobile homes down at the ranch. Vernon contacted me, and I conducted an auction down at the farm for them. I sold all the homes and arranged financing for the prospective buyers.

DR. E. O. FRANKLIN: Elvis didn't want to stay in the cattle business, so we had a sale and got rid of all of them. Then he just had the horses.

MIKE MCGREGOR: I guess Elvis just got tired of the ranch. You know, he had enough money; he could have kept the ranch a little while. If he got tired of owning it, playing with it, he could sell it tomorrow. People [who have money] like that, I don't understand why they do what they do.

BILL E. BURK: When he sold the Circle G Ranch [May 21, 1969], he got three hundred and fifty thousand dollars—that was with all the improvements he'd made and an extra forty acres he had bought right next to the basic property. So he lost at least a hundred thousand dollars on that deal. He moved the horses back to Graceland.

LOWELL HAYS *(jeweler)*: My father's doctor was Dr. Nick [Dr. George Nichopoulos]. One night Nick asked me if I'd like to go out to Graceland and meet Elvis. It was in early December. Elvis was in his backyard, shooting a gun at the walls outside his father's office. He was out there with the two local sheriffs, Bill Morris and Roy "Skip" Nixon. Elvis was wearing a mink coat with a big hood on it. It was raining, and he was laying down in his backyard, shooting at this target while wearing a full-length mink coat! That's how I met him.

:◎:◎:◎:

BILL BELEW: I got a call from Joe Esposito one day. The Colonel wanted to know if I would be interested in designing the clothes for Elvis's Las Vegas opening. Of course I said I would.

The first things I designed for Elvis were jumpsuits, and then he said he would like to experiment with some other things. I did some two-piece outfits—sleeveless outfits. They didn't give him the flexibility that he needed, so later we just went back to the basic jumpsuit design.

We both agreed that it was really the best look for him. It gave him a look of greater height and, being all one piece, it was just more comfortable for him; his shirttail didn't come out when he moved around.

RONNIE TUTT (musician): In 1969, a friend of mine told me Elvis was auditioning drummers. They had auditioned drummers for several weeks and they were getting frustrated. Larry Muhoberac, Elvis's keyboard player at that time, said, "I've got a drummer friend that's getting ready to move out to California." Elvis said, "Bring him in and let's see what he can do."

I flew in on a Saturday morning and got my equipment ready for that evening. They said, "Just sit here 'til we call you." Elvis was there to personally supervise the auditions. I'm waiting there when all at once some other drummer walks in. He comes over to me and says, "Hey man, they want me to audition next, can I borrow your drum set?" Rather reluctantly, I said, "Well, okay." So he starts playing the drums and everybody starts smiling like, "Yeah, we found the guy!" and I'm sinking lower and lower into the chair, thinking, "I'm not even going to get a chance to be heard. I've come all this way, this guy's using my drum set, and he's gonna get the gig!" Anyway, they auditioned me, too, and they kept me over an extra day because they said Elvis hadn't quite made up his mind.

MYRNA SMITH (singer): Our agency was called in 1969, after Elvis's Comeback Special. We didn't have to go for an audition. Whoever called our agency just asked if we were available and if we'd consider working as backup singers for Elvis Presley. Elvis had heard a song that we had recorded that was called "Sweet Inspiration," and he liked the sound we had. On the basis of that, he hired us. The first time we met him was at rehearsal in July of 1969.

RONNIE TUTT: When they told me Elvis had picked me for drummer I was really happy. They said he picked me because I watched him and we had that eye contact. It was part of our musical communication, so to speak. They said, "By the way, we start rehearsing tomorrow night!" I had the clothes on my back, so I immediately had to figure out how to live in L.A., where to stay, all of that.

The other musicians with him were great musicians, and it didn't take very long to fall into the whole show. It was just a matter of learning all of his stuff. Of course he had a tremendous repertoire, and he liked to be able to pull a song out of the air at any time; so it wasn't exactly a piece of cake, either.

GEORGE KLEIN: Elvis had played the Frontier Hotel in 1956, but Vegas wasn't quite ready for him then. He didn't play Vegas again until August of 1969. When the International Hotel opened, Barbra Streisand was their first star. They paid her one hundred thousand dollars to appear there. Elvis was booked to follow Streisand. An interesting sideline is that Colonel Parker said, "We'll play there, but we want more than Streisand. We want a hundred and five thousand dollars." So they paid Elvis a hundred and five thousand dollars.

Elvis went to Barbra's closing night, and he went backstage to her dressing room just to say he enjoyed her performance. He was going to have the very same dressing room the following night. Well, Barbra Streisand, as I understand it, can be very sarcastic and very rude—a typical "New Yawker."

When Elvis came in, he had on this big wide belt and sunglasses and the whole uniform that he wore wherever he went. That was Elvis and that's the way he dressed. Barbra started making very snide remarks about this belt, his sunglasses, whatever he had on. Elvis let the first remark slide off, and the second remark, but when she said something else critical of him, he just stood up (there were a lot of people in the dressing room) and he said, "Look, Barbra, we all know that you've got a big nose, and we all know that you've got bad teeth, and you're probably the ugliest movie star that ever made it to Hollywood. Why don't you just shut up and stop laying that reverse psychology routine on me. I've had that done too many times." Her mouth just flew open and she was shocked. She didn't know what to say.

Then she laughed and everybody laughed. She said, "Oh, Elvis, you're right." They became good friends after that because he put her in her place.

MYRNA SMITH: When Elvis walked onto the stage for that first rehearsal, we were already sitting there—the Sweet Inspirations and the Imperials. He walked in and had on a chocolate-colored suit. He had a tan, and he looked absolutely gorgeous. He walked over to us and introduced himself—like we didn't know who he was: "Hi, I'm Elvis Presley." From then on, whenever he'd see us, it was always a kiss.

We weren't Elvis fans at the very beginning because we had our own career going, but the songs we knew the backgrounds to, we sang. We embellished the backgrounds some; some of the stuff he liked, but if we did too much on a song he'd say, "Just leave that part out." (We would funk it up a lot, and sometimes it would get too far away from the original record.)

:◉:◉:◉:

FRED FREDRICK: Elvis flew two airplanes full of us out to Vegas for his opening because he didn't think anybody was gonna show up! Of course, the first night the line is all the way out across the whole hotel, out into the parking lot!

T. G. SHEPPARD [Bill Browder]: I had gone to work for RCA Victor in 1969 doing regional promotion. Ironically, I covered Memphis and a lot of the South. The Las Vegas opening [July 31, 1969] was quite wild. It was like a circus. Colonel Parker was a man who knew the carnival business. I was working record promotion for RCA then and the label went overboard. We brought people in from all over the world, radio and press. Elvis was a hit; he was on fire. It was just pandemonium.

BILL BELEW: The legendary Elvis scarves began when we went to Vegas; we remembered the idea from the TV special. He said, "Why don't you start making me some scarves because I perspire so much, and I can wipe off my face and hand 'em out to the audience." He started throwing them out to the fans, and that became a big thing. So I made tons and tons of different colored scarves that I would ship off to him.

MYRNA SMITH: We didn't realize before we worked with Elvis that he was so great. The first night we sang with him, when he opened in Vegas, I thought it was just a one-time occurrence—that opening night—because I didn't think anybody could possibly keep packing those people in, two shows a night, for a month. I thought, "This is phenomenal! But can he do it again tomorrow?" And then the next night came—"Yeah!"

RONNIE TUTT: Onstage you never knew what he was going to do. Yet we had great unspoken communication between us. I remember the first shows. They amazed me because they were incredibly electric, very, very high energy.

The first show each night, the audience was still eating dinner, which isn't a very conducive atmosphere for doing concert work; but even with that, people would go absolutely crazy. I saw the Beatles in the sixties when they came to Memphis. I stood right above them at the Mid-South Coliseum, and the people, the girls particularly, just screamed. With the Elvis show, of course, they weren't teeny-boppers in Vegas, and yet it was that same kind of intensity. Not many performers evoke that kind of wild excitement and intensity.

EDDIE FADAL: Whatever it took to get a rise out of his fans, Elvis would do it onstage. The stage was his living room. He even called it his living room. If it took sliding on his knees to the front of the stage, he would do it. If it meant lying down on his back, singing, he did it. He did everything to please his fans. It gave him the biggest thrill to see them excited, especially in Las Vegas.

T. G. SHEPPARD [Bill Browder]: He really was different when he came back to stage work. He was full of piss and vinegar. He had the eye of the tiger. Man, he went out there and just grabbed people by the neck and wore 'em out onstage. He was phenomenal.

MYRNA SMITH: When Elvis was in true form, he was fabulous. He had so much energy. His voice was a lot more remarkable than it ever came off on record, and his vocal pitch was much better than it came off on record. He was just a much better singer than could ever be captured. There are a lot of singers like that: You can't capture truly what they sound like. Some great singers' voices are just too big. Elvis was like that.

JUNE JUANICO: The last time I saw Elvis was in 1969. I watched him perform onstage at the Hilton [International], and he had never looked better—never. He was thin—even his black hair was okay. He looked wonderful, and he had incorporated karate moves into his act, which was a lot better because his dance rhythm left something to be desired. He had rhythm in his hands, he had rhythm in his feet, but as far as putting 'em together with his body [when he danced]—no, he couldn't.

MARY JARVIS: When Elvis opened in Vegas, he got Harry Jenkins [of RCA] to let Felton go out to Vegas with him. At that time Felton had a lot of other production responsibilities at RCA—Skeeter Davis, Floyd Cramer, Jim Ed Brown, Jimmy Dean, and Nat Stuckey. He was producing all of their records. I'm sure all of those artists began to get a little aggravated about Felton being off with Elvis week after week, so finally Chet told Felton he was neglecting his work and he'd have to take care of all of his artists or quit.

Felton resigned and Elvis took Felton on as an independent record producer. A few months later Elvis and Felton went into RCA Studio B in Nashville, and I believe Elvis cut forty songs with Felton. That was the most songs Elvis had ever recorded at one time. They did a country album, a gospel album, and a Christmas album. RCA must have been happy about that.

KANG RHEE *(karate instructor)*: He discover me 1970 to come to my institute in Memphis once to observation of the class. I was really surprised—everybody shocked—when four or five limousines pull into the parking lot and fifteen to twenty bodyguards surround him. So excited: It is Elvis! He want to study karate. He trying to call me "Master Rhee" and then order the bodyguards call me "Master Rhee." He tries to make bodyguard training through me for Priscilla and himself. He really trying to motivate everybody in his group to train under me.

He had trained in martial art at the Germany—it was Army days. Seems to be he told me his karate belt much more important prize to him than his fancy entertaining trophies like his gold records. He told me, "Master Rhee, I have a gold record, but I more appreciate and enjoy my black belt than my gold records."

He asks me many times, "Look at me please and tell me what you thinking about my different stances and kicks I do with my performance onstage."

Ronnie Tutt: I studied martial arts for a while so I could understand better what Elvis was doing onstage. I had to be able to catch those martial arts moves with the drums. I needed to be able to "read" what he was doing, anticipate him. We'd study together sometimes when we were out on the road, and then sometimes we'd have classes up in his suite at the hotel there in Vegas.

MYRNA SMITH: If Elvis was in Las Vegas when he wasn't performing, he would go down and gamble in the casino. Nobody would bother him. But if he was working Vegas, it was a different story. The hotel would be flooded with Elvis fans.

I remember one day during one of his engagements, he came down out of his suite on the elevator, alone. All of a sudden I see just hordes of people running toward the elevator. I had no idea what was going on, but it turned out Elvis had walked out of the hotel, gotten into a cab, and gone down to the gun shop to buy some guns. It was always like that if he tried to venture out while he was working. When he wasn't working there, somehow he kind of blended in.

RONNIE TUTT: His show was paced out pretty well, and we all had input in trying to make it pace as good as possible. There were a lot of times I thought to myself, "Man, this song is too fast!" Sometimes I felt like we needed to slow certain things down, and yet, if the songs weren't up to a certain energy level, Elvis felt like it wasn't exciting enough. That's the way he liked it—exciting. If it was going too slow for him, he'd look around at me and catch my eye, and either move his leg or kind of move his arm like, "Let's move it up a little bit," or "Crank it up."

Elvis was never trained in music. He was just a natural musician. He just played by feel, and if it felt right and did the right things to him, then he liked it. He counted on a few of us to make sure everything was right technically and musically.

:◎:◎:◎:

SONNY WEST: Elvis had a fear of someone shooting and killing him for no reason. When we had a death threat in Vegas in '70—just a few months after Charles Manson's people had killed Sharon Tate—Elvis broke down and actually cried in the dressing room. He called Red, Jerry Schilling, and me into the room and said, "I haven't done anything to anybody to get shot. I haven't hurt anybody. If some S.O.B. tries to kill me, I want you guys to get to him; and I want him done up right. I don't want him sitting around like Charlie Manson with a grin on his face or a claim to fame that he killed Elvis Presley."

I guarantee if anybody had really harmed Elvis, we would have got to the guy before the police. That's how much we loved Elvis.

MYRNA SMITH: The first time we were set to appear with Elvis outside of Vegas, we were excited. It was in Houston. The people were exceptionally nice to us. Later I found out the promoters had sent word that they were thrilled Elvis was coming but not to bring "those black girls" with him! Elvis had laid down the law that if we didn't come, he wasn't coming either. So when we did the show, I wondered why everybody was so nice to us. None of the guys told us 'cause they didn't want to hurt our feelings. I found out years later that Elvis had stood up for us.

CHERYLE JOHNSON: Elvis was the first person to play the rodeo in the new Astrodome in Houston [February 27, 1970]. He sold out three nights, and I had tickets to every show. They drove Elvis around in an open jeep so people could see him. No one had seen him [in person] in a long time because he hadn't been touring. It was hard to believe how beautiful he was.

During the concert Elvis told us, "I want to sing a song I like," and he sang "How Great Thou Art." It was one of the most incredible experiences I've ever had, to be there at a rock 'n' roll concert and hear Elvis sing "How Great Thou Art." The power of his voice in the Astrodome!

LOWELL HAYS: I was on the tour when they first did the "American Trilogy." It was thrilling every time you saw that flag roll down from the ceiling and all those spotlights hit that flag! It was unbelievable. Thousands of people would just stand up and cheer. I would just stand there and watch him and think, "There's never been anyone like him!"

JOAN DEARY: Elvis had great vocal range, and he continued working to expand his range and develop his voice. His music repertoire was unbelievable, from rock 'n' roll to "The American Trilogy." Who else do you know in rock 'n' roll that could sing "The American Trilogy" or "How Great Thou Art" and would do it live onstage?

:◎:◎:◎:

T. G. SHEPPARD [Bill Browder]: When Elvis did the tours following his Comeback [TV] Special, I got to travel with him some. RCA knew I was tight with Elvis, so they let me get away with murder. They didn't want to rock his boat. He was always a guaranteed sale. We spent most of our time at RCA working on other artists because Elvis was never a problem. People fought for his records, especially after '69 and '70. You never had to worry about getting Elvis's records sold.

Don Robertson: When Elvis sang one of my songs, I never had the feeling that he was just throwing the song away like some artists do. I always had the feeling that he was really into it.

I was really proud of the way Elvis did my song "I Really Don't Want to Know." He did it in a different way than it had been done before, kind of bluesy. He recorded it in 1970 in Nashville [at RCA studio] and it became Elvis's first Top Ten country hit since 1968. His version sold over one million singles.

Gordon Stoker: The Jordanaires worked with Elvis from January 1956 until 1970. When he went into Vegas and back out on the road, we just had so many recording sessions booked here in Nashville we couldn't work with him. We did some overdub sessions in 1971, but Elvis was never quite the same after that, it seemed to me. I think he kind of lost his family. All of us quit at the same time. We had to do what we thought was best for our families. Let me say, I've always regretted it.

D. J. Fontana: I didn't leave Elvis's band because anybody was mad. Scotty didn't leave because anybody was mad. It was just one of those things; people wanted to do other things. Elvis understood that. People make him out to be a bad guy, and I really hate that.

David Briggs *(musician)*: I worked on the last sessions that Scotty Moore and D. J. Fontana ever did with Elvis. It was kinda sad to see the changing of the guard. As far as I'm concerned, the best records that Elvis ever cut—I don't care what anybody thinks—are the ones that he did with Scotty and D. J. Everything after that was shit.

Elvis became so powerful that he didn't want to spend any time working on anything in the studio. In the early days, he would cut a song thirty or forty times [to get it right]. By the time I started working with him, he didn't want to cut anything more than once, maybe twice if you were lucky. He was impatient. He was tired. He was bored. That's why the records sounded so bad. Very few records did we even get to rehearse.

Faron Young: When Presley really got to making money, hell, he could have afforded to pay Scotty and D. J. and Bill Black a damn hundred grand apiece. It wouldn't have hurt him none. But Parker wouldn't let him pay them nothing but scale.

T. G. Sheppard [Bill Browder]: I'll never forget one time Elvis was playing Mobile, Alabama, on tour. We'd all gone out to eat at this big restaurant, and the Colonel always carried a bunch of little calendars in his pocket—Elvis calendars. Well, we ate probably three or four hundred dollars worth of food, and as we were getting ready to leave the girl brought the check. The Colonel told her, "Honey, I want to give you something real special for a tip. I mean, I could give you money, but this is going to mean more to you." So, he gave her an Elvis calendar! She said, "Thank you," 'cause I believe she was really in awe of who he was. But I bet after she got home that night and figured out how little she had made for that day, she was probably more than a little upset.

Dotty Ayers: In Portland, Oregon, in 1970, I went up to Elvis's hotel room after a show. It had been about five years or so since I had seen him, and I didn't even know if he wanted to see me. So I sent a telegram to Joe Esposito and told him that I was in Portland and would love to see Elvis and talk to him. I gave my phone number. Well, that afternoon Joe called me about an hour after their plane landed and said, "Elvis told me to call." Joe told me the hotel that they were staying at and to come up after the show.

Priscilla was there with Elvis, and I didn't know they were having trouble. Elvis seemed to be really tired. He got up and hugged me. Then Dr. Nick [Dr. George Nichopoulos] came in. This was the first time that I had ever seen Dr. Nick. They went into Elvis's bedroom with a little bag. Elvis was real slim then—almost skinny. I was sitting there on the couch with Vernon, and I said, "Vernon, what's wrong with Elvis?" He said, "Nothing. There's nothing wrong with him. He's just tired from the show. He just did a show of about sixty-five minutes on the stage." Vernon told me that Dr. Nick was going to give Elvis a B-12 shot. In a few minutes Elvis came back out, and he was just pacing. He just kept pacing and walking; it seemed like he was getting to feel better and better.

Elvis brought out all those jumpsuits to show me. He had started wearing jumpsuits on that tour. Then he started talking about old times—the times at Graceland and the kids that he used to run around with. He mentioned everybody's name, and he said, "We had fun back then, didn't we?"

CHERYLE JOHNSON: Elvis was the target of a number of threats in August of 1970. First, someone called a security guard at the International Hotel in Las Vegas and said he had information to the effect that two men were going to kidnap Elvis that night (August 26). The next day Colonel Parker's office received an anonymous call from a man claiming that Elvis would be kidnapped over the weekend. That was a Thursday. Early the next morning someone called Joe Esposito's house in Los Angeles and spoke to Joe's wife. He demanded fifty thousand dollars, saying that otherwise Elvis would be shot. Security around Elvis was beefed up as a result of these threats, but nothing happened.

SONNY WEST: Elvis got us weapon permits because that was our job—to protect him. (John Lennon might well be alive today if he had believed in armed bodyguards.) If you're going to have nuts with guns, you can't expect someone to be your bodyguard with no way to fire back—to just stand there like a dummy and be shot. Elvis said he would never ask any of us to do that, so he got us guns; and he wanted us to have backup guns in case one misfired. I used to say, "We're not going into a war, man. If I don't hit him in the first shot or two, I'm probably going to be shot down myself." But Elvis said he wanted us to have backup guns, so he gave us all kinds of guns for that reason.

At my wedding, Elvis had five guns on him in the church—one under each arm, one stuck in his belt, one behind, and one in his boot—a derringer in his boot—and a long flashlight!

ROY NIXON *(Shelby County Sheriff)*: Elvis was deputized under Sheriff Bill Morris. The special deputy commission was basically an honorary thing, but it did have legal authority. Elvis could have made arrests. To qualify, you had to be of good character and go to the pistol range and get qualified to carry a firearm. Elvis was the only one I know that had a chief deputy badge. A chief deputy is the top law enforcement officer that's appointed under the sheriff. Elvis didn't try to do any policing or anything with it. He just considered it an honor. Some of Elvis's friends took the badge that I gave him, and for a birthday present, had it gold-plated and had some little diamonds and rubies put in it.

DR. GEORGE NICHOPOULOS: Elvis spent a lot of time at the pistol range and used to ride around with patrolmen in patrol cars in Memphis.

ROBERT FERGUSON *(policeman, friend)*: Elvis would get out and cruise and patrol at night and answer calls sometimes, or try to. He had a police scanner in his car, and he'd just go to the scene. I've got ten hours of videotape of officers talking about Elvis doing this.

DR. GEORGE NICHOPOULOS: Elvis decided that he wanted to see the president, so he was just gonna go on up there [to Washington, D.C.]. He left Graceland without any money and just the clothes on his back. He went to Atlanta and called Jerry Schilling to bring him some clothes and money, and they went on up to see the president, uninvited! He'd had some conversations with President Nixon, and Nixon had invited Elvis to come up to visit (I'm sure, not unannounced).

SONNY WEST: Elvis had tremendously persuasive powers. He really did. I mean, how many people could drop a note off at the White House and an hour later be meeting with the president of the United States in the Oval Office and getting the president to give him a narcotics [agent's] badge—a legitimate narcotics badge!

DAVID STANLEY: Elvis started collecting badges after he met with President Nixon and got that narcotics badge. He already had a couple of badges he'd gotten from Memphis deputy sheriffs. But once Elvis had the badge from Nixon, whenever we'd go on tour that narcotics badge would help him get other badges. Almost every town we went to, he'd get an honorary badge for one thing or another.

Many people believe Elvis was an undercover agent, an FBI agent, but that's totally ridiculous.

SONNY WEST: Elvis had charm. He had ways of getting what he wanted. He "bought" some doctors. He bought them Cadillacs and stuff to get what he wanted. It never seemed that obvious; he was always thanking them for what they did, but we all knew exactly what he was doing, and it wasn't always in his own best interests.

:◎:◎:◎:

LOWELL HAYS: On Christmas Eve 1970, Dr. Nick called me and said, "Elvis is gonna be at the Memphian theater, and we're having a movie. He'd like to see some jewelry." I said, "Great. I'll be there."

About midnight I took a case of jewelry to the Memphian and they ushered me in and sat me down right behind Elvis. They told him, "Lowell Hays is here." Elvis turned around and acknowledged me and got up and motioned for me to follow him. We went into the men's room, opened one of the doors to a toilet stall, and he sat down on the toilet and said, "Let's have the case." I sat it down on his lap, and Elvis did all his Christmas shopping sitting there on the toilet in the Memphian theater in 1970. He made quite a nice purchase and we became fast friends. As far as I know, if I was anywhere near, for the rest of his life, he bought everything from me. From that day on I made the TCB necklaces, rings, and all of Elvis's jewelry.

Elvis knew exactly what he wanted. He used a little book of numbers, and if he had a specific person to buy for—a birthday—he would take their birth date, and with this numerical book determine what color stone they should have. He would buy a sapphire, emerald, ruby, opal, or whatever his little number book told him he should give to this particular person. Elvis always bought very nice pieces of jewelry. He was not cheap. And he used that number book a lot. I was surprised 'cause that's kind of a pagan thing, and I know Elvis was a Christian. I also know that he probably didn't know it was a pagan thing to do. But you didn't question him. Things like that, you didn't question him on.

JANELLE MCCOMB: In January of 1971, Elvis was named one of the Ten Outstanding Young Men of America by the Jaycees. He said that was the most prestigious award he had ever received and it was very humbling to him.

FRED FREDRICK: Receiving that award was the most proud thing that ever happened to Elvis. That ceremony was one thing that he didn't hesitate to agree to attend, and he was very respectful about it. He honestly, truly appreciated it 'cause he'd never gotten anything like that before.

EDDIE FADAL: Elvis received so many awards. He couldn't believe all the honors that were being bestowed on him. He'd say, "It's unreal," and his dad would chime in, "I can't believe how this all got started!"

GEORGE KLEIN: There was a mayor in Memphis who really liked Elvis and wanted to honor Elvis in some way. There were a lot of fans who kept saying, "Why don't you name something for Elvis?" So finally they decided to rename Highway 51 South, which runs [in front of] Graceland, as "Elvis Presley Boulevard." They asked me to find out what Elvis thought about the idea. Elvis said, "Look, I don't want to make a statement because either way I could look bad. If I said yes, it would look like I had a big ego; if I said no, it would look like I'm a snob or I'm not happy that they're doing this. I can't win either way—just tell them I'll be happy, I'll be flattered, I'll be extremely honored if they name a street after me. But by the same token, if they don't, I won't care; I won't get mad; it won't bother me in the least." So, I told them and they passed a resolution and named the boulevard after him.

:◎:◎:◎:

T. G. Sheppard [Bill Browder]: I think Elvis often thought he was a prophet. He was very religious. You know, the *Elvis Country* album, where he was on the cover as a child in a little hat? Well, on the top of the album there's a phrase saying, "I'm 10,000 years old," and there are excerpts between each cut from the back liner notes from "I Was Born Ten Thousand Years Ago." I often felt like he believed it. Everything in his life was connected to spirituality, numerology, colors. He was always searching: where do I go from here? What's my main mission in life. As he got older he always tried to seek out why all this happened to him, what might be the meaning of life. We all kind of do that as we get older: wonder what would have happened if we'd turned left instead of right, or hitchhiked to Nashville instead of going to Memphis. As Elvis got older, he was seeking and searching, and, therefore, in a strange way he became more religious as time went on. I don't know if it was just BS'ing or what, but he told me one time, "I'm very fortunate. There's not too many people in this world who just through word of mouth get self-image. Sinatra was a prophet, the Beatles, Rudolph Valentino, and Elvis Presley." There's only been a handful of people in our lifetime that had that magnetism, that just through word of mouth could sell fifteen, twenty, thirty thousand tickets without any advertising. He often wondered how that happened. But he felt it, you know. Maybe he was a minister of music.

Dr. George Nichopoulos: After a show there'd be a group of people waiting to talk to him, and he'd think nothing of sitting and talking to someone for two or three hours and leaving Priscilla to occupy herself for that time. He needed that time to come down after a performance. He met a lot of friends that way.

Shaun Nielsen: One night, standing on the roof outside his suite, he said to me, "Can you imagine what it's like to have anything you ever want for?"

I got to thinking that there was probably almost nothing that he couldn't have.

JANICE PENNINGTON: I think Elvis had achieved everything, the ultimate in success, but there were still the unanswered questions about life and about becoming closer to the "Oneness."

Elvis lived a lot in the outer world—the physical, material world. There were a lot of people who took from him on that level, and it was draining. There probably wasn't a lot of time in his life he could spend nurturing the spiritual part of himself.

LARRY GELLER: Elvis said to me many times, "Money, success, fame, being Elvis Presley, that's not the answer, not the whole answer. There's a reason for every person being born. Everyone has a mission. The whole idea is simply to find out what your purpose in life is."

:◎:◎:◎:

JERRY SCHILLING *(bodyguard)*: Elvis loved his home in Palm Springs. It was where he went to relax after a tour. People didn't bother him in Palm Springs. Elvis bought a black dune buggy from Liberace and we used to go riding on the dunes.

ALEX LOGAN *(maintenance engineer, Palm Springs)*: The Colonel had come to Palm Springs in the early sixties, and Elvis came a few years after. Elvis called his house [845 Chino Canyon] his motel—where he could get away from it all to rest. I kept the place for Elvis like I did for other celebrities that lived in Palm Springs—like Jackie Cooper and his wife. I had my pocket full of keys to celebrity houses.

Most of the people Elvis associated with were mechanics and plumbers. Sonny West would call and tell me to get some local boys and come up and play basketball. It would always be at night and you could never see the ball, and it was uphill and rocky, but it was fun.

CHARLIE HODGE *(musician)*: The living room of that Palm Springs house was the entertainment center. We had a lot of parties in that room. We used to fly in girls from Memphis or dancers from Las Vegas, and Elvis would tell stories about Jesus. He would stand up on the coffee table like he was preaching and hold out his arms. He was real serious, but he would get the stories all wrong. Joe Esposito and I would be sitting in the adjoining dining room, and sometimes we'd laugh so hard that Elvis would make us leave.

:◎:◎:◎:

BILLY STANLEY: Elvis had an affair with my first wife [Annie Hall Smith], and that really hurt me for a long time. I finally understood that all she really wanted from me was just to get close to Elvis, but it hurt for a long time. Looking back he actually did me a favor. It broke up my marriage, but that wouldn't have worked anyway, and in a strange way it eventually brought me closer to Elvis.

BECKY HARTLEY: I knew Elvis was not true to Priscilla because I was paying the bills from Palm Springs when they were married. Of course, you could always say that the bills were for the guys' girlfriends, but . . .

DR. GEORGE NICHOPOULOS: Elvis was dating other girls toward the tail-end of his marriage. I think Priscilla and a couple of the wives found some other girls in the house in Palm Springs. He knew it would eventually happen.

He was partly responsible for the divorce. He encouraged Priscilla to get involved in other things and not sit around the house.

BECKY HARTLEY: I do know that Priscilla was going with Mike [Stone] before she confronted Elvis—as far as leaving him and everything. Priscilla would bring her letters out to me; I mean, she talked to me about it. She would bring the mail out there for me to mail for her. I wasn't shocked. She knew at that time I wasn't going to tell anybody; I was not going to say anything. I knew what Elvis was doing.

It was New Year's Eve when she told him she was leaving. Elvis looked depressed that night at the house, and Priscilla was bubbly, going all around talking. I think he might have sensed what was coming.

MARTY LACKER: At times he was happy being married, but there were a lot of times he didn't like being tied down. That's the way it was. He wanted to be able to do what he wanted when he wanted. He didn't want somebody saying, "No, you can't." And with Elvis, what was good for the gander was not good for the goose.

LAMAR FIKE: He liked Priscilla, but there was nothing there. I think his ego took a bruising when she left him, but he was responsible for that.

BECKY HARTLEY: A lot of the fans think, "Oh, gosh, how could she have left him?" Well, you don't know what goes on behind closed doors.

I saw the divorce coming. I think one of the problems was that Priscilla was awfully young. Then Elvis, gosh, I guess it was hard for somebody like him to be settled; he had so many women flocking around and going after him. I guess he was just used to going with whoever he wanted.

DR. GEORGE NICHOPOULOS: Their custody arrangement was great. Elvis had a very good relationship with Priscilla after their divorce. He continued to do things for her and she continued to accommodate his wishes as far as Lisa Marie was concerned.

"He Tried to Behave Himself"
1972-1974

After Priscilla and little Lisa Marie leave Graceland to begin a new life in Hollywood without him, Elvis finds a steady girlfriend, Memphis beauty queen Linda Thompson. A new love by his side and a wounded ego to mend, Elvis picks up the pace of concert dates in Vegas, as well as destinations throughout the United States.

Looking for even greater horizons to explore, Elvis and the Colonel team up with RCA to produce the *Aloha from Hawaii* television special. Costume designer Bill Belew and RCA's Joan Deary give a personal glimpse into the brilliant event, which is beamed via satellite to a larger audience worldwide than the one that watched the landing of the first man on the moon.

Along with Elvis's incredible fame, however, comes the need for unprecedented precautions. Bodyguards Sam Thompson and David Stanley reveal the need to protect the king—even from those who love him.

For Elvis, the more his world expands, the more it shrinks. Dr. George Nichopoulos, Linda Thompson, and Sonny West tell of Elvis's efforts to cope with his increasingly unstable life as his future changes from one of possibility to one of limitation.

> "Onstage, a few times, Elvis said: 'My life's a fairy tale. It's like a dream. And I'm *living* it.'"
>
> LARRY GELLER

SHAUN NIELSEN: Elvis really liked Tom Jones. They were good friends, but Elvis got a secret kick out of walking in right in the middle of Tom's show. Tom's image was very macho and studly onstage, but when Elvis walked into his showroom the women forgot Tom was even there.

TOM JONES: I learned from Elvis to move while I was onstage. Most singers, when they go onstage, grip the microphone with both hands and just concentrate on what sound they're making. They are not really thinking about doing body movement. Elvis did. He was doing those moves that a lot of people would be scared to do. A lot of performers would think, "I shouldn't do this. It might look silly." He didn't care. He just did what felt natural. I did the same thing. I thought, "I want to go out there and do what I feel is natural for me." It worked. Yeah, I really got the whole idea from watching Elvis.

RED WEST: Elvis would have Tom Jones over when they were playing Las Vegas at the same time. They'd sing all night with Elvis's backup group. He never got tired. Andy Williams would come over, and Bobbie Gentry [recording artist]. Elvis would go do a show and then go backstage to talk to them. They'd end up over at the top of the Hilton singing 'til five, six, or seven in the morning.

MYRNA SMITH: Elvis loved to talk to you and delve into your spirituality. He was kind of a recluse in many respects, a loner to some degree, but he liked people. I think he had to grope to find where his place in life was. When he was alone or nearly alone, like with just Jerry [Schilling] and me, he was wonderful. He had a great sense of humor—always laughing, telling jokes, and reading to you. He liked Kahlil Gibran's books. Not only would he read to you, he'd recite a passage from one book or another. He'd deliver some long passage from a book from memory, and he always had something that he wanted to spiritually relate to you.

ROBERT FERGUSON: When I joined the police department, my partner was Fred Fredrick. He was good friends with Elvis, and we'd go by the Memphian theater, which Elvis would rent for all-night movies. I thought at the time, "This is an unusual person," because he would leave his group down front surrounded by girls and everybody, and he'd come and ask us, "What kind of calls have you had tonight?" I mean, it was just a living to me, but Elvis seemed very interested in police work. He would stand there for fifteen or twenty minutes or more and talk to us about that and ask us to come out to his house later on for a party.

Most of the time it was sort of embarrassing, because Elvis would just kind of stand back and listen to us. He wasn't doing the talking, we were. He had all this money and all these girls waiting for him to come back and sit with them, and he'd be out there talking to us. It kind of helped our egos because we'd say, "You know, this may not be a bad job after all. Elvis seems impressed."

FRANCES FORBES: I hadn't seen Elvis in years. One night another girl and I were out riding around and I saw Elvis's car at the Memphian theater. We waited until he came out, then we pulled up beside him. By then I'd become a blonde. He hollered at me, "Do you have on a wig?"

A couple of nights later we went back to the theater and went in. It was just like I'd never been away. He didn't seem changed at all to me. He walked up and hugged me. It was just like old times. He kept saying to different people, "I raised that child. I raised her." It was nice seeing him again. During this time, I don't know if he and Priscilla were divorced or separated—it was just before he met Linda Thompson.

LINDA THOMPSON *(girlfriend)*: I met Elvis on July 6, 1972. I was Miss Tennessee at the time, and we were introduced by a mutual friend when I was invited to go to the Memphian theater. My friend Jeanne LeMay (who was Miss Rhode Island at the time) and I went together, and Elvis and I met. From that moment on we had a real affinity for each other—a real common bond. We both had grown up in the same area, and we just kind of clicked.

JERRY KYLE: I saw Elvis and Linda together at the theater all the time, but they didn't go out arm in arm or anything like that. Maybe Elvis was the type not to show affection in public. I never saw it. I would have picked up on it if it was there.

LINDA THOMPSON: I know the first year that Elvis and I were together, there was no one else [he was dating]—there couldn't have been because I was with him twenty-four hours a day for three hundred and sixty-five days. Literally, we were together every moment: every sleeping moment, every waking moment. I even went to the dentist with him. So, for the first year, I think he broke his record. He was monogamous for the first year.

BECKY HARTLEY: When Elvis was going with Linda Thompson, they seemed to be happy. She seemed real good for him.

LINDA THOMPSON: Life was interesting at Graceland. There were times when it was like living a fairy tale, you know, and Elvis truly was Prince Charming. He was the most generous of men. He was the kindest, most sensitive, the funniest, most talented, most gorgeous and sexiest. He was all the wonderful things that only Elvis could be, and yet there were times when he was very, very difficult. His life was very difficult.

:◎:◎:◎:

MARTY PASETTA (*TV producer*): Elvis and I had a meeting; we were discussing the TV special *Aloha from Hawaii*. I outlined everything I had in mind and Elvis was very agreeable. When I got through with all my preamble, I said, "I would like you to go on a diet. I want you to lose weight." He said, "You know, it's one of the first times anyone's been honest with me." He said, "Yeah, I'll go on a diet for you." He lost twenty-five pounds for me.

BILL BELEW: When Elvis was getting ready to do the *Aloha* special he told me he really wanted to wear something that said "America" to the world. We batted it around awhile and I said, "Well, the flag has been done to death. The only other thing that really says America to the world is the American eagle. Why don't we do that?" He said, "Great! I love the idea." So we set about making an outfit and a cape and a great-looking jeweled belt. It was quite an elaborate costume, and many people were involved in making it; it called for a lot of embroidery and we attached jewels all over it. He loved it.

Elvis even decided he would wear it to his rehearsal—a rehearsal in front of a live audience there in Honolulu. But when that rehearsal was over I got a phone call from Joe Esposito. It was just one night before the live broadcast. Joe said, "Bill, you're not going to believe this. Elvis just threw his belt and cape out into the audience!" I said, "Joe, what are you talking about? He hasn't even done the show yet!" Joe said, "Well, we did a rehearsal, and he wanted the people that couldn't get tickets for the special to come and see him, so he did two run-through-type performances and he just gave his belt and cape away! So now we've got to have a new cape and a new belt!"

When I came out of my state of shock, I got on the phone and called everybody involved. That night we cut, embroidered, and did everything —nearly killed ourselves—and I called Joe and said, "Joe, in half an hour everything will be ready. However, I can't come to Hawaii. I'm doing a TV special with Lena Horne." He said, "Can you send someone?" I said, "Well, Nicki, who does the embroidery, will bring everything over there." He said, "Okay, our plane will be in the air in half an hour to pick him up."

Nicki took everything with him to Hawaii, and they were just wonderful to him. He even went to the show. But later that night, after they'd done the live satellite broadcast, Nicki called me and said, "Bill, you're not going to believe this!" I said, "Oh, please, what are you going to tell me now?" He said, "Elvis threw the belt and the cape into the audience again! I'm getting on the plane, coming back. We've got to make another cape and belt so he can go on with the tour."

At that time, the belt and cape were each worth about five thousand dollars, so Elvis threw ten thousand dollars into the audience two nights in a row!

JOAN DEARY: RCA paid for the whole *Aloha from Hawaii* special [aired January 14, 1973]. They paid for those [soundtrack] recordings and hired NBC to do the show. It was an RCA Records deal.

For the special Elvis had a prepared list of songs, but we did not know what order he would do the songs in. I was keeping track of the songs—keeping up with the time and how we were going to break. There was no music director and no choreographer. Elvis just got up there and sang, and everybody took their musical cues from what he did at the time. He made the decisions onstage and it was all timed out perfectly.

The special had a great dramatic effect. It certainly helped his record sales and contributed to the legend. When people went to see him, they didn't care what he said; what mattered was the feeling he put into a song. They knew he put everything he had into every song he sang. He and the audience had a love affair.

The special was broadcast live by satellite and was watched by an estimated one billion people in forty countries!

GEORGE KLEIN: The biggest untruth perpetrated on Elvis is that he was lonely and depressed and all that crap. He was just bored. If you've been around a big star, a super superstar, you know their attention span is short. They like to stay busy, whether it's publishing, writing, directing, acting—whatever. They want to keep moving. Well, Elvis was the same way. When he wasn't really active, he became bored. Some people misconstrued that for lonely and sad and all that crap.

LOWELL HAYS: When we were out on tour or in Vegas with Elvis, he insisted that we all go to his shows. He wanted to see us in the audience right there by the stage. I didn't blame him. He was paying all of our expenses—every penny of our expenses. So why shouldn't we be there? Between shows we all just goofed off and had a great time.

RED WEST: Elvis, on the other hand, was almost locked in his room whenever we did the four-week bookings in Las Vegas [twice a year], and that's a long time for anybody. He couldn't go anywhere. Out in public he was always stalked. When he would go out the crowds were unbelievable. We went to a gun shop once and looked up and here's a guy—bam, bam, bam—taking pictures. So we go back to the room. Actually Elvis was looking for a way to feel better, to just get out of the pressure. I would sit there in Vegas and I was going nuts, too. There's only one way that [kind of situation] can go; the way it did.

TOM JONES: One time when he was working the Hilton in Las Vegas, along the sides of the hallway to the nightclub they had statues of girls in crinoline dresses and men with three-cornered hats. I was there one night and he asked me, "What do you think of these statues along the walls here? What period of time is this anyway?" I said, "Looks like Charles II." Elvis said, "Charlton Heston?" I had to explain it to him.

For some reason, he didn't like these figures being there. One night very late, he went into the hallway with some of his bodyguards and painted them all black. The women in the crinoline especially. He made them into black people. He wanted to do something to make the hotel realize that these things looked funny up there.

DAVID BRIGGS: Elvis was having an open suite in Vegas one time. Of course, you couldn't get through security unless your name was on the list and you had that little gold lightning bolt. But this time he comes to the door himself, smoking a cigar and barefooted, wearing a T-Shirt and a pair of jeans. If you were with a girl, of course she's just floored already. He would say, "Oh my god, come in!" And he'd ask her, "What's your name? Well, my name is Elvis," as if she didn't know! Then Elvis would tell her, whether it was me she was with me or whoever, "Oh, you're with my favorite guy. I couldn't even work without this guy; he does everything . . . and blah, blah, blah." Well, your date is melting and messing her drawers by then. You could do anything you wanted with her. Then he would say, "Just make yourself at home. If you need anything, you just have David tell me." He did stuff like that. That's the good side of him I remember.

CHERYLE JOHNSON: In mid-February of 1973, Elvis missed three shows at the Hilton in Las Vegas. They said it was due to illness. A lot of fans were concerned. Elvis had almost never canceled shows before.

:◎:◎:◎:

MYRNA SMITH: When he'd walk onstage, it was like a light show. The arena would light up with people taking flash pictures, and you could just feel the electricity from the audience flowing onto the stage. It was like a roar of electricity, you know, and you just plugged into it and became a part of it while you were out there. I've never seen that with any other performer, and I've worked with some big names.

SHAUN NIELSEN: Liberace dropped in backstage once. Elvis had a great admiration for Liberace's talent; he felt Liberace was one of the finest entertainers in the world.

And Mohammed Ali came backstage after the show one night. They were good friends. I think Ali had a robe made for Elvis, and he had "The King" sewn on it. That was pretty heavy for Mohammed. He'd joke about being "the greatest," but he may have thought Elvis was even greater.

Elvis was very good at knowing how to pace his show, which is at times even more important than selecting the material. If you do too many slow songs you're gonna put 'em to sleep; too fast, you'll wear them out.

GEORGE KLEIN: Elvis liked the Righteous Brothers a lot. One night after Elvis's performance we were walking through the backstage hallway, and Bill Medley [one of the original Righteous Brothers] was out performing in the lounge. There were about ten people behind Elvis, just following him. Elvis walked right in front of Medley, who was performing, and said, "Hey, Bill, how are you doing?" and just kept right on walking. Medley dropped his microphone and just fell down laughing! Elvis would do nutty things like that.

:◎:◎:◎:

Don Wardell: In March of 1973 Elvis was in need of money, so the Colonel sold the royalty rights in all his early records to RCA. It was a $5.4 million deal, with another guarantee [for royalties] of five hundred thousand per year.

Joan Deary: I think the number-one reason the Colonel made the "buy-out" deal with RCA was money. He probably thought they had gotten all the use [sales] out of those masters that they could get. I mean, how many times can you reissue the same songs over and over again? Looking at it from that perspective, the criticism that's sometimes hurled at the Colonel for making the deal is incorrect. And the average person in our record company would have probably thought exactly the same thing. But looking at it from my perspective, knowing about all the unreleased outtakes and live performances—which RCA also bought in that deal—it was easy to see that we had just bought a gold mine.

You see, the fans were not just looking for the same songs over and over again. The Colonel was absolutely right about that. I felt what the fans were really looking for were the outtakes—something they didn't have. That's when I came up with the concept of the Legendary Performer series. I went to the president of RCA and said, "I'd like to do a series of collectibles, put a book with it, and use outtakes from our files that no one's ever heard." That's what kicked off RCA's Legendary Performer series. It was a big success. The first one by Elvis went gold [sold one million dollars worth].

Mac Wiseman: The consensus of a lot of people [in the industry] was that Parker really threw Presley to the wolves with a lot of that movie business and the Las Vegas bookings. What I heard from the inside track was that Parker began believing his own publicity, which is the worst thing you can do. He was becoming the star. Yeah, he'd go into Vegas and, you know, "Here comes the Colonel!" And rumor has it he dropped a ton of money there gambling.

BERNARD LANSKY: Parker had one product; he had Elvis. That was all he wanted or needed. He promoted Elvis and nothing and nobody else.

FARON YOUNG: After Presley was hot, I was out at Parker's one day (I used to go out there and visit him and Marie, his wife). I wouldn't call him "colonel." I said, "How you doing, Tom?" He said, "That's *Colonel!*" I said, "Naw, you son of a bitch, you ain't no fuckin' colonel." (He's got a picture on his wall of him and me—him in his Colonel suit.) I said, "You know, Tom, you've had a damn good career for coming out of a damn circus, but you got to remember, you've always had a good white horse to ride. You had Arnold when he was hot. Anybody could have booked Arnold when he was hot. Then you had Hank Snow. But when country music got rough, you couldn't even get Hank Snow or Minnie Pearl a fucking show date. Then comes Elvis. He's hot and you've got another white stallion. Well, my damn kid could have handled Elvis Presley! Goddamn, Parker, you ain't that brilliant!"

MARTY LACKER: I think Elvis, to a point, cared about the Colonel because of the early days. He knew the Colonel could get him these huge deals. Elvis basically was concerned with one thing (other than his entertaining): he just wanted to have enough money to do whatever he wanted to do, whenever he wanted to do it. He knew the Colonel had been providing him those things. In the later years, things slowly started changing.

There was times later on when Elvis wanted to get rid of the Colonel. Seriously. But the Colonel knew Elvis pretty good and he had a plan. Because Elvis's personal business was left up to Vernon, the Colonel conned them. When Elvis was going to break up with him, the Colonel handed Vernon a bill for over two million dollars that he said Elvis owed him for expenses and shit (which was total bullshit). That scared the piss out of Vernon and he talked Elvis into changing his mind.

:◎:◎:◎:

DAVID STANLEY: Elvis had a jet he leased to fly from show to show. There were threats to bomb that plane, as well as other threats.

We walked out of our hotel on Long Island [New York], where we were playing the Nassau Coliseum, and a guy pulled a switchblade on Elvis. I saw the blade reflecting in the sunlight. He had it down by his side. Elvis and I were walking together, and the guy moved forward as we moved forward, so I jumped across in front of Elvis and grabbed the guy by the back of the hair and slammed him against the wall. I had my gun down his throat until the others took him away.

We ran into that from time to time, but that was the worst situation we had.

Other times, some guy would try to punch Elvis out—jealous boyfriends, jealous husbands, even sometimes just fanatical women.

SAM THOMPSON (*bodyguard*): There were very few real threats to Elvis's person—threats as a result of malice—but there were threats that sprang from the love Elvis's fans had for him. They all wanted a piece of him, and there were millions of fans and only one Elvis.

I've taken Elvis into hotels and places where fans would literally pull his hair out. They didn't want to hurt him, but they wanted a piece of him.

After every show, Elvis would have claw marks on his hands, and he would have to wear Band-aids; if you see pictures of him after shows, you'll see Band-aids. People would accidentally claw him when reaching for him and reaching for scarves.

Somewhere out in the Midwest, I took a lady offstage who had scratched Elvis in an attempt to get to him. As I was taking her off, she was yelling excitedly to her friends, "Look, Elvis's skin!" It was bizarre.

MAE AXTON: Girls would try to get onstage with him, especially when he was throwing those scarves out. In Oklahoma City one night I saw a girl get so excited she jumped out of the balcony. It might have killed her, but the people below her broke the fall. It was scary sometimes in those concerts.

SHAUN NIELSEN: One time Elvis threw a scarf out to a lady, and the lady made the mistake of crossing it around her neck. Suddenly there was one woman on one side and another on the other, both pulling at that scarf, literally choking the middle woman to death! Elvis yelled, "Here now! Hold it! Hold it!" and he threw scarves to the women on both sides of her. I do believe they would have choked that woman to death right there on the front row, all because they were determined to get that scarf.

BILLY STANLEY: The hours we kept, the on-the-road time, was rough, and if you don't have that drive—some stimulant in you—you're not gonna make it. It almost killed me just trying to keep up that pace. That's why a lot of entertainers take drugs.

CHERYLE JOHNSON: Signs began to appear that Elvis just didn't have it anymore—you know, the music—or didn't care. You went to the concerts, and he sang the same songs concert after concert. I heard a lot of people say, "Well, it's plastic Elvis now," like just another Las Vegas lounge act. He went from the superstar of that great '68 Comeback Special (which was just wonderful, magnificent) to somebody who was just walking through his shows. The changes were very noticeable.

DR. GEORGE NICHOPOULOS: Unfortunately, Elvis felt that in order for something to be more effective, it had to be given by a shot. That's the reason that we gave him decongestants by injection at times.

Elvis had a phobia about going onstage and his voice cracking, or not being able to project as well as he could. Even though he may have felt all right before going onstage, he felt that somehow a shot would protect him from something bad happening. I don't know if he'd been embarrassed at some time or another onstage, or what may have happened, but it was difficult trying to get away from giving him shots all the time.

BECKY HARTLEY: I do know Elvis would get that "desert throat" out in Vegas. Before he would sing he would have to have shots and things.

Mr. Presley had me write a letter to one doctor because he was wondering why vitamin B-12 shots cost what they did, and exactly what all did they do? The doctor wrote back and said he couldn't, naturally, divulge that information. Vernon was concerned about it.

DR. GEORGE NICHOPOULOS: Every time Elvis got a shot, [the bodyguards] would think that it was some sort of narcotic or something, and that wasn't true. He was getting some allergy shots and B-12 shots (he was one of those people who thought that a B-12 shot helped him). He would feel better after one; whether it actually helped him or not, I don't know.

BILLY STANLEY: I had gotten off on drugs back when I was in high school. I wanted to fit in with what other kids were doing. Elvis didn't have anything to do with that. In fact, he wanted me to become a narc in my school. He was totally against acid, heroin, that kind of thing.

Elvis did do cocaine with me one time. I never saw him do it again, and I think he felt guilty about it even then.

SHAUN NIELSEN: Elvis came to the National Quartet Convention in Nashville several different times. They'd bring him around to the backstage door and he'd wait there until everybody was onstage, to make as little commotion as possible. They would just kind of sneak him in. We would always ask him if he wanted to be introduced, and sometimes he'd walk out and wave and go backstage. It was always quite an event when he was there.

JAMES BLACKWOOD: Elvis would always attend the convention if he could. I remember looking up one time and there he was backstage. The auditorium was packed—like four or five thousand people there. When Elvis came out onstage, it looked like a million light bulbs went off.

Elvis had a great feel for gospel music. The Grammys that he won were all for his gospel albums, and they were bestsellers. It's been said that Elvis copied his style originally from Jake Hess, who sang with the Imperials and the Statesmen Quartet. Like myself, he'd been raised in the Pentecostal church.

SHAUN NIELSEN: The first time I took the whole group (the group that was to become "Voice") to see Elvis, he flew us to Las Vegas. Tom Jones was having trouble with his backup singers, and we were gonna be like a "gift" from Elvis to Tom. We were put up in a nice hotel at Elvis's expense, and then he brought us up to his room to sing for Tom that night. This had to cost him a lot of money. We got up to sing, and I remember that right in front of us were Tom Jones, Bobbie Gentry, and Elvis Presley! I was intimidated, to say the least.

Anyway, Tom told Elvis that he had just signed a contract with The Blossoms, and if he got rid of them he'd probably be sued, so he didn't feel like he could use us.

Afterward, Elvis called us back up to his suite, and we sat there on the floor in the bedroom for a long time, just chatting. He said, "Well, I know you're probably disappointed, so I've drawn up this little contract." It was on a sheet of toilet tissue! The opening line said, "For the sum of one hundred thousand dollars . . ." we would travel and sing and work with him and write songs for his music publishing companies. He said, "Would you boys be interested in that?"

As soon as we revived ourselves, we said, "Sure! We'd love to do that." That was in 1973. That same one hundred thousand dollars would be equal to two hundred fifty to three hundred thousand dollars today.

After he signed the "contract" with us, Elvis went to the phone and called his dad. He said, "Daddy, I just want you to know I've finally got my own group." Those were his words. We were basically just to travel and sing with him when he felt like it. Sometimes he'd send a plane for us in Nashville, just to take us to Memphis to go to the movies! Then sometimes after the movies we'd go back to Graceland and sing all night. That basically was our job. We also opened his show at the Las Vegas Hilton for two or three years.

TONY BROWN (*musician*): For a year and a half I had a job with Voice. We were like Elvis's private musicians, you might say. You see, the regular orchestra and the singers in the show were all paid by the Colonel, but we were paid [out of Elvis's account] by Vernon, and our job was just to hang out with Elvis and be on-call twenty-four hours a day, seven days a week to entertain him. If he wanted to sing some old hymns, he wanted a group to sing harmony with him. That was our job. He would tell Esposito or whoever was around, "I'm going to Palm Springs. Get the guys [Voice] to come hang out with me." So someone would call us and tell us to fly to Palm Springs—or Memphis or L.A.— wherever, and we'd just go and wait in a hotel. Someone would call us and say, "Elvis is going to be hanging out in his living room tonight and wants you guys to come over." We'd go over and watch TV and hang out with him, and eventually we'd all end up around the piano.

When Voice disbanded I got with the big boys [the show band]. But I never was around Elvis again. Funny, when I had the lowly job of playing with Voice, we got to hang out with Elvis a lot. That's when I really got to see him as a real person. But once I got with the orchestra I was on the Colonel's payroll, and on *his* payroll hanging out with Elvis wasn't allowed. You weren't allowed to go backstage—not allowed to go to his dressing room or anything. 'Course Ronnie Tutt and some of those older guys that had been there a long time didn't care. They'd just walk in. But we were "encouraged" not to bother him.

CHERYLE JOHNSON: Elvis again had to cancel shows, this time [May 4–16, 1973] at the Sahara Tahoe [Stateline, Nevada]. He canceled out four days early because, it was reported, he was ill.

JAMES BURTON (*musician*): We cut "Are You Sincere" at the Palm Springs house. We had a remote truck brought up from Los Angeles. Elvis cut the record right in the living room with his pajamas and robe on the whole time. We did a couple more songs, but that's the only one that was a hit.

ALEX LOGAN: The Palm Springs house was different back then. The rooms were papered red and black, and the carpet was mostly red. I remember that Elvis had a big round bed and a red bedspread. I came into the room one day, and he was in bed by himself. I kidded him about how he knew what side of the bed to get up on.

Elvis had buttons that controlled all the lights, all the sound, and the security system. He finally had to have bars put on the windows because people would climb the fence and get in there.

We were building him a master bedroom that overlooked the valley, but after he and Priscilla split up, he never completed it. He never even put carpet in it; it just sat there. We put a playroom in for Lisa Marie. It took us about a year and a half to finish it. They had her fourth birthday party there.

CHARLIE HODGE: Elvis liked to lay out by the pool, but he didn't want to get his body tanned, just his face, so he wore his robe. He'd have [an electric] fan on him to keep cool.

He would eat a pan-fried hamburger steak and mashed potatoes from the kitchen, but he liked to grill steaks out by the pool and do a hot dog for Lisa Marie.

SAM THOMPSON: One time my sister Linda, my wife Louise, and I had been down with Elvis to see the old Circle G Ranch in Mississippi and were on our way back to Memphis in Elvis's Stutz Bearcat. We passed a little black boy, maybe ten or eleven years old, by the side of Highway 51. It was summer; it was hot—dust in the air. The kid was caked in dust, sitting at a little watermelon stand. We had this entourage, about four or five vehicles, and Elvis was in the lead.

[As we go by] Elvis pulls over. Of course, everybody pulls over after him. Everybody jumps out—Red and everybody. They're looking around. This is in the middle of nowhere. This little kid—I'll never forget his face. I know he knew who Elvis was, but he wasn't gonna let Elvis know that he knew. He was a businessman, this kid. He sat there and waited for Elvis to walk up. Elvis had to initiate the conversation, "How much are the watermelons?" A price was established. The kid was real tough and he wouldn't come off the price. So finally Elvis just turned around and said, "We'll take the whole stand. Pay him." That's the only time the kid's visage cracked.

Elvis took one watermelon, the choice one, and put it in the back of the car. Off we drove and left the entourage down there to settle up. Elvis bought the whole watermelon stand, bought all those watermelons, and took them back to Memphis.

:◉:◉:◉:

LARRY NIX *(recording engineer)*: About seven o'clock [on the night of July 21, 1973] here comes Elvis and his entourage—there must've been five or six cars go through the gate at Stax [recording studio, Memphis]. Elvis drives up in a white Stutz Bearcat. He steps out of this thing in his full garb: I mean cape, a round bolero hat, and the big glasses.

Elvis wasn't in real good shape, and the guys with him—they had a Winnebago out back they kept going to. Well, there was a lot of speed and stuff. Elvis's guys were going ninety to nothing.

One night during the sessions I'm in the control room, and they're doing a song. Elvis had all these RCA guys and his own little entourage in there. He had done a certain song and Kang Rhee, the karate guy, was sittin' on the couch to the left in the control room. After they recorded the song they'd all come up and play it back. All these RCA guys were saying, "Wow, another hit! Number one!"—blah, blah, blah—"Man, that's great! That's fabulous!" Elvis turns to this Kang Rhee and says, "What do you think?" The guy looks at him and says, "Oh, not so good." There was one honest guy. The engineer and I literally left the room and laid on the floor and just cracked up.

It was a crazy session. (Elvis was doing some Christmas songs.) They had gone shopping for a Christmas tree and decorations to make a lot of atmosphere. They set up a tree down in the lower left-hand corner of the studio to create a mood. Elvis walked in, ran down there, did a karate jump, and kicked it; the whole thing just fell over.

The recording sessions didn't go well at all; the rhythm section just broke up and didn't come back—left and didn't come back. They said they didn't have to put up with how Elvis was behaving.

I think right after the first session is when Elvis went into Baptist Hospital—between the two sessions. Maybe he went in there to dry out. Maybe he got it out of his system for a while.

:◉:◉:◉:

DR. GEORGE NICHOPOULOS: Elvis was always looking for shortcuts: "I oughta be able to lose weight faster!" In November of '73, I believe, he found this physician out in California who said he was giving Elvis acupuncture, but he was injecting him with syringes. He was using some local anesthetic, some Novocaine, some Demerol, and B-12, and of course Elvis felt great afterwards. This is how that illness got started. He'd had so much cortisone and Demerol in those shots he'd become addicted to Demerol and he was Cushingoid [his face and hands swollen, his body bloated] from too much cortisone. He was so sedated when he came back to Memphis, he was carried off the plane. I called an ambulance immediately. There were a number of different side effects; his ulcer was bleeding due to the cortisone, and the pain medicine was covering all this up. He was having a very difficult time breathing. He was near death. I hospitalized him and called in a couple of specialists to detoxify him. That was the first time I'd had to have him detoxified, and I've always felt this [overdose] was an accidental thing. While he was in the hospital we had to keep his chart locked up. Everyone wanted to look at his records.

That particular admission, the lab technicians were selling his blood and urine. It was crazy. A lot of things we didn't put in the chart because it was difficult to keep quiet. We didn't know how much Elvis was addicted, so we treated him like a Demerol addict. We stopped the Demerol and gave decreasing doses of Methadone. After he got well, Elvis was sorry; he tried to behave himself. He promised not to do it again.

LINDA THOMPSON: Life with Elvis wasn't all Camelot. There was a lot of heartache, and he exhibited a lot of self-destructive behavior, which was very difficult for me, you know—watching someone I loved so much destroy himself.

MARY ANN MOBLEY: In a way, Elvis was a victim of his fame. I think that the doctors gave him whatever they thought he wanted.

DR. GEORGE NICHOPOULOS: I became very conscious that Elvis was using prescribed drugs more heavily after the acupuncture incident. I felt if he could get sucked in on that so easily, he was a sitting target for anybody that wanted to play games with him. He was naive in a lot of ways about doctors.

Right after he got well from the acupuncture and started working again, I'd find him going to different areas of the country wanting to get something for pain, something I didn't think he ought to have. This was about the time he'd bought his airplanes, and it was convenient for him.

FARON YOUNG: I loved Elvis. He was a sweet boy. He was a good boy. He just got off into that damn dope. He'd take a few pills when he was tired, and he got to liking them son of a bitches—or they got to likin' him. Blacks always say, "You don't like that dope. It likes you."

DR. GEORGE NICHOPOULOS: Elvis would call other physicians to get extra drugs, so I had to get full cooperation from everyone around him on trying to limit those extras he was getting. I had to make everybody realize that if we didn't control the situation it would not only affect Elvis but also their jobs. If Elvis didn't work, they didn't work. Some of them may have thought they were doing him a favor by not telling what was going on, but they were only hurting him and themselves. There was [somewhat of] a turnaround about that time; if the pilots flew out, they'd call me; if someone had to go to the airport for Elvis, they'd call me. Sometimes they'd pick up a drug shipment and bring it by my office.

But if he really wanted something, it was easy for him to procure it. He would hide drugs everywhere. During Elvis's first major illness in '73, while he was in the hospital, Joe Esposito and myself went to his room to go through everything. He had three bottles [of drugs] that had a thousand capsules each: one was Dexedrine, one was Seconal, and the other was some other sedative—a thousand capsules in each bottle! We threw 'em all out.

This was a sporadic thing. There would be times when everything was fine and he would take nothing, times he was totally drug free.

SONNY WEST: Elvis was very strong on his convictions. If he had made up his mind that he was going to get off drugs and never take another one—if he'd really made up his mind to do it—he'd have done it and never taken another one again. I mean, he could have done that just like he done other things; he just had to make up his mind.

DR. FOREST TENNANT, JR. *(drug abuse expert)*: I think that Elvis Presley, himself, had a very poor understanding of what his drugs were doing, or why he was even taking the drugs.

When you get your drug problem all mixed up and you don't know why you're taking your drugs, and you don't admit to yourself internally why you're taking your drugs, that's when you get yourself into problems. That's exactly what happened to Elvis.

DR. GEORGE NICHOPOULOS: During one hospitalization some doctor mailed Elvis some drugs "to get well." We couldn't even identify the drugs because they were made locally. He didn't get to use them; we threw them away. Once a doctor came to visit him and gave him some medications without informing me. I called the doctor up and asked him what was going on. He said they were all placebos; not to worry, there was nothing in those pills. The bottle was sealed like from the factory. They were the real thing.

Dr. Forest Tennant, Jr.: Every internal medicine specialist, every general practitioner in the United States has some patients like Elvis Presley in their practice. It's well-known to doctors; and doctors, frankly, are at their wits' end in managing these cases. Doctors like myself are trying to work out what should be done with them, but it's a very frustrating thing for physicians. Elvis Presley's case is routine in some circles of medicine.

National surveys show that ninety percent of drugs prescribed by a doctor are taken as prescribed. However, doctors know that we have those few patients—that five or ten percent of patients that get these substances—that simply will not take them as prescribed. They have this compulsive drive to take more and more. We seem to be powerless to take them off of the drugs or to keep them from going from one doctor to another or one emergency room to another. They just keep taking the drugs on a compulsive basis, and they refuse to go into any kind of therapy from a psychological point of view, or they have failed these treatments.

There is quite a difference in having addiction that is well-controlled versus uncontrolled addiction. What we're finding out in those people who are going to compulsively take a drug to the point of addiction is that it's far, far better to have controlled medical addiction than uncontrolled addiction. In other words, it's the lesser of two evils.

Sonny West: There's times when Elvis woke up in the middle of the night and just took things. That's why he had someone watching him, so that he wouldn't take things and forget and accidentally take them again. There'd been a couple of times when Elvis almost OD'd but was saved.

Dr. George Nichopoulos: We had a confrontation and I told him that I couldn't trust him to continue taking his own medicines. I wasn't accusing him of overdosing or deliberately taking too much, but people with him would sometimes see him reach over and take something, and he'd be half asleep. He'd wake up and go to the bathroom and take a pill just to be sure he could go back to sleep ... and he didn't need it. This is where we had gotten into a lot of problems earlier on the tour. I said,

"Let me handle your medications. You call me if you need me." This put more demand on me as far as getting rest at night. It would have been easier to give them all to him and say, "Here, you take 'em," you know. We did real well with this for awhile, then he got to the point where he'd say, "Hey, I'm an adult. I'm a grown man. Why can't I handle my own medicines? Everybody else does. Why do you have to baby-sit with me?" I said, "We tried it the other way and you saw what happened. This is the only way I can be responsible for it." This came up every now and then, but he seemed to adjust to it.

:◎:◎:◎:

LARRY NIX: The second time Elvis came to Stax [December 10–15, 1973] it was a lot more upbeat. Elvis had his daughter and the girlfriend [Linda Thompson]. They brought a girl just to answer the phone. We had to keep a line open so Colonel Parker could call, I guess.

One of the things that struck me was when Elvis turned to one of his guys and said, "Hey! Hey, man, tonight's Monday night, right?" And the guy says, "Yeah," and boom! The guy leaves. It wasn't fifteen minutes later, this guy comes in with a big ol' TV—all the tags on it. He had run down and bought a TV and stuck it up there in the studio to watch Monday night football. When they left, they left the TV—just got it to watch Monday night football one time.

Another thing that surprised me was if a writer would bring a song in on tape, I would have to transfer it to a disc. Elvis wanted to review all the songs on *record*. That may have been because it was easier to play parts of a record than to rewind a tape, I don't know.

They'd bring the song in, I'd make the acetate [disc], and then I'd go in the studio while they were cutting it. Elvis would listen, and he'd go do it. The song would be done identical to the demo. That dumbfounded me. There was no imagination, no "Create a little bit here," you know! Felton Jarvis was the producer, but all the production was already done on the demos. They just copied them.

Elvis's daughter would be in there with him when he would perform. Most times about ten or eleven o'clock she'd fall asleep, and he'd pick her up and carry her. You could tell that, man, she was everything. I mean, nothing else mattered. He definitely took care of that girl.

DAVID BRIGGS: Elvis loved and worshiped Lisa Marie. That pretty well sums it up. He was crazy about her. He wanted everybody to really be nice around her. He really didn't want her to know some of the things that went on in his life. He was as protective as any dad. From what I saw, she was the most important thing in his life.

LINDA THOMPSON: Elvis was an enormously loving parent. I was with Lisa from the time she was four years old until she was nine years old. Every summer Elvis and I would have Lisa. Every Christmas she would come and spend time with us. We spent a lot of time with her. Elvis gave her, I think, the one thing that is vital for a parent to give to a child, and that is unequivocal love. She knew, unequivocally, that her daddy absolutely adored her.

Elvis was not always right. He was not always as strict as he should have been. He was not always as lenient as he should have been. But he was always, always as loving as he should have been. He let Lisa Marie know every waking moment how much he loved her. He had no hesitation, no qualms about saying, "Your daddy loves you so much," and he would get tears in his eyes telling her.

You know, Lisa was just this little kid; she soaked it up. She knew that her daddy adored her. He would laugh with her. He was very physically demonstrative in his affection, which is also very important. He was really a loving, wonderfully doting parent.

DAVID STANLEY: One time Elvis was booked [at the Sahara Tahoe Hotel] in Lake Tahoe [May 20, 1974] and we were upstairs in Elvis's hotel suite, which was at the end of the hall there. It was Elvis and myself and Red and Sonny and several of the guys, and Lisa Marie. This was during the time of the Patty Hearst kidnapping and a lot of terrorism was taking place. In fact, we were watching [on TV] the SLA [Simbianese Liberation Army] house burn down when the police invaded it. We were all sitting there watching the news, and all of a sudden the lights started going on and off. We were saying, "What the hell is that?" Elvis immediately grabbed Lisa and went right to his room. He was just real paranoid.

I walked out the door of the suite, and you know those emergency doors, there was somebody just banging real loud on that door. I opened the door and there stood a big guy, big red-headed guy. Had on a red coat and white pants. A real belligerent type—he had been drinking. He had a couple of girls standing with him. I said, "Hey, man, what are you doing?" He said, "Where's the goddamn party?" I said, "There is no party, sir. You're going to have to leave." Then the security guys down at the middle of the hall started walking toward us. He yelled, "I said, 'Where's the goddamn party?'" I told him again, "There is no party. Please stop turning the lights on and off" (the circuit-breaker box was right there in the stairwell). He started to move past me. I said, "You can't come in here." Well, he slammed his hand on my chest, pushed me across the hall, and stepped through the door. Just as he stepped through the door, Sonny came out the double doors of the suite, threw a right-hand lead with all his weight, and plastered the guy. I mean, Sonny put him down hard. It was pretty gory—lips and everything were flying. He hurt this guy. The guy goes down and Sonny holds him down (which he didn't have to do much of, 'cause the guy was almost unconscious). So the security guys came and cuffed him, put him on his feet, took him down the hall where the elevators are, and put him in a security room.

Well, I went into Elvis's room, and he was sitting in his bed with a Thompson submachine gun and a .45 [pistol], and Lisa sitting between his legs, and he's saying, "What the fuck's going on?" I said, "Elvis, we got a guy. He tried to come in. It's no big deal." And Elvis said, "Let's go check it out." So Elvis and I and Red go walking down the hall to the security room, and the guy is sitting there on the bed and he's handcuffed. He's regained consciousness and he's pretty upset. Elvis sat next to him on his left side; I sat next to him on his right side, and Elvis says, "What's going on here? What are you doing here?" And the guy's starting to cuss. He's really mad. Then he kicks at Sonny, trying to get people away from him. Just then Red dropped down with a right hand and hit him in the mouth again—while he's handcuffed! The guy falls back and is literally gurgling in his own blood. Elvis said, "Red, you son of a bitch!" Of course, all of us freaked out. I mean, we're not talking about a sweet shot; he hit this guy—broke his teeth and everything. The guy's just gurgling, blood pouring out of his mouth, so Elvis said, "David, help me." We pulled him forward so he wouldn't drown. Elvis began to help him, and Elvis was real upset with Red. I mean, real upset. You know, "You chicken shit; the guy's cuffed." I mean, he didn't like that at all. So we took the guy and we cleaned him up, and then Elvis's whole demeanor changed. Now he was merciful, trying to help the guy. We put him on the elevator. Elvis and myself took him downstairs with the police, and Elvis talked to him for a little bit, and he was gone.

The next thing I knew there was a lawsuit [6.3 million-dollar suit filed October 11, 1974, by Edward L. Ashley of Grass Valley, California]. I was puzzled because they didn't call me to give my deposition. Anyway, I think Elvis settled for six hundred fifty thousand dollars, something like that. I don't know that for sure, but I remember that figure. They settled out of court. It wasn't so bad that Sonny punched him coming in; it was that he got bashed when he was cuffed. That's what caused the lawsuit.

:◎:◎:◎:

DR. GEORGE NICHOPOULOS: I was on call to Elvis from maybe '74 'til the time of his death. He expected me to be around to chat and decide on what kind of activities we were going to do that day—racquetball, or movies.

It didn't work out too badly at first because Elvis wouldn't get up 'til six or seven o'clock in the evening, and that was after my office hours and hospital rounds, so it wasn't too bad to drop by Graceland. But once you got there you were stuck. He wanted you to stay three or four hours.

In those years I realized how important it was to keep him from being bored. We tried to keep him occupied so he wouldn't decide to fly off to Vegas or someplace. We all knew we had to keep him going physically to keep in shape and lose weight.

After a partnership meeting with my associates I had to come up with a figure to bill to Elvis when I was out on tour with him. We finally decided we would take two months of my time in the office, figure out what was the income from an average day, and charge a per diem on tour. The money wasn't paid to me; it was paid to the medical group I belonged to, to make up for my income loss while I was away from the office. I never charged Elvis anything for house calls. He was a friend, and although he could have afforded to pay me whatever I asked, we got so close I just couldn't charge him for anything.

JANICE PENNINGTON: About 1974 when I was twenty-nine, I met Elvis again because we had the same dentist, Dr. [Max] Shapiro in Beverly Hills. One day I told Max my little story about meeting Elvis years before, and to my surprise, he said, "I'm Elvis's dentist, and I'm going by his house today. Why don't you stop by on your way home?" Of course, I did. I told Elvis the story about my earlier experience with him, and later, when I became friends with him, I showed him my little pink diary with the rhinestone on the front. It was kinda sweet to read it all those years later.

Elvis asked me out, or rather, asked me over to his house for dinner; he wasn't able to go out in crowds the way most of us do. I said, "I'm sorry. I can't. I've just become engaged to a man from Aspen, Colorado, and I'm planning to get married, so I just can't." Elvis said, "Well, are there any more at home like you?" I told him, "Yes, I have a sister [Ann Pennington], a younger sister." He said, "One time when we have some people over to the house, please bring her over; I would like to meet her." So, several weeks later, I took my sister over to one of Elvis's little get-togethers and they started dating. They dated for about eight months.

ED PARKER *(karate instructor)*: Once Elvis asked me to come to Vegas. He said he wanted to buy me a car. I said, "Elvis, I own three cars." He said, "Yeah, but they're old." I said, "They're only a year old." He said, "There's ashes in the ashtrays." (He knew I didn't smoke.) I said, "Well, it looks like you just want to give me a car." Finally, he did. But to top it off, he said, "You know, I didn't get your wife anything," and he buys her a twelve-thousand-dollar mink coat!

FELTON JARVIS: Elvis told me he gave things to people sometimes to show them that it was no big deal. That their life would be just the same after they got it as it was before.

ED PARKER: One time a foreign reporter interviewed me about Elvis. She said, "He just gives gifts to people to buy their friendship, doesn't he?" I said, "No!" It kind of made me mad. I explained, "He gives things to people without even knowing who they are, and with no thought of ever seeing them again. That's what he does. He just likes to share his success. It's as simple as that."

SAM THOMPSON: That's the way Elvis was, but Elvis liked to give when he decided to give. He absolutely despised people who fawned and hinted and put him in a posture where he felt like he had to give gifts because they wanted them or asked for them. Elvis was tuned into all the people around him, his friends that needed things; but he wanted to be the one who initiated it. He didn't want you to hint, and believe me there were those who did that.

Elvis loved to see the surprise on your face when he gave you something. He loved to see your gratitude when it was genuine, and he liked nothing better than to sandbag you.

JANICE PENNINGTON: One night we were at Elvis's and he wanted to give me one of his jumpsuits. He had closets full of all these spectacular jumpsuits, but I said, "No, Elvis, that is not at all necessary. Thank you, thank you." It was enough just being around him and enjoying his company, but when he insisted, you didn't want to seem ungrateful. He kept on, "Take one of my belts." He grabbed one for my sister and one for me. The belt he gave me was one with a huge, foot-long buckle and all the chains and stones. I still have the belt.

LOWELL HAYS: In Monroe, Louisiana, Elvis visited a little girl who was terminally ill. She had written him a letter. Before he went to see her, he got a garnet cross from me which he took out there to the Crippled Children's Hospital and gave to her. He did a lot of neat things like that. Most of the time no one ever knew.

JANICE PENNINGTON: I sensed in Elvis more of a sadness sometimes, and that spiritual quest. He gave me a book that I treasure. It's called *The Impersonal Life*. He said, "This is a very special book to me," and he signed it and said, "It helped me." He hoped it would help me, too. It's a very deep book that talks about going within yourself and says the beauty of life and the treasures of life are all within ourselves.

DAVID BRIGGS: It kinda pisses me off sometimes to hear people say, "Oh, he was so dumb; he was a redneck." Elvis was actually very well-read, and he could talk to you on any subject for hours at a time because all he did was read. History, religion—you name it, he knew it. He knew every Confederate general and every battle in the Civil War. He was not a redneck, not dumb; he was brilliant. The guy that I knew [from 1972 to 1977] was a very cultured and well-read gentleman.

:◎:◎:◎:

LARRY STRICKLAND *(backup singer)*: I joined the group in the summer of '74, and things were starting to change at that time. Elvis's health was getting kinda funny. One week you would see him all bloated and not feeling good, and then a week later he would look normal. You never knew what he was going to be feeling like. He had stopped a lot of the socializing before I joined the group. The guys were telling me how they used to spend a lot of time with him in his hotel suite or at Graceland around the piano singing gospel music; by the time I joined, his health was bad and he'd stopped most of that.

SHAUN NIELSEN: At Graceland one night Elvis asked, "What do you think my very best selling single is?" We all guessed everything from "Hound Dog" to "Don't Be Cruel." "No," he said, "it's a song my mother played for me on the wind-up Victrola. Recorded way-back-when by a tenor named

Enrico Caruso. Caruso did it as "O Sole Mio." I recorded it as "It's Now or Never."

:◎:◎:◎:

GEORGE KLEIN: Barbra Streisand came backstage with Jon Peters to see Elvis [at the Hilton]. They wanted him to do a lead part in their remake of *A Star Is Born*. He liked the idea and Joe Esposito liked it and Jerry Schilling liked it. I was just sort of on the fringes of the group at that time; I wasn't there every day with him, but I put in my two-cents worth. I said, "Yeah, great idea." Then he turns the deal over to Colonel Parker and it gets bogged down in money. Colonel Parker told Streisand, "We will do it—million up front and fifty percent of the picture."

SHAUN NIELSEN: The Colonel made the demands for Elvis doing *A Star Is Born* so high, I think Streisand just couldn't afford to give him the part. I never understood why Elvis didn't just say, "Colonel, these are the things I want to do. Now if you want to go along, fine. If you don't, you just go your own way. I'm gonna do this." But I think the Colonel had been there for so many years, Elvis was afraid to go it alone.

EDDIE FADAL: Elvis wanted to do some heavy stuff. He wanted to do a picture like Marlon Brando did. He would recite some of Brando's lines from *The Wild One*. He could remember dialogue incredibly. Just hearing it a few times he could repeat it almost verbatim. That long speech at the opening of the movie *Patton*, he could recite that whole speech. He loved it.

:◎:◎:◎:

CHERYLE JOHNSON: In August, Elvis was again appearing at the Hilton in Vegas, and he canceled two more shows. They said it was because he had the flu, but a lot of fans were beginning to *seriously* worry about him.

ED PARKER: Once, at the Hilton, Elvis asked the guys to be quiet at the table; they didn't. He pulled his gun out and shot it five or six times into the air. He put some holes in the ceiling; he got their attention! It was his form of release. Some people try to make it mean something else, but it really didn't.

Another time Elvis asked the guys to turn the TV off because Robert

Goulet was on the phone. They didn't do it, so he came over and shot the TV out!

Some people said he was vicious—a madman; he was not. That was just his strange form of entertainment.

FRED FREDRICK: Elvis shot his Ferrari. It did something—ran off the road or stalled or whatever, so he just shot it. He said he "killed it." Somebody went down to get the car and towed it back up to the house. Elvis said, "Take that damn thing right back where I left it. It died!"

It still won't run. It's still shot.

KANG RHEE: We call him "Master Tiger," and myself, I am "Mr. Ox." Elvis like having title.

Tenth is highest degree. We qualify him seventh-degree black belt. That's exactly what he want to be. He said, "Master Rhee, this is spiritual number. Seven is really important to me." We promoting him under the TCB Martial Art Organization. He is founder, see. He is a strong role model. That's why we promoting him to seventh. Was he good enough for seven? If you compare to other seven? No. But he has sincere and dedicated attitude. That's why everybody gathering together to give him a seventh degree.

ED PARKER: Elvis was really hyped up about possibly doing a martial arts film. He wanted to show his fans that he could be a good actor, and he felt that if he could do his acting along with something he really loved—the martial arts—he felt it would boost him. But the Colonel said, "No," he would be changing his image too drastically.

LARRY GELLER: One afternoon in 1974, I got to the house in Holmby Hills about four in the afternoon, and as soon as I went into the house Elvis said, "Lawrence, we got to talk immediately." We went upstairs to his bedroom and he said, "I'm going to produce a film and I want you to write it." I asked, "What film?" He said, "It's going to be about the martial arts; the development, from Genesis all the way up to modern times. I want you to write the dialogue. I want you to put it all together." I said, "Fine." So I spent about two months putting together a thirty-page concept, a narrative outline. Elvis was not going to appear in the movie; he was going to narrate it. Ed Parker was going to be one of the producers along with Elvis. Colonel Parker was not going to have any say in the project. This was Elvis's baby, and this was his way of gaining some control, some independence. We started filming some karate tournaments in Beverly Hills and a few other places. We had a couple of reels of footage, but that's as far as we got. The whole project was squashed by his father and Colonel Parker.

:◎:◎:◎:

BECKY HARTLEY: I had been catching on to Vernon's affair with Sandy Miller for awhile because that was when he started coming in to the office all the time and going through the mail. He wanted to get Sandy's letters. Sandy would have addressed them to Elvis, and Vernon knew her handwriting. Sandy was from Colorado. One time (I think Vernon was in Vegas), he called and said, "Did I get a letter . . . ?" I said, "No." Well, after that, I opened the letter, you see, and I never told him.

Vernon even brought Sandy to Memphis while he was still married to Dee. Paulette [Shafer, another secretary] and I had to go to the apartment Vernon was renting for Sandy and sit and wait all day for them to turn on the utilities and all this stuff. It was kinda difficult because I really had no ill feelings toward Dee; she had never done anything to me.

Vernon didn't go into detail about what happened between him and Dee. I do know one time he made the statement that he could never be true to one woman.

Sandy was married before she started living with Vernon. She had three kids. I don't think the affair really bothered Elvis. I mean, just think how many women he had. I think Elvis just wanted his daddy to be happy.

:◎:◎:◎:

CHERYLE JOHNSON: Years later I found out that Elvis earned seven-and-a-quarter million dollars in 1974, and yet an audit revealed that he ended the year with a deficit of over seven hundred thousand dollars! It's no wonder Vernon was afraid they would one day be poor again. And yet, Elvis kept right on spending at a phenomenal rate.

"Down a Blind Alley"
1975-1976

Elvis is fat and forty" scream headlines throughout the world in January of 1975. Within the month, the king of rock 'n' roll is hospitalized. Extensive medical tests reveal various irreversible but manageable ailments—manageable for most people—but Dr. George Nichopoulos explains how Elvis is becoming his own worst enemy.

Despite failing health, Elvis returns to the road. Fan Cheryle Johnson watches with concern Elvis's downward spiral and his resultant bad press. Singers Shaun Nielsen and Myrna Smith describe E's grueling tour schedule and the alarming side effects of drug use and abuse.

While musicians Ronnie Tutt and Tony Brown relate stories of Elvis's bizarre behavior, jeweler Lowell Hays tells how Elvis's long-term relationship with Linda Thompson is coming to an end.

> "Elvis was despondent over his health problems, not over his career necessarily. He didn't look the way he wanted to look, and he wasn't able to sound the way he wanted to sound. There's nothing more demoralizing.... He couldn't be the Elvis he wanted to be at that point."
>
> WAYNE NEWTON *(recording artist)*

Dr. George Nichopoulos: It was exciting at first to travel with the entourage, but the excitement wore off in late '74 or early '75 when Elvis started losing control.

It was hard to convince his management that it was better for Elvis if he toured for ten or twelve days and got rest between tours. Colonel Parker didn't take me seriously at all.

Although he loved performing, Elvis could do just so much of it; then it produced stresses in him. A lot of his problems were the result of going through a tour of twenty to thirty days straight. In Vegas, Elvis was performing two shows a night, seven days a week, for a month at a time.

ED PARKER: You hear a lot of things about Elvis's diet. What he ate depended upon the mood he was in. Basically, he would eat scrambled eggs and very crisp bacon for breakfast, with toast and orange juice. Sometimes he might have a Spanish omelet. He usually drank black coffee without sugar, and he always drank lots of water.

The junk foods—the cheeseburgers and pizzas and peanut butter sandwiches and ice cream—he ate mainly when he got upset and wanted to comfort himself.

DR. GEORGE NICHOPOULOS: I'm sure Elvis's diet contributed to his health problems. My biggest problem was getting him to lose weight, and deciding what type of diet he should lose weight on. He had a bad habit of reading just anything—a tabloid or something: try this, that, or the other to lose weight. I remember one time, just before we toured, somebody came up with a no-calorie Jell-O, and he would eat Jell-O every day—ten times a day until he was full.

JANICE PENNINGTON: One night I was at his house in L.A. He was getting ready to do a show at the Hilton, and he had himself all wrapped up in Saran Wrap—his whole body was wrapped. He had a sweat suit over it 'cause he was trying to lose ten pounds. He was just jamming at the piano while he was kinda insulating himself, and he was pouring sweat. We were all having a great time listening to him, but it got to be four in the morning and he still didn't want people to leave.

BECKY HARTLEY: I look back and think how good-looking Elvis was in the early sixties, when I was fourteen. But I think how he got even better looking. He really did. His complexion was gorgeous; his smile was gorgeous. Of course when you're a movie star and singer, you've got to keep those looks up.

LAMAR FIKE: He hated his weight. I used to kid him. I'd say, "You got all this metal on [your costume], and if you keep gaining this weight you're gonna explode and kill the first three rows with shrapnel!"

DR. GEORGE NICHOPOULOS: If he could've just accepted that he was fat and forty and that his fans could take it or leave it . . . his singing was the same. So what if he didn't move around as fast; they weren't interested in that. They were interested in the man himself. He could've weighed a hundred pounds more and still been loved and admired by his fans, but you couldn't convince him of that. He still had that image of himself when he was more physical and thinner and more macho. Yet he couldn't hang in there and discipline himself to do what it took to get his weight down to where he really wanted it.

DR. DAN BROOKOFF *(associate director for medical education for Methodist Hospital, Memphis)*: Elvis looked like he was on steroids, all the weight gain. . . . We should mention that these are not the steroids that body builders use; these are not abused steroids. [Elvis was taking] steroids that people use for asthma [and for] colitis.

DR. GEORGE NICHOPOULOS: Elvis took steroids off and on from 1973 until the time that he died. At times it would be for his bowel problems, but other times it would be for infections.

He had steroid [related] problems after he came back from the West Coast in 1973. The guy out there was doing acupuncture and injecting him. [He gave Elvis injections of] Demerol, cortisone, xylocaine. Each time Elvis was put in the hospital, it was apparent that his adrenal gland was not up to par; we would have to suffer him other illnesses to be sure that he had enough cortisone to take care of that illness.

Elvis had involuntary bowel movements only a few times, and that was when he was overly sedated. This wasn't a common occurrence. This was in '73 (or '74) when he was controlling his own medications and was overly sedated. He couldn't wake up enough to realize he needed to go to the bathroom.

DR. DAN BROOKOFF: One problem Elvis had actually predated his use of narcotics. It's what they call a ganglionic fold. It's inherited. It's a disease where nerve fibers have not grown into the colon, and the colon does not have the muscle tone that it should.

The thing is that your colon does have bacteria in it, and the thing that keeps us alive is that things keep moving out fast; there's a flow. If your colon turns into a big flask or fermentation vat . . . it will give you problems.

DR. GEORGE NICHOPOULOS: We tried to get somebody to do a partial colostomy [removal of part of the intestine] on him in 1975, because his bowel problems were pretty serious. Not only did it hurt him, it hurt his appearance. The surgeon that saw him said, "No way. We don't remove [parts of] colons just for appearance."

Elvis's weight problem caused him to look a lot like he did when he was on the cortisone; his face would look swollen and puffy. He was putting on weight—most of it in his middle. The increased fat in his waistline and the problem he had with his colon made him look a lot bigger than he was.

DR. DURWOOD GRUBBS, *(doctor of pharmacy)*: The side-effects of steroid use are typically puffy cheeks, moon face, some swelling from the fluid in your body.

DR. GEORGE NICHOPOULOS: We would give him ACTH [an injectable cortisone] to try and build up his adrenal gland.

BECKY HARTLEY: After Elvis was released from the Baptist Hospital he would come out to my office. He would look kind of swollen and puffy and not as good as he usually did. Then he would bounce back.

While Elvis was in the hospital [January 29–February 14, 1975],

Vernon had a heart attack [February 5, 1975]. I remember my mother keeping Sandy's children when Vernon went into the hospital.

DR. GEORGE NICHOPOULOS: In early '75 we got a nurse to stay on the premises [at Graceland]. Before that Elvis would call me if he woke up at night and needed more medication to sleep. I'd have to drive back out to his house to give him something.

I don't think Elvis would've liked it if he had thought the nurse was just there for him. He had too much pride to admit he needed that [kind of] close supervision. I could justify someone being there twenty-four hours a day since Elvis's grandmother and father had been sick.

:◎:◎:◎:

CHERYLE JOHNSON: Despite the ups and downs of his health, Elvis went back to Las Vegas in March of '75 and did twenty-nine shows. Then toward the end of April, he hit the road and toured the South and Northeast doing almost sixty more shows.

DR. GEORGE NICHOPOULOS: Usually the routine, whether in Vegas or on the road, was that first one of us would wake him up. He would have some coffee and take his vitamins and some sort of appetite suppressant—sometimes these were innocuous and sometimes they were amphetamine-like substitutes. He would take a decongestant, his blood pressure medicine, and then he would eat. Then he'd kill a few hours before getting ready for the show. He had gotten into a routine in Vegas of getting what he called a voice shot, which was a combination of three or four different herbs that had no medical justification that you could find, but he was convinced that it helped his voice.

There were times we would even have to put some drops on his vocal cords. Then after he was dressed and ready, he would get a vitamin B-12 shot. If he still had some congestion, we would decide whether to placebo him—you had to give him something at that time 'cause he thought he couldn't perform without it—or give him a decongestant. Then he would leave and go to the show.

After we got to the show, about four or five minutes before he went on, we'd put some drops in his eyes. He kept getting conjunctivitis from hair dye that irritated his eyes—that and the bright lights. We would put a local anesthetic in his eyes, which he thought helped tremendously. Again, this had to be some psychological thing because the anesthetic wouldn't last very long.

After the show I'd give him his blood pressure pills again. I might also give him a sedative of some sort by injection to calm him down. It would depend on what kind of show it was, whether I felt he had really done anything as far as injuring his neck or back or something. A lot of times after a show he would want Demerol or something to calm him down. It got to the point where he would check the bottles. I would go to my bag in the next room and bring the shot back in, and many times it was a placebo. Then he got wise and said, "You bring the bag in the room." Then he'd watch me get it out of the bottle. I had a bottle that had saline in it, and I had another bottle with Demerol that had been diluted down with saline; there were various combinations of other things that we toyed with.

Elvis once went by a dentist's office in [Greensboro] North Carolina and loaded a box full of over-the-counter medications and stuff. I took the medications away from him. I made a mistake in taking them away because I did it in front of people. I think he would've accepted it better if it had just been a one-on-one situation. I guess I embarrassed him by taking them away from him. Then I embarrassed him even more by refusing to give them back. He stomped around the room for a little while, slammed a few doors.

Elvis's father had only been out of the hospital for a very short time after he'd had a heart attack, and he flew in to see him. Elvis walked out to greet his dad, and as he put his arm around him his pistol went off. The bullet hit some part of the chair I was sitting in and ricocheted off and hit me in the chest. All it did was give me a little burn on my chest. With his father just having had a heart attack, it could've been a very serious incident. Elvis tried to make a big joke out of it.

LOWELL HAYS: One night onstage, Elvis insinuated (right in front of the audience) that the Sweet Inspirations smelled like catfish. He was in a bad mood and things weren't going well. Well, a couple of them [were offended and] left right in the middle of the show. Then he said something smart to someone else onstage and they left. Before the show was over with, several people had walked offstage and left him to finish the show.

That night word went around the hotel that we were leaving for Asheville [North Carolina] the next morning at ten! Now Elvis was never even awake at ten o'clock in the morning, so nobody believed that. We were told we should have our bags out in the hall at nine and be ready to leave at ten. Next morning, we did get our bags in the hall at nine and we went downstairs. Elvis always had a bus for the ones that were on the plane with him—on his plane. So we got on the bus and we were on our way to the airport. We all agreed, eight or ten of us, "Look, he's not gonna be there even at eleven o'clock—probably not 'til late afternoon—and we're all hungry; let's stop and eat." We stopped at a Dairy Queen and we're having breakfast, and suddenly a motorcycle policeman and Elvis's limo came roaring by us. Well, we jumped up, ran out, jumped on the bus, and sped after him. When we got to the airport he was mad because we weren't there and didn't have the plane loaded. He left us all standing with our luggage in the middle of the runway and flew off without us! We had to wait two or three hours 'til he sent the plane back to pick us up.

Elvis got the kind of newspaper write-up he deserved about the [Greensboro] concert the night before.

By the time we finally got to Asheville, Elvis was in big trouble! Everybody was threatening to quit him. No one was going onstage that night, and even Elvis had figured out he was in big trouble. So he sent for me and started buying jewelry. He was buying everybody an "I'm sorry" gift. He made the biggest purchase of jewelry you can imagine! He bought almost everybody he'd angered a nice piece of jewelry. I didn't have that much merchandise with me. I had to call my brother, who brought another load of jewelry in our company plane. Elvis bought it all.

DR. GEORGE NICHOPOULOS: In Asheville, Elvis wanted me to give him a shot to calm him down. He wanted a narcotic. I told him I didn't think he needed it. At times like this, when I felt like it was going to be useless to argue with him, I'd just put a placebo in him and let it go at that.

A lot of times when he'd get depressed, the narcotics would give him an "up" feeling, as well as relieve his pain. He would always go back to something that made him feel good.

:◎:◎:◎:

BECKY HARTLEY: Elvis loaned people money all the time and would then write [the loss] off. You know, he didn't expect them to pay him back. One guy borrowed thirty thousand dollars from Elvis and never paid it back, and now he talks about how bad Elvis treated him.

There were different relatives coming around, you know, when they needed money and all. I don't think that stressed Elvis out; I think more or less he just accepted it.

DR. GEORGE NICHOPOULOS: There were some occasions where people who worked for Elvis asked him for loans which were not considered loans; they were never repaid.

I had trouble getting a bank loan one time—money for the construction of a house I was building. Elvis offered to give me the house, and I told him, "No." He said he'd finance it, and I could repay it any way I wanted to.... So we set up a schedule of interest and monthly payments just like a mortgage loan. I think it was about one hundred twenty five thousand, so I paid him back eighteen hundred dollars a month.

MARTY LACKER: The pitiful part of it was, Elvis left all his personal business up to Vernon, and Vernon had a third-grade education. That's why there were never any investments, except one (which was revealed after Elvis died) that Vernon made and lost like two and a half million dollars. It was some coal mine deal. Vernon was terrible as a business person, but unfortunately Elvis relied on him. Parker took care of the entertainment business, and Vernon took care of Elvis's personal business. Elvis just flat out didn't want to bother with business—period.

When me or Alan Fortas suggested things about investments and stuff to protect his money, Elvis would say, "That sounds good. Go to Daddy." So I went and talked to Daddy, and his daddy told me, "Mind your own fuckin' business!" Three times in a row I said, "No, Mr. Presley, wait a minute. Elvis told me to come and talk to you!" He said, "Mind your own fuckin' business!" He was that blunt. After he told me the third time, I said to myself, "Well, screw you." I never brought it up again. A month or so later Elvis asked me, "Did you ever talk to Daddy about that project?" I told him I had. Elvis asked me what his dad had said. I said, "He told me to mind my own fuckin' business." Elvis just looked at me and shook his head like, "What am I gonna do, man? That's my father."

Elvis trusted certain people. He would sometimes just tell them what he wanted. Same thing with his last will and testament. He told his father what he wanted in the will, and he trusted his father to put it in there. So when you'd come to Elvis with a document to sign, he'd just ask you, "Did you do what I asked you to do?" And the person could have lied to him and said "Yeah, I did it," and Elvis would sign it. He never read contracts as far as I know. He never even read his own will.

BECKY HARTLEY: People don't realize Vernon was self-educated. The thing about it is he had people to go to. Elvis had accountants and he had a very trustworthy lawyer when I worked there. If Mr. Presley couldn't find information, he had people that he could go to.

ANNIE CLOYD PRESLEY: Vernon loved a dollar better than anybody. Vernon loved money, and I blame him for a lot of it. Gladys never got high and mighty, and Elvis never got high and mighty; but Vernon did.

MARTY LACKER: In the last years, Elvis started paying people fairly decent. Joe [Esposito] left for awhile and then came back. When he returned, I think Joe was making a thousand dollars a week. I think he was the highest-paid guy, and that was still low when you consider the hours he worked and what all he did.

You see, you've got to understand something. Elvis couldn't tell you what a loaf of bread cost. Elvis could only relate to: "Hey, we're out here and we're having a lot of fun. I'm paying all the expenses and giving you a beautiful house to live in out in California." The only thing that Elvis could comprehend is what it would be like for some guy to have a brand-new car, nice shiny jewelry; that's why he gave those cars and jewelry away, because that's the only thing he understood. These gifts weren't like, "Hey, here's a bonus!" He didn't think of 'em in that context. See, he knew how he felt when he got his first new car. He knew how he felt when he sat on the curb in front of Lauderdale Courts and saw all those beautiful new cars go by. He and his family had nothing, so he knew what it was like to get something like that. It's the only thing he could really relate to.

Salaries and finances were mostly left up to Vernon. And Vernon (if he'd had his way): first of all, we wouldn't have been there; and secondly, if he had to pay us, it would have been ten dollars a week!

CHERYLE JOHNSON: Elvis bought that Delta Convair 880 jet in June of 1975. He named it the *Lisa Marie* and had the entire interior redone. By the time you added up the purchase price and the cost of remodeling it, Elvis had spent almost two million dollars!

:◎:◎:◎:

MYRNA SMITH: Normally, Elvis would fly out to the next city right after the show. As soon as he left the stage, he got in his limo, went straight to the airport, and flew to the next city. The rest of the show people, the band, the singers, we'd spend the night in the city where we had performed the show, and we'd travel on the next day. Elvis never had sound checks to make sure the mikes were all placed right and the sound was balanced properly, so we'd all be free the next day after we got to the new city—free until show time. Our group opened the show, so we'd get to the auditorium before Elvis did. The comedian followed us, and while the comedian was on we'd change into our backup singer clothes for Elvis's portion of the show. After the show was over each night, off he'd go to the next town. That's what had happened all along until I started dating Jerry [Schilling]. Then I'd have to leave immediately after the show in order to fly with Jerry on Elvis's plane. I'd have to get my stuff ready in a hurry and really move it.

RED WEST: Elvis was like a prisoner. He couldn't get out and do things like other people. Wherever we'd go, people were there; that comes with the territory. And anybody who reaches his level and can handle it, congratulations; 'cause I don't think anybody can do it.

SHAUN NIELSEN: One time, a girl had somehow gotten past the [arena's] security people and she came rushing up onstage. Out of the corner of my eye, I saw her running. I don't know what she was gonna do when she got there, but she looked like she was doing about sixty-five! If she had hit Elvis, she'd have knocked him down. But I reached out and grabbed her and picked her up with one arm and kept right on singing. I had this woman up off the floor, and she was screaming and her arms were reaching out to Elvis and her feet were still going ninety to nothing. Finally, one of [Elvis's] security guards came over and got her and escorted her away.

RED WEST: Somebody somewhere said Elvis's security team was better than the President's. That made me feel good whether it was true or false, but we really worked at it. We worked at keeping him from getting hurt.

TONY BROWN: Most all of [the bodyguards] around him claim that they loved him, and they probably did. But what they were doing was rationalizing. It was an abusive relationship between Elvis and those guys, unhealthy, and only in hindsight can we see it. But you know, that happens with a lot of big celebrities: it's easy to feel invincible when you're totally surrounded with yes-men.

DR. GEORGE NICHOPOULOS: We had some difference of opinion on what Elvis ought to be doing onstage because of some of his illnesses. He'd hurt his neck and back with some of those gyrations. He was notorious for breaking protocol, and it drove the band up the wall 'cause they didn't know what he was going to do next—and even Elvis didn't know what he was going to do next. Whatever the spirit hit him to do, he did.

SONNY WEST: Elvis didn't think he had that big a problem with drugs. He felt that he was in control, that he knew what he was doing, that he could quit when he wanted to, or something; but it wasn't working.

We finally told Vernon we were concerned about what Elvis was taking. Vernon went to Elvis and said, "The boys are concerned. What are you doing?" Elvis called us in and jumped all over us for getting his dad upset. We didn't upset his father. His father knew what was going on.

DR. GEORGE NICHOPOULOS: I think Elvis was like so many people who have alcohol or drug problems. I think that most of these people have the ability to rationalize and feel like they have control of the situation, that they can start and stop it whenever they want to. Therefore, they don't feel like they are addicted or really abusing the drugs.

Elvis's problem was that he didn't see the wrong in it if he was getting it from a doctor. He felt that by getting it from a doctor he wasn't the common everyday junkie getting something off the street. He was a person who thought that as far as medications and drugs went, there was something for everything.

CHERYLE JOHNSON: I saw Elvis in concert at least fifteen times over the years. I think the change was sudden, and even then it was up and down. Sometimes you'd see him and think, "Oh my goodness! What is wrong?" And the next time, he'd be right back. You'd see him in Vegas and he'd look good; then you'd see him a month or two later, and he would look worse than the time before.

TOM JONES: Elvis once asked me how I coped with my success. I said, "It's very easy because I've been wanting it for so very long." I said, "Isn't it a shame about The Beatles splitting up? They were such a wonderful group. But, I guess, it's all that drug business. They went through some funny changes." Elvis looked at me rather surprised and asked, "Well, haven't you ever gone through any of that stuff?" I said, "No. I stay away from it with my life."

Elvis told me that he had tried taking different drugs just to keep sane. He always seemed to be nervous about actually going onstage completely sober. He said to me he had gone through some changes, and at that time he had straightened himself out. Later on, he must have fallen back into it.

CHERYLE JOHNSON: I was starting to notice on his stage shows how he was coming apart. You could see the physical problems, and you could see that he just couldn't sing like he used to. He was slurring his words.

In Las Vegas onstage one night, Elvis held up a clipping, a review [of his show], and he was just ranting and raving. He said, "I can't believe somebody would write this about me!" More and more he was taking time away from performing and just getting into dissertations onstage. It was totally out of character for him.

Sometimes at the beginning of his shows, and even well into his shows, he was very lethargic. It was pretty obvious that he was bloated, too. I mean, you could see there was something wrong. The people that really knew him could just look in his eyes and see that the light just wasn't there anymore. He didn't have that fire any more. In mid-August he again canceled some of his dates at the Hilton. Many of us began to seriously worry about him. In the beginning we made excuses. Later on, we really worried.

DR. GEORGE NICHOPOULOS: If we could get Elvis to take his sedatives just before he ate, he could get through his dinner. What would happen frequently was someone would come in and start talking to him, and he'd have to order another tray; then he'd be falling asleep while he was trying to eat. There were times when I, Linda, and a couple of other people had to remove food from his mouth that he was choking on.

With him being under a lot of pressure and mental and physical fatigue, Elvis was demanding more medications for one thing or another. There were several hospitalizations. I felt this was leading down a blind alley. The only healthy changes I knew were to decrease the pressures that were put on him in all respects, not only his work stresses but his home stresses.

LINDA THOMPSON: When Elvis was in the hospital [September 1975], he was very possessive and fiercely needed me to be with him all the time, to take care of him, particularly when he was in that vulnerable state. While he was hospitalized, he was trying very hard to heal himself emotionally as well as physically.

We used to watch game shows in the daytime, but the TV used to go off at midnight, and those were his normal hours, so we used to watch the babies in the nursery and talk about one day having a child. We wanted to have a little boy together, so we had this running gag: "There he is over there. That could be him." We'd see a cute little baby and say, "That's him!" It was quite memorable and kind of a bonding time.

But there were other women, and it was very difficult for me because Elvis was my first major love. It was hard for me to know that if I was not with him, someone else would be. Women were so readily available to him. Considering the fact that he had so many women at his disposal, he did quite well. He showed a lot of restraint even though the press might not indicate that he did. He was Elvis, and all those women were clamoring to be near him.

You have to remember that Elvis was completely isolated from the world. He surrounded himself with about thirteen men and me. He was closed off to other people—other stimuli. I tried to understand that sometimes he just might need someone else to talk to. He might need someone to bounce an idea off, and he might need the ego gratification, too, of having another woman say, "Gee, you're so wonderful!" because we were together all the time. I think that, even though it was Elvis, you grow a little complacent, and possibly you don't always feed the person's ego like you should.

MYRNA SMITH: Some of Elvis's many romances ran concurrently. Sometimes he would overbook himself. It was like a revolving door. But the girls wouldn't know because they would be in different hotel rooms—sometimes different floors of the same hotel. He would ask me sometimes, "Well, Myrna, what am I gonna do now?" I'd say, "You can handle it."

Most of his relationships weren't sexual. Elvis just liked pretty women, and just spending the night in his room didn't necessarily mean it was sexual. Somebody always had to be in the room with Elvis. As you know, he'd take sleeping pills to go to sleep, and sometimes he'd get choked in his sleep. Lots of times someone would have to jump in to keep him from choking to death. Linda was very good at it. If she was with him, he'd do a lot better 'cause she took care that he ate and slept properly. There was always somebody there that had to do that, whether it was one of his stepbrothers, or a female. Didn't mean they were gettin' it on, it just meant someone was watching out for him.

LOWELL HAYS: Elvis insisted that I carry a briefcase full of jewelry everywhere I went. As time went on and we became friends, I began to feel like I was exploiting him. Once we went to Palm Springs and Elvis took a young lady (a cocktail waitress) he had picked up at one of the

Memphis football games. When we got to Palm Springs Elvis wanted to buy her some jewelry, and I said, "I didn't bring any." He said: "Why? You should have brought jewelry. You should always bring jewelry when you're around me. Why do you think I have you come around all the time? I want to be able to buy that jewelry." So I said, "Well, I feel like I'm exploiting you." He said, "Well, don't feel that way. I want the jewelry." Do you know, I had to go with him to a jewelry store in Palm Springs that night and help him buy jewelry for that girl!

GEORGE KLEIN: When they were building the interior of the *Lisa Marie*, they had it parked at an airport between Fort Worth and Dallas. At that time Elvis had another plane in Memphis. Well, we'd be out at Graceland watching TV, goofing around, and he'd say "Let's go look at the plane," like it was just outside. We'd say, "Okay, Elvis." He would call the airport and get [in touch with] his pilots and tell them he was going to be out there in thirty minutes or an hour. The pilots were always on standby. I'll bet we flew down to Texas at least fifteen times, man, showing different people the airplane. He'd take you through the plane and he'd say, "This is where my room is going to be. There's going to be a green chair here, and this is going to be closed-circuit television."

When the *Lisa Marie* was completed, I'd get on the intercom and I'd say: "Ladies and gentlemen, welcome to Presley Airlines. We'll be departing Memphis International in five minutes and landing in Las Vegas." Elvis got a kick out of it. He said, "One time I could hardly afford a new car, now I have five airplanes!"

LOWELL HAYS: Elvis loved guns, and he would get his guns out and play with them even on the plane. And you know, when you're flying along at thirty-five thousand feet in a pressurized plane and Elvis is playing with those guns, it really gets you nervous. Fortunately, nothing ever happened. He never shot out a TV on a plane!

DR. GEORGE NICHOPOULOS: There were a number of times that I was around when he had been unhappy with the TV—the vertical hold wasn't holding or something. He would get tired of adjusting it, and he'd shoot the set. They'd just go out and get another one.

Elvis shot so many sets that it was a little standing joke that there was a TV graveyard in the back of his house.

LOWELL HAYS: Lots of times Elvis would send for me and I'd sit around and wait for him three or four hours. Whenever I went upstairs [at Graceland] to show him things, Elvis would put the jewelry in the middle of his bed—it was bigger than a king-sized bed. He would get in the middle of that bed and sit cross-legged like an Indian with that jewelry spread all around him. That's how he bought most of the time. He was very selective in buying for people. I kept a list of what people had, and he would say does so-and-so have an emerald ring? "Well, let's get her an emerald ring." So we'd write her name on an envelope and stick the ring in it. That's how he'd do his Christmas shopping. When we'd get through, I'd put 'em all in boxes and write their names on 'em and hand them to Elvis before Christmas.

It was nothing for him to spend fifty or sixty thousand dollars at Christmas for his cooks, his grandmother, his aunts, his father, and all the guys. Today that would be equivalent to three hundred thousand dollars—for Christmas!

:◎:◎:◎:

T. G. SHEPPARD [Bill Browder]: My last trip with Elvis was for that New Year's Eve show in '75 when he played the Pontiac [Michigan] Silverdome. I had never seen that many people together in one room. It was really electrifying—a total sell-out—fifty or sixty thousand tickets! Elvis was just astounded and really excited. We flew up the day before and spent the night in Detroit. The next night we went over and did the show, and the crowd went crazy! We came back home late New Year's Eve night and went back to Graceland. Elvis was still [elated]; he said it was incredible.

KANG RHEE: I know Elvis for five year. I saw many times. He was perfectionist. He must have perfect look, perfect health, perfect shape—1970 to 1975 he has perfect shape. He is looking good and singing like bird. Everything is good and kind. He is very excited with the karate and the racquetball. Then at end of 1975 he starts gain weight and he don't want to show me he is out of shape. I think he shamed himself. The end of 1975 he goes to the hospital, and I lose contact after the end of '75. He go to the hospital every three months. His health is going down the hill and he has the eye problem and he has so many troubles with the health. He was out of the control. He doesn't have no more aim to be good, I guess. After that I couldn't contact with him anymore. He is locked in his room and he never comes out.

BILL BELEW: Toward the end, Elvis was like a lot of the women that I dealt with when they start fluctuating in their weight. They really didn't want to be measured because they really didn't want to know the truth.

It was something that I understood, so it wasn't a major problem; but, unfortunately, we only had about five good jumpsuits—one being the sunburst, one being the peacock, and a few others—that we were actually able to let out.

The tailor and I would watch Elvis's performance videos, and then I would talk to Joe Esposito on the road. I'd say, "It looks like to me he's gained a little bit." Joe would say, "Can you give me a couple more inches—let 'em out?" So we just literally did it looking at video and with Joe guessing what the changes should be. He'd send the suits back and we'd let 'em out and ship 'em back to wherever Elvis was going to be next. He didn't want to try 'em on, and he didn't want to be measured, so we just literally guessed at what his weight was doing.

DR. GEORGE NICHOPOULOS: I don't think Elvis really saw himself as being as heavy as he was. They were constantly letting his clothes in and out. (He once split his suit onstage.) I think he blocked this out somehow. He was just concerned with whether the people were getting their money's worth from coming to his shows. He never seemed preoccupied with how many albums he sold and hardly ever read the newspaper about any of his shows. He was just concerned with the audience response. This is what turned him on and really pleased him.

ED PARKER: Regardless of his weight, his fans loved him. They didn't care if he just sat and did nothing else but sing.

DR. GEORGE NICHOPOULOS: I don't think Elvis was using more or less drugs because of his weight. He used more or less drugs according to his stresses. I don't think he worried about his weight that much.

When Elvis was at Graceland, everyone waited on him hand and foot. Everybody knew how to please him. He felt comfortable there. Graceland was his security blanket. He had memories of his mother there. He certainly got into less trouble medically when he was there than he did other places.

:◉:◉:◉:

MYRNA SMITH: From 1969 on, when I joined Elvis, I remember a lot of good times. One that particularly stands out was his forty-first birthday

[January 8, 1976]. We were in Colorado—Vail to be exact. Linda Thompson and Elvis were still together, and I was with my ex-husband (who was my boyfriend at the time), Jerry Schilling, and the guys were all there. Elvis didn't want to celebrate his birthday, because he didn't want to get old. So he said, "We won't celebrate tonight," and the guys just kind of disappeared. Elvis and Linda were alone at the house.

He called Jerry and me and asked if we would come up. About ten-thirty or eleven, we went to the house and sat down and had cake and talked. Slowly he got into the fact that it was his birthday, and finally we sang "Happy Birthday" to him. He asked me if I had seen a movie called *Across 110th Street,* and I said, "No." He was really into those Super Fly movies. In fact, he wore Super Fly coats and Super Fly hats, and he had the whole outfit. He *became* "Super Fly" for a while. I remember when he finally grew out of that phase, he gave all of those outfits to a friend of mine in Memphis, a black guy who really appreciated those clothes because they were very expensive.

Anyway, since I hadn't seen *Across 110th Street,* Elvis said, "Let me tell you about it." And he started telling me the story—he did all the characters, all the dialogue, the whole film, from beginning to end. It took him as long to tell it as it took the film to run! I never saw that movie, but, you know, I don't ever need to, 'cause he told me the whole thing.

:◉:◉:◉:

LARRY STRICKLAND: I recorded a couple of albums with Elvis. The most notable one was the one we recorded at Graceland [*From Elvis Presley Boulevard, Memphis, Tennessee*]. We spent quite a bit of time [February 2–6, 1976] doing that in Memphis at the house every night. Some nights we would record, and other nights we'd just hang around. Some nights Elvis would want to sing, and some nights I guess he wasn't feeling like it. We never knew. We were always on call, and we would go over and spend the whole night there. Sometimes we wouldn't sing a note. But whenever he did come down [stairs] and sing, it was a lot of fun. That was the most intimate time I had with him.

Elvis was a real pro when it came to recording. I remember recording the song "Hurt," in particular. He hooked it about the second take from top to finish. I mean, he really sang it. With him it wasn't all this resinging and all that stuff. We would sometimes have to come back to Nashville and go back in and redo our parts to try to get ours better, but for Elvis, on the second or third take he'd get it right.

He was a frustrated bass singer and he loved that low part. During that recording session Elvis would come over to us while we were doing the harmonies and just sing along with us. He'd kinda sing bass along with me, and at the end of one of the songs he turned to me and said, "Hope you don't mind me singing with you." I said, "Oh, no, I won't let it mess me up." I didn't mean it the way it sounded, but everybody took a big breath, and all he did was just bust out laughing.

DAVID BRIGGS: We rehearsed "Moody Blue" before Elvis walked into the session. We cut it in his house. Nobody had the balls to tell him, "You ought to listen to that again." He only really paid attention to two or three people: James Burton, myself, and Ronnie Tutt. Felton would come to me and say, "Tell Elvis we need to do that again." I'd say, "Hey, Elvis, I made a mistake on that. Could we do that again?" And he would go, "Oh, okay." Nobody had the balls to tell him, "You could sing that better." He needed somebody to tell him that; he never had it after he got hot. He probably had it with Scotty Moore. See, Scotty Moore in my mind was his producer. And after Scotty left, it all changed.

ANITA FIELDER: Of all of Elvis's recordings, the one I was most touched by was his album *From Elvis Presley Boulevard, Memphis, Tennessee*. It has songs like "Hurt," "The Last Farewell," and "Blue Eyes Crying in the Rain." Every song in that album is for every woman in love with some man who doesn't appreciate her. My favorite cut is "Love Coming Down," because he seems really sorry he was so busy going up in the world that he couldn't see their love was coming down. He asks her forgiveness and promises to do better.

:◎:◎:◎:

DR. GEORGE NICHOPOULOS: There were times Elvis would go to California, Vegas, Palm Springs, to get drugs. A lot of the things he got we were able to throw away or exchange for placebos. If I was going to take care of him, I was going to take care of him. It's just professional courtesy that when another doctor treats someone that they call the primary physician and tell him what they're doing. Most of these doctors were embarrassed about what they'd done, so I'd have to find out the hard way what was going on.

FRED FREDRICK: Dr. Nick supposedly took pretty good care of Elvis. I don't know that he did or he didn't, but if it hadn't been Nick, it would have been somebody else.

DR. GEORGE NICHOPOULOS: Most doctors were delighted to be able to see Elvis, talk to him, and shake his hand, this kind of thing. They were just eager to please him. It wasn't for money, 'cause most of the doctors never charged Elvis anything.

V. L. LANE *(captain, Memphis Police Department, narcotics division)*: Elvis had shipments of cocaine coming in. I know he did. I sat up one evening and saw the shipment. It wasn't very much—a half pound, which would have been worth one million dollars. I don't know if it was his, but it had his name on it. He was supposed to pick it up at the Howard Johnson Motel [near Graceland, where Elvis often had guests stay]. I sat up waiting for him to show up, but he never did. He may have found out that we were on to it; I don't know. It could have been a lot of things. Anyway, we confiscated the cocaine and burned it.

PAUL DOUGHER: We stayed close friends, but later on it got to be such a hassle to try to see him, I gave up. Used to, you could just call and get right through. I could almost always get him on the phone or go out to the gate. They would let him know I was there and he'd say "Let him come up." But later with so many people trying to do that, I guess he wanted more seclusion. When I would call up there, Charlie Hodge would get on the phone, or Joe Esposito. They would say, "He's busy with something." They probably wouldn't even let him know I was on the phone. I finally gave up and would only see him when he came to see me. He would come by and I would say, "I tried to get hold of you." "Just tell them who you are," he'd say. "That doesn't always help," I explained.

EDDIE FADAL: The Memphis Mafia isolated him. They were afraid someone else would encroach on their territory, so they tried to keep everybody else out. It was a tough ring around Elvis, and I don't think Elvis realized that. There were a lot of people who called who had business being with Elvis. Some of these people were important recording artists and recording people that Elvis wanted to see, but they couldn't get through that group.

GEORGE KLEIN: Elvis knew that some of us, like Red West and I, weren't there for the money or to cash in on his fame—we'd been there before he became famous. Sure we rode with him to the top, but we weren't Johnny-come-latelys. We were friends with him when he was a nobody, and he never forgot that.

V. L. Lane: I didn't know what to do [regarding rumors of Elvis's drug abuse]. If I had gone to Elvis, that might have dissolved our friendship; he was getting paranoid. He thought everybody was against him, and I did not want Elvis to feel that I was against him. I didn't want to hurt him, so I didn't go forward. I wasn't afraid of Elvis, his publicity, and so forth; I was actually too closely associated with him, so I was wishing somebody else would do it rather than me.

Dr. Forest Tennant, Jr.: Celebrities pose a particularly difficult case to manage with their drug dependency, primarily because they do not stay in one place for very long. They're always flying around the country. In order to manage drug dependence well, a person has to be taken care of by a physician very close to where they live and work. The first thing you have to do in order to control drug dependency is maintain a regular lifestyle schedule. You've got to eat three meals a day at the same time, get eight hours of sleep a night on a regular basis, keep your nutrition up, and get into exercise. In other words, you have to develop a healthy lifestyle. An entertainer has the worst possible lifestyle of anyone I know.

Dr. George Nichopoulos: As far as some musicians are concerned, I think they're a different group of people—having to get up and down, getting ready for a show, and having to travel on buses with very little sleep. Their needs are different. Still, I think a lot of them don't take anything, and they do real well. Others feel like they can't do without drugs once they've gotten into them. The routine patient who's drug dependent feels they have to have a number of different things in their medicine cabinet in case something happens.

The only drug I think Elvis could have had that could change his personality [that dramatically] would have been cocaine. I know, from what some of the guys told me, he had used cocaine. Elvis never used any around me; he never even discussed it. He felt bent out of shape if anyone in the entourage was using drugs. He felt like if they got caught using drugs, it was going to come back on him.

V. L. Lane: [Police never searched Graceland because] nobody ever came forward, to my knowledge, and said that they had seen drugs. You see, you have to have someone to swear, "I saw drugs in such and such a house and here is where they were located," before you could obtain a warrant. I couldn't have gone to his house without a warrant—or anybody else's house.

MYRNA SMITH: Jerry was probably more aware of the changes in Elvis than I was. I knew he wasn't himself some nights when he came onstage; he wasn't quite awake yet. He slept all day and didn't get up 'til late afternoon. That's when he ate his breakfast. Then he got ready for his show. And sometimes when he came down, he would still seem half asleep. Even when he first walked onstage, he'd be half asleep. But he'd just be doing his show, you know, because he knew it so well. During the course of his show, whatever he'd had kicked in, and he woke up.

I've seen those times when he was having a hard time, but I'd be pulling for him so hard! He looked to us for a lot of inspiration. If you watched his show you'd sometimes see him looking over at us, pleading with those eyes. We'd be pulling for him. We'd make more racket, trying to get him going, you know. He'd pull it through somehow. I've seen him sometimes when it was scary: when he was glassy-eyed and not really awake. It was frightening to me 'cause I thought, "He is gonna fall."

RONNIE TUTT: I saw big changes in Elvis toward the end. There were nights I sensed he was so tired or so down I felt like I had to physically hit the drums much, much harder than I had before. There were times I would say to him in my mind, "Let's get up. Let's get going!" just like he would mentally "say" things to me at times. Sometimes he'd get my signal and he'd understand, but there were some nights when he just seemed so out of it, so down.

Also there'd be certain nights when the people were either too courteous, or too in awe, or too conservative, or whatever you want to say, but the audience wasn't responding like normal, or like what he was used to. He'd get frustrated and turn around and say, "Let's get the hell out of here!" I mean, he'd do his show—he always respected the public in that sense—but he certainly wasn't going to stay on and do extra encores or work quite as hard.

TONY BROWN: The band included the rhythm section, about twenty backup singers, and about twelve horn players. It was a big entourage. We'd sit around back there in the dressing room and talk about the situation: "Why can't somebody get through to Elvis?" "We should get Elvis on a health kick." "I wish we could help him." We'd say, "Ronnie Tutt, you know him really well. Why don't you go talk to him?" But we all knew it was hopeless because Elvis was surrounded by that little circle of people, you know, all those so-called friends and all those bodyguards.

If you dared to ask, "Can I have five minutes alone with Elvis?" the answer would be, "Absolutely not!" They probably figured you were gonna ask him for a Cadillac or something. If you did get five minutes with him, most likely they'd be opening the door, constantly checking to see what was going on. It was totally unrealistic to attempt to get thirty minutes alone with him so you could say, "Elvis, man, you could go on a program and clean yourself up, lose some weight. Man, you'd feel much better." Those kinds of conversations could never have taken place because when you got around Elvis, he controlled the conversation with idle chitchat.

:◎:◎:◎:

SONNY WEST: Sure, Elvis had a *P.D.R.* [*Physicians' Desk Reference*], but he didn't read the whole *P.D.R.* every night. He'd read about a certain drug and say, "I'd like to try that. It might work. I'll talk to the doctor about it."

Normally [at night], Elvis would take one packet (his "night packet" he called it) of drugs. Four or five hours later, he might take a second packet, then later, another. He usually took three packets.

People build up a resistance to drugs when they're taking so much. Elvis was using a lot of Dilaudid, which is very powerful. He was taking more of them at one time than you or I could possibly take. Elvis always thought he needed more of something.

BILL E. BURK: In the summer of '76, Red and Sonny West and Dave Hebler were fired [as bodyguards]. Vernon called them in and fired them. He gave them almost no notice or severance pay.

The story that was told to me by the "insiders" was that Elvis went to Vernon and said, "Let them starve out there a couple of weeks and bring them back on the payroll."

My understanding was that Vernon Presley did not want them back and went against Elvis's wishes. When they weren't brought back soon, they may have gotten a little bit mad. I don't know. I know that the book they wrote [*Elvis: What Happened?*] turned the fans against Red and Sonny. (Hebler had never been all that visible.)

DAVID STANLEY: Elvis loved Red and Sonny West, and I believe they loved Elvis. The public excuse for letting them go was that they were costing Elvis money due to a still-pending lawsuit. The lawsuit was for a sizeable amount of money—6.3 million dollars. Elvis himself was running into some serious problems, and it was not all financial. It was no secret. His drug intake was increasing daily it seemed.

There were a lot of gutless wonders around Elvis, but Red wasn't one of them. I mean, he would tell Elvis what he thought. Red went to Elvis and said, "You gotta back off." I think the only accountability Elvis had was through Red and Sonny; and when the drugs began to take over Elvis couldn't handle it anymore. He knew the only conscience left was those two guys; therefore, I think he fabricated an excuse to get them out of his life. He wasn't gonna listen to anybody else anymore. I believe that's why Elvis let Red and Sonny go.

:◉:◉:◉:

DR. GEORGE NICHOPOULOS: Linda was pretty much on every tour with Elvis. Occasionally he'd make up some story (when he'd met someone else on a tour) to get Linda out shopping or something and bring this other person in.

Linda and I were both striving for the same things; we wanted to see Elvis happy. We wanted to see him involved, out of his depressed states. We were trying to keep him away from certain situations. Linda was very helpful as far as letting me know what was going on. We had a good relationship. I discussed with her telling the cooks what food to give him and how much, but the cooks wanted to mother him, so they would just load him down. Breakfast was a pound of bacon with maybe eight or nine or ten biscuits, some eggs, and some cereal. He would not eat all that, but it was there if he wanted it. It was much easier to control his diet and food intake on the road than it was at Graceland.

LINDA THOMPSON: There were a number of things that led to the dissolution of our relationship. The primary one was just watching Elvis slowly self-destruct. It got to be too painful for me. I tried so many things—so many ways to get him to take better care of himself—to stop using so much prescription medication. Nothing seemed to work.

CHERYLE JOHNSON: For awhile people were willing to say, "Well, you know he's not feeling well. He's tired. The schedule is too much for him." The audiences really blamed it on his physical problems, overwork, the Colonel.

DR. GEORGE NICHOPOULOS: In 1976, Elvis was mildly hypertensive. He had a little glaucoma, and he was a mild diabetic. All these things were controlled. But his obesity would fluctuate; it was never really controlled. He had some arthritis in his neck and back, which were problems intermittently.

There were some internal conflicts with Elvis and Linda. I don't think his physical ailments had anything to do with that; I think it was more of an emotional thing. A lot of times he wouldn't think anything of spending three or four hours talking to somebody and leave somebody else hanging. Linda would be the one that was hangin' all this time, and she'd get bored; so she'd get involved with other people playing some card game or Monopoly or something, and this kinda irritated Elvis.

In June or July of '76, Elvis and I got into an argument and he flew off to Palm Springs. He was taking something—coke [cocaine], I believe—and had gotten sort of psychotic. He called me up at two o'clock and cussed me out about taking advantage of him. Something about the racquetball court [an Elvis investment that went sour]. He said he didn't need my services anymore. I said, "Fine."

I told him it might be healthier to get somebody else to go [on tour]. A day before he left, Elvis said he'd given it some more thought and talked this other guy into going. He didn't talk to me until his next tour. Houston was one of the dates on that tour.

CHERYLE JOHNSON: In Houston [August 28, 1976, at the Summit] people were actually sitting there crying when they saw Elvis. The show was like an hour-and-a-half late starting, which was unheard of for Elvis; his shows always started on time. They had a comedian, then the Sweet Inspirations sang; everybody sang. They were stalling, stalling, and stalling. When Elvis finally came out, people were just appalled at his appearance. His body and face were extremely bloated and his eyes were vacant, like nothing was there. His skin was a pale yellow. His hands were all puffy. He couldn't move. He started with "C. C. Rider" and he flubbed the words. He went into another song and the same thing happened. A lot of people were getting up and leaving. Some people thought he was on drugs and some thought he was drunk. He could hardly keep his eyes open. Half-way through the show he had the lights brought up and he apologized. He said he wasn't feeling well. He said, "You know, I have the creeping crud." He was slurring his words terribly. I thought it was a combination of being sick and being loaded.

I looked around at the fans sitting near me and I saw people just sitting there crying. You just couldn't believe what you were seeing. He stood there with the house lights up and shook anybody's hand that would come up to the stage. I mean, he would have stayed there all night shaking hands. Some girl wanted his ring. Elvis had a big turquoise ring on, and he started trying to pull it off but he couldn't. He was too swollen. It was sad, really sad. There was no encore. He walked off the stage. People just sat there. They really just couldn't believe what they had seen.

That night Elvis had invited some of us fan club members to meet with him. We drove out to his airplane and went aboard. He was a little more awake by that time, but he was very quiet, very subdued, and he looked horrible. He asked, "How did you like the show?" Everybody lied and said it was great. Nobody was telling him the truth. Maybe they didn't want him to feel worse than he already did.

The critics ripped him up. The newspaper reviews said something about the fans having witnessed the death of rock 'n' roll—that the Elvis we knew was dead. I went home and looked at pictures of Elvis, and I couldn't believe how quickly he had deteriorated.

I told my mom: "You know, Elvis looked horrible. I don't know what's wrong with him. I don't know if it's drugs or sickness or what, but I bet we are never going to see Elvis alive in Houston again." It was really an eerie feeling.

Dr. George Nichopoulos: What you were seeing were drug side-effects. He was using things to keep from having spasms in his bowels—things like Donnatal, which contributes to muscle and speech problems.

A doctor out in Vegas used to give Sparine to Elvis. It would just knock the bottom out of him. He would be that way all day. In fact, he couldn't perform or do diddly-squat.

Right after the Houston event, the Colonel called and said he'd appreciate it if I'd come back, 'cause he couldn't continue booking Elvis and canceling shows. They'd have to give the whole thing up if I wasn't going to go on the tours. The Colonel asked me to join them in Dallas. I said I wouldn't come unless Elvis apologized. Apparently he hadn't done much apologizing in his life. It was very difficult for him to come around and say he was sorry, but it all worked out.

Larry Geller: Every night after a performance, Elvis's blood pressure would shoot up. He would have to lay down with cold packs on his eyes because he couldn't see after a performance. He was literally blind for an hour or so.

Dr. George Nichopoulos: There were still illegal drugs coming in, but they were not coming in by the suitcase loads. Most of the stuff coming in was some form of codeine.

EDDIE FADAL: Elvis felt guilty whenever he disappointed his fans. He really loved them, and if you worked for him and you insulted his fans, that's one thing that could get you fired.

MYRNA SMITH: Elvis was easily angered due to the drugs he was taking. All the guys got fired at some point or another, but they were usually rehired—just like Red and Sonny probably would have been. It wasn't that they were permanently gone. He would have called 'em back. They were his friends.

I saw him angry a couple of times. When he heard about the book Red and Sonny and the other guy was writing he was angry, but he was really more hurt. He didn't want Lisa to read that stuff. They say their intent was to ultimately help him, but he said he felt betrayed.

LARRY GELLER: We found out about the book [*Elvis, What Happened?*] in the fall of 1976. It blew Elvis away. Man, I can't tell you the pain it created. This was a sensational (and controversial) major blast of an icon. Months later Elvis dismissed it. He thought maybe it was not going to actually come out—maybe this was just denial. But I knew it was coming out; we all knew.

BILL E. BURK: Red has said that shortly after the firing he and Elvis had a telephone conversation, and Elvis expressed disappointment that the book was coming out. Elvis knew what was going to be in it, but he never did say, "Don't print it." He just expressed his disappointment. Near the end of the phone call Elvis told Red, "Do what you've got to do."

LINDA THOMPSON: One day I said to myself, "I could be around here forever, and I could grow old, or I could die an untimely death from exhaustion just trying to take care of this person. Ultimately it's up to him. He's the one that's going to have to take care of himself. I can't do it for him." So I finally decided, "I don't want to live this kind of life for the rest of my life."

GEORGE KLEIN: I don't think Elvis really knew how sick he was. I don't think anybody knew. We knew he wasn't in the greatest of health, but we had no earthly idea that he was as sick as he was.

TONY BROWN: He'd be onstage some nights, and he'd suddenly just turn around and face us. He'd always pick out one person in the band, and he'd look at them and act silly. He'd just stand there, four or five minutes—not do anything. The audience would be screaming out song titles or applauding or stomping their feet. Elvis would have his back to the audience and he'd be going, like, "Just listen to them stupid people!" laughing, putting them on, and here we are with our hands on our instruments—ready—hoping he will call out something we know.

Instead, he's got his back to his audience and he's just being Elvis out of control saying, "These people, they don't care if I'm good or bad. I can do anything and they still love it!"

GEORGE KLEIN: Elvis never lost his will to live; he loved life. He enjoyed the tours. But he was putting on weight and he knew that he didn't look his best; plus the fact that you can't be good every night—there's no possible way. He was only human. Elvis, when he'd be feeling sick, he'd have to go out and perform in front of fifteen thousand people. Only when he was deathly sick or just flat on his back would he cancel. He went on the stage many times sick as a dog, with a bad cold or the flu or a sore throat. He hated to disappoint his fans. He loved those fans.

LARRY STRICKLAND: To me he was just a real simple kind of guy. I mean, he was always Elvis; he didn't act like "Elvis." He was very down to earth. He had a very normal side to him.

There was a part in the show where he liked to sing low on a couple of songs. He would drop down an octave, and it was my job to match tones with him and sing along with him, fill it out down there. Basically, if nobody looked at me, they would think that Elvis was singing those low notes. We got to where we could do it right together. He would never have had to let the audience know that it wasn't really him; but every night after our song, Elvis would walk over and point to me to let people know that it wasn't really him singing that low. He could have just gone right on and people would never have known. I think he truly, honestly loved the music and really loved anybody that had any musical talent.

BEN WEISMAN: Elvis invited me to come to one of those parties, you know, the last evening of the season [in Las Vegas]. I went upstairs and I kind of sat there real quiet. I'm not much of a party guy. Around maybe six o'clock in the morning he waved to me to come over. He said, "Ben, why are you so quiet?" I said, "I haven't got much to say." He said, "How many songs did I record of yours?" I said, "Fifty-seven." He said, "Fifty-seven!" He grabbed me, stood me up in front of the crowd, and said, "I want you all to meet Ben Weisman who wrote more songs for me than any other writer: fifty-seven. I want to hear it for this man." There was a big applause, then he took me over to the piano. He said, "Ben, I want you to hear this song. It's called 'Softly as I Leave You.' It's about a man who's going to die."

That was in 1976, a year or so before he died. Something wasn't exactly right. I think he knew it.

CHIP YOUNG: I played on just about all of Elvis's records from 1966 on. Once he knew you, really knew you, he was real friendly. He'd walk into a session and hug my neck.

The last session that I did, down at his house [Graceland, October 29–31, 1976] was kind of a fiasco. The production truck was set up outside and wires were run into the house. We did cut "Way Down" and "He'll Have to Go." But you know, it just wasn't technically good and I don't think Elvis was in the right frame of mind, either. Fact is, I never understood why he wanted to record at home.

He did two albums there. All the mikes were set up in that little den area in the back part of the house, the jungle room. All we did was move furniture around and set everything up there. The drums were right out in the open room. Unfortunately, their sound was bleeding into the other mikes. Elvis was standing in the middle of it all, so all the instruments were bleeding into his voice mike, too. They put up clear plastic material, but it just wasn't enough to keep the sounds separated. Elvis never paid attention to technical things like that. He was just not technical minded.

When we all finished the sessions, he went upstairs and gave each of us one of his personal shirts—the kind with a big collar and blousy sleeves. He hugged my neck and said, "Next time we record, I'll come to your studio in Murfreesboro and do it."

But he never recorded again. So other than his concert recordings, the last song he completed was done at that session at Graceland— November 1, 1976; the song was "He'll Have to Go."

LARRY STRICKLAND: When we'd have time off from Elvis, we'd book out as The Stamps Quartet. So we had a date booked over in North Carolina, but we were going to miss that date because his recording session [at Graceland] in Memphis was running overtime.

Well, Elvis wouldn't hear of us missing a date. He loaned us his Lear jet and had us flown from Memphis to North Carolina to make our little ol' booking. It probably cost ten times more money to fly that Lear over there and back than we made by performing.

We came back to Memphis and finished up the album, but we didn't have a way home to Nashville. We were going to have to fly home, which we couldn't afford. "Y'all just take my limo," Elvis said. "I'm getting a new one anyway." Just like that, he gave us the limousine.

:◉:◉:◉:

Jo Alden *(Ginger Alden's mother)*: Elvis had bought Linda [Thompson] a house. That was his way of providing for her. Linda was hanging in there as long as she possibly could. She tells it that she just couldn't take it anymore; but even Sam Thompson said it was over. I think Elvis just couldn't bring himself to say it.

Lamar Fike: I think Elvis came closer to being in love with Linda than anybody. He cared for Linda a lot.

Lowell Hays: When Elvis and Linda Thompson broke up [in November 1976], I think that's when he really went downhill. He was miserable after that. He had been miserable after he broke up with Priscilla. A lot of those songs he did, they were for her, you know. He never got over her. And then, I think he really loved Linda, but he just couldn't bring himself to marry her. When he broke up with her it was downhill from then on.

Linda Thompson: It was incredibly difficult for me to make the decision to leave, but I thought, "God forbid, if anything serious should happen to him. I have adored Elvis so deeply that it would be completely devastating for me to watch him die." So I had to sort of wean myself away from being that close, that bonded to him. It took eight months. When I left, I knew it was going to be rough for him. I had cared for him like he was a newborn baby; he was that needy. I thought, "Nobody else is going to do that. Nobody's going to know him that well; nobody's going to take care of him." But I had to go. For my own sanity I had to go. It was time.

Above: Shake, rattle, and roll the cameras! Elvis takes movie star-sweetheart Natalie Wood to see deejay Dewey Phillips at the WHBQ studio, Memphis, in October 1956. Dewey was the first to play an Elvis Presley record on the radio. (Jimmy Velvet)

Right: On the set of Clambake *in Hollywood during the spring of 1967, heartthrob Elvis waits for his cue. (Turner Entertainment Company)*

Opposite, top: In his first movie, Love Me Tender, *Elvis shares the screen with beautiful young costar Debra Paget. Elvis had third billing in the 1956 film, but it established him as a movie star. (20th Century Fox)*

Below: Elvis and Ann-Margret ham it up on the set of Viva Las Vegas *in 1964. Mutual fans, they dated for a number of years. (Turner Entertainment Company)*

Below, right: A happy-go-lucky Elvis Presley serenades young Memphis actress Stella Stevens and a bevy of beauties on the set of Girls! Girls! Girls! *The film was shot on location in Hollywood and Hawaii and ranked number six on Variety's top grossing movies of the year 1962. (Viacom)*

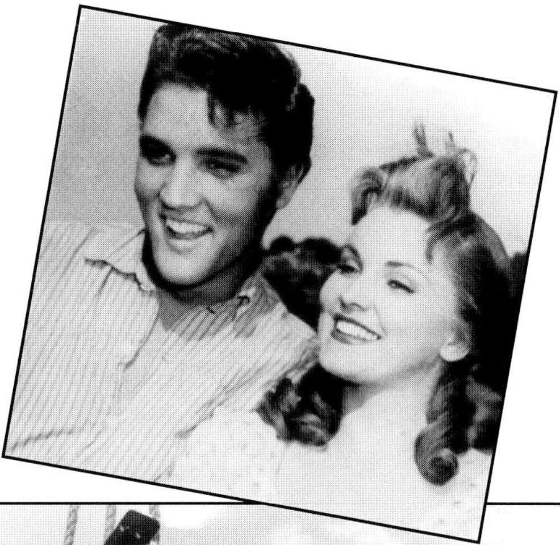

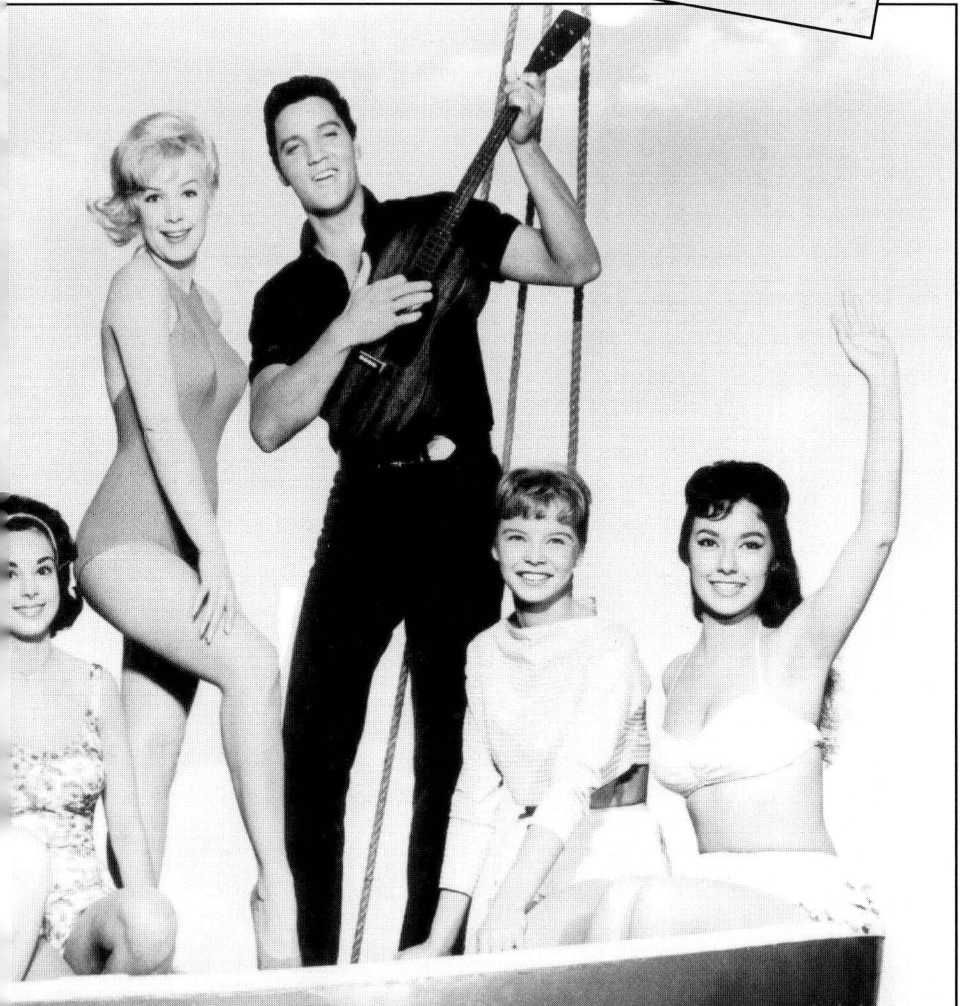

Right: Colonel Parker reportedly hired Nudie's of Hollywood in 1957 to design Elvis's "solid gold suit." It was a sensation with the press and the fans, but Elvis reportedly hated it. How much did it cost? One report says ten thousand dollars! (Sounds a little like Parker hype to us.) (RCA Records)

Below: Elvis loved the feel of a powerful motorcycle on the road and the tough look of black leather. The jacket inspired his costuming for the sensational '68 Comeback Special. (Jimmy Velvet)

Opposite: Elvis and friend Yvonne Lime in front of Graceland. (Jimmy Velvet)

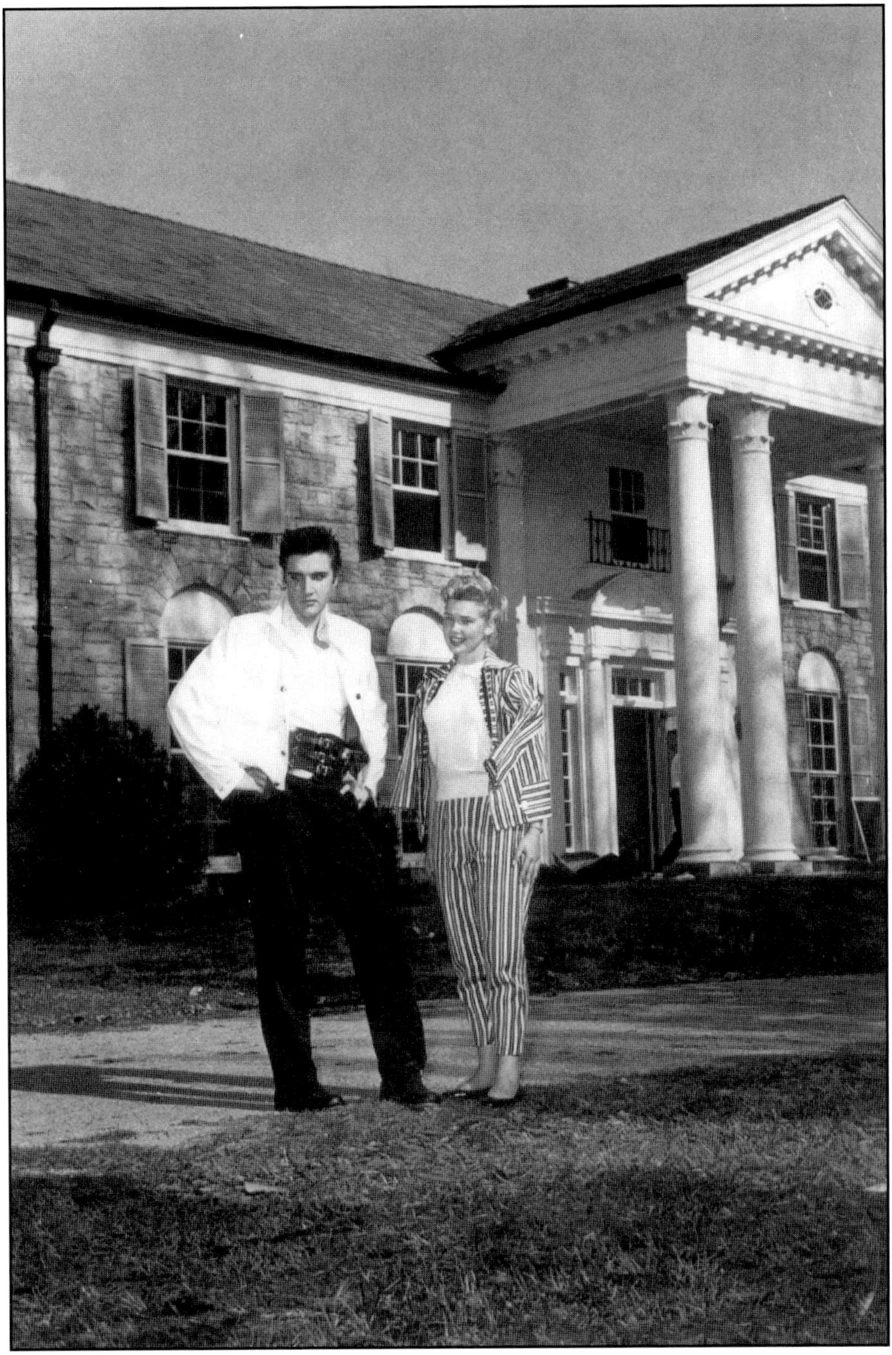

Above: With a wedding cake fit for a king–and queen–Elvis and Priscilla slice into their six-tier, five-foot-high confection following their marriage at the Aladdin Hotel, Las Vegas, Nevada, May 1, 1967.

Opposite, top: Elvis astride Rising Sun, his favorite horse, following a brisk ride. (Jimmy Velvet)

Opposite, bottom: Elvis, Priscilla, and Lisa Marie. (Michael Ochs Archives)

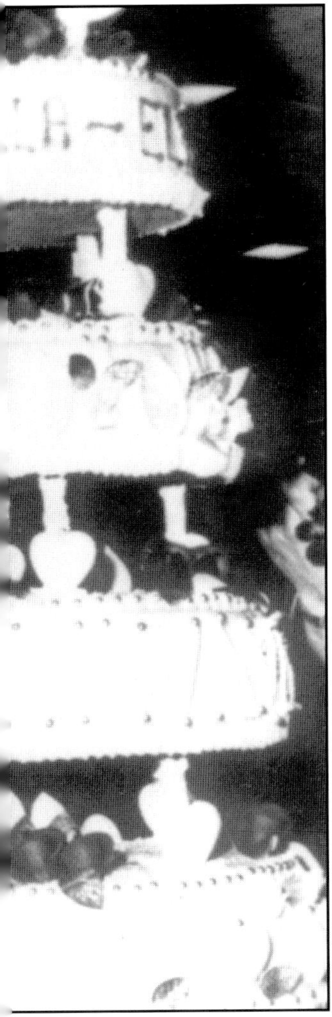

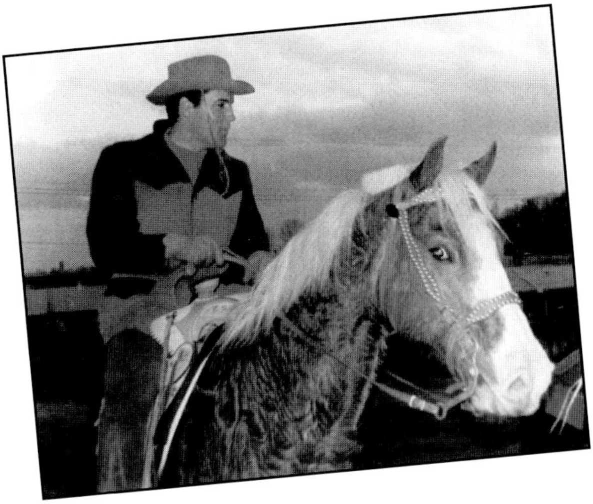

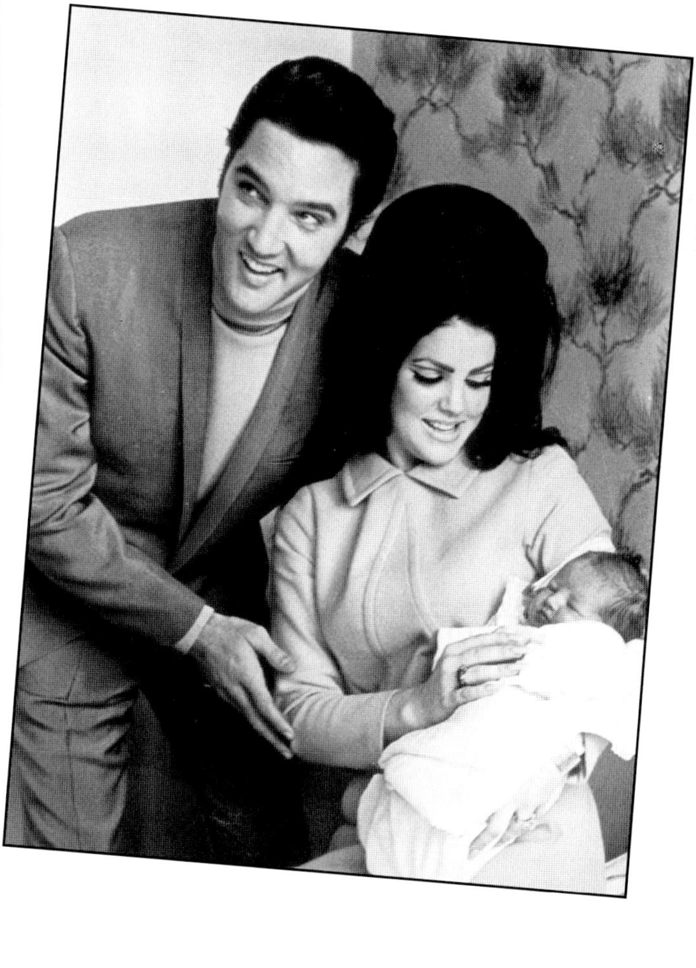

Above: Elvis gives a television press conference in June 1968 announcing the Comeback Special. (Robin C. Rosaaen)

Opposite: In April of 1972 the king performs on a fifteen-city tour being filmed for the full-length documentary movie, Elvis on Tour. *(Turner Entertainment Company)*

Below: Great Friends! Producer Felton Jarvis and Elvis share a laugh during a break in the recording sessions of September 10, 1967, at RCA Studio B in Nashville. (Bob Beckham)

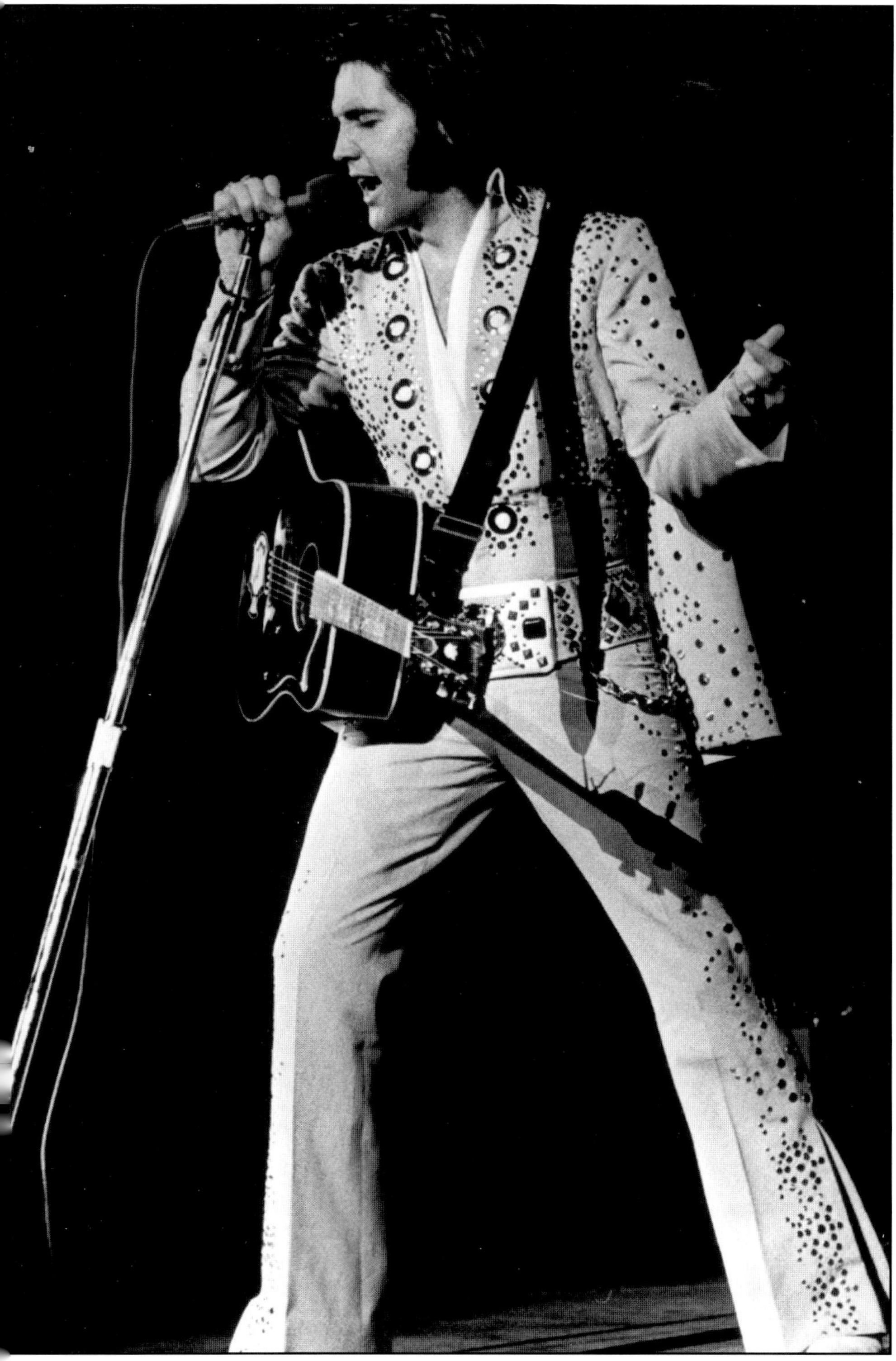

Above: Elvis performing in Las Vegas in 1973. (Robin C. Rosaaen)

Right: The cameras capture the king in his prime and prove once again that he's unbeatable. Here he is in the 1970 MGM documentary, Elvis—That's the Way It Is, *his thirty-second feature-length motion picture. (Turner Entertainment Company)*

Below: Elvis Presley, an American legend, is among those honored by the U.S. Jaycees as one of the Ten Outstanding Young Men of America at a ceremony held in January of 1971. It was the only award Elvis ever accepted publicly.

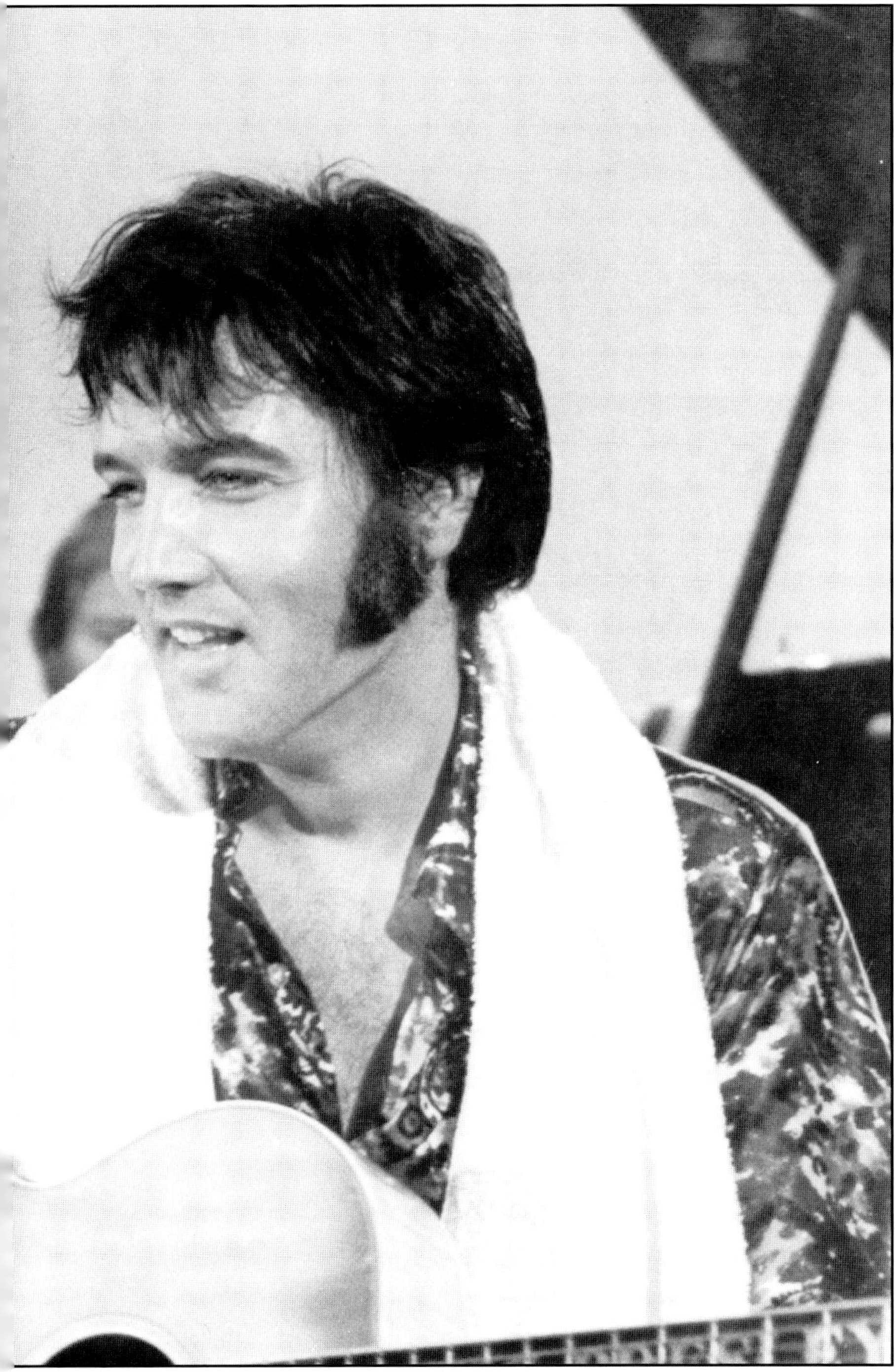

Above: A fan snapped this candid photo of the still costumed star preparing to ride away following a concert in 1973. (Robin C. Rosaaen)

Opposite, top: Typical scene following a late-1970 performance: Elvis is hustled through a backstage crowd by bodyguard-friend Red West. (Robin C. Rosaaen)

Right: Elvis and his entourage receive Shelby County, Tennessee, Deputy badges at Graceland in 1970. Standing left to right: Billy Smith, Bill Morris, Lamar Fike, Jerry Schilling, Sheriff Roy Nixon, Vernon Presley, Charlie Hodge, Sonny West, George Klein, Marty Lacker; front row: Dr. George Nichopoulos, Elvis, and Red West. (Michael Ochs Archives)

Below: Elvis and one of the great romances of his life, Linda Thompson, caught in a happy, candid moment. (Jeanne LeMay)

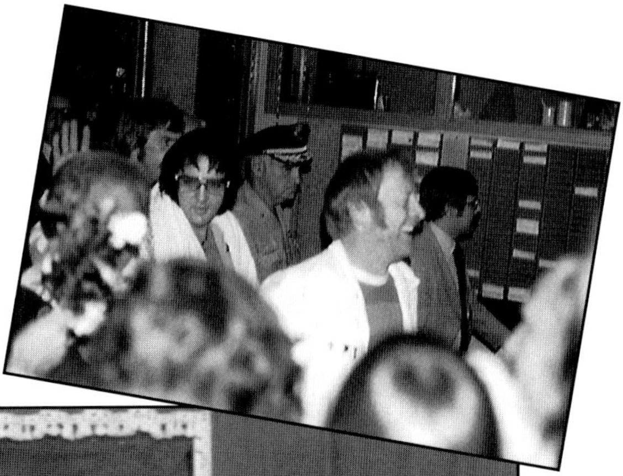

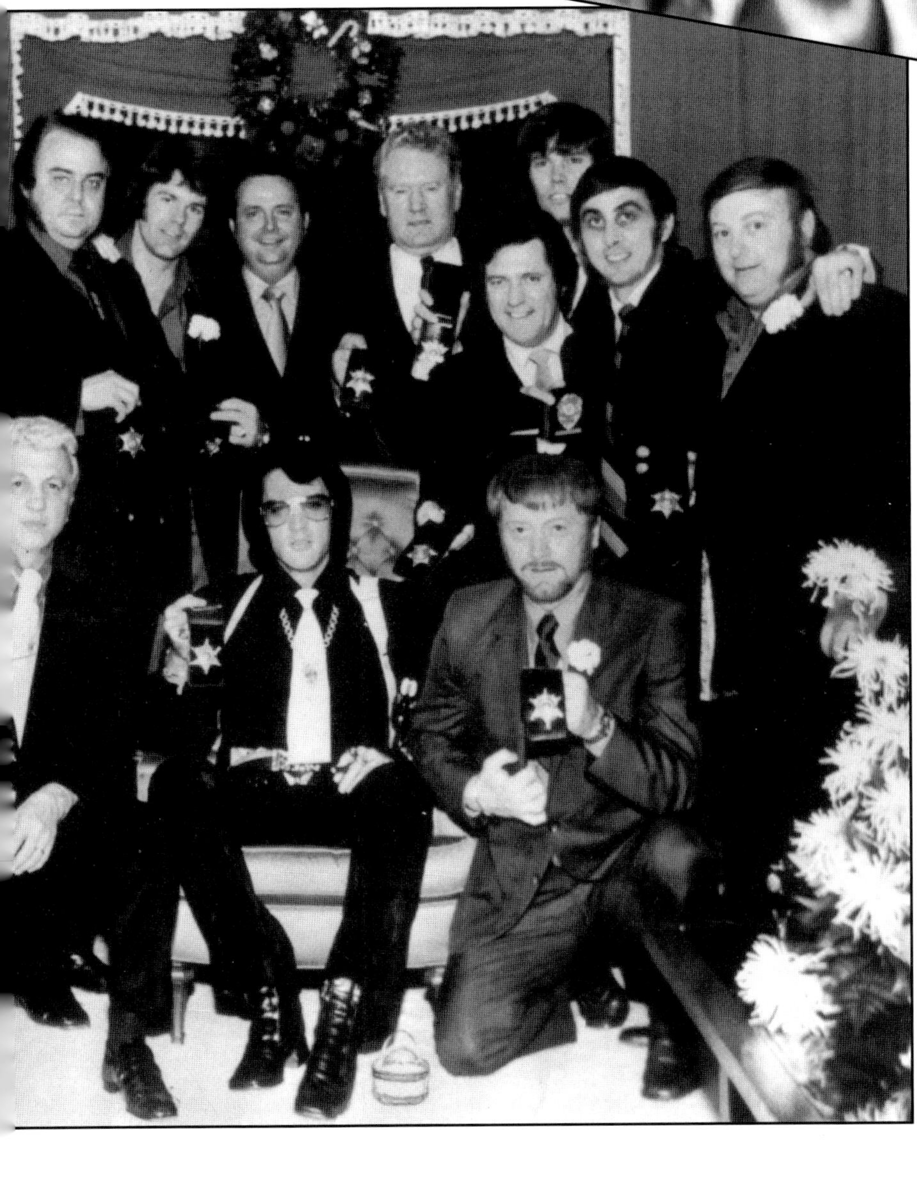

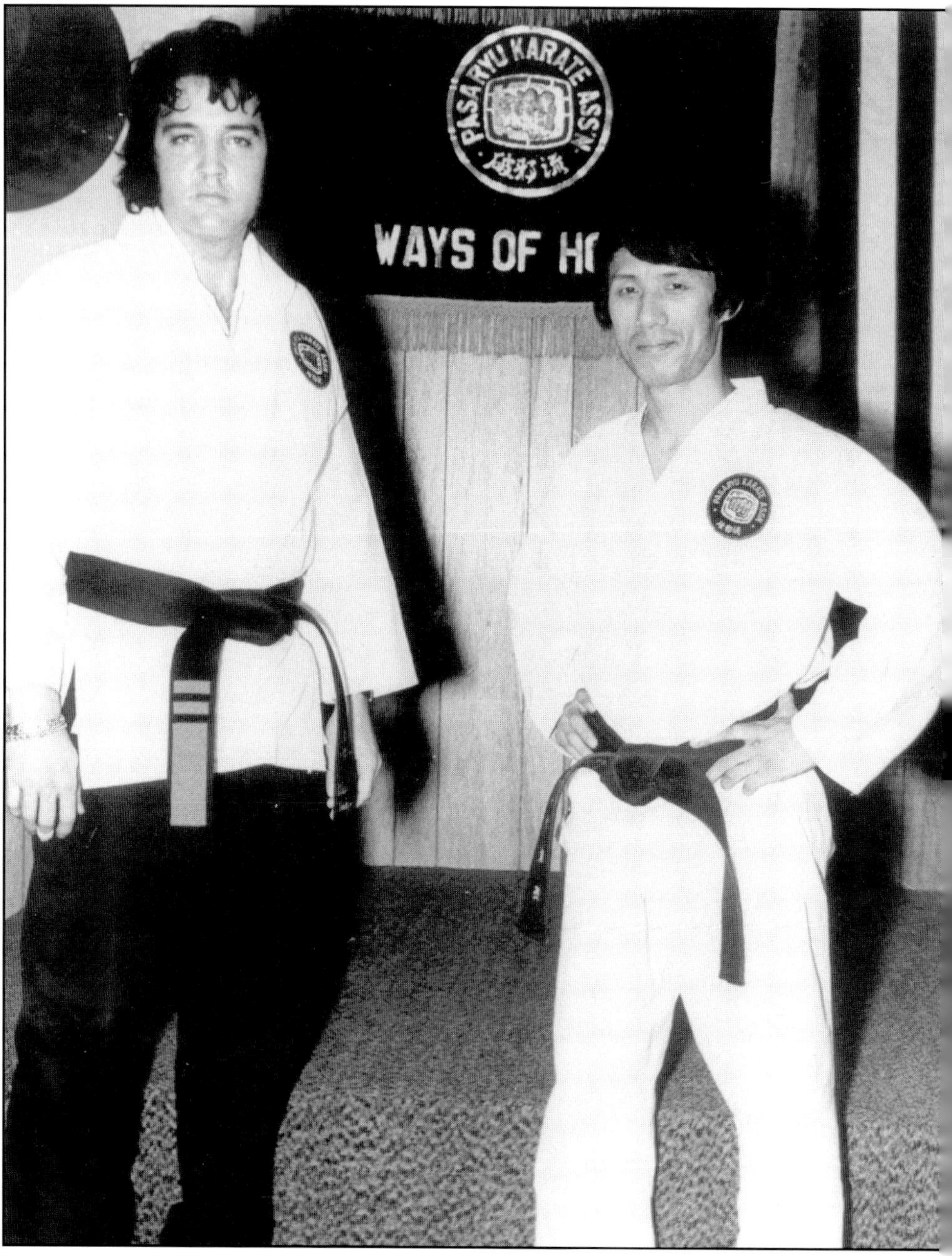
PASARYU KARATE ASS'N
WAYS OF HO

Above: On a Hawaiian holiday Elvis is flanked by the two beautiful Alden sisters– Rosemary (left) and Ginger (right).

Opposite: Seventh degree black belt expert "Master Tiger" (Elvis Presley) poses with his karate instructor "Mr. Ox" (Kang Rhee) in 1973. (Kang Rhee)

Below: Always good copy, Elvis has been both scandalized and idolized in the national media. (photo by Mark Hill)

This photo of Elvis and Joe Esposito's girlfriend, Shirley Dieu, was taken in the spring of 1977, five months before Elvis died. (Jimmy Velvet)

"Treadmill to Oblivion"
1976-1977

Appearing almost desperate to make changes in his life, Elvis becomes engaged—to someone half his age. Jeweler Lowell Hays makes the ring, while stepbrother David Stanley and old friend George Klein give conflicting stories regarding the sincerity of Elvis's marital plans.

As many of Elvis's close friends worry about his secret lifestyle, former bodyguards Red and Sonny West and reporter Bill E. Burk discuss the motivation behind the upcoming exposé, *Elvis: What Happened?* Hairstylist/guru Larry Geller reveals how Elvis fears its impact on his personal life more than on his career.

While Ann Marie McClain, a regular at the Graceland gates, reports how Elvis's sense of humor is still evident in his final few months, Lamar Fike relays how Elvis pushes himself beyond the limits of his physical endurance. Band members Tony Brown and Bobby Ogdin reminisce about the peaks and valleys of performing with the king during his final tour.

> "I think it was easier for The Beatles than Elvis. At least we all understood what was happening, you know. I mean, all the people around him couldn't understand it. He was on his own, and it showed, actually. As his life went on, he ended up more and more on his own."
>
> RINGO STARR *(drummer, The Beatles)*

LINDA THOMPSON: Probably the most valuable lesson that I derived from my time with Elvis is that there are no real heroes in life. There are people who are to be commended, people who are to be admired for their accomplishments, but never, never to be worshiped, because we are all subject to human fallibility. It wasn't fair to Elvis to put him up on a pedestal and not expect him to be human. That's too much pressure to put on another human being. We're not being fair to those whom we idolize when we do that to them, and we're also not being fair to ourselves.

LOWELL HAYS: Elvis was shielded from the world. We treated him like a little god. We just did, you know.

LARRY GELLER: Ginger [Alden] came on the scene November 29, 1976. That's when she came on tour with us. That day Elvis left Linda in San Francisco. That afternoon, when I went to Elvis's room, he was in his bathroom shaving. He said, "I'm bringing Ginger." That was the last time he saw Linda Thompson. Ginger flew in that day. She had just turned twenty. I liked Ginger very, very much; she was a very sweet lady. But I did not think Ginger was good for Elvis. Ginger was young—too inexperienced. They were just incompatible. And Elvis was dying; he was! I thought Linda was fabulous for Elvis, just fabulous.

We were in Vegas one time, outside on the balcony overlooking the city at six in the morning. Elvis looked at me and said, "Larry, do you realize I will never know if a woman loves me or 'Elvis Presley.' I'll never know, man, do you realize that?" I said, "Elvis, as far as I'm concerned you've only had one real lasting love affair in your life." Elvis said, "Who?

What are you talking about?" I said, "Your fans—the public." He said, "You know what, man? You're right. That's true."

TONY BROWN: You know what? I honestly believe that when Priscilla left him, he just gave up. A lot of us thought that. Linda Thompson was the closest person to Elvis after Priscilla. I knew Linda really well. She really tried to help Elvis, but I think she finally just gave up, because how can one person fight against ten rogues who are just along for the ride, you know?

LARRY GELLER: Elvis said to me many times, "Hey, man, [Priscilla] was just the dress rehearsal for the real thing." He said, "It took me a long time to realize she's like my sister. You know, for a long time, I thought maybe she was my soul mate."

LINDA THOMPSON: I know that Elvis loved Ann-Margret. He used to talk about what a wonderful lady she was, how he would have married her but circumstances just kind of got a little convoluted. Apparently the press got hold of information that they were very serious and that she was about to let go of her career and become Mrs. Elvis Presley. Elvis was very shy about that kind of press.

I know he loved Anita Wood, too. And I'm sure he loved Priscilla. Elvis had a great capacity for love, which I think is commendable. You know, he was not nearly as promiscuous as people might assert. There were a lot of women friends that Elvis had, even when he was with me, and they truly were just friends.

DR. GEORGE NICHOPOULOS: Elvis wanted to know what you thought about the girl he was dating—whether she was good for him. He wanted to be sure he had the prettiest girl, and that she was always decked out with the necessary jewelry and stuff to stand out as "his" girl. He'd buy her cars, jewelry, and different things. A lot of times if he had a problem, he'd ask me to talk to the girl and try to get some feel about it.

JO ALDEN: Of all the women that Elvis had dated, including Priscilla, I think Linda was the favorite because she was a big buddy to everybody. Ginger was shy and didn't have much to say.

DR. GEORGE NICHOPOULOS: Elvis was jealous up to a point. He expected [all of the girls he was dating] to be one-man girls, and no shenanigans.

BILL E. BURK: In late 1976 I saw Elvis in Vegas, and I thought he was looking and acting like he was totally worn out. I suggested to him that maybe he should take a year off and just rest. (At that time I didn't know what his finances were.) He said, "Naw, I've got thirty-nine people working for me, and they're depending on me. What are they gonna do if I get out of this for a year?"

LARRY GELLER: We were in Elvis's room in the Hilton Hotel [between December 2 and 12, 1976], and I remember Charlie Hodge came in right in the middle of the conversation. Elvis said, "Charlie, what you are about to hear is between the three of us; that's it. I'm letting go of . . . I'm going to get rid of the Memphis Mafia. I don't like the term; it has been an embarrassment my whole life. I don't need all these people around me. Daddy wants them gone; he always has. All I need is a few people around me. I want to change my life; I want a whole new life. I want a new career and I want to be an actor again. I'm going to stop the tours. I want to get rid of . . . (Elvis told us who he was going to let go) and I want Tom Huelett to be my manager. If it can work out with Ginger, I would love to be married again. I want to have a son. I want more children."

ANN MARIE MCCLAIN: I saw Elvis perform thirty-three times—most of them in Vegas. I have eleven [Elvis] scarves.

SONNY NEAL: I was in Vegas working with Charlie Rich when Joe [Esposito] called. Elvis was playing his last dates in Vegas, and that was the last time I really talked to him—about eight months before he died. I knew he was sick—very sick. I asked Joe how Elvis was doing, and he said, "We're getting ready to take him home." I said, "I will appreciate it if you don't come by 'cause we've got a lot of problems over here." It was opening night for Charlie Rich, and I said, "You know how Charlie is. It would probably warp his head if Elvis comes in and is in real bad shape." I talked to Elvis for just a minute, then Joe got back on the line and said, "I'm going to take your advice." That was the last I heard from him.

ANNIE CLOYD PRESLEY: It made me sad to know that Elvis's life was so miserable. I blame Vernon with a lot of it—and Tom Parker—but Elvis was a grown man. He should have made his own decisions. I've always said it and I'm not gonna back down now. Elvis had been raised in the Holiness church. As far as I know, that's the only kind of church he ever went to. They taught a perfect life.

Here Elvis is out doing things that he knew they taught was wrong, which made him miserable. So here he is studying all these other doctrines—different cults and things—trying to find peace. That's what he was trying to find.

BROTHER FRANK SMITH: I really felt pressed, as the preacher that I was, to go and see Elvis and to talk to him about salvation and a relationship with the Lord. But I did not. I believed he would have seen me; I'm sure he would have, but I didn't go. I just delayed in going until it was too late; then I really felt bad. I should have gone to see him.

JAMES BLACKWOOD: Reverend [Rex] Humbard related to me that he went back to Elvis's dressing room in Las Vegas one night, and Elvis's first question to him was, "When do you think the King (referring to Jesus) is coming back?" Reverend Humbard said, "Well, I think very soon, Elvis." Elvis said, "I do, too."

Reverend Humbard said that they sat and talked for some time. Then he said, "Elvis, I know you have things to do; you've got another show." Elvis said, "No, wait a minute. I don't have to go yet. I want to talk some more about the Lord." So they talked about the Bible and the Lord. Before Reverend Humbard left he said to Elvis, "Could I pray with you?" Elvis said, "Sure." So they held hands and prayed. Reverend Humbard said, "I felt the presence of the Lord and felt very impressed with Elvis— his knowledge of the Bible and his feel for the Lord."

ANNIE CLOYD PRESLEY: I feel like if Elvis could have stayed in the church, even though he sang these kind of songs, he could have served God better and been a happier man. I'm not saying he was wrong in the way he lived; I'm saying he would have been a happier man, because that was the way he had been raised.

DAVID STANLEY: Elvis came home from the [final Vegas] tour, and I went to the airport to meet him. I had crutches because I'd banged up my foot pretty good in a motorcycle accident.

Well, Elvis comes down the steps [of the *Lisa Marie*] with Ginger; they had developed a relationship in Vegas. And Elvis said, "This is my new girlfriend, Ginger Alden." I said, "Hello, Ginger," and then Elvis hugged me.

Jo Alden: They say Elvis did one of his best shows ever in Pittsburgh on New Year's Eve. Lisa was there; she sat on Ginger's lap.

Elvis celebrated his last birthday [January 8, 1977] with Ginger in Palm Springs. I never thought of Elvis as being forty-two years old. I've had the question asked me: "Why did you let your twenty-year-old daughter go with a forty-two-year-old man?" I always said, "Ginger is twenty years old and she has a mind of her own. I have a son who's ten years younger than Elvis, and Elvis doesn't seem to me to be any older than my son."

Dr. George Nichopoulos: Elvis asked my opinion of Ginger, and he had talked about the possibility of marriage. He felt that if he could work this out, everything would be where he wanted it. Everything would be in place. The situation waxed and waned, but it never reached a point where he was comfortable with it. If he could've gotten that part of his life worked out, I think he would've been happier and would not have felt so stressed.

Lowell Hays: One night, Elvis had one of the guys call me about one o'clock in the morning. He said, "Elvis wants to talk to you." Then Elvis came to the phone. "Lowell, I'm gonna get engaged tonight [January 26, 1977] and I need an engagement ring." I said, "What do you want?" He said, "I want a diamond just exactly like the one in my TCB ring." I said, "Well, I don't have a diamond that big [11.5 carats]." He said, "Well, find me one." I explained, "I'm not gonna be able to find you one in the middle of the night." So he said, "Well, I'll find one," and he hung up. I went back to sleep, but he called back an hour later and said, "I can't find one. You've got to find me one. Don't you have some friends in New York? I can send you to New York. You can take my plane and go to New York." Well, I made a phone call to a diamond-cutter friend of mine—the only one I thought might possibly have a diamond that large, or at least have the right connections. He just laughed. He said, "There's no way to get a diamond that size in the middle of the night!"

So I called Graceland back and said, "Elvis, there's just no way to get that thing done tonight." But he just wouldn't take "no" for an answer. When I hung up I was trying to get back to sleep, but I kept thinking. All of a sudden I thought, "I know how to do this." So I called him back and said, "Elvis, give her the diamond in your TCB ring. I can replace it tomorrow." "All right!" he said. "Come out here and get it." So at about three o'clock in the morning, I went out to Graceland, got his TCB ring, brought it back to my shop, mounted it in that mounting that Ginger Alden has, with three diamonds on each side of it, and Elvis got "engaged" to someone he didn't care anything about—who absolutely didn't care anything about him! It just made me sick that I was the one that made that ring.

DAVID STANLEY: Elvis proposed to Ginger Alden. He asked her to marry him—point blank. He sure did. I was there when he gave her the ring. He put it on her hand and he said, "Would you marry me?"

Charlie Hodge and I were sitting right there when he did it. It was in his bedroom. He was sitting on the bed and she was sitting on the chair.

LOWELL HAYS: Ginger was also dating somebody else. I heard she was out on a date the very night that Elvis gave her the ring. Ginger was not one of my favorite people.

DAVID STANLEY: As far as loving Ginger and wanting to marry her, I think Elvis was so far gone and had missed reality bad. It was like he just said, "I think I'll pick you. Here's a ring. Let's get married." I don't think the feeling was mutual.

GEORGE KLEIN: A lot of the guys in Elvis's inner circle of friends said he wasn't going to marry Ginger, but Elvis told several people that he was going to marry her. He told me on more than one occasion.

LARRY GELLER: Was he going to marry Ginger? Absolutely not.

DAVID STANLEY: Elvis always had women. That was just his life. I mean when he married Priscilla he had women; after Priscilla he had women. But toward the end of his life, when he began to get on medication, I'm sure these women were frustrated, because he really just got to where he couldn't do anything.

Elvis and Linda kind of went their own ways. Then Ginger Alden walked into Elvis's life. She was twenty-one or twenty-two years old. The only thing she knew about Elvis Presley was sideburns, high collars, and hound dogs.

In Ginger's case it was probably more family motivated—"Hey, if this guy likes you and you can be friends, it sure could be beneficial." Not to put Ginger down; I like Ginger. She walked in and I think she felt sorry for Elvis, but greed has a strange way of doing things to people. I think she was motivated by her family, "Stick it out and stay with it."

Jo Alden: I think Elvis was so perceptive of people. He sized you up as soon as you walked in. There was something about him; he could just tell.

David Stanley: There was a thing in Elvis's entourage that I call the "loyalty factor." You couldn't be around Elvis unless you were loyal. When I first went to work for Elvis Presley, that very first day, Lamar Fike sat down with me and said, "You don't show press to Elvis. You don't criticize his shows. You never talk to the media, and you don't discuss any of his personal life whatsoever with anyone."

Bill E. Burk: In February of 1977, Red called me and told me they [Red, Sonny West, and Dave Hebler] were doing a book [*Elvis, What Happened?*] with a ghost writer. He told me that the reason for the book was not primarily to make money; their motive was that they were dissatisfied with Elvis's way of life, and they felt like they had done all they could to get him straightened out. They felt that by writing the book, the fans would get fired up and put pressure on Elvis to straighten up, because he loved his fans so much. I actually believe to this day that this was the original motivation for the book.

Sonny West: We wrote the book to put a challenge to Elvis. Of course, we knew we would make money from the book, but that's beside the point, really. Red and I and Dave had jobs when we went to work for Elvis. We knew we could get other jobs. We wanted to put a challenge to Elvis. No one had done that before. No one had written anything that would wake him up and make him see what he was doing. We had kept our mouths shut for years. That was our loyalty to him, and our love for him. When we saw him going downhill we tried to stop him, and he didn't like it.

So Elvis decided to teach us. He seemed to have lost the control he had over us before: when he spoke, we jumped [when they worked for him]. When he fired us, we were very hurt. I was almost in a state of shock. And when I couldn't reach him, and he wouldn't talk to me, I told them: "Relay the message. Tell him I won't be calling back," and I meant it. I was cutting him loose, right then, just like he had cut me loose. Then after the hurt, anger moved in. Why? How could he do this to me? We would have given up our lives. We were even willing to take a bullet for him. Elvis bragged about us to people and said, "I've got guys that'll get in front of a knife, a bullet, or anything else to save me. I'm proud of that. They've made that commitment to me." Then for him to cut us loose like that, the anger came in. After we thought it out, we knew it wasn't Elvis. It was the drugs that was making him act that way.

RED WEST: I was showing [in the book] what it was like the whole time that I was with him. I was showing the good, the bad, the good times, the bad times, what drugs can do to people.

T. G. SHEPPARD [Bill Browder]: I really think the reason that they did that book was to try to make Elvis understand what was going on in his life—that he was too close to the forest to see the trees. I believe they thought the book would jolt him into realizing something was wrong. Red and Sonny were too close to him to sell out. Elvis just wouldn't listen to them.

DR. GEORGE NICHOPOULOS: His main defense [when there were problems] was work, especially in the last few months of his life. There were many times he was having problems (other than health problems) when he'd call the Colonel and say, "Let's get another tour together."

GEORGE KLEIN: He didn't even think about retiring. He thought that he could always go out and do a tour and make money if his bank account got low.

LAMAR FIKE: He had to keep working. Elvis had a payroll that was phenomenal, and he had to keep a lot of people employed. By all rights, he should have never worked the year before he died. Everybody kept telling the Colonel: "Hey, back off. The guy's sick. The guy's really in bad shape." But Elvis had to pay his bills, and I suppose the Colonel had to pay his. I was on the payroll like everybody else.

Today it wouldn't happen. Who goes to Vegas and works four weeks and does two and three shows a night? I mean this is unbelievable. The hotel put in a special, larger concert room that holds four thousand people because Elvis only wanted to work one show a night.

I think Fred Allen put it great when he said, "It's called a treadmill to oblivion."

FELTON JARVIS: I remember Elvis telling me, "I'm just so tired of being Elvis Presley."

LOWELL HAYS: Toward the end, Vernon had the staff trained so that when I came on the premises they would call him and let him know I was there. Vernon would come up there and stay with me the whole time, trying to keep me away from Elvis. Elvis was having financial problems, you know. He had really made some bad business moves, and he was also in trouble with those airplanes. He didn't pay me for a long time. I never really worried about being paid. It wasn't nothing for him to be behind one hundred-fifty thousand dollars for months at a time. That was kind of hard on me, but I banked at the same bank he did, and they knew; so the bank would loan me money when I needed it.

LARRY GELLER: Near the end of March 1977 we were in Baton Rouge. Elvis was feeling horrible.

I was in my bedroom, and at seven in the morning my phone rang. Elvis wanted me to come to his room. I went in and he was sitting propped up in bed. He kept shaking his head. He said: "Lawrence, man, I'm sick. I don't feel good. There's something wrong. I can't sleep and I've got to be onstage tonight."

That afternoon he still felt rotten, and he canceled the tour. When he did that, I knew I had to give him some information he did not want to hear. No one was speaking the truth to him. Everyone was just placating him—being obsequious. In Elvis's mind, a book [*Elvis, What Happened?*] was coming out, but he wouldn't admit it was *really* coming out. But I knew for sure it was.

When I think about it, I just cry. I cringe within myself. We went into the bathroom. Two grown men are standing there crying—tears rolling down our faces. I said, "Elvis, I love you. I'm only telling you the truth because you need to know it."

He said to me, "What is my little girl going to think when she grows up? What is she going to think of her daddy?" I said: "Wait a minute, Elvis, what the hell are you saying, man? What do you mean, what is she going to think of her daddy? You're going to be there with her. She'll be by your side. She'll know the truth."

He said: "And my fans will be my fans. They are not going to believe lies. All I'm concerned about is my daughter and my daddy. The book is going to hurt them. That's the only thing I give a shit about. The fans are not going to believe it."

Elvis went into the hospital the next day, but he did not let the doctors do any extensive testing. He should have. He knew the end was near. There's no doubt about it.

GEORGE KLEIN: It had gotten to where he didn't want many people up at Graceland. He went into seclusion. It had gotten to the point that he couldn't even come downstairs in his pajamas or with his hair messed up in his own home. So the last six months that Elvis was with us, he said, "Look, guys, I don't have anything against you, but I'm not feeling all that well; so why don't you call and check before you come up to Graceland, to see if everything's cool."

DR. GEORGE NICHOPOULOS: There were times I think Elvis really enjoyed being a recluse. There were other times he had no choice. He couldn't go out even if he wanted to because the crowds at the gate would follow wherever he went. He did a lot of meditating. He also enjoyed reading, watching TV, and not having somebody hovering over him all the time, like it was on the road.

ANN MARIE MCCLAIN: The first time I met Elvis was about five months before he died. I was washing everything I owned in the laundromat across the street [from the Graceland gates]. I had thirteen washing machines full of clothes because Elvis had been in town so long that I hadn't had a chance to wash my clothes—I was always at the gates. I'm across the street, and here he goes. I saw the motorcycle go by. I had my binoculars and I saw him pull into the Vicker's gas station. Well, I rushed to my car, drove halfway into the lot of the gas station (just stalled the car), and ran over to him.

Elvis was showing off a little necklace Lisa Marie had made him. It was a little bead-type thing. He goes, "See what my daughter just made me?" We were trying to see everything and just get as close as we could. Elvis had a new ring with a white diamond/black diamond, white pearl/black pearl design, and he said, "I want you to see the new ring you just bought me." (He meant the fans.)

Then he showed us the new motorbike. One of the other girls goes, "Elvis, can I ride on the motorcycle with you?" He said, "Sorry, honey, no. I've got to go on my paper route. I've got to earn some spending money."

DR. GEORGE NICHOPOULOS: Elvis was having this problem with Ginger, and he wanted to be on the road more. He knew he was happier performing, but he also knew by these frequent tours he kinda had her over a barrel: she couldn't be going home [every night if they were out on tour]. He had many other girls available, but he was obsessed with this one individual and would do all kinds of things to keep her around.

LARRY GELLER: In either March or April of '77 we were in Elvis's bedroom —him and I—on the floor. There were two large trunks filled with his favorite books, over a hundred of them, and we were looking at a book or two. We were talking, and Elvis stood up and said, "Come with me a minute." As we were approaching the living room, he stopped in the doorway and stood toe to toe with me. He put his arm on my shoulder. He said, "Lawrence, the fans, they know 'Elvis' but they don't know me. They have no idea of the truth. If you don't tell the story, my story, to the world, they'll never know it. They'll never know the truth. I want to know right now, are you with me? Are you going to do something?" Well, in my mind I figured we were going to write a book together, to offset that bodyguard book.

:◎:◎:◎:

DR. GEORGE NICHOPOULOS: Elvis was having some of his security watch Ginger's house to see if she was seeing somebody else. He had her followed. He'd be overly in love with her one day, then awfully suspicious of her the next.

BILL PERRY: Ginger was a gorgeous lady. She really was. We [sheriff deputies] all knew who she was. We all kept a very good eye over there where she lived on Royal Crest 'cause that was our job. It's not that we were interested in seeing Ginger, it was just that we wanted to protect her, 'cause that was our job. We knew that Elvis would appreciate it.

ANN MARIE MCCLAIN: In public Elvis and Ginger weren't exactly lovey-dovey. It was sorta like she was just there. One night Elvis was on his motorcycle and Ginger was riding with him, and they pulled into Vicker's gas station. He saw this car all dressed up with a fancy paint job and stuff—one of these hot rods with the wheels extended in front and the flames painted on the side, and so on. Elvis stopped to look at it. He got off his motorcycle and he forgot all about Ginger. He was looking at the car, and she was standing about two feet behind him—standing out of the way.

These two French girls were with me, and one of them was just gibbering. Elvis goes, "What did she say?" I said: "I don't know; they're speaking French. I know she's got some holy sand from Israel she wants to give you." One girl is just sorta standing there in one spot screaming and holding her hands. Turns out one of the girls was a Canadian nun. They were both Elvis fans, and they had come down to Memphis to see Elvis.

Anyway, Elvis got back on his motorcycle and was starting it up. Then he looked around and said (as a kind of afterthought), "Oh, Ginger, get on the bike." She did, and they took off.

Dr. George Nichopoulos: Elvis had expressed to me on many occasions that he would like to have another child.

He had gotten over his financial stresses and some other problems he'd been having, but he was still having girlfriend problems. Probably the biggest stress was Ginger. He was very wrapped up in her 'cause apparently something about her eyes or facial expressions reminded him of his mother. He wanted her to be around more. He'd want her to go on the tours, and sometimes she did, sometimes she didn't. Her behavior just kept him in emotional turmoil. I don't think he'd ever been faced with a female companion that he didn't have the upper-hand with; it really got to him.

Jo Alden: Elvis gave us so much in such a short length of time. He gave our whole family things, you know. He gave me two fur coats. I guess he gave Ginger five. He gave my daughter Terry one—a leather and mink stroller—and my daughter-in-law one. I have three beautiful rings that he gave me, and, of course, Rosemary [Ginger's other sister] had four. Then he gave Terry one that was really gorgeous. One of mine has multicolor stones. They're diamonds, but they are colored diamonds. He loved doing those things, and I think that some of the others around him resented it. There was so much jealousy there, they sorta took it out on us.

Bill Perry: Elvis bought Ginger a green TR6 [automobile]. He put her a pool in the back of the house, and I think he had the house painted or something. He had a lot of work done. It was a nice house to begin with, but Elvis was just that way. He would just do things for people.

Dr. George Nichopoulos: Elvis and I discussed that you can't buy someone's love; it's either there or it isn't, or you have to win it. He couldn't continue to try and win Ginger over with more cars, more jewelry, or more this and that. He had done a lot for her and her family. He thought for sure that each time he did something then everything would be fine, but it never was fine for very long.

Jo Alden: Elvis would talk with Priscilla all the time when Lisa was there and when Ginger was there. They had a good relationship because of Lisa, you know. Priscilla was kinda taking advantage of Elvis. Along in the spring Priscilla was going to get into the jewelry business. Elvis would laugh and say, "Oh, Priscilla is always trying something, something new, and something different." Way up toward the last, Priscilla called. She wanted to go on a trip overseas, and she wanted to use Elvis's plane. Elvis told her, "No. You fly commercial." Then what was it? Oh, she wanted Elvis to set her dad up in the imported wine business. Elvis wouldn't do it.

:◎:◎:◎:

Tony Brown: We got to where we performed ten days every month. They tried to make it the same ten days. We'd tour like from the twelfth through the twenty-second. They had a little [scheduling] formula going so everybody could plan their month. We'd go out and play various venues, various cities.

Elvis would come on tour looking real heavy and really bloated and groggy. I saw him get out of the limo once, and he walked straight into one of those big concrete pillars underneath the arena—he was so groggy. He'd walk with his head down, you know, that Elvis stance, shaking his hands. The strange thing was that all those people around him, who should have been taking care of him, were just looking around, strutting their stuff 'cause they just rode in with the king, you know. They're looking around, sort of going, "Hey, man, I'm Elvis's bodyguard." And they're so busy with their own egos they let the king walk right into a damn pillar! Of course, he made a joke of it. Elvis always had a comeback. Still, it was sad to see him embarrassed. I've seen him get out of a limo with no one helping him and just fall flat on his face.

Onstage you had to really be on your toes during those final few months, and it sort of got to be a pain in the butt. Elvis would suddenly call out songs onstage that none of us knew. One night he called out "Blueberry Hill." Of course nobody had rehearsed it. I said, "What key? What key's it in?"—in front of twenty thousand people! Somebody shouted, "Try C," and I'm sitting there with my mind just whirling 'cause

Elvis is telling twenty thousand people he wants to sing "Blueberry Hill" and I don't even know the damn song! So I just started playing some sort of something as an intro, and Elvis whirls around and says, "That's not the way it goes!" He comes over to the piano in front of all those people and sits down and tries to show me how to play it. Joe Guercio [Elvis's orchestra leader] is over there just spitting bullets. So finally, I think David Briggs or somebody hit an intro. Elvis sings a verse and a chorus and says, "I don't want to sing that!" and stops.

By then I'm a noodle! He did it to [James] Burton, too. Somebody requested an old song from one of his movies, and he said, "Kick it off, Burton." Of course, he embarrassed Burton 'cause Burton couldn't remember the damn song. So I wasn't the only one. But Elvis didn't care. It was like he was just sitting around singing in his own living room.

BOBBY OGDIN *(musician)*: When he was onstage, Elvis was always on somebody, teasing and playing. He got me with a big cup of water one night—one of those big cups of water he kept up there. Every now and then he'd just look around at somebody onstage, and he'd look just like a mischievous little kid; then all of a sudden, he'd throw water all over you. He did it to me. He did it to the girls. He would fake it sometimes with an empty cup. He loved clowning, something to break the monotony a little bit.

At some point in the show, Elvis always leaned forward and pulled a scarf from around his neck and threw it to some lady up front in the audience. Charlie Hodge would immediately wrap another scarf around his neck. Elvis would be on the front edge of the stage and it would just freak out the women. They'd be hysterical with excitement. But before he did that, Elvis would always take off his rings, those big, really expensive diamond rings, and hand them to Charlie Hodge for safekeeping. One night he got mixed up and handed Charlie a scarf and threw his big diamond ring into the audience. He did it totally backwards! I have no idea what that ring was worth, but I'm sure it was worth a small fortune. Elvis was real cool about it when it happened, though. He didn't say a thing or let on that he'd goofed.

SHAUN NIELSEN: Elvis got sick onstage in Baltimore. He had to leave the stage, and we all had to fill in. When he came back, some people in the audience booed him, but they were certainly outnumbered by the ones who were just happy he was back.

BOBBY OGDIN: During the time I worked for Elvis, we never did a sound check, never did a rehearsal either, as I recall. We had scheduled rehearsals in Memphis during that last year—scheduled 'em before four different tours. Everybody flew in from all directions, and we'd go down and set everything up at Graceland in the racquetball court. We'd get it all ready, check out all the microphones, and wait about an hour or two. Then Elvis would decide he didn't want to rehearse and call it off. We'd all go back to the hotel or go out to eat. We'd do that for about three nights in a row, and then we'd just take off on tour, no rehearsal, no sound checks.

One time Elvis scheduled a rehearsal on the road. There was some song he wanted to work up. The entire band came in that afternoon, set up and waited, but Elvis didn't show up. There was an Elvis impersonator there that Felton knew, so he just called the guy down on the stage and got him to run through a few songs—songs we never did on the regular shows. It was just kind of spinning wheels. Then we all went back to the hotel. The show was pretty well set as it was.

:◎:◎:◎:

DR. GEORGE NICHOPOULOS: There was one tour near the end where Ginger decided to go home and Elvis [immediately] developed some "illness;" we had to stop. He just didn't care about continuing the tour without her. She had quite a hold on him.

JO ALDEN: Elvis wanted Ginger with him onstage. I don't think another girl ever sat onstage. The first time Ginger was there, Elvis told her he wanted her to see the ending of his show. After that, during the last song that he always sang to end his show, "Can't Help Falling in Love," one of the bodyguards would help Ginger outside. She would be in the limousine when Elvis rushed offstage and got in.

BOBBY OGDIN: Even on his final tour, Elvis Presley's shows created the strongest audience electricity of anybody I've ever worked with. When Elvis walked onstage it was like an explosion of response and screaming and flash bulbs and everything. It was probably just caused by the limited access to him. People stored up all that desire and excitement.

JANELLE MCCOMB: Elvis made every member of an audience a part of all he acquired. When he stepped on that stage, that little secretary became the office manager, and that little intern became chief of staff. He gave hope and inspiration to all those kids who dared to dream some impossible dream. In Elvis they saw a kid born in a two-room house in Tupelo, Mississippi, who rose to fame and stardom, and it gave them hope.

ARLENE COGAN: I went on most of the last tour, followed the show from city to city, mainly because I was just worried about Elvis's health. I felt that he was unhappy, and I felt for the first time in my life that it was more important for him to see me sitting there than it was for me to see him. I wanted him to know somebody was there that cared about him. I went with a friend, Rose Clayton, to see him in Knoxville, Louisville, Philadelphia, Baltimore, Binghamton, Omaha, and Lincoln. (He canceled two dates during that tour for health reasons.) I had planned on going on to Indianapolis, but for some reason, I just came on back home to Memphis and didn't see that last concert.

MYRNA SMITH: I saw a change in Elvis physically, but not so much while it was occurring as when I reflect on it now. The concerts [filmed for the CBS TV special] weren't shown on TV immediately. While we were doing them, I thought he looked great. You know, being around somebody all the time, you don't notice so much how they really look. I knew he had put on weight, but I didn't think, "Gee, he looks bloated," or any of that until I saw one of the concerts on TV later.

BOBBY OGDIN: No matter how he was feeling, Elvis always nailed "How Great Thou Art" in his stage show. It was really pretty magical. His voice was always great for that song even when he wasn't "in voice." It was real special, real heavy.

BILL RANDLE: The last time I saw Elvis Presley, he came to a class of mine. I was teaching at the University of Cincinnati. He came anonymously, only three or four people saw him. He was bloated and fat.
 I'm a martial arts person, so wherever I work I always have a kicking board or a punching board on the wall. Elvis was a student of Mr. [Ed] Parker, who was a very good karate fighter. He practiced on my wall for about fifteen minutes and told me he was very happy with his life and left. I went to see him at his concert that night.

BOBBY OGDIN: In Indianapolis—the very last show we did with him—he was overweight, but he went back and forth a lot on his weight, so he didn't seem any different from normal at that show. We really didn't have any indication he was sick. Oh, before that sometimes he'd come onstage sleepy, you know, from having just gotten up an hour or so before. But other times he'd be full of energy and ready to go. When he'd come to the stage sleepy the energy would always pour in from the audience. It was like a tidal wave. He'd feel that big wave, and about a song or two into the show he'd get really into it. It must have been a huge boost to have had twenty thousand people directing their energy onstage to you.

Jo Alden: Ginger was with Elvis in Indianapolis [June 26, 1977]. She always had to leave just before he ended his show and go wait in the car, because the crowd would be right behind him and he had to get away fast.

It's so sad; at his last concert she was already in the car when he walked offstage for the very last time.

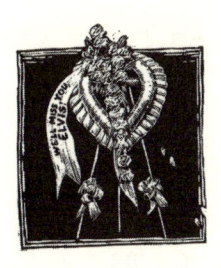

"When the Light Is Gone"
1977

In the heat of August, Elvis prepares for yet another tour, but this one is different: for the first time in his career Elvis will have to face a public newly made aware of his imperfections. It is a confrontation he dreads. But on the morning of August 16, 1977, fate intervenes...

Larry Geller and bodyguard Sam Thompson are among those giving behind-the-scenes accounts of the king's final night at Graceland. Then, after awakening to find that Elvis is not asleep beside her, girlfriend Ginger Alden makes a startling discovery. Paramedics Charles Crosby and Ulysses Jones describe what they find when they answer the emergency call to 3764 Elvis Presley Boulevard.

Many of Elvis's closest friends and loyal fans share their reactions to shocking news that stuns the world; they describe with anguish and sorrow the heartbreak of the days that follow.

> "It's hard for me to watch documentaries of Elvis's life because it's such a sad and tragic story: he seemed to be a happy, generous, sweetheart of a guy in the early years; then they get to his decline, and it starts becoming one of the saddest stories. It just breaks my heart and I can't watch anymore."
>
> CLINT BLACK *(country music recording star)*

LARRY STRICKLAND: This is really weird; and so help me, I wouldn't tell something that was not true. We were out on a tour with The Stamps—on the bus. I was back in my bunk sleeping and I had a bad dream. I dreamed we were singing at a funeral, and the casket was down in front of us. When we stood up to sing, the figure in the casket sat up. It was faceless (I didn't recognize any face), but it made an awful noise. I woke up with just the sickest feeling, got out of my bed, and went up to sit with the bus driver that night—to try to shake off the feeling. So help me, it wasn't much later that we were singing at Elvis's funeral! We were standing over behind the casket, singing as we had in my dream. It was the most weird thing I've ever known in my life.

T. G. SHEPPARD [Bill Browder]: I last saw Elvis in early August; I just went up to visit. I saw Charlie Hodge, and George Klein was there. And I saw Elvis. He was in the racquetball court. That's the last time I saw him alive.

There's a look that people get in their eyes when they're not well, and there's a look in their eyes when the light is gone—and it was already gone. When I left I even made a statement to my concessions manager, Gary. He asked me, "How was Elvis?" I said, "I don't know *where* he is." He said, "What do you mean?" I said, "I don't know, man. Something's not right. I don't think he's long for this world."

FELTON JARVIS: I'd told Elvis that I had to quit. He wanted me to stay for the next tour, and then, he said, he'd take some time off. It was hard for me to tell Elvis I had to stop touring with him. He was my best friend.

Elvis saved my life when I was dying because I needed a kidney and was on a long waiting list. He didn't just take over, 'cause he knew how I felt about that. Finally he called and said, "Felton, I've stayed out of this and let you do it your way, but it ain't working. You're dying, man, and I need you. Do you mind if I call somebody and try to help you get a kidney?" I had been on the list a long time, and they told me they couldn't match me; but when they found out that Elvis was interested in helping me, they found me a kidney. In a week I had a transplant.

Elvis knew how hard it was for me on the road. We were all tired and Elvis knew it. I had a lot of trouble getting to sleep at night. It's hard to have balance in your life when you're in rock 'n' roll. I was the Sunday school superintendent at my church—First Presbyterian in Franklin, Tennessee—and I missed being there. My wife [Mary] had to take care of everything at home. But man, Elvis didn't have nothing but the road. He couldn't go to church.

GEORGE KLEIN: The last two or three weeks I went up to Graceland quite a bit, and we would sit and rap in his room. It wasn't like he told everyone to get lost. If Joe or Jerry or Alan or Billy wanted to come up, Elvis would say, "Yeah, come on up to the room. I'm watching TV." We'd go up and shoot the bull with him. I saw him two or three times the last two weeks of his life.

DR. GEORGE NICHOPOULOS: Elvis had respect for Colonel Parker and for what he'd done for him in the past; but they had some problems getting together and talking about things. Toward the last, Elvis would avoid conversations with him.

LARRY GELLER: Elvis gradually lost respect for the Colonel because he felt he was being used. He didn't feel the Colonel really cared for him as a human being. Elvis respected the Colonel for how he launched his career, but he felt it was mishandled later on.

GEORGE KLEIN: Elvis listened to the Colonel's advice up until the later years. His phrasing was, "Okay, I don't agree with the Colonel, but the ol' fellow got me this far, and I'm doing pretty good, so I think I'm gonna continue to listen to him." Later, right toward the end, he started to stand up to the Colonel more.

LARRY GELLER: Elvis was the most loyal person I've ever met in my life. He couldn't say "no" to people, and he didn't want to upset the applecart. At the end he was going to fire the Colonel, and he wanted Tom Huelett to become his manager. (Tom Huelett was a concert promoter.) Elvis really wanted the Colonel out; he knew when he was going to do it, and we spoke of it. After that next tour Elvis was going to let the Colonel go.

Elvis wanted to make the big break from Parker. But the big break came only when he left this planet.

DR. GEORGE NICHOPOULOS: Elvis was looking forward to another tour. He was looking forward to having Ginger to himself and working again.

BILL BELEW: There was a new look in development for Elvis. We had literally gone as far as we could go with the jewels and the embroidery work, and I was working on this new idea: it was a costume with lasers. We had a prototype of it that we had shown Elvis, and we were all very excited. We knew that if and when he went to Europe, it was going to be almost like the Beatles coming to America. He would have to have something really spectacular to wear.

We designed all the wires and everything so that when he walked onstage in the jeweled cape there would be a remote control he would press and eight lasers would shoot out from different points all over the suit. That's what we were working on, because lasers were becoming *the* thing. Between the spotlights hitting the jewels and the lasers coming from the suit, it would really have been spectacular. We decided we might even try it here in America if the European tour didn't come through.

DR. GEORGE NICHOPOULOS: Ginger and I talked about a number of things, but not about their relationship. I never felt comfortable discussing it with her. I had touched on it with her, the confusion she was creating: "You're going; you're not going" and "You need to make up your mind. Don't dangle Elvis on a string. It's creating problems for all of us." I mentioned it a few times, then let it go. It was affecting him to a great extent.

Elvis's health had really been controlled. His high blood pressure was being controlled. But at times his sugar got out of line; that's another thing steroids do, they will elevate your blood sugar to the level of a diabetic. Elvis really didn't have anything life-threatening going on.

I went by early that evening [August 15, 1977] and didn't stay very long 'cause I had a lot to do to get prepared for the tour. I left the medications I thought he was going to need that night. He didn't say anything at the time about his toothache. He did mention he wasn't sure whether Ginger was going to go or not. He thought she was going to stay behind, and he was talking about, "bringing somebody else in." He said, "I've had it. I'm not going to worry about it. If she's not going to go, then she's not going to go." He was resigned to it.

SAM THOMPSON: We were all getting ready to go on the tour. I thought I was flying Lisa Marie (who was visiting at Graceland) back to Los Angeles that day to be with Priscilla, but Elvis was always one to put off things that were unpleasant. It was unpleasant for him to leave his daughter, and for her to leave him. We put it off 'til that night. We sat around that evening, Dick Grob and I; the others played cards, drank coffee, and basically just waited for Elvis to decide how he wanted to handle this.

DR. GEORGE NICHOPOULOS: Apparently his tooth started hurting that night, and he went to the dentist.

SAM THOMPSON: Sometime after midnight, I remember Elvis leaving with a group of people to go to the office of [his dentist] Dr. Lester Hofman. He waved at me and said, "When I get back, Sam, I want to talk to you about Lisa, and we'll work things out. So stay around." I did.

ANN MARIE MCCLAIN: We saw Elvis as he was coming back through the gate from his dentist appointment. We heard the horn honk and we all looked up; then it honked again coming in the gate. He was just a-waving. He waved and I waved back. That was it.

LARRY GELLER: He came into the house and stopped and gave me a look as he was going up the stairs. He took his glasses off and gave me a look. I knew precisely what he meant: he meant he was struggling; he was hurting. I hadn't seen Elvis in approximately six weeks, and when I saw him he just didn't look right. He still had his beauty, but when I saw his face a thunderbolt went right through me. I was speechless. He walked upstairs like a zombie—like a robot.

I went into the other room, slumped into a sofa, and I was just totally absorbed with that devastating experience.

The next thing I knew, a phone was being handed to me. It was Elvis. And the most remarkable thing happened, his voice was so unlike I had ever heard it before. It was so soft and so childlike. I kept thinking, "He sounds like he's five or six years old." His voice was so innocent, and it took away the memory of the earlier experience. He said, "So, Lawrence, you want to come upstairs?" I did, and we spoke for awhile. I gave him three books.

He said to me, "Lawrence, don't forget, angels fly because they take themselves so lightly." He had the best sense of humor. Elvis was pure soul—pure soul, an astute human being.

DR. GEORGE NICHOPOULOS: I got a phone call about two or three o'clock in the morning that Elvis was having severe pain and that the dentist's pain pills weren't helping him any. Elvis said he'd send somebody by my house to pick up a prescription, and they could take it to the hospital to get it filled. He asked specifically for Dilaudid, so I wrote one [prescription] out for three or four Dilaudids.

Since my car had been broken into several times, I didn't have the medication at home that I had gotten together for the tour, so I couldn't placebo it. I wasn't at Graceland, so I couldn't really know how much pain he was really having. I talked to some people who said he did go to the dentist and was having some problems. Apparently the pain went away after he started playing racquetball with Ginger, his cousin Billy, and Billy's wife Jo; so he never took the medication.

SAM THOMPSON: I don't know what time it was—early—when Elvis went upstairs and said a word or two to me. He called down and told me that he was going to maybe play racquetball and get a few hours sleep, that I should come back early in the afternoon and book a later flight to fly Lisa home. So I made our reservations from Memphis to Los Angeles and went home. It must have been four in the morning—something like that.

BILLY SMITH (cousin): We played racquetball from four o'clock until about seven o'clock that morning—that Tuesday morning.

JO ALDEN: Ginger and Jo sat out and watched Elvis and Billy play, but Elvis was just clowning around. It wasn't a hard game of racquetball. Then Elvis came out and played the piano, I guess, for the last time he ever sang or played.

BILLY SMITH: I went upstairs with Elvis, and I was blow-drying his hair. He was a little bit depressed from the fact that *Elvis: What Happened?* was coming out. Excerpts had already been in a magazine. He was angered by it and wondered if he was going to be confronted about it while he was onstage. But from all I gathered, Elvis had hopes of it being one of the best tours he had ever done. That was at seven o'clock in the morning.

Jo Alden: Ginger was in her period and she said something to him about waiting a couple of days and joining the tour later when she got to feeling better. She said that since they had talked that night about announcing their upcoming wedding, maybe she would do some shopping before she left. He told her he wanted her to go with him. He said, "I need you for inspiration. You can shop on tour."

Ginger Alden: I was ready to fall asleep. I told him he needed to get some sleep, too, but he said he couldn't sleep and went into the bathroom to read. It was a book on religion or psychology.

Dr. George Nichopoulos: Apparently Ginger went to sleep. Elvis was wide awake at eight o'clock in the morning and talking coherently [on the phone] to my nurse. He had already taken the sedative I'd left that night, but he said he couldn't sleep. He knew he had to sleep 'cause he had a show to do that night. The nurse called me to get [permission to give] the reserve envelope of his pills. We gave him one placebo and one sedative. To my knowledge, that's all he took.

After he talked to my nurse and she distributed the sleeping pill, no one heard anything else from him.

There was a group of six guys who alternated nights staying in the room adjoining Elvis's bedroom, so they could hear him. They were supposed to get up any time he got up, 'cause in the past he had fallen down stumbling over some things. The guy [Rick Stanley] who was supposed to stay with him [that night] was downstairs in the rec room. He never checked on Elvis. They had tried to get Rick to go over to the nurse's house to pick up the sleeping pill [for Elvis] but they couldn't rouse him, so Elvis's aunt [Delta] went over and got it. Apparently the guy had taken something and they couldn't get him up.

David Stanley: People say: "Where were you, Ricky? Where were you, David?" Hey, when Elvis says, "Don't bother me 'til four o'clock in the afternoon," you don't bother him. He was with Ginger, so we didn't just sit and watch him sleep. When Ginger wasn't there, we were around him all the time.

We had been scheduled to leave that afternoon for Portland, Maine, to start the tour. I went to Graceland about noon on the sixteenth to relieve Ricky. When I came in, Ricky was downstairs. He left, and a friend of mine, Mark White, and I started shooting pool—just kinda hangin' out, you know.

Dr. George Nichopoulos: About two in the afternoon Ginger woke up and, not finding Elvis in bed, went to his bathroom door and called his name.

Ginger Alden: I said, "Elvis?" and he didn't answer, so I opened his bathroom door. That's when I saw him there. I slapped him a few times, and it was like he breathed once when I turned his head. I raised one of his eyelids and his eye was just blood red, but I couldn't move him.

I thought at first he might have hit his head, because he had fallen out of his black lounging chair and his face was buried in the carpet.

Joe Esposito: I just happened to walk into the house to talk to Al [Strada] when Ginger phoned downstairs and said something was wrong with Elvis. We rushed upstairs. Ginger thought he had just collapsed. Al and I went to pick Elvis up because I thought he had fainted; then I realized he was not breathing.

Charles Crosby *(paramedic)*: The emergency call was received at the fire station. The caller said that "someone was having difficulty breathing at 3764 Elvis Presley Boulevard." At that point we only knew it was Elvis's house. Ulysses Jones and I jumped into the ambulance and took off.

Ginger Alden: When Joe turned Elvis's head I think he knew Elvis was dead, because he didn't want me to see him and sent me into the other room.

Dr. George Nichopoulos: Seems like it was somewhere around two in the afternoon when I got beeped at the hospital. I called Graceland, and they weren't sure what was wrong. They said Elvis was in serious trouble and for me to get out there as fast as I could.

David Stanley: Mark and I were shooting pool in the basement when Amber, Lisa Marie's friend, walked into the room and said, "David, I think Elvis is sick."

I wasn't that alarmed, but I said to myself, "Well, I need to get Mark off the premises." So I walked out to the car with Mark, and we drove around to the front of the house. Just as I was headed down into the driveway I saw Patsy [Presley] Gambill running out the front of the house screaming. She was freaked out; I'm thinking, "What the hell is going on?" So I rush down the drive, and just as I get to the bottom of the driveway near the gates an ambulance comes tearing in. Then I began to worry. I dropped Mark off across the street, sped back up to the house, jumped out of the car, ran in the house and up the back steps into Elvis's bathroom. By the time I got there the ambulance guys had just walked in.

CHARLES CROSBY: As soon as we got to the house, we were shown to an upstairs bedroom where several people were gathered around the body of a large white male. I didn't recognize him immediately. A woman was giving him mouth-to-mouth resuscitation.

DAVID STANLEY: Charlie Hodge was in the room along with Al Strada and Joe Esposito. Vernon had just arrived. His girlfriend, Sandy, was trying to help revive Elvis. When I walked into the bathroom Vernon was crying, and he began to slowly start sliding down against the bathroom wall, screaming, "Oh, Son, please don't die!"

ULYSSES JONES *(paramedic)*: Several people were huddled over the body of a man clothed in pajamas—a yellow top and a blue bottom. From his shoulders up, his skin was dark blue. His sideburns were gray.

DAVID STANLEY: The ambulance guy said, "What happened here?" And I said very directly, "He's OD'd!" I know now that sounds blunt, but at that instant there was no time to play games. The main thing was to try to save Elvis.

ULYSSES JONES: I knelt down to the body, checked his pulse, and shined a penlight into his eyes to see if there was any reaction. There was nothing. The people around me were weeping.

DAVID STANLEY: I looked around and began to see some pill packs laying around. Instinctively, I began to pick them up and put them in my pocket.

ULYSSES JONES: I inserted an airway tube into his throat and gave the nearest man a squeeze bag for pumping air into his lungs.

DAVID STANLEY: Charlie was massaging Elvis's chest. Joe said, "Let's get him on the stretcher." I think Joe knew Elvis was dead, but I think he didn't want to let on to Vernon that it was hopeless, because Vernon had a history of heart trouble and was crying and obviously very stressed; I'm sure Joe must have wanted to give Vernon whatever hope he could. And I think maybe we all had a singular thought, "If there is any hope . . ."

So I took Elvis under his arms, and Joe and Al grabbed him by the feet, and we lifted him onto the stretcher. One of the ambulance guys helped and we began to roll him out. When we got down the stairs and out the front door we put him in the ambulance, and Joe and Al got in the ambulance with him just as Dr. Nick pulled up.

DR. GEORGE NICHOPOULOS: When I got there they were putting him in the ambulance. Joe told me when he had turned Elvis over [up in the bathroom] he heard some air move, and I thought that if this was true it may *just* have happened, and we ought to try and resuscitate him.

I got in the ambulance and we took off.

DR. KEVIN S. MERIGIAN *(pharmacologist/toxicologist)*: Whenever you move a body, it's not uncommon to hear a rush of air from somewhere. There may be some air in the chest, and when you move the body from one position to the other, it may squeeze it out.

DR. GEORGE NICHOPOULOS: I should've realized that as stiff as Elvis's body was that he'd been dead for some time. We intubated him, got an I.V. started, and massaged his heart (the usual things) for the ten to fifteen minutes it took to get to the hospital, and I guess another twenty to thirty minutes there.

DAVID STANLEY: As soon as the ambulance left, I ran through the house and out the back door to where the cars were parked. Billy Smith was there and said, "What's going on?" I said, "Billy, come with me right now!" We jumped in the car and shot down the driveway headed for Baptist Hospital.

When we got there, Elvis had already arrived. Billy and I showed our IDs and were taken into a room adjacent to where they were working on Elvis. Joe and Al were there. And we all just stood by and waited.

We could not see into the room, but every once in awhile someone would rush through the doors going in or coming out, and when the doors would swing open you could see this large crowd working furiously on Elvis.

MARIAN COCKE *(nurse)*: When I walked in, the emergency room was full and Dr. Nick just looked at me, as did John [John Quartermous, who was performing CPR on Elvis]. I read what was in their faces because I couldn't really see Elvis. I touched one of the interns on the arm and moved him aside so I could see Elvis. When I did, my knees got weak. I said, "Please stop!" It was evident that the soul of this boy had long since left his body, and I could not bear to see them continue. Dr. Nick told John to hold up on the CPR, and when he saw there was absolutely no complex on the EKG, he agreed they should stop.

DAVID STANLEY: Finally Dr. Nick came back into the room where we were waiting. He just shook his head and said, "He's gone."

DR. GEORGE NICHOPOULOS: There's no way to know if things would have turned out differently if the regular procedure [at Graceland] had been followed. There's certainly a possibility that if there'd been someone in the next room (as there should have been), then when Elvis had a cardiac arrhythmia and passed out they would've heard it. Whether they could've done anything or not, there's no way to know. When Elvis was found, his face was down in the pile carpet. If somebody had heard him fall and gone in there, they could've afforded him some breathing room and called somebody.

:◎:◎:◎:

CHARLES CROSBY: We drove Dr. Nichopoulos back to Graceland and waited while he went in to inform Mr. Presley. I think Dr. Nichopoulos was worried about Mr. Presley's heart condition and wanted to have us there just in case. We waited in the living room–dining room area. Elvis's daughter was there. She was crying. A lady was holding her and comforting her.

SAM THOMPSON: My dad was going to drop me off at Graceland and go home. As we were driving up to the mansion, David Stanley was [again] coming down the driveway. He stopped us, and he was obviously overwrought. He said, "Have you heard? Elvis is dead." And then he drove off.

I remember my dad and I just looked at each other and said, "We didn't hear this right. What's going on?" We drove on up and the ambulance was sitting out front. As it turned out, that was the ambulance that had brought Dr. Nick back to the house to break the news to Vernon. We drove around to the back and I parked. My dad and I walked in through the back door, not really knowing what to expect. We walked into the jungle room; Vernon was sitting there. I got there just at the time Dr. Nick walked [back] in and leaned over and whispered something in Vernon's ear. Vernon let out a yell and cried, "My baby's dead!" Tish [Henley], the nurse [who was stationed at Graceland], was there, and she was ministering to Vernon. The whole place just filled, and people were crying and moaning. It was chaos.

I went into the other room just to get away from it for a minute and sort of collect my thoughts, and Lisa was in there. She was just a little girl then. [Lisa Marie Presley was nine years old when Elvis died.] It really hit her. She came up to me and said, "Sam, my daddy's dead." She just said it so matter-of-fact. I couldn't even answer. She said, "I'm going to call Linda." She went into one of the bedrooms and called my sister—had her number memorized. I took the phone from Lisa and Linda said, "Is it true?"

I said, "Yes, it's true. He's dead."

CHERYLE JOHNSON: I heard on TV that Elvis had been taken to the hospital in respiratory distress. The last time I saw him I knew he was sick. I had been expecting something to happen.

DAVID STANLEY: The hospital officials made the announcement at about 3:30 P.M. that Elvis had died, and that an autopsy was being performed.

DR. JERRY T. FRANCISCO *(Shelby County Medical Examiner)*: Elvis Presley died in a matter of four short minutes of coronary arrhythmia, an irregular beating of the heart. Death occurred between 9:00 A.M. and 2:00 P.M. There's no way to be more precise than that. [The autopsy revealed] that there was severe cardiovascular disease present. He had a history of mild hypertension and some coronary artery disease. These two diseases may be responsible for cardiac arrhythmia, but the precise cause was not determined. Basically it was a natural death. The precise cause of death may never be discovered.

:◎:◎:◎:

HAROLD LOYD: I was asleep and it was about time to get up for work anyway—a little after four. I had to be at work [guarding the gates at Graceland] at six. My wife saw it on TV at home, and she came runnin' up there to the bedroom yellin'. She was choked up, screamin', "Oh, my god, Harold, wake up! Wake up! Elvis is dead!" I can still hear her voice ringin', "Elvis is dead!"

It took me a while to really get awake. My wife took off back down to the livin' room. I jumped up and grabbed my pants (I think I got one leg in), flopped downstairs, and sank down on the couch in front of the TV set. It was showing them takin' Elvis out of the ambulance at the hospital emergency room earlier in the afternoon.

I kinda flashed back to real early that morning, when he had come home from the dentist. He had been in good spirits, man, just cuttin' up and laughin' and jokin', havin' a ball.

And just a few hours later, it was all over.

JANICE PENNINGTON: We were taping *The Price Is Right,* and I was walking down the hall toward the set when someone announced on the P.A. that it had just come on the news that Elvis had died. I was just shocked, stunned. I didn't want to accept it. It was that denial, I guess. He was a special, special person.

LOWELL HAYS: Someone called me and told me that Elvis had died and I just laughed. I said, "Oh, that's bull!" Elvis was timeless to me. He could never die. I just didn't believe it. Then I had to believe it.

BEN WEISMAN: On August 16, 1977, I was on a show called *The Young and the Restless,* a soap opera on CBS-TV. I was playing the piano in a nightclub scene in the show. In between takes, someone said, "Ben, we've got some bad news for you. You're not going to believe it, but you better sit down." I said, "What?" The guy said, "One of your good friends died." I said, "Who? Elvis? Come on, it isn't true." I called my wife and she said, "It's on all the TV shows that Elvis is gone." Well, I started shaking, and it took me a long time to get through that scene so I could get out of there.

BETTY COCKERELL: I had just come home about 3:30 or so from Methodist Hospital in Memphis, where I was working as a nurse, and the news flashed on the TV screen: "Bulletin! Bulletin! Bulletin! Elvis Presley died today at Baptist Hospital." You know, I just remember the total shock, the way I felt. I immediately went to the phone and called a friend of mine [Anita Fielder] who lived in Nashville and told her, and she started crying, and I did, too.

GEORGE KLEIN: Driving out to Graceland at breakneck speed after I heard about his death, I put in one of his tapes; and right at the beginning of "Can't Help Falling in Love With You," the tape stopped! It was broken right at the beginning of the song, just like he didn't want to sing any more. It was a strange coincidence.

BOBBY WOOD: I was in Nashville doing a Joe Tex recording session, and when the news reached us Joe called the session off. He couldn't work no more. It shook him up 'cause Elvis was his biggest hero.

I was shocked. We were all shocked. I just couldn't believe it. [At first] somebody said, "That's a sick joke," or something like that; but they said, "No, it's true."

BILL E. BURK: I was out playing golf, and when I got through with nine holes I came in for a lemonade break before going out for the second nine. The golf pro remarked to me, "Too bad about Elvis, ain't it." I looked at him rather surprised and asked, "What?" And he said, "He's dead! Forty-two years old and dead from a heart attack."

WILL "BARDAHL" McDANIEL: I was at home when I heard the news. I walked out to the back porch and sat down and cried.

JOAN DEARY: I was in California. I came back from lunch and walked into my office [at RCA] and the phone was ringing. I picked it up, and it was a fan from New Jersey who had just heard the announcement on the air. He was crying, and the news was such a shock I couldn't believe it. I flipped on the radio and it came over the air. Then suddenly, because the New York office was closed when the news broke—two o'clock L.A. time—suddenly, all the phones in my office lit up! People and reporters from all over the world started calling RCA's Hollywood office.

Grelan Landon [head of RCA publicity at that time] came running in and said, "Refer all the calls to me!" The phones at RCA just went crazy.

T. G. SHEPPARD [Bill Browder]: I was back in Nashville at my manager's office and the phone rang. The secretary said, "There's a radio station wanting a quote from you." And you know, instantly I knew what it was. I hadn't heard any radio that day, but something just went off in my head as I picked up the phone. It was a local disc jockey in Nashville saying, "I need a quote about your friend passing away—Elvis Presley." Yeah, I knew. There are some things in life you just know.

MARY JARVIS: I had dropped Felton off at Stevens Aircraft—a small private airport where the show plane was supposed to stop and pick up Felton and the Nashville contingency, and I was driving home. It was raining so hard! I switched on the car radio and the announcer said, "It has been confirmed that it was not Vernon Presley but Elvis Presley who died today in Memphis." I wheeled the car around and headed back to the airport! The show plane had landed by the time I got there, and Felton had received a call from someone (I think the Colonel), so he knew. Felton had to go on the plane and tell all those musicians and singers that Elvis was dead. But all he could bring himself to say was, "The tour is off. Act of God. Go home and we'll call you."

He immediately flew out to Memphis on the show plane to help out at Graceland.

BILLY STANLEY: I'd gone to a liquor store to get a keg of beer; I was going to throw a party for my brothers before they left on tour that night. When I walked into the store the sales people, who knew me, looked at me kinda funny. I said, "What's going on?" They told me they'd just heard on the radio that Elvis was dead. I said, "That's a sick joke! You shouldn't be kidding around like that!" They said, "We're not kidding." I called the house to check them out, and one of the secretaries answered and said it was true. I just went numb and dropped the phone. I ran outside, crying like a baby, standing out in the hot sun.

I went to Graceland, and it was a madhouse.

MAE AXTON: I was going to a rock festival over in Georgia and I had left my office and gone by my apartment to pick up something. When I got there and was trying to get the key in the door, the phone was ringing. I finally got in and picked it up and said, "Hello," but nobody answered. Finally Elvis's secretary came on the phone and said, "Mae, Vernon was trying to call you. Elvis is . . . Mae, he's . . . gone." I couldn't believe it. I just couldn't handle it.

RONNIE TUTT: My wife's mother called me and said, "You're not going to believe this, but they're saying—a bulletin just went across on TV—that Elvis is dead!" Obviously I was stunned, so I called Graceland to try to reach Felton. By chance, he answered the phone, and I said (I could tell he was shook up just by the way he answered the phone), I said, "Felton, this is Ronnie. Is it true?" That's all I said, and he said, "Yes, it's true."

MYRNA SMITH: We [band members and singers] were in the air going to Portland, Maine, on our charter plane for the show that night. We were over Tempe, Arizona, I think, headed east, and someone radioed instructions to our plane to turn around and go back to L.A., but instead of turning around we landed, and Marty Harrell, who played trombone with the band, went to call and find out why they wanted us to turn the plane around. I just assumed we had left somebody in L.A. So when Marty said for everybody to get off the plane, I didn't get off. But Marty came back and said, "Myrna, would you please get off because I have something to tell everybody, and I can only say it once."

I got off the plane, and Marty told us that the tour was canceled—Elvis was dead. I was totally shocked. I found myself running around the airport, hysterical. They had to give me Valium.

As soon as the plane landed back in L.A., I made a reservation to go to Memphis the next day. It was lucky I did, because two hours later the airlines were all booked solid and you couldn't get a flight into Memphis. Linda Thompson couldn't get a flight out, so my ex-husband Jerry gave her his ticket and he flew on the plane they sent for Priscilla.

IRA JONES: I was in California when Elvis died, but somehow the reporters found me and came to me for a comment. I said, "He was one of the nicest guys I ever met." They said, "But what about all the dope he used?" I said, "What?" They could have knocked me over with a stick. That was the first I'd ever heard about it.

LAMAR FIKE: I don't think Elvis ever thought he'd live long. I think he knew deep down in the back of his mind there was not much long life in that family. Fact is, there's nobody left in that family—period. It's gone. There's literally nobody to carry on the Presley name.

BILL E. BURK: I called Joe Beaulieu, Priscilla's stepfather, and offered him the use of my car while he was in Memphis. He said thanks, he didn't need it, but maybe I could help in another way. He said, "Elvis told me that if he died before me that he wanted a military color guard at his body during his wake. I know that you're in the Tennessee Air National Guard, and I believe your unit has a color guard. Would they do the honors?"

About nine o'clock the morning of the seventeenth, I brought the color guard to Graceland with their silver helmets, white gloves, and white leggings.

GEORGE KLEIN: That night me and Larry and Charlie, and, I think, Jerry and Joe, were sitting in the garage apartment watching TV, and when the ten o'clock news came on with the story about his death, all the TVs in the house went out!

LARRY GELLER: Elvis's body was being prepared for the funeral at the Memphis Funeral Home. I went there on behalf of his dad to prepare Elvis's hair, so that when he was laid out for all the fans he would look proper. I went to the funeral home at eight o'clock that morning. Someone said, "Mr. Geller, this way please." When I saw his body, I just froze. I said, "Oh no, God!" One of the policemen grabbed me (to steady me), and I said, "No, no. Leave me alone. I'll be all right."

Let me tell you something, I have seen Elvis thousands of times, when he was sleeping, when he woke up, in just about every possible situation. When I stood over his body, I looked hard at him. Despite rumors to the contrary, that *was* Elvis Presley, I'm sorry to say. I would want him alive just as much as anyone else.

JIM ORWOOD: The Shelby County deputies were the honor guard [at Graceland when Elvis lay in state]. We lined both sides of the driveway from the gates to the entrance of the house for two days.

I worked right there at the steps to the entrance of the mansion. I was on duty as a paramedic. People were screaming and hollering, "Don't really be dead, Elvis!" and all that. Men and women both.

ARLENE COGAN: Frances [Forbes] and Darlene [Daughtry] and myself, and my son Randy, went up to the house the day after they brought Elvis's body back. I did not want to bother Vernon 'cause I knew what shape he had to be in. To tell the truth, I was very worried that it might end up being a double funeral. Vernon had a very bad heart condition. We walked up. One or two of the sheriff's deputies that were there knew us. They stopped the people so we could go in privately.

It was something I was totally unprepared for. I could never imagine him being gone or being in that state. I had a very hard time accepting it.

NAOMIA STIERS: Mary Lou said, "Mama, do you want to go up to Memphis?" I said, "No, I don't think I do." She said, "You've got to go." She finally got a nurse to work for her. So we got in the car and left, and we ran into the hardest rain just out of Nashville. We got in behind a big truck going about ninety miles an hour and we stayed right behind him until we drove out of that rain.

When we got to Memphis we had to park about a mile from Elvis's house and walk. The streets were partly closed off, and what traffic was on 'em was just barely moving. We had to walk the rest of the way to his house in that hot, broiling sun. But when we got up there (oh, it was within fifteen or twenty feet of the gates), we couldn't get through the crowd. People were just packed up there. But they started calling for medical help, so Mary Lou told them she was a nurse. They let her get through the crowd, and she went inside the gates to help with the people that were fainting. After she'd been in there a little while, she told 'em, "My mother's a nurse, too. If you'll page her, let her in, she'll help." They paged me, but nobody would move to let me in. So I got down and crawled through the crowd and under the barricade.

Later, I walked up the hill to the mansion behind one girl (she was crying), and when she saw Elvis she started screaming, threw herself on the casket, and said she'd been loving him for years. They had to carry her away.

I went up there—I didn't want to—but I walked by there real fast because I wanted to remember Elvis as I'd seen him last. That was a traumatic experience.

BETTY COCKERELL: On the day they were to let people into Graceland to view the body, [Anita Fielder and I] went out there. The line was two abreast, and it stretched all the way from the street up to the house. It seemed like the line kept growing all day 'til it was way out along the street. People were converging on Memphis from all over the world. Both sides of the driveway were lined with flowers—flowers and arrangements of every possible description, wreaths and bouquets and single roses, thousands of flowers, hundreds and hundreds of gorgeous arrangements. I remember going along looking at the cards.

I got in the line with my friend and it must have taken us at least two hours to get up to the house. People seemed to be making a real effort to stay orderly and calm, respectful.

When you got to the front of Graceland, the door was open (I can still see it, just as plain as if it was happening right now). That casket was at an angle almost facing the door, so when you walked in you were looking right at Elvis's head. I would say that from what I saw, he had to have weighed over two hundred and fifty pounds. I mean, it was an enormous body. And I remember his hair was as black as you could ever imagine.

They had dyed it, and they had done a poor job because it looked terrible. That was bad in itself, but I remember he had on a white suit. I just remember white, white, white, like the casket was white. And people, when they took the first look . . . it was so bad they just kinda turned away. The woman right in front of me fainted. She did. And then I was up there myself. My friend was right behind me, and I said, "Don't look!" And with that, very slowly, the line passed on by, and people, when they got outside, were crying and screaming.

JIM ORWOOD: [Early that evening] the sheriff's department got us all down to the gate, and they said, "Okay, when we give you the signal, close the gate." We shut the gate against probably ten thousand people that were still out there. It was something; I swear it was something.

RONNIE MCDOWELL *(country recording artist)*: I went to Memphis that Wednesday after Elvis died, and I stood in line from eight o'clock in the morning 'til five o'clock; people were four abreast for three miles. I got about fifty feet from the gates before they closed them, so I never saw him, alive or dead. It really hurt me. I just climbed in my Camaro and headed back to Nashville. On the way back I told my friend, Bill Huntsman, "I'm going to write a song about Elvis. I've got these words going through my head."

SAM THOMPSON: I spent the night at Graceland, Wednesday night [August 18, 1977]. It was my function to guard over Elvis's body. The body was placed in the foyer, the casket was open, and the house was dark. There wasn't anybody there but me and a pot of coffee. I sat beside that body because there were rumors going around that people were going to steal it. We had perimeter security set up with the police department, and I sat up 'til five the next morning when I was relieved by Dick Grob.

MYRNA SMITH: I remember I went right to the house, and we were all sitting in the jungle room—the room with the waterfall and all that strange massive furniture. I hadn't seen Vernon yet, and I didn't know how I was going to react when I saw him. Joe Esposito's ex-wife, Joanie, was there taking care of all the women, and when Vernon came in and we looked at each other, we just both broke up crying. We went and hugged each other. I remember Joanie walking over to me and telling me to pull myself together. I thought, "Elvis is dead! And she's telling me to pull myself together!" I've never forgiven Joanie for that because I was just doing what my heart told me to do. Other than that, about all else I remember was the people coming in to the view the body, Caroline Kennedy, James Brown, and other big names.

JOAN DEARY: The day Grelan and I left L.A. to go to Elvis's funeral, it was pouring rain. The San Diego Freeway was a madhouse. We got the last two seats on the flight, and when we arrived in Memphis, we had no hotel reservations. There was a Shriner's convention going on, and there were no rooms to be had.

JAMES BLACKWOOD: We were in Charlie Hodge's apartment [at Graceland] planning the funeral service. There was a Church of Christ minister who was Dee's pastor, or at least she went to his church. He was there, and Reverend [Rex] Humbard was there, and Charlie Hodge, J. D. Sumner, and me. We were talking about who would do what.

Kathy Westmoreland was going to sing "My Heavenly Father Watches Over Me." And the numbers that the Stamps Quartet were going to sing was already set. Some of the Statesmen were there; they were going to sing a song or two. Charlie turned to me and said, "James, I think Elvis would want you to sing his favorite song, 'How Great Thou Art.' Will you do it?" I said, "Well, sure." When Joe Guercio found out that I was going to sing it, he came to me and said, "Mr. Blackwood, I have directed Elvis singing 'How Great Thou Art' hundreds of times. Would you give me the privilege of directing you singing it for him this last time?" I said, "Sure."

BILLY STANLEY: Joe Esposito kind of took control and handled everything for Vernon until the Colonel came in town. Then the two of them handled all of the arrangements.

BERNARD LANSKY: I put his first suit on him, and I put his last suit on him. It was a white suit that I had made for him. I put his shirt on him and a white tie; that's what Elvis was buried in.

BETTY COCKERELL: It was a hot, hot day, and people were falling out—fainting. There was a Red Cross ambulance and fire trucks that were giving assistance to people passing out in the heat.

BRENDA FIELDER: Every florist shop in the area was swamped with orders for all kinds of wreaths: guitars and hound dogs and hearts. We went into a couple of flower shops. They were going crazy trying to fill orders.

Marquees all over town said "We love you, Elvis," and "In Memoriam," and that sort of thing.

BILL E. BURK: There were so many floral arrangements ordered that week from all over the world that every Memphis florist sold out of every flower they had. They had to have more flowers flown in from Denver and other cities.

RUSSELL CHEST *(fan)*: There were not really any parking places in front of Graceland. There was a sidewalk, and cars were just parked on the sidewalk; they would turn in off the street with their two front wheels up over the curb, and they'd park like that, one car after another. It was about midnight [the night before the funeral] when we got there, and there were people and kids sleeping in the trunks of their cars, and there was just a general feeling of bewilderment. Once they got there, it was like people didn't really know what to do. They were just there.

It was very early when they delivered the morning paper, the *Commercial Appeal*, and they brought big stacks of them to a convenience market down the street from Graceland. These were all quickly bought up by people hoping for a souvenir or whatever. Of course, the headline and the photograph on the front was about Elvis. I can remember just a real run of people wanting to grab those papers.

BRENDA FIELDER: There were people from all over; there were license plates from Canada, many different states—bikers, Elvis look-a-likes, women in go-go outfits with boots, real die-hard fans, and curiosity seekers, too. And then there were the people who were selling the snow-cones and T-shirts. It was almost a carnival atmosphere, but very solemn, very sad, very strange. And it was quiet and respectful.

RUSSELL CHEST: The day of the funeral was very, very hot. It seems like the temperature was in the upper nineties. It felt like it may have even been over one hundred. Folks had been up all night long. There was an automobile accident just an hour or so prior to us getting there. An intoxicated teenage boy, I think, was speeding down through the street and hit and, I believe, killed at least one or two kids.

BRENDA FIELDER: A lot of people had come in and just camped out. They were sleeping in their car trunks, back seats, putting up little lean-to tents in the area. Hotels were booked solid, and none of us wanted to leave. I don't know why, but we all just felt we had to be there for Elvis.

A lot of people were crying. There were women who were really, really hysterical. Some people were writing on the [stone wall in front of the house], farewell writings, love notes to the king, last respects. It was the last chance they felt that they had to be close to him.

RUSSELL CHEST: You could tell some of the people were true Elvis fans, that he really meant a lot to them. There were some people that were just shaken to their souls.

BETTY COCKERELL: People that know I had walked up that hill and seen him lying in that casket have asked, "Tell me how he looked." Well, I do not mean any disrespect, but he looked horrible. I wish I could have been left with the memory of seeing him look like he looked in the sixties. I really do. I've wished that so many times. Outside, the people who had gone through seemed to be in disbelief that he was that dissipated-looking. You didn't want to believe it was Elvis, but it *was* Elvis.

:◎:◎:◎:

ED PARKER: When I went back to Graceland and saw all the many people who were at his funeral, even I was amazed. I don't think Elvis ever realized just how popular and famous he was. Had he been there in spirit alongside of me, I think even he himself would have been in awe.

JOAN DEARY: We came in through the back gate. The security guards had our names. They had a list of names of who could go in because, after all, the house would hold only so many.

SHAUN NIELSEN: I wasn't invited to the funeral, but I was there. I went up to Graceland when all the musicians came in from L.A. I viewed him laying there in state. It was so sad, I felt so helpless.

JOAN DEARY: I can remember the funeral vividly, and yet it's like some vague memory floating away somewhere in my mind. I wasn't really with it, because it was still such a terrible shock. It was almost like you were in another world. I couldn't tell you one word that was said at those services—not one word. I wasn't thinking or listening. I was just staring at that coffin in total disbelief.

LARRY STRICKLAND: The whole scene is such a hazy memory for me. I remember being in the piano room, there in the little area by the living room where the funeral took place. I remember when we first walked in, Charlie Hodge was standing beside the casket. He really loved Elvis, you know. He was just stroking, stroking Elvis's hands. I walked into a room and there was Ann-Margret, Priscilla, and a bunch of famous people, but I didn't even recognize them. It just didn't dawn on me, you know, that everybody there was just like me; they were really mourning. It was a terrible thing.

JOAN DEARY: It was in August and it was so hot; they turned off the air conditioning in the house so people could hear what was being said. Still, I couldn't tell you one word of what they were saying. The place was jammed with people. Most of us were standing. There were a few seats for Vernon and Priscilla and little Lisa. The casket was directly in front of me, and I was just mesmerized. I was glued to it—to the absolute mental-blocking-out of everything else.

JAMES BLACKWOOD: The casket was in front of the French doors, and they were closed. The singers were all behind the doors and couldn't be seen. As I sang "How Great Thou Art," Mr. Guercio sat over to the side and directed, tears rolling down his cheeks.

MYRNA SMITH: I remember part of the funeral. I remember being next to Ann-Margret and Roger [Smith]. I remember Kathy [Westmoreland]—I think she sang "My Heavenly Father Watches Over Me"—and the Stamps sang, too. I was in such a daze. I went to the cemetery, to the burial. Jerry was a pallbearer, I remember that.

SHAUN NIELSEN: I don't know if Lisa Marie fully understood. She must have known her daddy wouldn't be back, but she just kind of sat there and looked.

JOAN DEARY: I will always remember the Colonel was wearing a Hawaiian shirt, and I thought that was rather strange. To me, when you go to funerals you wear dark clothes. That's the way I grew up, and I was rather surprised to see some of the women in sun-back dresses. Maybe that's the way it is today.

MARTY LACKER: What would your opinion of somebody be if he supposedly cared for someone and at the funeral all he did was stand outside and lean up against a car and smoke a cigar and look at all the people going in? I'm willing—I might lose it, but I'm willing—to bet a thousand bucks the Colonel was responsible for those vendors being out there in front of Graceland selling flowers. I never had any use for him. He knew it. My loyalty was to Elvis.

NAOMIA STIERS: Some people, they give way to their emotions and scream and carry on, and they get that hurting out when it's somebody they love that's passed away. Other people suffer silently, and there was a lot of them there that day. There was just something about Elvis (I don't know what it was) that people *really* loved.

JOAN DEARY: Finally we were told by Joe Esposito to pay our last respects—anybody who wanted to—so I went up. I don't know how many other people went up, but after that we went outside.

BILLY STANLEY: Ricky and David and I went up to the casket by ourselves. I started crying. I was thinking, "I'd really love to be able to tell you how much I appreciated you and what you did for me." Plus, after the affair that Elvis had with my first wife, I never had the chance to actually go forward and tell him, "Hey, I forgive you for that." That's the hard part. I didn't want him to go to his grave thinking that he hurt me. I wanted him to know that our love was stronger than what happened.

LARRY GELLER: Right after the ceremony at Graceland, a few of the guys—Jerry Schilling, Charlie Hodge, Vernon, Joe Esposito, and myself—were standing by the casket. Right before the lid came down, Joe took the ring off Elvis's finger (you know, the TCB ring), and as we were putting the lid down, I put my hand in and touched him on his forehead. I wanted to be the last person to touch him; and I was.

BILLY STANLEY: As we were coming out of Graceland, there was a tree branch that fell for no apparent reason, just fell off the tree beside a couple of the limos. Sometimes I would take it that he was kidding, but Elvis always said that when he died there would be a sign that showed he was happy. And you know, that branch fell. It caught everybody by surprise. It was almost like there was the sign that we were all looking for, that he was happy.

BETTY COCKERELL: I took off from work the day of the funeral and went back out there. It comes back across my mind: there wasn't just one white funeral car carrying him away, there was a white hearse and a long, long line of white limousines. Seems like the whole city was paralyzed. People were numb. Everything came to a standstill. Businesses didn't open. It was a city in grief.

Russell Chest: At some point, I think about midday, the gates opened and the hearse and the accompanying cars came down the hill slowly and turned into the street to head for the cemetery. When that happened, there was a surge in the crowd, toward the street, like everybody was hoping to get a last glimpse. There was almost a feeling of fear in the air, fear that the crowd might get out of control, 'cause it just surged toward the street from either side, and people were being shoved together. It happened very fast. The cars weren't really going that slow once they turned. They were moving on. I guess they were wanting to get on through the crowd before anything might happen. As I was standing there, watching, I noticed a young woman, probably in her mid-thirties, standing in front of me, and she seemed relatively calm. She had sunglasses on and was well dressed, high heels, skirt and blouse. And it astonished me that when the hearse was about to reach our point, she went busting out into the street and tried to throw herself on the hood of the hearse. The hearse driver had to slam on his brakes to avoid hitting her. A policeman, who was standing nearest to us, went running out behind her and just scooped her up in his arms and carried her on to the other side of the street. Then the hearse took off again. It was very intense. The funeral procession moved on by very quickly, and that just left people feeling bewildered again. It almost seemed purposeless to be there in a way, but a lot of people felt so strongly about Elvis they didn't really know what else to do.

Joan Deary: I remember the ride in the limo, going down the driveway and out into the street. There were so many people all along the street, and flowers like you wouldn't believe.

Larry Strickland: In the funeral procession, we were in our bus. We went behind the limousines and motorcade. We drove past throngs and throngs of weeping people. What it reminded me of was when Kennedy was assassinated, that huge motorcade in D.C.—except Kennedy's motorcade was all black, and Elvis's was all white.

Brenda Fielder: As the motorcycles drove past, everything hushed. Everybody was straining to see, and then that white hearse—you knew that's where he was. It was eerie, so quiet, so solemn. It was strange to feel that in the middle of a huge crowd.

BILLY STANLEY: I always thought Elvis would live forever. On the way to the cemetery the only thing I saw was all the people lining the streets. I thought to myself, "All these people came to pay their respects for Elvis," and that really warmed my heart.

LARRY GELLER: I'm not surprised that people want him alive, but Elvis Presley was laid to rest on August 18, 1977. He will live forever.

ANITA FIELDER: I still love to hear him sing—always have, always will. And I know he will be in heaven and sing for me there.

"Something That Was Lasting"
1977-1994

With his untimely death Elvis's image takes on a different dimension: Elvis the idol becomes Elvis the icon. RCA's Joan Deary and Don Wardell tell how the record label is astounded by the transformation.

Then, less than two years after Elvis's death, Priscilla re-enters the picture, and strong reactions are forthcoming from members of the Memphis Mafia, Marty Lacker, and Lamar Fike, and from stepbrothers David and Billy Stanley. Devotees Naomia Stiers, Janelle McComb, and Cheryle Johnson share what Elvis's loyal fans do to memorialize the king of rock 'n' roll.

But soon some former Elvis associates sell their confidentiality for cash, beginning a proliferation of tell-all stories that expose the innermost secrets behind the image of the world's most famous entertainer.

Meanwhile, rumors and speculations regarding Elvis's drug use and abuse continue to surface as the media scramble to find the "real" answer to what killed Elvis. Doctors Dan Brookoff and Kevin Merigian give expert opinions, and their conclusions are startlingly simple.

Finally, former girlfriend Linda Thompson closes with a heartfelt reminder that one is remembered not so much by how one dies as by how one lives—and so Elvis lives on.

> "He was great when he started, and he was still great when he died. There's very few singers that are that way. Listen to his first records and listen to his last. Man, he was something!"
>
> WAYLON JENNINGS

JOAN DEARY: A few weeks after the funeral I was in the supermarket, and there was this rag-sheet, that *Enquirer*, with a picture of Elvis in his coffin! I can tell you, I almost passed out! I thought to myself, "Who in the world would have taken a picture of him lying in his coffin and sold it to the *Enquirer*?" That to me was just the final betrayal, a betrayal of the fans who didn't want to remember him like that.

LARRY GELLER: Somebody, some distant relative in the family, had a camera hidden in their jacket that day. Everyone was told, "No one can take in cameras," and a lot of them were confiscated by us as fans lined up for hours to view his body. But that person took a picture, and they took a picture with an inferior camera in low lighting, at an angle that no one would normally use to take a picture. It was the only angle from which the person could sneak the picture. So when the picture came out, it looked like he had a funny little nose. People said, "That wasn't Elvis." Yes, it was. The picture was an air-brushed picture, or a combination of airbrushing and bad angle and bad lighting. That's why people doubted it was him.

DAVID STANLEY: It was reported that in the month following Elvis's death more than a million people visited his tomb. The crowds became a serious problem for the cemetery, and so Vernon made the decision to relocate the bodies of both Elvis and Gladys to the Graceland property. They are there today in the meditation garden, and thousands and thousands of people come by every year to pay their respects.

JOAN DEARY: The public's reaction to the death of Elvis Presley was phenomenal. People must have thought that that would be the end for his records, that RCA would stop pressing them. So they started buying them by the thousands, and RCA had every pressing plant in the country just making Elvis Presley records 'round the clock. It was almost like panic buying. People were desperate to have everything. We just could not keep enough records out there in the stores.

I had to go to England to the RCA London pressing plant, and you couldn't even walk in the halls without tripping over Elvis material—covers, records stacked up. They couldn't handle the demand 'cause they pressed for the whole European market. It wasn't just the United States; demand was worldwide. RCA was shocked. Yes, they were definitely shocked.

DON WARDELL: Trying to determine exactly how many records Elvis has sold is like calculating how many people have seen *Gone With the Wind*; nobody really knows. People will give you all kinds of estimated guesses, but some of them are very bad. They forget that Elvis's sales went through the era of the ten-inch shellac, the 45, the EP, the 8-track tape, the cassette tape, the LP, the CD, the DAT, the VHS, and the laser. Then you have to add "worldwide." I'd like to meet the man who knows exactly how many records Elvis has sold. Nobody knows, but it is safe to say that Elvis Presley has sold in excess of a billion records worldwide. That is absolutely a fact.

:◎:◎:◎:

RONNIE MCDOWELL: As soon as I got back to Nashville after the funeral, I went into the Scorpion Records office. Lee Morgan was in there, and he said, "Ronnie, let's do a tribute to Elvis—a song. Look at these words I've been writing and listen to this melody." Then I said, "Hey, first, you look at these words I've been writing and listen to what I've been working on." And so we did "The King Is Gone." We combined together what we had, and that was the song. We went in the studio that Thursday night, only two days after Elvis's funeral. There were some of Elvis's musicians in town that were supposed to have gone to Portland, Maine, to play [that last concert] with him. A bunch of them came over and played on this session. We picked a studio at random, and unbeknownst to me, it turned out to be Scotty Moore's place. Elvis had helped finance that studio. Is that not an ironic twist?

We rush-released "The King Is Gone" and it was a huge hit. It was my way of paying my respects. It made me feel good to pay tribute to Elvis. He had meant so much to me, and still does.

MARTY LACKER: After Elvis died, I was living in California and was getting ready to move back to Memphis. Priscilla called one day and asked if she could come over to say goodbye. I thought that was very nice of her and said okay. When she arrived, she asked if I would be seeing Vernon when I got back to Memphis. I said yes. She said she was worried about what would happen to the estate in case of Vernon's death, and would I help talk Vernon into naming her [in his will] as an executor of Elvis's estate? I knew then why she'd been so nice to stop by.

ARLENE COGAN: A while after Elvis died, Vernon told me on the phone that he didn't know what he was gonna do about Graceland, being that Elvis was gone and Miss Minnie [Elvis's grandmother] was so old. He said that he didn't really want to do it, but he felt he had no choice but to name Priscilla as an executor of the estate, because if for nothing else, she would oversee Lisa's best interests. Vernon died in June [26], 1979, from heart failure.

DAVID STANLEY: The day before Vernon's funeral, Priscilla came from California, and I saw her at Graceland. I said, "Hello." And she goes, "I'm glad that son of a bitch is dead! That greedy son of a bitch, I'm glad he's dead!"

Dee was crying, and Priscilla said, "I didn't cry that much over Elvis." That's what she said! I just kinda looked at her and thought, "Well, shit!"

Back then she was working on a video of their home movies, and she wanted me to sign a release. She said, "That son of a bitch didn't take care of you boys. *I will.*" So she wanted us to sign this release, and I just wasn't real gung-ho about it. I mean, Vernon's body wasn't even cold yet. I wasn't into talking a lot of business.

Before she left to go back to L.A., I finally signed the agreement, which I never got nothing on. She used the footage, and there's footage of us at Elvis's wedding and playing at Graceland at one of her birthday parties. You might say she screwed us—more ways than one.

BILLY STANLEY: We weren't really that close to Priscilla after she and Elvis separated. When Elvis died, we only saw her at the funeral. She came to Memphis when Vernon died and told us that we needed to sign our movie rights over to her, and stuff like that. She said that if anything came of it she'd make sure we were taken care of. But the story was shown on TV, and we never heard anything from her.

LAMAR FIKE: Priscilla changed. She was in control. [Vernon had named her his successor to oversee the estate.] She knew where she was going. She'd had five years out there [in California] on her own, doing stuff she wanted to do. She came on pretty strong. She was the only one who had the Presley name. She had the daughter. Everything was left to Lisa. It was not left to Priscilla. People have a tendency to forget that. Elvis didn't leave a penny to Priscilla, not a red cent; but she was the mother of his [minor] daughter.

Some people still call her Elvis's widow! Damn! They were divorced for five fucking years when he died! Does that make her a widow? Anyway, she is Lisa's mother. She's blown off all the friends she had down the line, but that's just the way it is. She is rude to everybody; that's her style. When you're a bitch, everyone knows you're a bitch. Not a lot of warmth in Priscilla. She's got more plastic than a Corvette.

:◉:◉:◉:

CHERYLE JOHNSON: The fan clubs ultimately accepted total control by Priscilla and the estate, because they hadn't been given any alternative. If you want to go to Graceland, if you want to participate in the activities there, you do it the way the estate wants to do it.

PRISCILLA PRESLEY: [June 7, 1982] Elvis was very proud of his home, and any time guests would come in he was more than willing to show them through the house. I think he'd be very pleased to know that the house is shown [open to the public] in this way—very happy. There is no kind of construction going up on the grounds that's permanent. If Lisa ever decides she wants to maintain it as her personal home, it's here for her.

You always get criticism when you're dealing with reality and you're dealing with economics. I mean, we have no choice in this matter. People are not always going to think you are doing the right thing. If there is to be a Graceland at all, this is the way we have to do it. Thank god, we're doing it privately; we have control. We're doing it in a way I believe Elvis would love and appreciate. We're maintaining it and preserving it for him.

LAMAR FIKE: I think Priscilla gets 2.5 percent, or something like that, of the estate. I've heard numbers from 2.5 to five. Just figure what that brings in! The estate does very, very well, 'cause it's a well-oiled machine. Lisa's protected, and I think that in itself is very good. None of us ever wanted anything from this.

:◎:◎:◎:

NAOMIA STIERS: I was in Memphis the night the candlelight service was started. By this time, Elvis's body had been re-located to Graceland. It was August 15, 1979. There was a small group of the members of the Elvis Country Fan Club, and they wanted to go inside the gate and have a little prayer and sing or do something in Elvis's memory. They talked to the different Graceland people who let us go in. I guess there were probably about fifteen of us that first year. We lit our candles, and we sat in a little circle by the gate and said a prayer. Now that's the way that the candlelight service started. The next year we wanted to do it again, and each year it just kept getting bigger and bigger. It has become like a tradition. Each year on the anniversary of his death, fifteen to twenty thousand people from all over the world come to pay their respects. When the gates open, they light their candles and slowly walk up the hill single-file to the gravesite, where they say a little prayer. It is a sad and touching time.

JANELLE MCCOMB: I asked him one time, "Elvis, if you were ever to have anything done in your honor or your memory, what would you like?" He said, "I would like a chapel so my fans would have a place to meditate." I thought it was a beautiful idea.

After Elvis died, a foundation was formed [in Tupelo] to actually build a chapel close to the little house where he was born. They asked me to head the fund-raising effort. I really wasn't up to it, so I drove up to Graceland. Vernon was still alive at that time. He was sitting in the house, and I said, "Vernon, I just don't believe I can handle this project. I'm in the middle years of my life, and just when I'm able to enjoy life . . ." He started crying. "But you knew what my boy wanted." I took a deep breath and thought, "Well, if it's meant to be . . ." My daddy always said to me, "Hands were not made to dangle or to just fit in your pockets."

The first donations, the seed money, came from fans in Tupelo. Then I started out on a quest that carried me to seven foreign countries (places where I couldn't even speak the language) to tell people about it. We got donations from Belgium, Holland, France, and England, and it turned out to be a very beautiful project, with the help of a lot of people. Rick Nelson even did a benefit for us.

You know, I never let [Elvis and Vernon] down in life, and I had no intention of letting them down in death. But building a chapel in a small town in Mississippi, I sometimes felt like the Flying Nun trying to quarterback for Notre Dame. It was almost impossible. Yet the doors opened [August 19, 1979]. People came. We did it. It was probably the only thing I ever heard Elvis ask for in his life.

CHERYLE JOHNSON: After a year of planning, fans and fan club presidents from literally all over the world met in Memphis [August 17, 1980] to discuss what kind of tribute we would do for Elvis. George Klein was there and Eddie Fadal and Charlie Hodge, and that hairdresser [Larry Geller]—I mean, what a dingbat! I had written to them and asked them to come and talk about what they felt would be a good memorial to Elvis.

We all had this big meeting and decided we wanted to form some kind of an organization that would do positive things for Elvis because it was a huge waste of money just sending flowers to Graceland year after year. Larry Geller said that he had seen Elvis heal people, and that kind of power didn't end after death. He suggested building some kind of a healing center (he said he could get Elvis's body!). I mean really! Not to be disrespectful, but we were all: "Well, why didn't he heal himself?" Geller said he was a teacher, and he and Elvis had read about all of these different religions, and he wanted to minister with that.

Well, about that time the meeting just came apart! Other people like Eddie Fadal stood up and said Elvis would never want anything like that. That was just a crazy idea. Eddie said he didn't think that Elvis had any special healing powers. So there was a lot of turmoil.

Then a representative from the city of Memphis came in—Wyatt Chandler—and he said what he would like to see us do was to have the fans and the city take over Graceland and open it up to the public. Well, it was too soon after Elvis had died to bring up something like that. The fans in the room went ballistic! They said, "You can't take Elvis's house! That's a shrine to Elvis! Nobody should be in that house!" I mean, everyone was ready to explode. I thought we were going to have to get security to get that man out of the room because the fans just came apart. We had people standing up and screaming and crying, "You can't take Elvis's house!"

By then Geller had been booed down. He was trying to build a constituency, but nobody was going for it.

Finally we started talking about forming a foundation to do good works. That part went really well. The next day, I was introduced to Harold Stribeck [a Memphis attorney]. Stribeck said that he was really an Elvis Presley fan and that he would like to see a foundation that worked to support charities in Memphis. As things progressed, we established the

Worldwide Federation of Elvis Presley Fan Clubs to raise money for the foundation [the Elvis Presley International Memorial Foundation]. Harold helped us charter it; we got nonprofit status [from the state of Tennessee], and we were rolling along pretty well. I went to the county commissioners, and we talked them into naming the new trauma center at the City of Memphis Hospital after Elvis. We made a commitment to do fund-raising for it. But then . . .

Things changed at Graceland. Vernon had died and Priscilla had been named in Vernon's will to be one of the successor coexecutors of the estate. The coexecutors began trying to prevent people from using Elvis's name. The estate was trying to control the money and the licensing of all souvenirs. The federation got a letter saying we could no longer use Elvis's name without paying a licensing fee to Graceland—which was ridiculous because we already had been given permission by the state of Tennessee. We were already chartered.

Well, that was the beginning of the end. We needed to initiate a lawsuit [to prove our right to continue the foundation], but we had no money to finance it. We held a banquet and tried to raise funds, but we didn't make any money on that. We didn't have the necessary monies for the legal fees, so the federation was dissolved.

:◎:◎:◎:

DON WARDELL: People still make their living off Elvis's memory, people have their self-esteem and their wish fulfillment granted through it.

FARON YOUNG: We used to go out there to Parker's little place in Madison, [Tennessee]. He was going to make a fucking museum out of it last time I was over there visiting him. He paved the whole yard and all that shit. I said, "You're gonna make a Presley museum?" He said, "Hell no, it's gonna be a Colonel Tom Parker museum!" I said, "Who the hell cares about Tom Parker?"

JOAN DEARY: In a lot of the books written about Elvis, people are trying to magnify their own importance in Elvis's life—magnify it far beyond what it actually was. But the fans can always spot a phony. A lot of fans know more about Elvis than the writers of some of these books. You can't go out and mix with his fans unless you really know what you're talking about.

LARRY GELLER: [The late] Albert Goldman's biography, *Elvis*, was ludicrous. Here he spends a whole chapter on me, the "Swami"—and never once interviewed me. He said I pasted Elvis's sideburns on at the funeral—and this, that, and the other—and none of it was true.

:◉:◉:◉:

Cheryle Johnson: There are a certain number of fans who don't even believe Elvis is dead. After we started the foundation, I got a call at my job from somebody in Illinois, and they told me that they had a tape they wanted me to hear that proved Elvis was not dead. So I said, "Well, play me the tape. I'd love to hear it." So they played me the tape, and, you know, on the phone, it did sound a lot like Elvis; there's no doubt about it, and a song on the tape was new. (It was someone who sounded like Elvis singing Eddie Rabbitt's song "I Love a Rainy Night.") Some fans said, "Well, look, it's Elvis and he's singing this new song. He must be alive!"

That was something the foundation had a hard time overcoming, a certain element of fans honestly didn't believe Elvis had died—especially after a cover story "Elvis Is Alive" appeared in the *National Examiner* [October 4, 1988].

ALAN FORTAS: If you'll notice, there were never many books written or any talk ever spoken about Elvis's private life until just before he passed away. [*Elvis: What Happened?* reached bookstores after Elvis died.] There was almost never anything derogatory said about Elvis. We felt his entourage was a sacred group, and that nobody in it would ever talk about his private life, especially to the press.

DAVID STANLEY: I didn't start discussing Elvis's life until 1990 when I told Albert Goldman that I thought Elvis committed suicide [*Life* Magazine, June 1990]. Up until then my loyalty was so strong that I said, "There's no way that Elvis would take himself out. Elvis did a little bit of drugs, here and there, but . . ." Then I began to realize if people are going to look at this guy as a human being, we've got to talk about what really happened.

When I walked into Elvis's bathroom, they were about to roll him over. There were the empty attacks [envelopes that had contained medication] laying around—attack one, two, and three. Now Elvis would take this medication starting around 2:00 A.M. He'd take the first around two, another one around four-thirty or five, and another around eight in the morning. Elvis played racquetball that night. He didn't take an attack before he played racquetball because he couldn't have even stood up. So, obviously, he hadn't taken any drugs. He got the attacks right on schedule. Rick [Stanley, who was the bodyguard on duty the day Elvis died] took a couple up, and Delta [Biggs, Elvis's aunt] took another load up, and so he got them all. Elvis didn't go to his room—it's documented that he didn't go to his room—'til around 7:00 or 7:30 A.M. Now usually Elvis ate breakfast, but that day he ate no breakfast. Around eight or nine was the last conversation he had with people downstairs: "I'm just kicking back."

The next thing we know, we find Elvis is dead. Now, when I walk in, I see the three empty attacks, and I see the syringes laying around his body. It was obvious to me Elvis took them. Now it's one thing to take these pills through an eight-hour span, but if Elvis retired at seven-thirty or eight in the morning, and they found him dead around one in the afternoon [It is reported that the ambulance was called at 2:33 P.M.], somewhere between eight and noon he took the medication, 'cause he had been dead for a couple of hours. So if you take all three attacks (that's thirty-three pills and nine shots of Demerol) at one time, you're gonna die.

JO ALDEN: Ginger saw Elvis take the medication each time it was brought up, so he didn't take it all at one time.

DR. GEORGE NICHOPOULOS: Elvis got the packs the night before he died. The packs were something that were made up by me, or me and the nurse, and this was a known quantity of something. He had to take what was in the pack; he couldn't deviate from that. These packs weren't loaded with all kinds of drugs. They were either something for sleep or something for his colon, or whatever—his blood pressure. They weren't happy pills.

DAVID STANLEY: I was on a [television talk] show [discussing whether there was a cover-up regarding Elvis's death]. This guy said, "Well, wasn't that obstructing justice? Why didn't you tell [what you saw] to the authorities?" They didn't ask; that's why I didn't tell them. I picked up. There was a clean-up. That room was completely scraped before any authority walked in there, and I was doing my small part by just picking stuff up. Even after I did that, there was much more of a clean-up before the authorities actually came in and investigated what was going on. My mind was thinking "TCB, take care of business, take care of business."

BILLY SMITH: There was no such thing as a suicide note. If Elvis killed himself, he did it out of pure mistake, because when you deal with that many drugs there's always that possibility. But it never entered his mind to commit suicide. In Elvis's own words: "That is a cheap cop-out to life." So, you know, that was just not his way, or his way of thinking.

Sonny West: Elvis Presley would never commit suicide in a bathroom! If he was going to commit suicide, he would have looked sharp. He would have died in his bed. He would have laid there and gone to sleep with whatever he wanted to kill himself with.

Bill E. Burk: No! There was no way possible that Elvis Presley would have committed suicide that morning and let Lisa Marie be a witness to that! He would never have done that to Lisa.

:◎:◎:◎:

Dr. George Nichopoulos: I was in on some of the autopsy findings initially, but for some reason Elvis's father said that he didn't want anybody but himself to have a full report of the autopsy. I got bits and pieces but never really knew what was going on completely.

Cheryle Johnson: According to a lot of different people, especially the media, there was this big cover-up conspiracy to hide the "real" cause of Elvis's death. It was first reported that he had had a heart attack.

Dr. George Nichopoulos: After the autopsy [conducted at Baptist Hospital with Nichopoulos present] the only thing we could find of any significance was hardening of one of the heart vessels. We felt that this was the most likely thing [causing the arrhythmia], especially after he'd been exercising early that morning, playing racquetball. They found that Elvis had an enlarged heart, and the risk factors were that he had hypertension, and really that is all. If someone has a heart attack, the pathologist specifically says that.

Dr. Kevin S. Merigian: A heart attack is where something goes wrong with the blood vessels that nourish the heart with oxygen while it is beating. Your heart is really beating; it's a high-metabolic organ. It's really moving; and all of a sudden it gets no oxygen. Boom. You kill it. That's one way. Or, you can get a blood clot that forms in there when there is a lot of plaque from coronary artery disease, or arteriosclerosis. When there is a lot of plaque formation [in the arteries leading to your heart], the blood can't get through, and finally it forms a clot. Well, [Elvis] didn't have any clot in his heart.

He didn't have a heart attack. More than likely, what he had was a cardiac arrhythmia, which means his heart didn't beat right. The electric activity was jumbled; it just did not make his heart pump.

DR. DAN BROOKOFF: Elvis died suddenly. There is a limited number of things that can kill you suddenly, like a stroke (which he did not have). Cardiac arrhythmia could have done it.

DR. JERRY T. FRANCISCO: The cause of death *was* cardiac arrhythmia.

DR. KEVIN S. MERIGIAN: Just looking at the [toxicology] report from Bio-Science Laboratories [in Van Nuys, California], if Dr. Francisco said that Elvis died of a cardiac arrhythmia, he's right on. I don't think he's lying. I don't think he's covering anything up.

DR. GEORGE NICHOPOULOS: There were two conclusions as to the cause of death: One probability was that this was a cardiac problem, not a drug problem. Then one pathologist at one hospital thought Elvis's death was due to polypharmacy. The coroner, who had the benefit of watching the autopsy and had gotten all the toxicology reports, still felt that none of the drug levels were high enough to contribute to Elvis's death.

DR. KEVIN S. MERIGIAN: It couldn't have been an overdose. None of the drugs [found in Elvis's system] are associated with arrhythmia or causing the heart to fail—none of these.

DR. DAN BROOKOFF: If Elvis [purposely or otherwise had taken] a massive overdose of sedating drugs, which there doesn't seem to be any evidence of [from Bio-Science findings released in October 1977], he would have gone to sleep. He would have been in a dense coma for hours and hours—one that they could have reversed, one that they could have supported him on—and he would have come out of it. Elvis seems to have had a sudden event.

Elvis did not have enough drugs in him to make him sleep. The drug overdose theory just doesn't fit at all. Of people who die of drug overdoses, there are two types. Some are injecting drugs, and they die very suddenly, usually because they are injecting something that contains foreign material or is contaminated. Some people take too many tranquilizers, and it takes hours and hours to die. They are not awake; they are in a deep coma.

Dr. Kevin S. Merigian: You have a dead person, you have this finite set of data; that's all you have. You [contact] a bunch of experts and you say, "Now, what do you think happened?"

If you ask a toxicologist, he's going to say [Elvis] died of an overdose. If you ask people that just look at specimens from autopsies, they're going to think it's a morbidity [death] from an overdose; but this is *not* a morbidity from an overdose. I can tell you that I disagree totally with the Bio-Science report conclusion. I don't know who their consultants were, but if [Elvis] was alert or awake when this happened [judging from the position of his body], it could not have been an overdose from these drugs. It's just that straightforward. We're not talking about a case in which somebody was found down in coma and then stopped breathing.

The reality is, yes, there were a lot of drugs [in Elvis's system]; but you're looking at very minimal concentrations of each of these drugs. None of these drugs in and of or by itself would have caused a problem.

[The Bio-Science Laboratories report says:] "Of particular note is the combination of codeine, ethchlorvynol, and barbiturates detected in body fluids and tissue. The levels in the body fluids and tissues exceed some other known identifiable multiple drug overdose cases where codeine has been implicated." I disagree with that. This death is not the result of a multiple drug ingestion. That's quite frankly silly. It's conjecture and it's totally without foundation.

Again, I can't tell you what happened—but most people who [actually] die of these kinds of overdoses literally die when they're in a coma and they stop breathing. This is not the scenario of a conscious person walking around and then all of a sudden having a cardiac death episode from these kinds of drugs in his system.

Now, if the person had cocaine, if he had amphetamines, if he had mostly stimulants in his system, then one would make the case that he had a cardiac arrhythmia from those stimulants; but these drugs [found in Elvis's system] are all downers: they will slow your heart, they keep your blood pressure fairly maintained at a low level, make you very sleepy, very tired—and then you die in a coma of a respiratory arrest.

The technology of state-of-the-art forensic medicine is such that they can't always tell you why people die. There are many, many cases that are signed out as unknown. Elvis would be a classic case. They found some drugs in his system, but we knew he was on these drugs; however, there was no sign that he really overdosed on them.

So what if there is polypharmacy? Doctors prescribe lots of drugs to people all the time. The average elderly person is on seven drugs at a time, and that is polypharmacy. If someone is maintained at a therapeutic level on those, the toxicities really don't interact. Elvis's body contained some drugs that could have interacted, but even if you added them together, they would not have amounted to a high dose of anything. Furthermore, most of these drugs are "cross-tolerant," which means, your body does not perceive any of them in a category that is any more severe than the other; so they are all acting as the same type of drug.

DR. DAN BROOKOFF: The report says Elvis had some phenobarbital [in his body]. I'm sure that it comes from one of the bowel drugs he was taking: Donnatal, which is a common little-old-ladies' drug that has phenobarbital in it. People are not abusing that as a sedative; they are trying to calm down their bowels.

DR. KEVIN S. MERIGIAN: Sedation means to take someone who is in a very anxious state and bring their level of anxiety down to where they can function in a normal way, and that's what those profiles of drugs [in Elvis's body at time of death] at those levels would imply: that Elvis was being sedated.

DR. DAN BROOKOFF: There are other drugs Elvis was on that could make him a center for other problems. He was on either steroids or ACTH for his bowel problems. Elvis had colitis—they found at his autopsy what they call megacolon [enlarged colon].

DR. KEVIN S. MERIGIAN: [The autopsy reports that] "Elvis had taken mass amounts of cortisone in Las Vegas which distended his colon."

DR. GEORGE NICHOPOULOS: Elvis did have an enlarged colon, which in some cases may be two, three, four times the normal-size colon. You can have this for legitimate reasons; there are not enough nerve endings to cause stimulation and get the colon to contract down and do its job.

I think Dan Warlick [investigator for the Shelby County Medical Examiner's Office] felt like Elvis had had some kind of cardiac event because Elvis was found far enough away from the toilet that he did not just sit down on the toilet and fall over. He had carpet material on his tongue—in his mouth. Elvis had a seizure or something, and he had bitten his tongue. There was blood.

DR. KEVIN S. MERIGIAN: It's plausible that Elvis was sitting on the toilet and straining to have a bowel movement. Then all of a sudden, he had a cardiac event, stood up, grabbed his chest, and hit the floor. That is a whole lot more plausible than him dying from a [drug overdose]. When you strain your body and your bowels, that puts a real pressure on your heart.

DR. DAN BROOKOFF: When you strain—even if you were just straining down real hard—you could slow your heart down, and sometimes you can have what is called an "escape rhythm" from that. That can happen especially if you are on medications like steroids or things like that, if you are dehydrated (Elvis had been fasting), if you are kind of chemically unbalanced; usually you have some kind of underlying disease before that happens. They did not find any evidence of [severe] heart disease.

DR. KEVIN S. MERIGIAN: Now, if Elvis had had a cardiac arrhythmia and then lost blood pressure, that is very classic for having a seizure. He may have stood up, clutched his chest or something, and then fallen over. That is a sudden cardiac death episode.

[Elvis's death] is not a drug overdose from any of these drugs. I'll testify to that in any court. The reality is, you cannot use only laboratory information; you have to get the clinical picture. He just would not have had a seizure from any of the medicines in his system.

There is no way for a coroner to tell you exactly what happened. But just reading this [Bio-Science Laboratories] report, with that limited information, you cannot come to the conclusion that he died of an overdose. Believe me, I have seen a lot more drugs [than that] in a lot of people who have not died.

:◎:◎:◎:

CHERYLE JOHNSON: Another popular theory was that Elvis died from an allergic reaction to codeine—that he mistook codeine for the Dilaudid that Dr. Nick had prescribed. However, Elvis must not have taken the Dilaudid, because it wasn't listed in the toxicology report. So, some people wondered if codeine shock was the cause.

Dr. Kevin S. Merigian: Elvis did not have anaphylactic shock [allergic shock reaction]. This occurs when people get something like a bee sting, and they are dead within minutes. They get real tight, they might have massive hives, they can't breathe, their throat swells up, their blood pressure goes out, and they die. It is a tremendous histamine release that kills them. Codeine is far from causing something like that; it is so low on the list it is absolutely preposterous.

Dr. Forest Tennant, Jr.: When you die of an overdose from codeine, your lungs fill up with fluid. Elvis did not have that.

Dr. Jerry T. Francisco: The lungs were clear.

Dr. Kevin S. Merigian: Codeine would only be significant if all the drugs [in the body] were at toxic levels. It would be one thing to say that they found a very high level of codeine in his blood and in his liver, but of all the drugs they are talking about, [from the autopsy] they found very little in his liver.

The Bio-Science report shows codeine at 1.08 MCG/ML in the serum; he had a 1.6 MCG/GM in the liver and 2.3 MCG/GM in the kidney. An average codeine level in someone who is thought to have had a fatal codeine overdose would be 2.8 MCG/ML, and *his* level was only 1.08 MCG/ML; so literally that's not a fatal codeine overdose. [In an overdose] the liver is about 6.8 MCG/GM, and his liver was 1.6 MCG/GM. So, you can see that there was not a huge dose of the drug [codeine] in his system. Now, he also has Morphine, .03 MCG/ML in the serum, .04 MCG/GM in the liver, and .04 MCG/GM in the kidney. What that's telling you is that he probably took codeine, because codeine metabolizes to Morphine.

Elvis may have taken the Valium [listed in the report] twelve hours prior to when this [sample] was procured.... All that's remaining is metabolite, and there's not a lot here, actually. That's what's very curious about the whole thing. Usually if somebody has a high dose of [Valium] diazepam in their blood, then they are considered dead. When I say high we're looking at 30 MCG/ML; his is .01 MCG/ML, so it's very, very small in comparison. It's like 1/600th of what it should be for an overdose.

[The report also shows] ethchlorvynol, which is a sedative/hypnotic, very common in the fifties and the sixties. And looking at the averages, the blood concentration in a fatal ethchlorvynol case would be roughly around 84 MCG/ML. Elvis has got 7.5 MCG/ML, so he's not even at 1/10th of what a fatal concentration would be.

Amobarbital is reported. It is a short-acting barbiturate, again usually used as a sedative/hypnotic or sleeper. In fatal cases on average you're looking at blood levels probably around 100 MCG/ML, and he's got 11. Here again he's only got one tenth of what one would consider to be a high dose.

Phenobarbital is reported at 5 MCG/ML; that's not even in the therapeutic range. That probably wouldn't even make you sleepy.

As far as Methaqualone (quaalude is the common term) is concerned, a fatal case [might be] 6.4 MCG/ML; well, Elvis has a 6.0 MCG/ML, so that may be consistent. However, his liver was positive and his kidney was positive, and you would have thought there would be very measurable levels. In a fatal textbook case, the person's blood was 6.4 MCG/ML, but their liver was 58 MCG/ML, so the liver [concentration] was ten times higher than the blood. We don't have that listed here. They did not quantitate that. That means to me that Elvis did not have a high dose that went into his system and caused a death.

Certainly the Demerol was found in the liver and in the kidney, but nothing measured in the blood or in the serum. Then he's got the phenyltoloxamine (these are a lot of drugs) in his serum and in his blood; some were present in his urine. But the reality is I don't see anything here, with the exception of the quaaludes, that could even be implicated in some kind of fatality, that would suggest he just overdosed, stopped breathing.

The thing that you have to realize is that the way you die from the drugs listed in the report is that you go to sleep and stop breathing. That's the only thing.

:◉:◉:◉:

CHERYLE JOHNSON: At the end of September 1981, the Tennessee State Board of Medical Examiners brought Dr. Nick [Nichopoulos] to trial, charging that he had overprescribed painkillers and other drugs to Elvis [and other patients]. The implication was that Elvis might have died from polypharmacy, overdosed on drugs possibly prescribed by Dr. Nick. It was a full-blown jury trial and very dramatic. However, [on November 4] the jury handed down a "not guilty" verdict on all charges.

DR. KEVIN S. MERIGIAN: If they had brought me up at the trial, I would just have said there are not enough drugs in this man's system—or a clinical scenario that anyone has told me about—that would be consistent with his dying a death related to any of these drugs [in the Bio-Science report]. There is not a lot of codeine there at all. All this has nothing to do with his death. I mean, he just has some drugs in his system; so what?

So, the reality is, if Elvis Presley had been brought in literally in a full cardiac arrest, there's nothing they could have given him to wake him up and make him go on his jolly way, because there was nothing in here [the toxicology report] that needed an antidote. Nothing in here even comes close to being enough to cause his death.

DR. DAN BROOKOFF: A lot of things can happen in the end. The question is what kicked it off in the beginning. For some people that have a cardiac problem and are straining real hard with stool, that can slow their heart down so much that they can develop an arrhythmia.

There are so many causes of sudden death. Elvis was awake and then he died. That's not a drug overdose death.

DR. KEVIN S. MERIGIAN: You can only conclude that he died a mysterious death, probably related to his heart. Since he did not have any seizure history in his life, it was probably a sudden cardiac arrhythmia.

I think for this guy—it may sound absolutely "hokey"—it was just his time. However you look at it, divine intervention, the Lord, or the forces of nature, it was just his time; and it wasn't a result of drugs. His heart, and he, perished.

:◎:◎:◎:

LINDA THOMPSON: I guess that whatever could have been said about Elvis, whatever conjecture could have been made, whatever hypothesis—it's all been said, and it's all been done. There's not a lot I could say that could dispel any myths or notions that people have about him. I can only reiterate the positive, and that would be that he was an incredibly generous human being, very loyal person, very loyal friend, very loving man, very funny; he loved to laugh, loved life, loved living, loved people—and there was the down side, too. There was the self-destructive side, the bad temper, self-absorbed, and all the things that come with an ego of that magnitude; but there were so many wonderful things about Elvis that life with him was never dull.

Those Who Knew Him Best

GINGER ALDEN dated Elvis as his steady girlfriend from November 1976 until his death on August 16, 1977.

JO ALDEN is the mother of Ginger Alden, Elvis's last girlfriend. Jo accompanied Elvis and Ginger to numerous shows during the last eight months of Elvis's life.

STEVE ALLEN was the host of a popular early TV show [*The Steve Allen Show*]. He gave Elvis valuable public exposure [July 1, 1956].

MAE BOREN AXTON is a multitalented lady who commands great respect in Nashville. She gave early concert exposure to Elvis in Florida and cowrote his first huge hit, "Heartbreak Hotel." They remained friends for the rest of his life.

DOTTY AYERS (BOOTH) earned her introduction to Elvis after writing letters to Gladys in support of the young rocker in the early years when he was being panned by the press.

JERRY BAXTER was one of Memphis's top boppers, whom Elvis loved to watch dance. He was a member of Elvis's touch football team during the sixties.

PRISCILLA BEAULIEU (PRESLEY) was fourteen years old when she met the singer-soldier in Germany, where her stepfather, an Army officer, was stationed. Two years later Priscilla arrived in Memphis to complete her senior year in high school. She became Elvis's bride in May of 1968, and gave birth to their daughter, Lisa Marie, nine months later. Priscilla separated from Elvis and was later divorced by him in 1973.

ELOIS BEDFORD (SANDEFUR) was Elvis's very first girlfriend. They were sweethearts from second to fifth grade.

BILL BELEW is the costume designer who developed many of Elvis Presley's best known outfits—the jumpsuits, the capes, the belts. Just before Elvis's death, Bill and the singer made plans for a "new look"—a laser-equipped costume—for Elvis to wear in his much-discussed future tour of Europe.

CLINT BLACK is a much-acclaimed country music songwriter and recording artist.

JAMES BLACKWOOD, a member of the Blackwood Brothers gospel group, met Elvis when he attended the First Assembly of God church in south Memphis. James sang at the funerals of both Gladys and Elvis.

EDDIE BOND was a popular country music band leader and one of the city's top disc jockeys in the fifties.

OWEN BRADLEY is one of the founding fathers of Nashville's music industry. A chance meeting between Owen and Colonel Tom Parker at a Florida racetrack almost landed Elvis on Decca Records instead of RCA.

DAVID BRIGGS, a respected session keyboardist, played piano and organ in the Elvis stage show and on many studio sessions beginning in 1970. He dated Linda Thompson briefly after she parted ways with Elvis.

DR. DAN BROOKOFF is associate director of medical education at Methodist Hospital in Memphis.

BILL BROWDER—See T. G. Sheppard.

TONY BROWN is one of the most successful record producers in Nashville (Reba McEntire, Vince Gill, etc.). He became associated with Elvis through the group Voice and moved up into the full orchestra when pianist Glen D. Hardin quit.

BILL E. BURK was an entertainment columnist for the *Memphis Press-Scimitar* who obtained many exclusive interviews with Elvis, Vernon, and Priscilla. Bill has written and published several books about the king.

PAUL BURLISON was an electrician at Crown Electric when Elvis started working there as an apprentice. He is the now legendary guitarist of the Rock 'N Roll Trio.

JAMES BURTON was first seen by Elvis in his role as the guitarist for Rick Nelson's band in the TV series *The Adventures of Ozzie & Harriet*. Elvis hired him in 1969 for his Las Vegas opening. James played lead guitar for Elvis from 1970 until his final concert.

JOHN CALLENDER was a squad leader in Germany during Elvis's Army days. Elvis sometimes drove a jeep for him.

JOHNNY CASH came out of rural Arkansas to find tremendous success first on Sun Records and later on the Columbia label. He often toured with Elvis in the early years.

RUSSELL CHEST became an Elvis Presley fan when his dad, who worked in record distribution in Nashville, brought home a handful of Elvis 45s. On the evening before Elvis's funeral, "Rusty" drove to Memphis (with Brenda Fielder) to pay his respects.

ODELL CLARK was Elvis's neighbor and childhood playmate when they both lived on Kelly Street in East Tupelo. He retired as a captain from the Tupelo Police Department.

JACK CLEMENT got his first experience in the record business by working for Sam Phillips in the heyday of Sun. One night he flipped on the control room tape recorder and captured the impromptu Million Dollar Quartet (Elvis, Carl Perkins, Jerry Lee Lewis, and Johnny Cash) for posterity.

MARIAN COCKE met Elvis in 1975 during his stay at Baptist Hospital, Memphis. They became good friends, and Marian remained one of his personal nurses until the end of his life.

BETTY COCKERELL was a Presley fan from the instant she heard Elvis's early RCA recordings. Never wavering, she drove to Graceland to pay her last respects to the star that hot August day in 1972.

ARLENE COGAN (BRADLEY) met Elvis at a press conference in Chicago when she was fourteen and became a member of his "gang." She palled around with him for close to five years. Arlene kept in touch with Elvis through the years and traveled with Rose Clayton to all but the last concert on his final tour.

CHARLES CROSBY was one of two paramedics who answered the distress call from 3764 Elvis Presley Boulevard, on August 16, 1977.

JEAN CROWE, wife of Jim Crowe, was still a high school student when she and Jim spotted Elvis's entourage one night and followed the group to the Memphian theater. After the movie, they were invited to Graceland.

JIM CROWE, Jean Crowe's husband, became one of the regular Graceland guys and regularly played touch football on Elvis's team, Elvis Presley Enterprises.

T. TOMMY CUTRER was one of the earliest disc jockeys to play a record by Elvis Presley. He now laughingly admits to one of the biggest mistakes of his life: turning down a chance to manage the fledgling star.

MAC DAVIS first saw Elvis at a promotional appearance in Lubbock, Texas, in 1955. Mac penned Presley's hits: "Memories," "In the Ghetto," and "Don't Cry, Daddy."

JOAN DEARY, now retired, had a lengthy career with RCA Records, first as a secretary, then as an assistant to producer Steve Sholes, and later as an executive in the label's Artist and Repertory department. She was one of the key behind-the-scenes individuals who prepared Elvis's albums for release and actually produced many later projects.

BILL DENNY, a successful Nashville businessman, is the son of the late John Denny, the man often quoted (or misquoted) as having told young Elvis, after his first Grand Ole Opry appearance, that he should go back to truck driving.

TROY DERAMUS is a Louisiana musician who watched a young Elvis Presley completely captivate the Louisiana Hayride audience.

LITTLE JIMMY DICKENS, a star of the Grand Ole Opry, Nashville, witnessed the first and only appearance of Elvis Presley on the show.

DINAH DODD (MCINTURF), as a young girl, twice met Elvis as his train traveled through her hometown. She still has the souvenirs.

PAUL DOUGHER was a neighbor and close friend of young Elvis when they lived at Lauderdale Courts. He remained a friend for life.

RICHARD EGAN received top billing over Debra Paget and newcomer Elvis Presley in the 1956 Twentieth Century-Fox movie *Love Me Tender.*

JOE ESPOSITO served in the Army with Elvis and then went to work for him. When Elvis began touring in 1970, Joe became his trusty road manager. Joe was among those who tried to revive Elvis when he was found on his bathroom floor, shortly before Elvis was pronounced dead.

EDDIE FADAL was a Texas disc jockey when up-and-coming singer Elvis Presley walked into the radio station where he worked in 1955. They remained close friends throughout Elvis's life. In the spring of 1994, on the day before he passed away, Eddie called the writers of this book to say that he was mailing them some of his treasured photographs of Elvis and hoped they could publish them.

LAVERNE FARRAR (CLAYTON), the first girl to be included in Elvis's circle of friends, was a playmate in E's neighborhood from "as far back as Elvis goes." Laverne remembers Elvis as a person with "a tender heart" who never forgot his friends.

ROBERT "FERGY" FERGUSON, an Elvis policeman-buddy, first saw Elvis perform at the Eagle's Nest in 1954 and admits he didn't like him "because Elvis was cooler than I was."

ANITA FIELDER claims she became an Elvis fan because her daughter Brenda "fell madly in love with him" when she was only four years old. A fan 'til the end, Anita journeyed to Memphis to pay her respects following Elvis's death.

BRENDA FIELDER admits she liked to tap dance to the rockin' rhythms of the Hillbilly Cat when she was just a kid. When Elvis died, she drove to Memphis with her boyfriend, Russell Chest, to pay her respects and to photograph the crowds.

LAMAR FIKE was a close friend and confidant of the king. Legend has it that Lamar met Elvis by crawling through the back window at the young star's Audubon house, but Lamar claims he first met Elvis at Sun Records. He should know. He was a friend for the rest of Elvis's life and worked for him in varying capacities.

D. J. Fontana is one of Nashville's most acclaimed studio musicians. Hired from the Louisiana Hayride to round out Elvis's first road band, he traveled with the artist from coast to coast in the early years. D. J. played drums on all the early Elvis Presley recordings and movie soundtracks.

Buzzy Forbes, a neighbor and friend of Elvis's from the Lauderdale Court days, remained his friend throughout Elvis's life.

Frances Forbes (Lively) met Elvis while hanging out at the gates to his home on Audubon Drive when she was fourteen. She was a member of his "gang" for more than five years.

Alan Fortas was a member of the so-called Memphis Mafia and worked for Elvis in various capacities from 1960 on. Alan succumbed to cancer only a few weeks after being interviewed by Dick Heard for this book.

Dr. Jerry T. Francisco is the Shelby County Medical Examiner who determined that Elvis died from cardiac arrhythmia. He has been suspected by the media and some Memphis politicians of down-playing the involvement of drugs in Elvis's death. As this book goes to press, a Miami pathologist, hired by the Tennessee Registrar of Vital Records, is reexamining the unpublished autopsy report filed by Francisco, plus samples of specimens from Elvis's autopsy. These specimens have been stored at the Baptist Memorial Hospital since Elvis's death.

Dr. E. O. Franklin, a veterinarian, arrived at Graceland in the early sixties to care for the menagerie belonging to Elvis. Doc Franklin helped buy, care for, and later sell much of the livestock on Elvis's Circle G ranch.

Tillman Franks is a well-known country music promoter and manager of talent. Tillman helped gain early concert exposure for young Elvis by booking him on shows in the Ark-La-Tex area.

Fred Fredrick met Elvis in wood shop class at Humes High School. He later became a police officer. Fred has donated much of his time to helping Graceland restore Elvis's vehicles and cataloging warehouses full of items belonging to Elvis. He says Elvis "never threw anything away."

BILL GALLAGHER, a longtime big-league record executive, attempted to negotiate with Tom Parker for Presley's contract, but his company, Columbia Records, was beat out by an offer from RCA.

LARRY GELLER, a hair stylist, began working for Elvis in 1964. Larry became known as Elvis's "guru" because of his knowledge of the occult and his influence on Elvis.

KEITH GIBSON served with Elvis in the Army and they became buddies. He claims Elvis's so-called desire for privacy was sometimes overshadowed by his desire to be recognized.

BARBARA GLIDEWELL gained an introduction to Elvis after being hit on the head at a concert. Gladys invited Barbara to visit their home on Audubon Drive, and she soon became a "regular."

DR. DURWOOD GRUBBS, RPH, has been a practicing pharmacist in Memphis for more than forty years.

MACK GURLEY picked up Elvis in 1950 while he was hitchhiking and gave him a ride home. Remaining friends through the years, Mack was one of Elvis's guests at the king's final Las Vegas engagement in December 1976.

GUY HARRIS was a neighbor and playmate of young Elvis in East Tupelo even before they started elementary school. Guy was a sergeant with the Tupelo Police Department when Elvis died.

ED HART met Elvis in Germany. Then a first lieutenant, this West Point graduate ultimately retired as a full colonel.

BECKY HARTLEY (YANCEY) gained access to Elvis through a party at Graceland, and Elvis hired her as a secretary for his office behind the mansion. She often palled around with Priscilla.

LOWELL HAYS is the Memphis jeweler whom Elvis hired to make the original TCB jewelry from 1970 to 1977. He flew with Elvis to most of the king's concerts during that period.

CHARLIE HODGE served in the Army with Elvis and later became his rhythm guitar player. He lived at Graceland for many years.

CHARLES HOLMES was an Army draftee from Memphis, who trained at Fort Hood, Texas, and was assigned to the Third Armored Division in Germany. On returning to Memphis, Holmes worked as a reporter for the *Commercial Appeal*.

WANDA JACKSON was already signed to a recording contract when, as a young girl, she toured the Southwest with Elvis Presley. Offstage, they dated and Elvis gave her a ring—as was his custom with most young ladies he truly liked.

WAYNE JACKSON was the trumpet player Elvis hired for his sessions at American Studio in 1969 and at Stax in 1973. He is now a member of the world-famous Memphis Horns.

FELTON JARVIS succeeded Chet Atkins as Elvis's record producer at RCA, Nashville, in 1964. He later went to work for Elvis as an independent producer and became one of E's closest friends. Rose Clayton often interviewed Felton about Elvis. Their final interview occurred in 1980, a few days before Felton's fatal stroke.

MARY JARVIS was the secretary to Chet Atkins at RCA Records in Nashville when he produced Elvis. She later became the wife of Felton Jarvis.

WAYLON JENNINGS, now a major country recording artist in his own right, remembers the favorable, lasting impression Elvis's first records made on him.

CHERYLE JOHNSON (SMITH) joined an Elvis fan club when she was only nine years old and first met Elvis at Graceland shortly after he returned from the Army. She often traveled long distances to see him perform. Cheryle was a principal organizer and founding member of the Worldwide Federation of Elvis Presley Fan Clubs and the Elvis Presley International Memorial Foundation.

IRA JONES greeted Elvis Presley when the singer stepped off the troop ship to serve with the Army in West Germany. Elvis became Ira's jeep driver and they spent most on-duty hours together.

SHIRLEY JANE JONES (GILLENTINE) was a fifth grade classmate of Elvis's at Lawhorn Elementary in East Tupelo when she won first place in a talent contest and, she reveals, Elvis won fourth place.

TOM JONES is a recording star who became one of the hottest acts in Las Vegas. He spent a great deal of time offstage with Elvis, and they were close friends.

ULYSSES JONES was on of two paramedics who answered the distress call from 3764 Elvis Presley Boulevard, on August 16, 1977.

JUNE JUANICO (from Biloxi, Mississippi) was mesmerized by young Elvis during one of his early tours and ended up dating the hot new star for several years.

HAL KANTER, the Hollywood director and cowriter of Elvis's film, *Loving You*, was one of the first influential people in Hollywood to recognize the big screen potential of young Elvis. He later wrote the screenplay for Presley's, *Blue Hawaii*.

MARION KEISKER, who passed away in 1989, once complained to Dick Heard that she never really got the credit she deserved for being one of the first people in the music business to recognize the potential of young Elvis Presley. An employee of Memphis Recording Service, she called Elvis to the attention of Sun Records owner Sam Phillips.

STAN KESLER was an engineer at Memphis Recording Service, "Sun Studio." He has the distinction of having written five of Elvis's Sun singles.

BUDDY KILLEN, then a struggling Nashville musician, helped kick off one of the hottest music publishing companies in the history of country music when songwriter Mae Axton handed him and Jack Stapp, his partner in Tree Publishing, the rights to "Heartbreak Hotel." It turned out to be Elvis's first million-seller.

MERLE KILGORE was a hot new recording artist and performer when he befriended young Presley and toured with him on a string of Ark-La-Tex dates. Years later Merle gave up his recording career to become manager of Hank Williams, Jr. Today he's "happy—and rich, very rich!"

GEORGE KLEIN was a "big wheel" at Humes High School in Memphis where he graduated with Elvis in 1953. George became a disc jockey at radio station WHBQ, and he and Elvis remained close friends until the end. George was a pallbearer at Elvis's funeral.

GERALDINE KYLE met Elvis after becoming close friends with his stepmother, Dee Presley.

JERRY KYLE, the son of Geraldine Kyle, was a close friend of Elvis's young stepbrother, Rick Stanley.

MARTY LACKER remembers meeting Elvis Presley at Humes High in 1952. He traveled for many years as part of the king's entourage and was largely responsible for convincing Elvis to record with Chips Moman at American Studios. The sessions revived Elvis's sagging record career in 1969.

V. L. LANE is a retired captain of the Memphis Police Department, Narcotics Division, who first met Elvis in 1953 when he was a patrolman.

ANGELA LANSBURY portrayed Sarah Lee Gates, Elvis's mother, in the 1961 film *Blue Hawaii*. Although she has been highly successful for several decades in movies, she is currently best-known as the star of the TV series, *Murder, She Wrote*.

BERNARD LANSKY is a Memphis clothier, who with his brother Guy owned Lansky Brothers on Beale Street where Elvis shopped. Bernard fitted Elvis for his high school prom tux, dressed Elvis for early stage and TV shows, and provided the white suit in which Elvis was laid to rest.

MIKE LEECH was a Memphis session musician and arranger who belonged to the American Group at American (studio).

LANCE LeGAULT coached Elvis on where to stand and when to move in movies from 1960 to 1968. They became good friends.

MARLO LEWIS was producer of the tremendously popular *Ed Sullivan* [TV] *Show* when, in 1956–1957, rising young star Elvis Presley made three appearances on the show.

ALEX LOGAN was the maintenance engineer at Elvis's Palm Springs home at 845 Chico Canyon Road.

HORACE LOGAN was—and is—the executive at radio station KWKH, Shreveport, Louisiana, who first booked Elvis as a substitute act [December 11, 1954] and shortly thereafter signed him to a long-term contract.

HAROLD LOYD was Elvis's first cousin (his mother, Rhetta, and Elvis's mother, Gladys, were sisters). Harold lived with the Presleys for awhile in East Tupelo and later went to work at Graceland as a gatekeeper.

BECKY MARTIN was a fifth-grade classmate of Elvis's in East Tupelo. She remained a welcomed guest at the Presleys' homes, where she and Elvis would sing together at the piano or ride go-carts.

NEAL MATTHEWS is a longtime member of the Jordanaires on whom Elvis often relied for backing in the recording studio.

JOHN W. MCAFEE, SR., was the newsreel cameraman assigned to cover the major events in Elvis's life for Theatrical Newsreel and for the television networks. He was also one of the union projectionists who screened movies for Elvis at Memphis theaters. John is the father of Rose Clayton.

ANN MARIE MCCLAIN became a Presley fan at age ten when she first saw an Elvis movie. She saw Elvis perform many times and became a "regular" at the Graceland gates.

JANELLE MCCOMB was a family friend who never lost touch with Vernon or Elvis. She once asked Elvis a question that ultimately led to the building of a memorial to him near his birthplace in Tupelo, Mississippi.

CHARLIE MCCOY, a talented Nashville studio musician [harmonica, bass, guitar, etc.], was called in one night as a substitute picker on an Elvis session and ended up being hired back time and time again.

WILL "BARDAHL" MCDANIEL first met Elvis when the young singer rented the Rainbow Skating Rink, where Will worked. Elvis nicknamed him "Bardahl," and they remained friends until the end.

RONNIE MCDOWELL was, in 1977, a struggling young recording artist signed to a small country label distributed by Dick Heard's company. Distraught following Elvis's death, he wrote and recorded the huge, best-selling tribute record, "The King Is Gone."

MIKE MCGREGOR lived at both Graceland and the Circle G ranch during the nine years that he worked for Elvis taking care of Elvis's horses.

KEVIN S. MERIGIAN, M.D., is a clinical pharmacologist and toxicologist at the Toxicology Center in the Elvis Presley Trauma Center in Memphis, Tennessee.

GEORGE MICHAEL is a major songwriter and recording artist, and a former a member of the group WHAM!

MARY ANN MOBLEY, a "Miss Mississippi" who became "Miss America" in 1959, had a lead role with Elvis in *Girl Happy* and later costarred with him in *Harum Scarum*. Although she never dated Elvis, she was a friend for many years.

CHIPS MOMAN, one of the most successful producers in the history of Memphis music, helped revitalize Elvis's recording career with such hits as "In the Ghetto," "Suspicious Minds," and "Kentucky Rain."

BILL MONROE, known as the "father of bluegrass," was a star of the Grand Ole Opry, Nashville, when Elvis came there to perform one of Monroe's compositions: "Blue Moon of Kentucky." Elvis apologized to Bill for jazzing up his song.

DICK "BUCKY" MOORE transacted business with Elvis while working as a paint salesman, car dealer, and owner of Dick Moore Mobile Homes.

SCOTTY MOORE was Elvis Presley's first manager and lead guitarist. After he left Elvis, Scotty pursued a successful career as a musician and studio owner in Nashville. In 1968, at Elvis's request, he appeared in the king's (so-called) "Comeback Special," entitled *Elvis*.

SONNY NEAL is the son of the late Bob Neal, who managed Elvis from 1955 to 1956. As a young man Sonny often traveled the show circuit with Elvis and his band. He maintained contact with Elvis through the years.

GENE NELSON hoofed his way to stardom in movies like *Working Her Way Through College* before turning to directing. He directed Elvis in *Kissin' Cousins* and *Harum Scarum*.

WAYNE NEWTON, a recording artist and mega-bucks performer, was a great admirer of Elvis Presley and still pays tribute to Elvis onstage.

DR. GEORGE NICHOPOULOS became Elvis's personal physician in 1967 and continued to treat Elvis through a number of hospitalizations and up until Elvis's death. Nick was a regular member of the touring entourage. In 1980, the Tennessee Board of Medical Examiners brought charges against Dr. Nick, claiming he over-prescribed drugs to Elvis and others. After a month-long trial, a jury acquitted him of all charges in 1981.

SHAUN NIELSEN was a member of the group Voice, which Elvis hired as his own personal backup group. Shaun then became part of the larger stage show entourage and remained in the group through Elvis's final performance.

LARRY NIX was an engineer on Elvis's Stax sessions in Memphis in July and December of 1973.

ROY W. NIXON was the Shelby County sheriff who commissioned Elvis as a chief deputy.

BOBBY OGDIN is a successful keyboard player who toured with Elvis during the final months of the king's life.

JIM ORWOOD was a member of the Shelby County Sheriff's Department who originally met Elvis as a fan and later served as part of the honor guard when Elvis's body lay in state at Graceland.

FRANK PAGE was one of the primary announcers on the Louisiana Hayride. He is still employed by—and a big wheel at—the Hayride's parent station, KWKH, Shreveport, Louisiana.

ED PARKER first met Elvis in Los Angeles in 1960 when they both attended a karate exhibition. He became one of Elvis's karate instructors and friends.

COLONEL TOM PARKER (an honorary Colonel) was Elvis's controversial manager from 1956 until the singer's death.

MARTY PASETTA produced the 1973 TV special *Elvis: Aloha From Hawaii*, which was seen by one billion people in forty countries—more people than had watched the first man walk on the moon.

JANICE PENNINGTON, a star of *The Price Is Right* TV show for many years, first met Elvis as a fan in 1957 and ultimately became good friends with him during the later movie years.

CARL PERKINS was a Sun Records recording artist and writer of "Blue Suede Shoes."

BILL PERRY was the paperboy for the Presley household when they lived in Lauderdale Courts and often played football with Elvis on Saturdays. He is now a member of the Shelby County Sheriff's Department.

SAM PHILLIPS was the owner of Sun Records. He is credited with discovering Elvis, producing the famous Sun sound, and then selling Elvis to RCA. Elvis and Sam remained friends through the years.

BARBARA PITTMAN was the only female recording artist on the Sun label and recorded for that company longer than any of its other artists. Barbara also grew up in the projects and, like Elvis, sang at the Eagle's Nest in the mid-fifties.

MARY LOU POPE is the daughter of Elvis super-fan Naomia Stiers. She often helped her mom with fan club activities.

ANNIE CLOYD PRESLEY was Elvis's cousin-in-law. She married Sales Presley, Vernon's cousin.

CHRISTINE ROBERTS PRESLEY was Elvis's great aunt. She was married to Noah Presley, the brother of J. D., Elvis's grandfather. Christine was one of the few people Gladys would allow to take care of Elvis when he was a baby.

VESTER PRESLEY was Vernon's brother and worked at the gates of Graceland.

WAYNE E. PRESLEY was Elvis's cousin and played with him as a child in East Tupelo.

JOAN PRICE (ADAN) was a young fan from east Tennessee who met Elvis when she boarded the train on which he was traveling to New York to appear on the *Ed Sullivan Show.*

BILL RANDLE, of radio station WERE, Cleveland, Ohio, is reported to have been the first disc jockey above the Mason-Dixon line to ever play an Elvis Presley record. Randle also introduced the young singer on his first network TV appearance.

MARY REEVES DAVIS is the widow of country music superstar Jim Reeves. When Jim was a regular on the Louisiana Hayride, he and Mary often welcomed young Presley to their home for dinner.

KANG RHEE is a martial arts instructor in Memphis. In 1970 he became a *tae kwon do* instructor to a grateful Elvis Presley, who reportedly gave Rhee fifty thousand dollars to start his own karate school.

DON ROBERTSON, a successful full-time songwriter, has many hits to his credit. Elvis recorded fourteen songs Don either wrote or cowrote, including "I Really Don't Want to Know."

JOE SAVERY was Elvis's sixth grade classmate at Milam Junior High in Tupelo, Mississippi.

JERRY SCHILLING was a teenager when he met Elvis during a touch football game. He became a member of the Memphis Mafia and worked with Elvis for twelve years in varying capacities. Jerry was a pallbearer at Elvis's funeral.

ABE SCHWAB is the proprietor of the A. B. Schwab Dry Goods Store on Beale Street in Memphis.

T. G. SHEPPARD is the stage name of Bill Browder. He met Elvis at Rainbow roller rink and remained his friend for life. As an adult he promoted Presley product for RCA.

BILLY SMITH was Elvis's first cousin. Billy traveled and worked for Elvis intermittently beginning in the late fifties. He played racquetball with Elvis a few hours before Elvis's death and was one of the last people to see Elvis alive.

BROTHER FRANK W. SMITH was pastor at the First Assembly of God church, which the Presleys attended in Tupelo before moving to Memphis. He taught Elvis to make chords on his guitar. Brother Smith often sang "Old Shep," which was one of Elvis's favorite songs when he was young.

CORENE RANDLE SMITH is the wife of Brother Frank W. Smith.

MYRNA SMITH went to work with Elvis as a backup singer and was a member of the Sweet Inspirations group. She stayed with the Elvis show to the end, eventually marrying and later divorcing Elvis's close friend and confidant Jerry Schilling.

RONNIE SMITH was a musician in south Memphis who began playing guitar with Elvis in 1951. Elvis sang in Ronnie's band before he signed with Sun Records.

BILLY JO SPEARS, a country singer, met Elvis very early in his career and literally helped Elvis pull (or pin) himself together.

BILLY STANLEY became Elvis's stepbrother when his mother, Dee, divorced his father in 1960 and married Vernon Presley.

DAVID STANLEY, brother of Billy and stepbrother of Elvis, grew up in and out of Graceland. Later, as a young adult, he helped work tour security for Elvis. David claims to have helped clean up evidence of Elvis's drug use immediately following Elvis's death.

RINGO STARR, Beatles' drummer and Elvis fan, visited the king during the group's American tour in 1965.

NAOMIA STIERS was, is, and always will be an Elvis Presley fan. Early in Elvis's career, Naomia performed thousands of hours of volunteer work to help promote Elvis, who became her friend for life and who welcomed her often into his home.

GORDON STOKER is a longtime member of the Jordanaires who sang backup on countless recordings by Elvis Presley and other artists.

LARRY STRICKLAND sang bass with the Stamps when they did backup for Elvis. Now a Nashville businessman, Larry is currently married to country star Naomi Judd.

J. D. SUMNER was one of Elvis's favorite bass singers from the time Elvis was sixteen and first sneaked into his gospel music shows.

DR. FOREST TENNANT, JR., was, at the time of his interview, the executive director of a UCLA-affiliated clinic for research on drug abuse.

LINDA THOMPSON (FOSTER), a former Miss Tennessee, was Elvis's steady girlfriend from 1972 to 1976. Linda's gentle attentiveness and spontaneous sense of humor were a source of strength in Elvis's life, and she was almost constantly at his side. Linda, currently an actress, starred for many years on TV's *Hee-Haw*. She is also a Grammy Award-winning songwriter.

SAM THOMPSON is Linda Thompson's brother. He was a member of the Shelby County Sheriff's department before he served as Graceland's chief of security and as a bodyguard on Elvis's tours. He is now a circuit court judge in Memphis.

RONNIE TROUT was a classmate of Elvis's at Humes High School and worked part-time at Lansky Brothers on Beale Street.

RONNIE TUTT is the drummer who played on Elvis's live shows as well as many of his recording sessions beginning in 1969.

JIMMY VELVET first met Elvis backstage at a Florida concert and maintained his friendship with Elvis throughout the years. He eventually became one of the world's biggest collectors of Presley memorabilia, and in 1994 he auctioned off a portion of his vast collection for 2.4 million dollars.

PORTER WAGONER was a hot new country music writer and recording star in the late fifties when he toured with and befriended a rising star named Elvis Presley.

BILLY WALKER first met Elvis when Billy performed (with Slim Whitman and others) in Memphis in 1954. Elvis was brand-new at the time, but Billy says Elvis stole the show.

RAY WALKER has been the bass singer with the Jordanaires since he joined the group in 1958. He first lent his vocal talents to Elvis's recordings of "I Need Your Love Tonight" and "Now and Then There's a Fool Such As I."

DON WARDELL worked on the powerful European station Radio Luxembourg before coming to the U.S. to work on Elvis Presley projects for RCA. Don recently retired and is still considered one of the world's foremost authorities on Elvis Presley's recording career.

BEN WEISMAN wrote and cowrote more songs recorded by Elvis Presley than any other writer. Included in his Elvis repertoire are the title songs to six Presley movies.

RED WEST befriended Elvis at Humes High and remained extremely close friends with him through most of the ups and downs of Elvis's life. He appeared with Elvis in many movies. On July 13, 1976, Red, together with Sonny West and Dave Hebler, was fired by Vernon Presley. Red subsequently pursued his career as a stunt man in Hollywood. He is now a drama teacher in Bartlett, Tennessee, where he owns his own school.

SONNY WEST is the cousin of Red West and first met Elvis at a skating party. Elvis served as best man in Sonny's wedding, and they were together until a year before Elvis died. A long-term member of the Memphis Mafia. Sonny ultimately coauthored *Elvis: What Happened?* in 1977.

SLIM WHITMAN, a major country artist, took news of "a hot new singer" back to his base at the Louisiana Hayride in 1954 following a concert in Memphis. The rest is history.

MAC WISEMAN was a fifties record executive (Dot Records) and was very knowledgeable about trends in the country music recording field. As an artist, he was once managed by Colonel Tom Parker but split with him because he was so hot with his hit "Davy Crockett" that he didn't need Parker's help getting bookings.

ANITA WOOD (BREWER) was a vivacious beauty who cohosted a popular TV show in Memphis and dated Elvis several years before and after he was in the Army. They broke up when Anita learned about Elvis's infatuation with Priscilla Beaulieu.

BOBBY WOOD played piano as part of the hot rhythm section at American Studios, Memphis, where Elvis recorded in January 1969. Out of those sessions came some of the biggest hits of Elvis's career.

CHIP YOUNG is one of Nashville's most respected session guitarists and producers. He picked on many of Elvis's sessions, as well as the Presley recordings that were polished for release immediately following Elvis's death.

FARON YOUNG, a country superstar beginning in the fifties, befriended young Elvis and showed him the ropes on the road. Faron taught Elvis how to "movie fight."

JUDGE DAVID ZENOFF was a member of the Nevada Supreme Court when he was asked to officiate at a wedding in Las Vegas. To his surprise the groom turned out to be Elvis Presley.

Index

Adams, Nick, 97, 105, 126, 128
Alden, Ginger, 318, 322–24, 328–30, 332, 335, 339–42
Alden, Jo, 315, 319, 324, 329–30, 334, 340–41, 370
"All Shook Up", 184
Allen, Steve, 103
Aloha From Hawaii, 259, 262–63
American Sound Studio, 227, 235, 238–39
Ann-Margret, 201–202, 218, 228, 319, 357
"Are You Lonesome Tonight?", 170
"Are You Sincere", 271
Atkins, Chet, 48, 59, 169
Axton, Mae, 55, 65–68, 75–76, 81, 84–86, 88, 90, 100, 149, 158, 170–71, 215, 268, 349
Ayers, Dotty, 100, 109, 118, 125, 130, 138, 146–47, 161, 167–68, 175, 193–94, 250

Baxter, Jerry, 42
Bedford, Elois, 9, 23, 25, 28
Belew, Bill, 233, 242, 244, 259, 262–63, 302, 338–39
Bienstock, Freddy, 95, 115, 168, 197
Black, Clint, 336
Blackwood, James, 37, 93, 100–101, 149, 232, 270, 321, 354, 357
Blue Hawaii, 182, 183, 185
"Blue Moon of Kentucky", 49–50, 51, 56, 58, 59, 83
Bond, Eddie, 44, 46–50, 78
Bradley, Owen, 81–82, 84, 93
Briggs, David, 249, 277, 282, 264–65, 277–78, 282, 304
Brookoff, Dr. Dan, 289–90, 361, 372–75, 378
Browder, Bill. *See* T. G. Sheppard
Brown, Tony, 271, 287, 296, 307–08, 312–13, 317–18, 330–31, 319, 330
Burlison, Paul, 45–46, 51, 78, 105, 162, 224
Burk, Bill E., 128, 147, 166, 205, 222–23, 241, 308, 312, 317, 324, 348, 350, 355, 371
Burton, James, 271

Callender, John, 135, 154–55, 158–62
"Can't Help Falling in Love", 185
Cash, Johnny, 66, 86, 88, 106
Change of Habit, 241
Charro, 235
Chest, Russell "Rusty", 355–56, 359
Clambake, 214, 226
Clark, Odell, 7, 16–20, 22–28
Clement, Jack, 31, 44, 46, 48, 49–50, 51–52, 81, 87, 89, 106, 118, 133
Cockerell, Betty, 104, 347, 352, 354, 356, 358–59
Cocke, Marian, 345
Cogan, Arlene, 109, 117–18, 125–27, 130, 138–40, 145, 149–53, 161–62, 166–67, 173, 175–76, 182, 188–90, 193, 198–99, 333, 351, 364
Comeback Special, 1968. *See* Elvis
Crosby, Charles, 335, 342–43, 345
Crowe, Jean, 174
Crowe, Jim, 165, 173–76, 191–93, 200, 202, 217
Crown Electric, 45
Cutrer, T. Tommy, 56, 61, 66, 77

Davis, Mac, 64, 236
Davis, Mary Reeves, 8
Deary, Joan, 83, 88, 144, 169–70, 197, 207, 213, 215, 234, 240, 248, 259, 263, 266, 348, 354, 356–59, 361–63, 368
Denny, Bill, 59
DeRamus, Troy, 76
Dickens, Little Jimmy, 58, 59
Dodd, Dinah, 103, 110–11
"Don't Be Cruel", 91, 170
Double Trouble, 220
Dougher, Paul, 31–36, 40–41, 42, 50, 96, 109, 111, 176–77, 200, 304

Easy Come, Easy Go, 221
Ed Sullivan Show, The, 89, 103, 104
Egan, Richard, 95
Elvis (1968 Comeback Special), 227, 233–35
Elvis, What Happened?, 308, 312, 317, 324, 326, 369
Esposito, Joe, 227–31, 342

Fadal, Eddie, 74, 135, 141–48, 151–52, 169–70, 196, 245, 253, 283, 312
Farrar, Laverne, 16–17, 20–21, 24, 26–27, 30
Ferguson, Robert, 252, 261
Fielder, Anita, 304, 346, 352, 360, 382
Fielder, Brenda, 129, 183, 221, 354–55, 359
Fike, Lamar, 126–27, 135, 146, 155, 162–63, 177, 224, 228, 257, 289, 315, 317, 325, 350, 361, 365
Flaming Star, 178–79
Follow That Dream, 181, 185, 186,
Fontana, D. J., 55, 65, 91, 140, 144, 233, 249
Forbes, Buzzy, 31–36, 40, 42–43, 101, 102, 168
Forbes, Frances, 109, 130–32, 136–37, 145, 161–62, 167–68, 180, 191, 193, 195, 261
Fortas, Alan, 119, 125, 130, 135, 146, 165, 176–77, 188–90, 201–202, 205–206, 209, 235, 369
Francisco, Dr. Jerry T., 346, 372
Franklin, Dr. E. O., 205, 221–23, 241
Franks, Tillman, 55–57, 60–61, 65, 71
Fredrick, Fred, 31, 36, 39–40, 41–43, 45, 102, 124, 135, 138, 141, 217, 232, 244, 253, 284, 304
"From Elvis Presley Boulevard, Memphis, Tennessee", 303–304
Fun in Acapulco, 202

Gallagher, Bill, 83, 84, 87, 88
Geller, Larry, 44, 208–10, 216, 255, 260, 284, 311–12, 317–20, 323, 326, 328, 335, 337–39, 350, 351, 358, 362
G.I. Blues, 164, 177, 178
Gibson, Keith, 135, 154, 156–57, 163
Girl Happy, 181, 186, 210, 214
Girls, Girls, Girls, 181, 189–90
Gleason, Jackie, 89–90

Glidewell, Barbara, 97–99, 109, 111, 115–16, 118–19, 125, 128, 133, 136–38
Graceland, 109, 112, 115–18, 123–26, 128, 131, 165, 167, 171–72, 174–77, 181, 186, 191–92, 194, 196, 198, 200, 202, 221–222, 227, 235, 237, 259, 262, 280, 300–301, 314, 317, 327, 335, 337, 339–42, 345, 349, 352–54, 356, 358, 364–65
Grand Ole Opry, 55, 58, 59
Grubbs, Dr. Durwood, 290
Gurley, Mack, 36–37, 39, 118, 123–24, 127–28, 135–36, 145, 168, 170, 190, 196

Harum Scarum, 211, 212
Harris, Guy, 7, 16, 18, 20–23, 27, 29
Hart, Ed, 135, 154–59
Hartley, Becky, 165, 181, 191–94, 196–98, 200, 202, 216, 218, 224, 231, 256–57, 262, 269, 289–91, 293–94
Hays, Lowell, 241–42, 248, 252–53, 264, 282, 287, 292–93, 299–301, 315, 317–18, 322–23, 347
"Heartbreak Hotel", 85–86, 90, 114, 119
Hill and Range Music Publishing Co., 88, 91, 95, 115, 185, 207, 237, 239–40
Hodge, Charlie, 255, 272
Hofman, Dr. Lester, 339
Holmes, Charles, 141, 144, 153–54
"Hound Dog", 91, 170
"How Great Thou Art", 100–101, 220, 248, 333, 354, 357
How Great Thou Art, 219
Hunt, Dr. William Robert, 9

"I Really Don't Want to Know", 249
"In the Ghetto", 236–38, 240
It Happened at the World's Fair, 199
"It's Now or Never", 169–70
"It's Only Make Believe", 139
"I Got a Woman", 114

Jackie Gleason's *Stage Show*, 89–90, 92
Jackson, Wanda, 55, 66–67, 72–74, 82, 95, 131
Jackson, Wayne, 238, 241
Jailhouse Rock, 121

Jarvis, Felton, 219, 226, 281, 326, 336–37
Jarvis, Mary, 219, 246, 349
Jennings, Waylon, 56, 73, 362
Johnson, Cheryle, 172, 178, 183, 198, 200–02, 214, 220, 248, 251, 265, 268, 271, 283, 285, 287, 290–91, 295, 297–98, 309–11, 346, 361, 364, 366–69, 371, 375–77
Jones, Ira, 135, 153–58, 160, 350
Jones, Shirley Jane, 23–26, 30
Jones, Ulysses, 335, 343
Jones, Tom, 213, 233–34, 260, 264, 270, 297–98
Juanico, June, 55, 69, 70, 94, 95, 99, 100, 102, 115–16, 190, 195, 245

Kanter, Hal, 93–94, 109, 112–115, 129, 182–83
Keisker, Marion, 31, 44, 45, 46
"Kentucky Rain", 239
Kesler, Stan, 31, 46–49, 77–79
Kid Galahad, 187, 188
Kilgore, Merle, 60–61, 72–73
Killen, Buddy, 58–59, 86, 90
King Creole, 139, 145
"King Is Gone, The", 363
Kissin' Cousins, 206–208
Klein, George, 31, 37, 38–39, 41, 121, 126–27, 167, 176, 205, 210–11, 216, 221, 237, 241, 243, 253–54, 264, 265–66, 283, 300, 305, 312–13, 317, 323, 325, 337, 348, 351
Kyle, Geraldine, 181, 192–93, 195, 202, 217–18, 229, 231–32
Kyle, Jerry, 181, 192, 196, 231, 261

Lacker, Marty, 49, 53, 123–25, 140, 180, 187–88, 215–16, 224, 227–29, 235–36, 256, 267, 294–95, 357–58, 361, 364
Lane, V. L., 305–306
Lansbury, Angela, 181–83
Lansky, Bernard, 41, 43, 102, 103, 267, 354
Las Vegas, Nevada, 101, 227, 229, 243, 246–47, 249, 251, 259–60, 264–66, 269–71, 281, 291, 304, 312, 318, 320–21

Leech, Mike, 238
LeGault, Lance, 179, 189, 207, 210–12, 214, 221, 234–35
"(Let Me Be Your) Teddy Bear", 122, 124
Lewis, Jerry Lee, 106, 119
Lewis, Marlo, 89, 103, 104
Logan, Alex, 255, 272
Logan, Horace, 55–58, 60–62, 77, 97, 106, 107, 203
"Lonely Blue Boy", 139
Louisiana Hayride, 55–58, 60–77, 86, 106, 107
"Love Me Tender", 94–95
Love Me Tender, 94–95, 100
"Loving You", 115
Loving You, 93–95, 113, 114, 129
Loyd, Harold, 7, 8, 10–14, 18, 21, 25, 28, 30, 31, 32, 44, 111–12, 148, 186–87, 346

Martin, Becky, 7, 20–25, 30, 96, 102
Matthews, Neal, 128, 169
McAfee, John W. Sr., 104, 105, 117, 211
McClain, Ann Marie, 186, 317, 320, 327–29, 339
McComb, Janelle, 8–10, 32, 253, 332–33, 361, 366–67
McCoy, Charlie, 213, 220
McDaniel, Will "Bardahl", 119, 124, 136–39, 173, 177, 194, 348
McDowell, Ronnie, 353, 363
McGregor, Mike, 224, 241
Merigian, Dr. Kevin S., 344, 361, 371–78
Michael, George, 110
Miller, Sandy, 343
Mobley, Mary Ann, 205, 210–11, 234, 274
Moman, Chips, 227, 235–41
"Money Honey", 114
Monroe, Bill, 50, 59
Moore, Dick "Bucky", 102, 241
Moore, Scotty, 31, 46–48, 50–52, 55, 62, 64, 65, 76, 227, 233
"My Happiness", 44–46

Neal, Bob, 50–51, 65–66, 81–83, 85, 86, 88
Neal, Sonny, 50–51, 88, 320
Nelson, Gene, 206–208

Newton, Wayne, 288
Nichopoulos, Dr. George, 223, 250–52, 254, 256–57, 259, 269, 273–77, 280, 287–94, 296–98, 300, 302, 304–306, 308–309, 319–20, 322, 325, 327, 329, 332, 337–42, 344–45, 370–72, 374
Nielsen, Shaun, 219–20, 254–55, 260, 265, 268, 270, 282–83, 287, 296, 330, 356–57
Nix, Larry, 273, 277
Nixon, Roy, 251
"Now and Then There's a Fool Such As I", 144

Ogdin, Bobby, 317, 331–33
Orbison, Roy, 162
Orwood, Jim, 97, 351, 353

Page, Frank, 55, 57, 60–61, 66, 106, 107
Paradise Hawaiian Style, 215
Parker, Colonel Tom, 77, 81–88, 91–96, 99–105, 115, 135, 140–41, 148–49, 155, 170, 182, 185, 200, 202–203, 205–206, 208, 211, 215–16, 228–30, 243–44, 250–51, 255, 259, 267, 271, 276, 283–85, 288, 311, 325, 337–38, 368
Parker, Ed, 281, 283–84, 288, 302, 355
Pasetta, Mary, 262
Pennington, Janice, 109, 121, 122, 255, 280–82, 289, 347
Perkins, Carl, 47, 88, 106
Perry, Bill, 32, 34, 38, 98, 328–29
Phillips, Dewey, 48–49, 56, 77–78
Phillips, Sam, 31, 44, 47–48, 56, 66, 79, 87–88, 106
Pittman, Barbara, 35, 38, 78, 81, 87–88, 93, 132, 141, 146, 148–50, 182
Pope, Mary Lou, 157, 171
Presley, Annie Cloyd, 7, 11–17, 19, 21–22, 26, 81, 100, 321
Presley, Christine Roberts, 7, 8, 11–17, 29, 81, 105
Presley, Dee, 192
Presley, Elvis Aaron, 10
    birth of, 8, 9
    burial and reburial of, 355–60, 366
    death of, 341–45
    fan reaction to, 345–55
    doctors, 223
    drugs, 138, 289–93, 297–98, 302, 304–306, 308, 310–12
        discussion of involvement in Elvis's death, 370–78
        experiments with, 217, 269
        first use, 138
        overdoses, 274–75, 343
        prescription, 250, 269, 274–77, 289–92, 298, 308
    early gigs, 45–46, 60–77, 338, 340–41
    early musical training, 13, 15, 17–19, 24–29, 36–37, 39, 41–42, 48
    early schooling, 22–26, 28–29, 33, 36, 38–41, 43, 44
    estate of, 364–65, 368
    films
        Aloha From Hawaii, 259, 262–63
        Blue Hawaii, 182–83, 185
        Change of Habit, 241
        Charro, 235
        Clambake, 214, 226
        Double Trouble, 220
        Easy Come, Easy Go, 221
        Flaming Star, 178–79
        Follow That Dream, 181, 185, 186
        Fun in Acapulco, 202
        GI Blues, 164, 177, 178
        Girl Happy, 181, 186, 210, 214
        Girls, Girls, Girls, 181, 189–90
        Harum Scarum, 211–12
        It Happened at the World's Fair, 199
        Jailhouse Rock, 121
        Kid Galahad, 187–88
        King Creole, 139, 145
        Kissin' Cousins, 206–208
        Love Me Tender, 94–95, 100
        Paradise Hawaiian Style, 215
        Speedway, 234–35
        Spinout, 214
        Stay Away, Joe, 221
        Trouble With Girls, The, 186, 235
        Viva Las Vegas, 201, 218
        Wild in the Country, 179–80, 182
    first girlfriend, 25

first public performance, 45–46
first hit record, 49, 57, 66
   reaction to, 49–51, 56–59, 66
funeral of, 355–60, 364
homes: Hollywood, 188
   Memphis, 109, 112, 115–18, 123–26, 128, 131, 165, 167, 171–72, 174–77, 181, 186, 191–92, 194, 196, 198, 200, 202, 221–222, 227, 235, 237, 259, 262, 280, 300–301, 314, 317, 327, 335, 337, 339–42, 345, 349, 352–54, 356, 358, 364–65
   Palm Springs, 255–56, 272
   Tupelo, 7, 8–10, 13, 16, 20–23, 26–28, 30
karate, 183, 246, 273, 284–85
Las Vegas, 101, 227, 229, 243, 246–47, 249, 251
medical problems, 374
Memphis Mafia, 176, 305, 320, 361
move to Memphis, 30, 32
relationship with Gladys, 11, 13–19, 21–23, 25–26, 29, 33, 125–27, 142, 147, 150
relationship with Vernon, 11, 18, 111–12, 225
tours, last, 291–93, 298, 301, 310–11, 314–15, 320–22, 330–33, 338–39
U.S. Army, 139–163
   drafted into, 133, 135, 139
   assigned to Germany, 152–53
   reactions by Germans, 155–57, 159–60
   training, 141–45, 150–52
wedding, 229–231

Presley, Gladys, 8–19, 21–23, 25–26, 28–30, 33–36, 44, 93, 96, 98, 100, 102, 104, 109–110, 117–18, 124–27, 142–43, 145–51, 175
Presley, Jesse Garon, 9–11
Presley, Lisa Marie, 232, 257, 272, 277–78, 312, 321, 326–27, 339, 345–46, 365
Presley, Priscilla Beaulieu, 163, 165, 167, 181, 191, 193–96, 200–202, 217–218, 227–32, 256–57, 319, 330, 339, 364–65

Presley, Vernon, 8–13, 15, 16, 18–20, 26, 28, 30, 32, 34–36, 93, 96, 104, 111–12, 117–118, 142, 145–49, 175–76, 182, 192, 202, 225, 267, 271, 285, 291–92, 294–95, 343, 345–46, 362, 364
Presley, Vester, 8–9, 21
Presley, Wayne E., 7, 12–14
Price, Joan, 110–11

Randle, Bill, 81, 89, 92, 333
RCA Records, 81, 83–85, 87–103, 112, 135, 144, 169–70, 236, 244, 246, 248–49, 259, 262, 266, 273, 348, 362–63
"Return to Sender", 189, 190
Rhee, Kang, 246, 273, 284, 301
Robertson, Don, 88–89, 115, 185–86, 189, 197, 207, 249
Roustabout, 208, 210

Savery, Joe, 7, 9, 81, 104
Schilling, Jerry, 176, 247, 252, 254, 260, 282, 296, 303, 358, 392, 394
Schwab, Abe, 48
Sheppard, T. G., 165, 174, 228, 234, 244–45, 248–50, 254, 301, 325, 336, 348
Sholes, Steve, 83–84, 87, 169, 140, 169
Sinatra, Frank, 170, 177–78
Smith, Billy, 340, 370
Smith, Brother Frank W., 25–26, 321
Smith, Corene Randle, 15–16
Smith, Myrna, 227, 242–45, 247–48, 260, 265, 287, 295–96, 299, 302–303, 307, 312, 333, 350, 353, 357
Smith, Ronnie, 31, 37, 40, 44, 45–46, 49, 52, 97, 109, 111
Snow, Hank, 70–72, 74–75, 86, 92
Spears, Billy Jo, 63–64
Speedway, 234–35
Spinout, 214
Stanley, Billy, 176, 181, 185–86, 194, 235, 256, 268, 317, 349, 354, 358, 361, 364
Stanley, David, 181, 192, 195, 252, 259, 267, 278–80, 308–09, 317, 320–21, 323–24, 341–46, 361–62, 364, 369–70
Stanley, Rick, 192, 341
Stanley, Dee, 175–76, 182, 192, 202, 364

Stanwyck, Barbara, 208, 210
Starr, Ringo, 318
Stay Away, Joe, 221
Stiers, Naomia, 129, 171–73, 178, 351–52, 358, 361, 366
Stoker, Gordon, 112–13, 136, 140, 184–85, 249
Streisand, Barbra, 243–244, 283
Strickland, Larry, 282, 303–304, 313–15, 336, 357, 359
Sullivan, Ed, 103
Sumner, J. D., 37, 100
Sun Records, 31, 44–46, 78–79, 81, 84, 86, 87, 119, 133
"Suspicious Minds", 237, 239

Tennant, Jr., Dr. Forest, 275–76, 306, 376
"That's All Right (Mama)", 47, 51, 56, 58, 64, 170
"That's When Your Heartaches Begin", 44
Thompson, Linda, 259, 261–62, 274, 278, 287, 298–99, 309, 312, 315, 319, 361, 378
Thompson, Sam, 259, 268, 272, 281, 335, 339–40, 345–46, 353
Trouble With Girls, The, 186, 235
Trout, Ronnie, 31, 33, 35, 38, 39, 41, 43
Tupelo, Mississippi, 7–10, 13, 16, 20–23, 26–28, 30
Tutt, Ronnie, 227, 242–43, 245, 247, 287, 307, 349

Velvet, Jimmy, 9, 55, 67–68, 73–75, 90, 101, 119–20, 128, 139–40, 182, 194, 212
Viva Las Vegas, 201, 218

Wagoner, Porter, 55, 62–63, 67
Walker, Billy, 51, 55, 57, 64, 88, 107
Walker, Ray, 144, 168–69, 220, 224
Wallis, Hal, 93–94, 111, 183
Wardell, Don, 232, 241, 266, 361, 363, 368
Weisman, Ben, 95–96, 109, 115, 120, 129, 139, 188, 205, 212, 313–14, 347
West, Red, 74, 165, 177–80, 183, 185, 188, 199, 201–202, 205, 208, 210, 215, 221, 260, 264, 296, 317, 325
West, Sonny, 214, 247–48, 251–52, 259, 275, 276, 297, 308, 317, 324–25, 371
Whitman, Slim, 51, 55, 57, 72
Wild in the Country, 179, 180, 182
Wiseman, Mac, 70, 78–79, 81, 86–88, 91, 266
Wood, Anita, 104, 109, 122, 123, 128, 130–133, 150, 180–81, 190–91, 319
Wood, Bobby, 236–39, 348
Wood, Natalie, 97, 105

Young, Chip, 205, 219, 314
Young, Faron, 55, 58, 59, 70–72, 75, 92, 112, 114, 116–17, 249–50, 267

Zenoff, Judge David, 227, 229–30

Acknowledgments

A sincere effort was made in shaping this oral biography to retain the conversational style and integrity of the persons interviewed. Whenever possible entire passages from interviews were used verbatim; nevertheless, it was sometimes necessary to combine parts of several statements and edit others for clarity.

Although the majority of interviews presented in *Elvis Up Close* were conducted specifically for this book, some earlier statements were taken from the editors' seventeen-year collection of interviews with those who knew Elvis best.

With special thanks: To our agent, Sally Hill-McMillan; and Brian Curtis, who put us together; to the staff at Turner Publishing, especially Walton Rawls, Kathy Buttler, Lauren Emerson, Marty Moore and Karen Smith.

To those who gave of their time so generously for interviews we were not able to include in this book: Eddy Arnold, Chet Atkins, Garth Brooks, Steve Binder, Peter Brown, Kenny Buttrey, Bill Carlisle, Jerry Carrigen, June Carter Cash, Jim Castle, Jerry Chestnut, Johnny Christopher, Skeeter Davis, Jim Denson, Carolyn Dodson, Rev. Walton Duncan, Jo Cathy Elkington, Dick Grob, Kenny Herman, Dr. Jim Hickman, Cordell Jackson, A. J. Kotona, Jeanne LeMay, Billy McAfee, Reba McEntire, Ronnie Milsap, Tom Morgan, Heba Namataelia, Don Nix, Tommy Oswald, Knox Phillips, Sheriff Harold Ray Presley and Charlene Presley, Dr. Richard Ranta, Georgeann Reynolds, Gary Rossington, Mitchell Savery, Bill and Vacil Speer, Clyde and Wilma Starkman, Henry Strzlecki, Billy Swan, Travis Tritt, Justin Tubb, Leann and Tony Joe White, Jerry Yancey, and Trisha Yearwood.

To Kathy Lee and our entire staff: Brandee Anderson, Ralph Dailey, Clay Elder, Alan Farmer, Aileen Jackson, Philip Smith, and Jayne Sparks.

For assistance with contacts and research: Patsy Andersen, Jenny Bohler, Bill E. Burk, Tom Foster, Paula Haynes, Brenda Horn, Cheryl Kagen, Ken Kragen, Leonard Lubin, Dianne Magrum, Margaret McAfee, Todd Morgan, Janie Osborne, Nancy Russell, Evelyn Shriver, Norman E. Soloman, Cheryle Smith, Jerry Strobel, Joe Taylor, Hugh Waddell, and Kathy Sue Velvet.

Sincere thanks to Clay Smith and Greg Travis in Nashville, and Barry Berk, Jim Van Messel, and the staff of *Entertainment Tonight* in Los Angeles.

Our very special gratitude to our families and friends, who have spent years listening to our "Elvising."

And to the king: "Thank ya' very much."